A SOLDIER
to the LAST

Also by Edward G. Longacre

Grant's Cavalryman: The Life and Wars of General James H. Wilson (1996)

Mounted Raids of the Civil War (1975)

The Man Behind the Guns: A Biography of General Henry Jackson Hunt, Chief of Artillery, Army of the Potomac (1977)

From Antietam to Fort Fisher: The Civil War Letters of Edward King Wightman, 1862–1865 (1985) (editor)

The Cavalry at Gettysburg: A Tactical Study of Mounted Operations during the Civil War's Pivotal Campaign, 9 June–14 July 1863 (1986)

To Gettysburg and Beyond: The Twelfth New Jersey Volunteer Infantry, II Corps, Army of the Potomac, 1862–1865 (1988)

Jersey Cavaliers: A History of the First New Jersey Volunteer Cavalry, 1861–1865 (1992)

Pickett, Leader of the Charge: A Biography of General George E. Pickett, C.S.A. (1995)

General John Buford: A Military Biography (1995)

Army of Amateurs: General Benjamin F. Butler and the Army of the James, 1863–1865 (1997)

Custer and His Wolverines: The Michigan Cavalry Brigade, 1861–1865 (1997)

Joshua Chamberlain, the Soldier and the Man (1999)

Lincoln's Cavalrymen: A History of the Mounted Forces of the Army of the Potomac, 1861–1865 (2000)

General William Dorsey Pender: A Military Biography (2001)

Lee's Cavalrymen: A History of the Mounted Forces of the Army of Northern Virginia, 1861–1865 (2002)

A Regiment of Slaves: The Fourth United States Colored Infantry, 1863–1866 (2003)

Gentleman and Soldier: A Biography of Wade Hampton III (2004)

The Cavalry at Appomattox: A Tactical History of Mounted Operations during the Civil War's Climactic Campaign, March 29–April 9, 1865 (2004)

Fitz Lee: A Biography of General Fitzhugh Lee, C.S.A. (2005)

The Commanders of Chancellorsville: The Gentleman Versus the Rogue (2005)

Ulysses S. Grant: The Soldier and the Man (2006)

A SOLDIER
to the LAST

Maj. Gen. Joseph Wheeler in Blue and Gray

E D W A R D G. L O N G A C R E

Potomac Books, Inc.
Washington, D.C.

Library of Congress Cataloging-in-Publication Data
Longacre, Edward G., 1946–
    A soldier to the last : Maj. Gen. Joseph Wheeler in blue and gray / Edward G. Longacre.
        p. cm.
    Includes bibliographical references and index.
    ISBN 1-57488-591-X (hardcover : alk. paper)
    1. Wheeler, Joseph, 1836–1906. 2. Confederate States of America. Army—Biography.
3. Generals—Confederate States of America—Biography. 4. United States—History—
Civil War, 1861–1865—Campaigns. I. Title.
    E467.1.W5L66 2006
    973.7'3092—dc22

                                                                                    2006007766

ISBN-10 1-57488-591-X
ISBN-13 978-1-57488-591-0

Potomac Books, Inc.
22841 Quicksilver Drive
Dulles, Virginia 20166

First Edition

10 9 8 7 6 5 4 3 2 1

In memory of my kinsmen,
John and Benjamin W. Longacre,
murdered by Union militia,
Johnson County, Missouri, July 17, 1862

CONTENTS

List of Maps   ix
Preface   xi
Acknowledgments   xv

1   Not Length or Breadth or Thickness   1
2   An Example of Cool, Heroic Courage   17
3   Bluegrass Bound   33
4   Praise and Promotion   51
5   Defending in Front, Attacking in Rear   65
6   Targeting Ships, Forts, and Trains   83
7   At Long Last, Victory   99
8   War Child   115
9   Essential to the Efficiency of the Cavalry   133
10 Countermarching Through Georgia   149
11 The Pursuer and the Pursued   165
12 All That Human Exertion Could Accomplish   185
13 New Fields of Battle   205
14 A Soldier to the Last   219

Notes   237
Bibliography   267
Index   281
About the Author   288

MAPS

Shiloh, about 4 PM, April 6, 1862   28

Kentucky   48

Wheeler's Raids: Stones River Campaign, December 29–31,
1862, and Railroads Raid, April 10–11, 1863   76

Wheeler's Sequatchie Valley Raid, October 1–9, 1863   120

Wheeler's Atlanta Campaign Raid, August 10–September
17, 1864   170

The Carolinas   188

Monroe's Crossroads   197

Santiago de Cuba Campaign, June–July 1898; Central Luzon,
Philippine Islands   223

PREFACE

One of our best-known Civil War historians, told that I was planning a biography of General Joseph Wheeler, wrote me to complain that Wheeler was perhaps the most overrated of the Confederate generals and to express the hope that I would "give the little son of a bitch what he deserves." Other historians—including several who have published studies about the Army of Tennessee, whose cavalry Wheeler commanded from mid-1862 almost to war's end—have expressed a similar opinion, albeit in more temperate language. They have portrayed Wheeler as a leader who failed to inspire or discipline his troops, who was neither an adept tactician (despite authoring a wartime treatise on mounted infantry tactics) nor a skillful gatherer of enemy intelligence, and whose ambition-driven support of equally inept superiors—especially Braxton Bragg, the army's longest-tenured commander—retarded rather than advanced Confederate fortunes in the western theater of the war.

To some degree, each of these criticisms has merit; but each is also overblown. To be sure, both as an administrator and as a combat leader Joe Wheeler had his flaws and limitations. These deficiencies loom larger when he is compared to other commanders of mounted troops in the West who won the laurels and the reputation that eluded him—notably Nathan Bedford Forrest and John Hunt Morgan, both of whom served under Wheeler in 1862–63. Forrest and Morgan exerted an extraordinary hold over their men, who regarded them with reverence and admiration as well as respect and trust. The short, wiry, sometimes unkempt Wheeler lacked their imposing stature and physical grace. He did not share Forrest's ability to put the fear of God in his own men as well as in the enemy. He did not possess Morgan's oratorical power, courtly charm, or theatrical flair. Nor did he display their aptitude for detached service and independent command. Forrest and Morgan were especially skillful at long-distance raiding, one of the most visible features of cavalry operations in the vast territory that was the western theater. While Wheeler conducted more than his share of raids, he never matched the success that Forrest and Morgan achieved while attacking communications lines and supply depots in the Union rear.

Wheeler's deficiencies as a field commander were counterbalanced by certain gifts and strengths. If he fared poorly when operating beyond the reach of his superiors, he was adept at close tactical support of the main army, a skill shared by few cavalry leaders in the West. If he sometimes failed to tap the intelligence-gathering potential of his command, he usually did a creditable job of keeping Bragg and his successors informed of enemy positions, movements, and intentions. And if he did not possess Forrest's and Morgan's tactical brilliance, he never demonstrated the unprofessional behavior and insubordinate attitude they sometimes displayed toward superiors they did not admire or appreciate.

Wheeler may not have made the most of his opportunities when on the offensive, but he could be counted on to defend his army's front, rear, and flanks with skill and dogged determination. As he demonstrated on many occasions, especially during the early stages of the Stones River and Chickamauga campaigns, he was adept at fighting and falling back, delaying the advance of a larger, better-equipped enemy and shielding his own army from its blows. He was unrelenting in pursuing enemy raiders, as he proved early in the Atlanta Campaign, when he captured, virtually intact, a division of Yankee horsemen intent on breaking Confederate communications and freeing the inmates of Andersonville Prison. He performed just as energetically, if less successfully, in pursuit of what was in effect the war's longest raid—William T. Sherman's foray from Atlanta to the Georgia coast, then northward through the Carolinas. During this campaign, as on some earlier occasions, Wheeler was roundly criticized for failing to curtail his men's tendency to loot and destroy on a par with Sherman's "bummers." Yet he himself was a model of rectitude and decorum, qualities he quietly but tirelessly attempted to impart to his officers and troopers.

When elevated to the command of the cavalry of the Army of Tennessee, Wheeler was barely twenty-five. His youth, which a long and bushy beard failed to disguise, contributed to his friction-laden relationships with older, more seasoned colleagues and subordinates. Yet it also enabled him to make military contributions to his nation thirty-three years after the close of the Civil War. In 1898, at the outbreak of hostilities with the Spanish Empire, Wheeler—then a several-term congressman from Alabama—was appointed by President William McKinley a major general in the regular army of the United States. Subsequently he took command of a brigade of cavalry that included the celebrated "Rough Riders" of Col. Leonard Wood and Lt. Col. Theodore Roosevelt. Although intended as a public-relations gesture in furtherance of national unity, Wheeler's appointment enabled him to see active service in the field against Spanish forces, a distinction denied to the five other ex-Confederates whom McKinley appointed general officers at war's beginning.

In Cuba between May and August 1898, and in the Philippines for seven months stretching into the following year, the venerable officer served with distinction to himself and his region. His service, however, was not without controversy—much of it caused by the jealousy of regular officers who lacked his opportunity to win renown. Whether or not he uttered the famous cry attributed to him when pursuing some fleeing Spaniards ("We've got the damned Yankees on the run!"), Wheeler's well-publicized exploits in blue came to overshadow those he had achieved in Confederate gray, making him—three decades after he fought against the Union cause—a hero to the entire nation.

It is difficult to explain why a soldier celebrated for conspicuous service on so many fields, an officer noted for professionalism, devotion to duty, and combativeness (a trait that earned him at least two nicknames, the rather prosaic "Fightin' Joe" and the more poetic and evocative "War Child"), has lacked a book-length biography for so many years. The last full-length study of Wheeler's life and career and the only scholarly attempt to assess his contributions to the Confederacy and his reunited nation, is John P. Dyer's *Fightin' Joe Wheeler*, published in 1941 by Louisiana State University Press and reissued twenty years later, at the outset of the Civil War centennial, under the title *From Shiloh to San Juan.*

Dyer's competent volume strives to define its subject's character and personality while highlighting his most dramatic military operations. Yet the author gives scant attention to less highly publicized but equally important episodes in Wheeler's career, relegating his role in several raids, skirmishes, and battles to a few sentences or a single paragraph. Then, too, the size and composition of Wheeler's command changed markedly and often during the war, but Dyer rarely enumerates the units at the general's disposal or identifies those senior subordinates who came and went with confusing frequency. The present study, which concentrates heavily on Wheeler's Civil War career, attempts to rectify these and other omissions. It also strives to correct some of the errors and misconceptions about him that have become a part of the public record. Above all, it seeks to make Joseph Wheeler's life and career accessible to a new generation of readers.

ACKNOWLEDGMENTS

I am deeply indebted to the following persons, who helped me research this work and prepare it for publication:

David Arthur and Rick Russell of Potomac Books, Inc.; Rich Baker and Steve Bye of the U.S. Army Military History Institute; Paul Beck of the University of Wisconsin at La Crosse; Darla Brock of the Tennessee State Library and Archives; Mike Brubaker and Micki Waldrop of the Atlanta History Center; Larry Carr and Mike Veach of the Filson Historical Society; Jody Cary and Lauren Eisenberg of the Gilder Lehrman Collection; Cathy Clevenger and Cheryl Nabati of the Bateman Memorial Library, Langley Air Force Base, Virginia; John Coski of the Museum of the Confederacy; Paul Dangel, Berwyn, Pennsylvania; Linda Woodward Geiger, Jasper, Georgia; Jenna deGraffenried of the Rosenberg Library; Randy Gue and Naomi Nelson of the Robert W. Woodruff Library, Emory University; Lisa Gayle Hazirjian, Durham, North Carolina; Jan Hilley of the New-York Historical Society; John M. Jackson of the Newman Library, Virginia Polytechnic Institute and State University; Claire McCann of King Library, University of Kentucky; Linda McCurdy of the William R. Perkins Library, Duke University; Debbie McKeon-Pogue of the United States Military Academy Special Collections and Archives; Phil Montgomery of the Rice University Library; Kathryn Page of the Louisiana State Museum; Anish Parikh, Yorktown, Virginia; Ranee Pruitt of the Huntsville-Madison County (Alabama) Public Library; Anna M. Rabb and Anne Skilton of the Wilson Library, University of North Carolina; Suzette Raney and Jim Reece of the Chattanooga-Hamilton County (Tennessee) Bicentennial Library; David Rich, Montgomery, Alabama; Steve Sansom, Jackson, Mississippi; Tim Smith of Shiloh National Military Park; Sarah Starr of the Western Reserve Historical Society Library and Archives; John Varner of the Auburn University Archives; Jean B. Waggener, Franklin, Tennessee; John Wheat of the Center for American History, University of

Texas; Elizabeth Wills of the Kentucky Historical Society; Eric J. Wittenberg, Columbus, Ohio; and Noelle Yetter, Vienna, Virginia. Finally, as always, I thank my wife, Ann, for her untiring assistance and support.

1

NOT LENGTH OR BREADTH
OR THICKNESS

*L*eroy Pope Walker was new to the business of soldiering, and it showed. The bewhiskered, forty-four-year-old Alabamian had garbed himself in a spanking-new greatcoat of gray, its sleeves awash in the gilt lace that signified a brigadier general in the Provisional Army of the Confederacy. Despite custom tailoring the uniform seemed a poor fit; it hung loosely on his lanky frame as if intended for a man of more martial stature.

In fact, Walker was used to wearing the morning-coat of a politician, his profession for the last twenty years. His resume included several terms in the state legislature, a circuit court judgeship, and three stints as a Democratic presidential elector. One of the leaders of Alabama's secession movement, in 1860 he had been a delegate to two of his party's presidential conventions—one in Charleston that had deadlocked over sectional candidates and the subsequent gathering in Richmond that had endorsed the Deep South's nominee, John C. Breckinridge of Kentucky. Because another Democratic convention had nominated Senator Stephen Douglas of Illinois, the party was fatally split, a condition that in November threw the election to the "Black Republican" candidate, Abraham Lincoln of Illinois, and transformed secession from ominous possibility to tragic reality.

When, following Lincoln's election, the lower South banded together for mutual defense, a government was formed at Montgomery, Alabama. As one of the state's leading politicos, Leroy Walker was virtually assured of a prominent position in that government. In late February 1861, three months before Virginia joined her neighbors in secession and the Confederate capital was moved to Richmond, Confederate President Jefferson Davis appointed Walker his secretary of war.[1]

The selection had been dictated by political expediency rather than the man's fitness for the position. As it turned out, Walker's lack of military experience

1

and his modest administrative abilities made his seven-month tenure a nightmare. Handicapped by a general paucity of resources—everything from canteens to cannons—Walker proved unequal to the task of organizing, arming, equipping, and staffing a large army on short notice. By the time he resigned his post on September 10, 1861, the impossible burdens of his office and the overwork they had produced had broken his health. Even so, Walker wished to continue to serve the Confederacy—now in a military capacity. As a reward for his diligent labor, President Davis appointed him a general officer and gave him command of four regiments of Alabama infantry organizing in Walker's hometown of Huntsville. There the newly minted brigadier repaired in late September, ready to shoulder a new round of administrative responsibilities, possibly as onerous as those he had borne in Montgomery and Richmond.[2]

Upon reaching Huntsville, Walker established his headquarters in an office building only a few blocks from his home. Within hours of his arrival, he assembled the commanders of his regiments. Most of his subordinates were well known to him, for they, like he, had forged flourishing legal and political careers in northern Alabama. After exchanging salutes, Walker shook hands with the commanders of his 14th, 17th, and 18th Alabama—Cols. Thomas J. Judge, Thomas H. Watts, and Edward C. Bullock, respectively. Each officer was resplendent in a uniform of rich gray broadcloth bearing three stars on the collar and three loops of lace on the sleeves. Their ensemble included elegant headgear, boots of burnished leather, and exotic weaponry: French-made pistols and sabers of the finest Sheffield steel. The accoutrements marked their owners as men of prosperity and prominence, successful professionals who also expected to succeed in their new calling.[3]

The fourth officer standing at attention before Walker's desk offered a marked contrast to these well-heeled civilians. Georgia-born Joseph Wheeler, the newly appointed commander of the 19th Alabama, wore an inexpensive woolen uniform. Designed for a first lieutenant of artillery, it had only recently been transformed into the raiment of a colonel of infantry. Unlike his solidly built colleagues, each of whom was of at least medium height, Wheeler stood five feet, two inches in his jackboots. His narrow-waisted tunic suggested that he weighed no more than 120 pounds soaking wet. And although a full beard was in cultivation on his thin, smooth face, it failed to disguise his lack of maturity. In fact, Wheeler had turned twenty-five less than two weeks earlier.

Had General Walker not possessed a keen memory, he might have wondered how this scrawny youngster had risen to such high rank so early in this war. In fact, it had been Walker's doing—he had made the appointment upon the recommendation of the line and field officers of the 19th Alabama when that regiment had organized the previous month. These officers, civilian-soldiers all, had become well acquainted with then-Lieutenant Wheeler during a stint of duty at Pensacola, headquarters of Brig. Gen. Braxton Bragg's Department of Alabama and West Florida. These gentlemen were not the only observers to be impressed by the young subaltern's industry, military knowledge, and professional poise. Along with "a large number of the company officers," the colonel of the 7th Alabama, also training at Pensacola, had petitioned the War Department in Richmond to appoint Wheeler to field rank in his regiment.[4]

More than anything else, Wheeler's education and experience had recommended him for promotion. Of Walker's ranking subordinates, he alone was a graduate of the United States Military Academy. Although he had ranked near the foot of the Class of 1859, Wheeler had acquired at the Academy a working knowledge of the tactics and duties of all three combat arms. Upon graduation he had been posted to one of the army's two regiments of dragoons (soldiers trained, armed, and equipped to fight both mounted and on foot as conditions warranted), but he had never served in that capacity. Instead, following a stint as an instructor at the Cavalry School of Practice at Carlisle Barracks, Pennsylvania, Wheeler had become a brevet second lieutenant in the Regiment of Mounted Riflemen. He had served a brief tour of frontier duty, then resigned his commission days before the opening shots of the Civil War pounded a United States Army garrison in Charleston Harbor, South Carolina. As a loyal Southerner, Wheeler had placed himself at the disposal of Georgia Governor Joseph E. Brown. Soon afterward, he had been commissioned into the Confederate army as a first lieutenant of artillery.[5]

Given the ease with which prominent civilians with no military qualifications attained high rank, Wheeler must have been chagrined to find himself elevated only one step above his prewar grade. Although he came from a financially strapped family and lacked political clout, Wheeler was as ambitious, as eager for promotion, as the best-connected civilian in arms. Thus he had leapt at the chance to gain regimental command in the Provisional Confederate Army, even if it meant serving under a politician-general such as Leroy Walker.

Wheeler's superior would have been forgiven if, during their first meeting, he entertained doubts about Wheeler's ability to whip his assigned unit into fighting trim. According to a Huntsville newspaper, the recruits of the 19th Alabama—most of whom hailed not from the local area but from Blount, Cherokee, Jefferson, and other counties in the middle of the state—were among "the sturdiest, most athletic, civil, well-behaved men, the very bone and sinew of the land." The hyperbolic correspondent who rendered this judgment failed to mention that few, if any, of these would-be warriors had received military training, even in the notoriously lax ranks of the militia. The great majority knew nothing of military life beyond what they remembered from the patriotic lore of their youth.[6]

In addition to being ignorant of the profession they had embarked upon, the recruits lacked uniforms, equipment of all kinds, arms, and ammunition. In time, state quartermasters would furnish clothing and camp equipage, but weaponry would prove impossible to come by for months after training camp opened at Huntsville. This critical lack threatened to vitiate any instructional program to which the 19th was exposed.

Another deterrent to proficiency was the general ill health of the regiment. Prior to the 19th's arrival at Huntsville, the commander of the state's militia, Gen. Jeremiah Clements, had laid out a campground amid a "beautiful grove" along the banks of Big Spring, the largest body of water in the area. Camp Jones (named for Col. Egbert J. Jones, an Alabama hero of the July 21 victory near Manassas Junction, Virginia, the first sizable land battle of the conflict) abounded in picturesque vistas. Yet the camp also sprawled across low, marshy ground that proved to be a fertile source of disease. Within weeks of the first arrivals, infectious maladies of one form or another had infiltrated Camp Jones. By the time of Wheeler's commissioning, a frightening proportion of the 1,000-man regiment had been laid low by measles, chicken pox, and diphtheria.

Another commander might have thrown up his hands and importuned General Walker for relief. Wheeler merely rolled up his gilt-encrusted sleeves and got to work with a will. His first act was to move the camp to an abandoned militia training ground at Blue Springs, several miles north of Huntsville. The new location, like its predecessor, afforded access to shade and water, but it sat on higher ground and had the additional advantage of being far enough from town to isolate the regiment, thus promoting unit cohesion and discipline. Wheeler dubbed the new site Camp Bradford in honor of a local widow who had helped nurse the sick of the 19th.[7]

The move to Blue Springs produced a notable improvement in the corporate health. As inmates left the hospital to return to active duty, Wheeler began to organize the regiment into companies and battalions. At the same time he strove to acquaint himself with the material at his disposal and to identify promising candidates for commissions and sergeant's stripes. He was careful to keep every relationship strictly professional. This was largely a matter of personal preference—naturally diffident and reserved, Wheeler did not easily forge close ties; nor, once they were in place, did he casually break them. In his capacity as regimental commander a sense of detachment served him well, for it prevented him from incurring personal obligations to the officers and men he would have to order about on the drill plain and later on the battlefield.

Once small units had been formed and staffed, Wheeler concentrated on perfecting the training program that had originated at Camp Jones under his predecessor (Col. W. E. Hill, a graduate of the Virginia Military Institute) but that had faltered due to illnesses and ennui. Wheeler's instructional regimen was a rigorous one. John Witherspoon Du Bose, an Alabamian who would serve under Wheeler and write a history of the general's service in the Army of Tennessee, noted that "in the forenoon every day the officers' school of instruction, the sergeants' school, the corporals' school, were called. Company drill, battalion drill, inspection, dress parade, occupied the hours of daylight every day, and the colonel was always present. Every soldier saw him absorbed in his duties. . . . His motions were quick, his decisions prompt and firm, his judgment just and accurate." Not even the prolonged absence of shoulder-arms slowed the pace of instruction. In place of rifles the men toted fence rails and tree branches. They became so conversant with these ersatz weapons that when finally issued the real article they felt they knew everything there was to know about being a rifleman.[8]

General Walker, who visited Camp Jones throughout the summer, was quickly impressed by the leadership, energy, and organizational skill of his youngest subordinate as well as by the growing proficiency the men demonstrated under his tutelage. Equally impressed was the officer who finally supplied those men with the infantry arms they sorely lacked. While making the rounds of his far-flung department, Braxton Bragg, Walker's imperious and sometimes irascible superior at Pensacola, had an excellent opportunity to study at close range the 19th Alabama and its colonel. He so liked what he saw that he made a note to support the regiment with as many rifles and accoutrements as he could scare up.[9]

He had not always felt this way about Joseph Wheeler, whose rapid ascent to regimental command originally had stoked his ire. It had also involved Bragg in a prolonged debate with Walker's successor as secretary of war. The argument pivoted on Wheeler's youth and lack of seniority, not his ability to command a regiment, even though Bragg may well have harbored reservations about the Georgian's academic record at West Point and his limited army experience.

In fact, while at Pensacola Lieutenant Wheeler had given his superior a dramatic illustration of his industry and technical expertise. During the early weeks of the war, Bragg, whose mission was to defend the Gulf Coast as far west as Mobile, had been striving to refurbish the several fortifications that guarded the entrance to Pensacola Bay, including the venerable Fort San Carlos de Barrancas. Shortly before hostilities began, the United States forces who had garrisoned that mainland fort had evacuated it in favor of Fort Pickens on Santa Rosa Island. Before departing Barrancas, they had spiked, dismounted, or otherwise rendered inoperable the fort's heavy cannons. Bragg wished to repair and remount them in order to repulse a possible attack by Federal land and naval forces and also to help reduce Fort Pickens. No member of his staff, however, had the required engineering expertise, and the citizens in arms who predominated at Pensacola refused to form labor details unless supervised by an experienced officer.

The dilemma persisted until one evening Lieutenant Wheeler appeared at Bragg's office and volunteered to oversee the project. Although unacquainted with the callow subaltern and thus unfamiliar with his abilities, Bragg accepted his offer. The following day Wheeler took charge of the work parties—which probably consisted, at least in part, of slave labor—and set to work with such zeal and determination that within a fortnight several guns had been mounted and placed in operation.[10]

Bragg was equally surprised and gratified by Wheeler's enterprise, which helped deter the enemy from attacking Barrancas during the next eight months. Yet some weeks later, when Wheeler gained his colonel's commission and command of the 19th Alabama, Bragg felt compelled to protest his promotion. The old soldier considered Wheeler's jump over the heads of hundreds of more experienced officers prejudicial to the morale of his command. In late September Bragg—himself recently promoted to major general—wrote Walker's successor, the brilliant, multitalented Judah P. Benjamin, to complain about the extraordinary honor accorded the young Georgian. While acknowledging that Wheeler was "a very excellent officer, and none envy him his good fortune . . . they cannot see the justice of the apparent reflection on themselves. The jealousy with which professional soldiers look upon military rank is second only, my dear sir, to that of honor." Bragg relied on, and felt indebted to, many of the officers past whom Wheeler had advanced. Now he shared the "mortification which has been inflicted on them," which he ascribed to political meddling and War Department apathy.[11]

Bragg's protest availed him nothing except a certain amount of embarrassment. In his reply, which did not reach Bragg until early October, Secretary Benjamin called the general's protest "wholly without foundation" and pointed out that Bragg himself was in large measure responsible for Wheeler's meteoric rise. Benjamin recalled that around the time the officers of the 7th Alabama had sought Wheeler's promotion, the lieutenant had applied to Bragg in his own behalf, asking either for the higher rank or for authority to raise a regiment in the Confederate Provisional Army. Bragg had forwarded the correspondence to the War Office with a "full and cordial indorsement of Lieutenant Wheeler's application."[12]

Benjamin's mild reproof failed to mollify the argumentative Bragg, who, despite his own role in it, decried the precedent thus set. He said as much in a second letter of protest. To this missive Benjamin did not reply, forcing Bragg to drop the matter.[13]

In later weeks, although his view of the issue at hand did not change, Bragg's appreciation of Colonel Wheeler's military abilities continued to grow. During an inspection trip early in the fall, the departmental commander scrutinized the conditions at the training station at Huntsville and made a detailed report of his findings. He concluded that General Walker was not only an inefficient administrator but lacked the skill required of a field commander. On the other hand, he was so impressed by the training program at Camp Bradford that he decided to reward the 19th Alabama. In early November, with Benjamin's approval, he called the regiment to Mobile, where from a variety of sources including hospitalized soldiers he furnished it with enough shoulder arms to make it a fighting force in fact as well as in name. This gesture—which Bragg did not grant any other outfit at Huntsville—suggested that he had revised his earlier assessment of the commander of the 19th. It had become obvious that Colonel Wheeler was the right man at the right time in the right position.[14]

———

Joseph Wheeler III, the youngest son of Joseph Wheeler Jr. and Julia Knox Hull Wheeler, had been born in Augusta, Georgia, on September 10, 1836. His ancestry was Anglo-Saxon: the first Wheeler had come to America from Kent, England, in 1640 to settle in the colony of Massachusetts Bay. The lineage of Joseph's mother, a native of Newton, Massachusetts, was especially distinguished, she having descended from another early New England Puritan, Richard Hull. A more notable ancestor was Anne Boleyn, the second wife of Henry VIII. Julia's father was Gen. William Hull, a stalwart of the American Revolution whose lustrous reputation had been tarnished by his surrender of the garrison at Detroit to an English force during the War of 1812. That unhappy event resulted from circumstances beyond Hull's control, including the poorly situated and lightly defended fortifications his troops had been forced to occupy and a lack of naval support on Lake Erie. Even so, the general's reputation never recovered from the devastating effect of his capitulation.[15]

Julia was the second wife of Joseph Wheeler Jr. Joseph's first spouse, the former Sara Bradford, had long suffered from various illnesses, the only possible cure for which was removal to a more salubrious climate than Massachusetts could offer. Sara's physical condition was one of two factors in the Wheelers' move to Georgia in 1819, the other being the economic depression that crippled New England commerce in the wake of the War of 1812. For a time the couple appeared to prosper in their new home on the Savannah River near Augusta. Joseph forged successful careers as a banker, real estate promoter, and gentleman farmer. The move, however, had come too late to salvage Sara's health; less than two years after settling in Georgia, her thirty-two-year-old husband became a widower. He shared his grief with relatives back in Connecticut and Massachusetts, whom he visited frequently. It was in the latter state that he met Julia, a widow with a son from an earlier marriage. They were married in September 1825.[16]

Soon after the wedding, Joseph Wheeler returned to Georgia with his new wife and stepson, determined to live a more pleasant life than heretofore. In fact, his second marriage, though relatively brief, was happy and fruitful. Over the next eleven years two sons and two daughters were born to the couple. The youngest was originally known as Joseph Wheeler III, although early in life he inherited the suffix "Junior," the elder Wheeler having dropped it upon the death of his own father. The boy also inherited many of his father's traits. John P. Dyer observes that "the physical characteristics of the two were much the same— the same slight build and mildness of countenance. In temperament they showed similar traits, especially a mixture of shrewdness, impetuosity, and caution. Too, there was in both father and son an aloofness and a reserve which few men ever really penetrated." Furthermore, both exuded a sometimes exaggerated sense of dignity and formality. Although these characteristics were off-putting to some, they helped further the careers of father and son as, respectively, civilian businessman and professional soldier.[17]

While his family life flourished, the elder Joseph's business interests suffered a sharp decline within a year of his namesake's birth. The Panic of 1837, the first major business depression in American history, struck the South as hard as it did Joseph's native region. The businesses that it ruined and the capital it siphoned off, combined with unwise decisions by the elder Wheeler including the cosigning of notes for friends and relatives less business-minded than he, eventually took most of his cash and property. The transplanted Yankee was forced to settle his debts by selling not only stocks and bonds but also parcels of land in Georgia and New England. He was left with nothing beyond the family's sixty-acre farm, which he operated with the support of a few slaves, and part ownership of a textile mill in Derby, Connecticut.

Joseph's business reverses seem to have affected the health of his second wife, who died in 1842 at age forty-three. Again left disconsolate and rootless, the two-time widower returned to Connecticut, where he and his children moved into a modest house in Derby. When they came of age, the children attended the common schools of the area. In 1847, two years after his father sold his interest in the mill and returned alone to Georgia in a futile attempt to regain prosperity, Joseph Jr. entered a more highly-regarded educational institution, the Episcopal Academy of Connecticut (later the Cheshire Academy). This came about through the largess of Julia Hull Wheeler's two sisters, both of whom were comfortably situated.[18]

Little is known of young Joseph's term at the Episcopal Academy, which—typical of secondary institutions of the time—schooled youngsters between the ages of ten and fourteen. Dyer claims that Joseph's fellow students regarded him as "stiff, polite, and very serious." Yet he loosened up enough to take part in a traditional feat of the student body, one calculated to increase his popularity among his classmates. In the darkness of night, accompanied by his close friend, future financier extraordinaire J. Piermont Morgan, Joseph climbed a waterspout at the rear of the school building and carved his name in the oaken beam that supported the school bell. Dyer notes that other than this single out-of-character exploit, "his conduct seems to have attracted no special attention. He passed his courses in Cheshire, he did the chores around his aunts' home, and in the course of time [the spring of 1851] finished his secondary school work."[19]

Upon graduation, Joseph left Connecticut for New York City. There he boarded with his sister Lucy, now Mrs. Sterling S. Smith, wife of a prominent local businessman. Apparently the arrangement proved unsatisfactory, for by the summer of 1853 the teenager had become the ward of one of his aunts, Mrs. Augusta Hull Platt, in whose Brooklyn home, presumably, he resided.[20]

Mrs. Platt and her husband secured for the boy a clerkship in a mercantile office, where Joseph toiled for more than a year. It must have been a long and trying period; perhaps mindful of his father's disastrous commercial ventures, he had no desire to enter the world of business. Nor did he intend to take up permanent residence in New York and its environs. His preference was for an extended stay at an institution fifty miles to the north, nestled among the Hudson Valley highlands.

Since early youth Joseph had been keenly aware of his family's military tradition. He had been weaned on tales of William Hull's Revolutionary War achievements (to the conspicuous neglect of the general's later, more problematic, career) and had gloried in the gallant deeds of the general's brother, Abraham Fuller Hull, a Harvard-educated officer in the regular service who had died a hero in the July 1814 battle of Lundy's Lane. Though he may not have looked the part, William's grandson and Abraham's grandnephew fancied himself soldier material. By his late teens Joseph Jr. was ready to put his aspirations to the test at the tuition-free United States Military Academy. A West Point education would not only provide entry into his chosen field but would spare from additional financial burdens those relatives who had already supported him so generously.[21]

Family lore has it that Joseph made numerous applications for an Academy appointment, only to encounter repeated rejection. In reality, his request for an appointment languished for less than a year in the office of New York's sixth district congressman, John Wheeler (no relation to the applicant) before it was submitted to Secretary of War Jefferson Davis. The nomination may have been owed, in part at least, to the congressman's Connecticut roots and his Episcopal Academy education. Then, too, Representative Wheeler must have been influenced by the character references provided by prominent acquaintances including Reverend Francis Vinton, D.D., rector of Brooklyn's Grace Episcopal Church. Vinton pronounced Joseph Wheeler Jr. an "excellent young man, of pure morals & of good intellect & of sufficient learning" to turn a West Point education to good advantage.[22]

On June 8, 1854, only two days after the congressman sent in Joseph's name, the War Department notified the applicant of his acceptance into the West Point class of 1859 (the institution was experimenting with a five-year course in contrast to the four years of schooling it had offered since its founding in 1802). His appointment was contingent on Joseph's passing the entrance examinations, mental and physical, that the Academy demanded of all plebes. Joseph's acceptance bound him to serve his country "eight years unless sooner discharged." He happily acknowledged receipt of his appointment, never suspecting that events and sentiments would prevent him from honoring his commitment to the army.[23]

Although his prior educational experience was sufficient to enable him to pass the far-from-rigorous entrance exams, it did not ensure him academic success at West Point. In fact Cadet Wheeler would make a rather dismal record at the Academy, one that started poorly, then went downhill. At the end of his first (or "fifth-class") year, which was taken up with mathematics courses and

English studies, he ranked twenty-fourth among thirty-five cadets. The following year, when French was added to the course load, he finished eighteenth in his reduced class of twenty-nine. During his third-class year, which introduced him to military drawing, the bottom fell out and he sank to twenty-first of twenty-three cadets. He fared even worse during his next-to-last year at the Academy, which included courses in chemistry as well as civil engineering, the core of the Academy's curriculum. He ended that term next-to-last in a class of twenty-two.

Joseph's record was atypical of his era. Many other cadets, including those who went on to successful military careers, lacked the skill or diligence to master such demanding subjects as engineering and algebra. Most of them excelled, however, at the Academy's tactical courses, offered during the last year of study. Not so Joseph Wheeler Jr., who did almost as badly in the military-specific courses as he did in the core subjects of natural and experimental philosophy, mineralogy, geology, and ethics. At the close of his first-class year, he ranked sixteenth out of twenty-two cadets in infantry tactics, eighteenth in ordnance and gunnery, twenty-first in artillery tactics, and dead last in the tactics of the mounted arm.[24]

Given the success he was destined to achieve in his chosen profession, especially in cavalry operations, his showing appears to defy rational analysis. His deficiencies were not due to want of studious application; by all accounts, he spent a great deal of time reading in the Academy library and in his barracks room. Nor did his overall class standing suffer, as many classmates' did, from an inordinate number of violations of the Academy's strict disciplinary code. He never came close to the number of demerits—200 in a given year—that meant instant dismissal. During his five years of study, he accumulated, respectively, forty-three, eighty-two, six, forty-eight, and thirteen demerits. Many were the result of poor performance on the drill plain rather than misbehavior out of the classroom. His delinquency log is replete with instances of "neglect of duty," "allowing disorder in ranks," and being "inattentive at cavalry drill."[25]

One has to look beyond infractions and demerits for an explanation of Wheeler's abysmal academic record. Perhaps his abiding shyness proved a handicap during classroom recitations and tactical exercises. Perhaps he was one of those students who, although able to absorb knowledge, are poor test-takers. Perhaps, like many of his fellows, he spent his time in the library reading novels and light verse rather than textbooks or tactics manuals.

If Wheeler was no scholar, neither was he an athlete. Undoubtedly due to his slight build, he took little interest in, and in fact seems to have avoided, the Academy's embryonic physical education program. One would not imagine that his stature was so different from that of his classmates as to provoke public comment. Yet it prompted one classmate, a devotee of geometry, to dub him "Point," a moniker that stuck. As John Du Bose explains, the nickname referred to the fact that in the flesh Cadet Wheeler displayed "neither length, breadth, nor thickness."[26]

Wheeler's appellation was not a term of derision, indicative of unpopularity among his fellow cadets. Although his introverted nature and serious demeanor militated against his acquiring a bevy of close friends, he managed to form a number of attachments—some of which endured for decades—and was well-thought-of by his peers. One recalled him as "always earnest and quiet . . . a true gentleman always," adding approvingly that Wheeler "rarely spoke when he had nothing to say"—which seems to have been quite often.[27]

Wheeler's final class standing was nineteenth of twenty-two cadets. Ironically, of those twenty-two he alone would achieve military fame. Few members of the Class of 1859 gained high rank, let alone professional distinction. Besides Wheeler, only Northern-born Martin D. Hardin and Edwin H. Stoughton became general officers during the Civil War, and the reputation of neither survived the conflict. Lesser-ranking officers such as Confederate colonels Charles R. Collins and Robert F. Beckham made distinguished reputations, but their careers were cut short by death in battle.

It would appear that in his personal relationships, Wheeler preferred the company of Collins, Beckham, and other Southern-born cadets to those classmates with Northern roots, especially those who argued politics. Despite his years in the North and his family's ties to New York and New England, Wheeler was a Southerner by birth, and he considered himself one at heart as well. His innate dignity and decorum and the importance he ascribed to gentlemanly behavior made him responsive to the Southern ethos, which prized honor, virtue, and pedigree while condemning so-called Northern traits such as materialism and demagoguery. As the son of a Georgia farmer and slaveholder, Wheeler was a proponent of the agrarian economy. And as a scion of a politically conservative family, he accepted the view of most Southerners that their way of life was threatened by Yankee agitators who would trample the Constitution in their frenzied quest for political advantage.

As a microcosm of the society from which it drew its student body, West Point during the late 1850s was a hotbed of political ferment and sectional conflict. As the volatile decade drew to a close, cadets from the North, South, and Northwest expressed divergent views with heated words and sometimes with clenched fists. Wheeler's innate reticence kept him out of the louder vocal clashes, while his physical stature would not permit him to fight. Still, he closely monitored the points of contention among his classmates while quietly supporting the Southern view of national affairs. Despite his desire to avoid confrontations with cadets who did not share his political views, he must have suspected that the country would eventually fall victim to the sectional divide. By the time he left West Point, a national tragedy of epic proportions was drawing near, and he doubted he would escape involvement in it.[28]

— — — —

By the narrowest of margins, Wheeler graduated with his West Point class on July 1, 1859. It was a day of triumph in more than one sense. Had he deliberately mismanaged his academic career, he could not have been more fortunate in the duty assignment it brought him. The Academy's highest-ranking graduates were usually offered positions in the army's elite units, the corps of topographical and construction engineers. Graduates of lesser standing could expect to be posted to the artillery, the infantry, and the mounted service, in order of desirability. Wheeler, who had loved horses since youth and had developed into an accomplished equestrian despite his poor grades in cavalry tactics, must have been overjoyed to receive a brevet second lieutenancy in the mounted arm. The brevet was a provisional rank at which a young officer would serve until a vacancy opened in his assigned unit through the promotion, resignation, or death of he who was next in seniority.[29]

Presumably, Wheeler was no less pleased to find himself assigned to the 1st United States Dragoons. America's oldest and, arguably, most distinguished mounted outfit, the 1st Dragoons had served the nation since its organization at Jefferson Barracks, Missouri, in 1833. For the first thirteen years of its existence it had guarded travelers' routes and settlers' communities from the Kansas Territory to the Rocky Mountains. The regiment had also served with distinction in the Mexican War of 1846–48, winning renown in the battle of Buena Vista, where a detachment under Maj. Enoch Steen attacked in flank a column of Mexican lancers that had attempted to waylay an American supply train. Steen's hell-for-leather charge cut the enemy column in two and dispersed it, saving the train.[30]

The 1st, one of two dragoon regiments in the service, was a model of organizational and operational flexibility, combining the talents of horses and foot soldiers. In 1846 the economy-minded Congress that had created these hybrid units had also authorized the formation of a regiment of mounted riflemen—soldiers who regarded their horses mainly as transportation and who, upon reaching the scene of battle, dismounted to fight with infantry weapons. Not until the year after Wheeler's matriculation at West Point did Congress come to the realization that three mounted outfits—cavalry being necessary to combating fast-moving hostiles—were insufficient to patrol a frontier that stretched from the Rio Grande to the Canadian border. In 1855 two regiments formally designated as cavalry were added to the army. Their officers and men fought primarily on horseback, with sabers, pistols, and carbines (short-barrel shoulder arms).[31]

Brevet Second Lt. Joseph Wheeler's maiden service with his regiment was not in the field but at a training facility, the Cavalry School of Practice at Carlisle Barracks. He arrived at that venerable post in the shadow of South Mountain in the early fall of 1859 at the close of the three months' leave granted to Academy graduates. He may have spent his furlough with his sister and aunt in Brooklyn, or perhaps he returned to Georgia, where his other siblings, including his businessman brother, William, continued to reside.

Little is known of Brevet Second Lieutenant Wheeler's first stint of active duty. Dyer speculates that he was sent to Carlisle for additional training, a logical supposition given his terrible showing in cavalry tactics. Yet it is more likely that he went to Pennsylvania to tutor those raw recruits whose grasp of mounted service was even weaker than his own. It is likely, too, that the routine at Carlisle was much as it had been when Lt. William Woods Averell (USMA Class of 1855) was posted to the Cavalry School, then at Jefferson Barracks, Missouri, four years earlier. Averell left a detailed account of a typical day at the installation:

"Reveille at 5 A. M., followed by 'stable call,' which we attended until 7 o'clock. We walked up and down the line while the men were grooming the horses and also inspected the stables. Each of us had charge of about thirty horses. . . . Guard mounting was called at 8 A. M., and at 9 mounted drill began and lasted until 11:30. At 1:30 P. M. there was a dismounted drill which lasted until 4:30 followed by stable call again at 5 o'clock. After that we had the evening to ourselves, those of us who were not on duty as Officer of the Day or Officer of the Guard. Sometimes, with leave, we used to gallop into the city, eleven miles, to social entertainments or to the theatre."[32]

Six days a week (excepting only Sunday), the School of Practice was a hive of activity and a Babel of voices as closely-spaced columns of riders and horses went through the various evolutions of mounted drill to the accompaniment of shouted commands from instructors. Averell recalled that "the great plain outside the Post presented the most attractive and animated spectacle during drill hours. Nearly a thousand mounted men were instructed there daily in all the schools—from that of a trooper mounted, to that of a squadron [the standard maneuvering unit, consisting of two 100-man companies], and finally of the regiment. . . . Within sixty days over eight hundred men and horses had been broken in and formed into coherent troops or squadrons. Every manoeuvre [sic] known to tactics could be executed with rapidity and precision. The men could use their arms and fight mounted or dismounted. And beyond all, for without it everything else would have soon disappeared, they had learned to care for their horses, arms and equipments, how to pitch camp or establish bivouac and to guard it, how to handle their rations and the best way to prepare their food. It was a wonderful performance. It tested the qualifications of every officer to the utmost."[33]

At Carlisle Barracks, Wheeler could observe at close range the different horse units. The Regiment of Mounted Rifles impressed him the most; in time he decided he preferred it to its sister outfits. In contrast to the dragoons, who fought mounted approximately half the time, and the cavalry, who fought predominately in the saddle, the officers and men of this regiment fought almost entirely afoot. Because they had no need for the weapons and accoutrements of the other units they were more lightly equipped and thus enjoyed greater mobility.

Too, their tactics were less complex and thus took less time to master, meaning that a mounted riflemen could devote himself to the nuances rather than the basics of his arm. Wheeler also noted that there was a decided difference in the firepower of which the three forces were capable. While a rifle could be cumbersome and time-consuming to load, it could do greater damage at longer range than a dragoon's musketoon or a cavalryman's carbine.

—— —— —— ——

When Wheeler's stint at the Cavalry School ended in the late spring of 1860, he hastened to Washington, D.C., to seek a transfer from his assigned outfit to the one that had captured his imagination. Either he had learned of a vacancy in the latter or his timing was fortuitous, for on June 26 he was notified of his posting to the Mounted Riflemen. Given no time in which to celebrate his good fortune, he set about to join his new unit in the New Mexico Territory.[34]

Given the limitations of military transportation, the journey west promised to be an ordeal, especially as it was to be made by mule train. Wheeler's ultimate destination was Fort Craig, which occupied the crest of a small plateau on the right bank of the Rio Grande, in south-central New Mexico. Since 1854, the garrison had coordinated operations aimed at protecting land and water travelers from marauding Apaches. It was at this spartan but bustling installation that Wheeler would spent much of the next nine months, interspersed with trips to other territorial outposts, including Fort Fillmore on the lower Rio Grande and Fort Union along the Santa Fe Trail.[35]

In addition to being slow and bone-wracking, the trip to Fort Craig was replete with danger. According to a highly dramatized account written by Wheeler himself and repeated at length by his most recent biographer, the young subaltern commenced fighting Indians before he was halfway to his destination. At the outset of the journey, he was detailed to guard a wagon that carried not combat troops but a surgeon and a pregnant woman, the wife of an officer at Fort Craig. Several days into the westward trek, the woman went into labor, forcing the wagon to halt. While the surgeon prepared for the delivery, assisted by Wheeler and the wagon's half-breed teamster, the rest of the column continued west, leaving the little party isolated and vulnerable.

No sooner had the child been delivered and the wagon returned to the trail than an Apache war party attacked amid volleys of war-whoops and arrows. The three men in Wheeler's party opened fire, the driver dropping one attacker with his rifle. With that, as Wheeler wrote, "the Indians were after the driver in a bunch. The air seemed filled with arrows. That was my chance. I engaged the crowd, knocking down a horse with a shot from my musket. Then I threw away my gun and went at them with my Colt pistol. The driver came in with his Colt and the Indians were on the run. . . ." Suddenly the danger was past, and the wagon caught up with the balance of the train. Once the other travelers heard of his role in the fight they bestowed on the young lieutenant praise, congratulations, and a nickname: "Fightin' Joe." The sobriquet would adhere to him for the rest of his life, replacing the less flattering appellation he had acquired at West Point.[36]

In the wake of his harrowing introduction to life on the Indian frontier, the balance of Wheeler's service in New Mexico must have seemed anticlimactic. Years later one of his Civil War subordinates claimed what Wheeler took part in "several Indian engagements" as a Mounted Rifleman. Dyer, however, states that Wheeler's service in New Mexico was "one of comparative quiet among the Indians of the Southwest. . . . border duty consisted largely of drill and maneuvers, with now and then a brush with small bands of wandering Apaches."[37]

The record appears to bear out Dyer's version. While Wheeler was in New Mexico, detachments of mounted riflemen had fewer than a half-dozen encounters with hostile warriors, and his company took part in only two or three. Wheeler's only opportunity to participate in a pitched battle appears to have occurred only days after he arrived at his new duty station, when more than half of his outfit engaged Apaches at Canada de los Penavetitos, during the so-called Canadian River Expedition. The record does not indicate whether on that occasion Wheeler—still two months away from becoming a full-rank second lieutenant—strengthened his claim to the nickname he had gained on the trail to Fort Craig.[38]

———— ——

Although the majority of its enlisted personnel were Northern- or foreign-born, a majority of the officers in Wheeler's regiment including its colonel, William Wing Loring, and its lieutenant colonel, George B. Crittenden, were Southerners who adhered to the doctrine of states' rights and believed their home states were entitled to withdraw from the Union if the federal government oppressed them. If the sectional crisis boiled over into war, family ties and regional alliances would compel them to resign their commissions and return home to defend their regions against the government they had served ever since joining the army. As the presidential election of 1860 drew near, these officers declared that if a Republican won the White House and attempted to hold the South in the Union by force, war would surely come, and quickly.[39]

Because his regional allegiance did not appear so clear-cut, one would assume that Second Lieutenant Wheeler would have had a more difficult time determining how he would react to secession and conflict. Although he had been born in the Deep South, his family's roots lay in the soil of New England and its history was dramatically entwined with that of the United States Army. Yet after November 6, when former Illinois Congressman Abraham Lincoln was elected president despite having polled fewer votes than his combined Democrat and Whig opponents, the portents became ominous. Wheeler's Southern-born colleagues began to tender their resignations in the wake of South Carolina's December 20 announcement that the bonds tying her to the rest of the nation were "hereby dissolved." For two weeks after her precipitate action, an uneasy calm settled upon the country. The lull ended in January 1861, with the secession of Mississippi, Florida, and Alabama. Soon a secession convention was convening in Milledgeville, Georgia's capital, and there seemed little doubt that a majority of the conferees would vote to take the state out of the Union. By now Wheeler was firmly convinced of the path he should take. As he wrote his brother William, "much as I love the Union, and much as I am attached to my profession, all would be given up when my state, by its action, shows that such a course is necessary and proper."[40]

On January 19, by a vote of 208 to 89, Georgia adopted an ordinance of secession. Within days, William Wheeler had begun to recruit in Augusta a battery of artillery, whose services he planned to offer to Governor Brown. Even as he wrote the governor about his intention, William sought a commission for his younger brother. He commented on Joseph's military education and experience. He mentioned his brother's Northern upbringing but testified to his allegiance to his native state. "I have just received a letter from him," William added, "which states that he will resign his present position and return to this State. It will probably be two or three weeks before he arrives here where he will offer his services to you."[41]

William Wheeler correctly judged his brother's intentions, but he was premature in predicting the date of his resignation. Not until February 27—by which date seven states had declared themselves out of the Union, with four more to follow over the next two months—did the lieutenant submit his resignation to the adjutant general's office. Although it is doubtful that he knew it, his brother's efforts had secured for him a lieutenancy in Georgia's state forces.[42]

Although Wheeler had postponed his resignation for nearly a month after his state seceded, his decision predated by six weeks South Carolina's bombardment of the U.S. Army garrison inside Fort Sumter, Charleston Harbor, the act that touched off the powder keg of war. By the time the fort surrendered, Joseph Wheeler, clothed in civilian attire, was traveling by wagon, steamboat, and railroad to the place of his birth. There he would join thousands of other Georgians in striving to defend their state against a hostile nation perched almost on their doorstep.

2

AN EXAMPLE OF COOL, HEROIC COURAGE

*I*t is not known whether Wheeler returned directly to Georgia or traveled first to Montgomery, Alabama, seat of the fledgling Confederate nation. The only certainty is that one week before the firing on Sumter, the commission his brother had acquired for him in Georgia's defense forces was superseded by his appointment as a second lieutenant of artillery in the Regular Army of the Confederate States of America. This force, whose projected strength mirrored the small size of the regular army of the United States, was expected not only to help fight the war now imminent but also to do peacetime duty once the South won her independence. The burden of the war, however, would be carried on primarily by the soldiers of the much larger Confederate Provisional Army, which was organizing at the same time. Wheeler was destined to transition to the provisional ranks; the regular service was regarded as something of a holding organization into which former U.S. Army officers were taken until their qualifications could be matched against the military needs of the Confederacy.[1]

By about late April Wheeler had returned to Augusta for a joyful reunion with his family. There, in the aftermath of the firing on Sumter, he received the orders that called him to Braxton Bragg's headquarters at Pensacola. He delayed only long enough to complete his military wardrobe. Its centerpiece was a gray tunic whose collar carried the gold bar that denoted his rank and whose sleeve cuffs were trimmed in scarlet, the color of his service branch.

When entraining for Florida—which, like Georgia, was brimming over with the secessionist spirit—the lieutenant undoubtedly expected to see early service against the U.S. Army units that garrisoned various works along the Atlantic and Gulf coasts. If so, he must have been disappointed when, upon his arrival in Pensacola, he found that the nearest enemy, a detachment of the 1st United States Artillery under Lt. Adam J. Slemmer, had abandoned readily accessible Forts Barrancas and McRae on the mainland below the city in favor of

Fort Pickens, which sprawled across the southern tip of Santa Rosa Island. The isolated position of the incomplete yet formidable installation that guarded the entrance to Pensacola Bay caused Wheeler to doubt that Slemmer's garrison could be taken by anything less than a prolonged siege. Even that hope died when cargo vessels from the North, convoyed by U.S. Navy warships, began regular supply runs to the fort.[2]

The close cooperation between Slemmer's artillerists and their naval comrades prompted Bragg to remount the guns at Barrancas, the project that brought Lieutenant Wheeler to the attention of his departmental commander. It was the competence and self-confidence he displayed on that occasion that gained him the opportunity to transition so abruptly from artillery subaltern to colonel of the 19th Alabama. And it was his conspicuous ability in regimental command that brought him to Mobile, where his weaponless outfit was armed, outfitted, and readied for field service.

If Wheeler expected that promotion and transfer would be springboards to an active combat career, he was again disappointed. Although it enjoyed the distinction of being the Gulf Coast's most important defensive position (with the possible exception of Galveston, Texas), Mobile proved to be no more a hotbed of military action than Pensacola. If the Yankees seemed disinclined to challenge the guns that Wheeler had helped return to service, they appeared just as unwilling to attack the less formidable defenses of coastal Alabama. They did, however, clamp a shipping blockade on Mobile. The presence of the sidewheel steam frigate *Powhatan* along the outer reaches of Mobile Bay discouraged larger ships from entering the harbor. Yet sleek, shallow-draught blockade runners, operating under cover of night, evaded the U.S. Navy barrier with relative ease.[3]

With no war in progress on the local scene, Wheeler used the fall of 1861 and the following winter to perfect the organization and training of his regiment. He did so with single-minded determination and an abundance of energy and zeal. He allowed nothing to interfere with his duties, and he did not spare himself from the hardships and discomforts stemming from his rigorous training program. Some of his colleagues were not so self-sacrificing. By early December, General Walker and the rest of his brigade had been transferred from Huntsville to Mobile. Wheeler's immediate superior had not lost his taste for the genteel side of military life, nor had the well-heeled citizen-soldiers who commanded the other regiments in his command. According to John Du Bose, Walker established his headquarters in a comfortable private dwelling on Government Street, "hung a painted tin sign at the front door indicating his presence within, distributed his regiments on the suburbs and seemed to wait, in ease, developments." Taking a page from him, his subordinates declined to rough it in the field; they booked rooms in the finest hotel in Mobile, "riding their horses from the livery stables daily or occasionally, perhaps, to the encampment."[4]

By contrast, Colonel Wheeler "was present on duty night and day." He slept under canvas and took his meals in the officers' mess. He rode his horse only within the boundaries of the encampment he had carved out of a stand of pines south of the city. The young officer, his beard at last dark and luxuriant, instructed his would-be soldiers in the manner of an old and accomplished drill-master. The daily routine lasted from 6 AM until sunset. It featured an hour of officers' drill followed by an hour of drill by the regiment as a whole, an hour of tactical recitation by the officers, another hour of recitation by the noncommis-sioned officers, an hour of drill by companies, two hours of camp policing, ninety minutes of drill by the entire regiment, a dress parade at evening, and finally a posting of camp guards. An hour (7 to 8 AM) was allotted for breakfast; dinner hour began at noon or twelve-thirty; and the supper hour followed im-mediately after the second period of regimental drill.[5]

The tactics in which the regiment was instructed derived from a manual compiled by Confederate general William J. Hardee, a Georgia-born veteran of seventeen years in the United States Army, a former commandant of cadets at West Point, and one of the most highly regarded military theorists of his day. Hardee's two-volume *Rifle and Light Infantry Tactics*, first published in 1853, had been the product of an effort by Secretary of War Davis to replace earlier textbooks based on the widespread use of the musket with a work that took into account recent, revolutionary developments in small-arms technology.

Thanks to the introduction in the early 1850s of the conical, hollow, expandable minié ball, the rifle had become the standard shoulder-arm of the United States infantry. Sensing that this weapon would be wielded by the major-ity of soldiers on both sides, Wheeler believed it imperative that a work such as Hardee's guide the movements his regiment would make when it set foot on a battlefield.

Hardee's manual was a decided improvement over its highly limited predecessors. Chief among the latter was *Infantry Tactics; or, Rules for the Exercise and Manoeuvres of the United States Infantry*, a three-volume work published in 1852 by Winfield Scott, now, as then, the commanding general of the United States Army. Based on French manuals heavily influenced by the campaigns of Napoleon, Scott's tactics were predicated on the widespread use of muskets, which had an effective range of a couple of hundred yards. Hardee's text, how-ever, took into account the killing-power of the rifle, whose grooved barrel im-parted a methodical spin to the minié ball it fired, enabling an infantryman to strike a target 600 yards away and inflict some damage at twice that distance.[6]

To factor in the increased range of the rifle, Hardee made several ad-justments to the tactics of Scott and other earlier tacticians. His main contribu-tion was an increase in the rate of advance advocated for an attacking force. Theoretically, a longer stride and a more rapid pace would enable the attacker, after drawing the enemy's fire, to reach his line before a second volley could be unleashed. This was indeed an improvement over earlier tactics, but regiments including Wheeler's 19th Alabama experienced difficulty adopting the faster pace and unnaturally long stride.

The most serious defect in Hardee's system was that despite his best efforts it failed to account for the increased firepower of the rifle. That weapon would inflict heavy damage on any attacker before its wielder reached the enemy. This revolutionary effect would not become fully evident, however, until many months into the conflict. By then thousands of young men would have fallen prey to advanced technology and inadequate efforts to adjust to it.[7]

—— —— ——

By the early months of 1862 the war in various theaters was dragging on without decisive results. In the aftermath of what would become known as First Bull Run (or First Manassas), the antagonists in Virginia appeared to have taken a breather. The Rebels had imposed a partially effective blockade on Potomac River shipping, and the Yankees had regrouped inside the Washington defenses, where a new commander, George B. McClellan, was attempting to turn them into something more like soldiers. In late October a detachment of McClellan's army botched an offensive and suffered for it at Ball's Bluff on the upper Potomac, but at about the same time Union forces emerged victorious from small engagements in the western corner of the state. His defeats at Cheat Mountain and Carnifix Ferry heaped opprobrium and discredit on one of the South's best-known soldiers, Robert E. Lee. With these exceptions, the war in the Old Dominion remained generally quiescent.

Elsewhere in the divided nation, operations had been proceeding with comparable sluggishness. In the weeks following Bull Run, the only military activity of any scope had taken place in the Trans-Mississippi, especially in Missouri, where bloody engagements had been fought at Wilson's Creek and Lexington. Then, in early November, a Union force under an obscure brigadier named Ulysses S. Grant drove more numerous Confederates from their camps at Belmont, Missouri, across the river from Columbus, Kentucky, before retreating in confusion in the face of an unexpected counterattack. Farther south and east, from August through November, expeditionary forces had seized and occupied Confederate forts along the Carolina coast.[8]

Even Florida had seen action of some consequence. On November 22, shortly after Wheeler's regiment left the state for Mobile, a major artillery duel had broken out in Pensacola Harbor, where Lieutenant Slemmer's garrison, supported by two men-of-war, engaged Confederate land batteries including the remounted guns inside Forts Barrancas and McRae. The two-day engagement inflicted minimal damage and little loss of life but served to confirm Wheeler's belief that Fort Pickens was impervious to capture by Bragg.[9]

Early in the new year, things began to heat up in the western theater. On January 19, 1862, near Mill Springs and Logan's Cross Roads, Kentucky, Federal troops led by Brig. Gen. George H. Thomas repulsed an attack by raw recruits under Maj. Gen. George B. Crittenden, Wheeler's old superior in the

Mounted Rifles, then drove the Confederates from the field. Thomas's victory demonstrated the weakness of the primary Confederate defense line in the West.

Soon after Mill Springs, the reputation of the man who had built that line, Gen. Albert Sidney Johnston, suffered an even more devastating blow. Early in February Grant, at the head of 15,000 men, sailed up the Tennessee River, his transports convoyed by a fleet of wooden and iron-plated warships. On the sixth, as Grant prepared to attack Fort Henry on the east bank of the river just below the Kentucky border, his naval comrades shelled the small but strategically positioned installation into surrender.

At once Grant marched his reinforced command, now 27,000 strong, overland to Fort Donelson on the Cumberland River, twelve miles southeast of Fort Henry. Fearing to lose this vital position, Johnston rushed troops from Bowling Green to Donelson, increasing its garrison to 17,000. Most of these troops fell into Union hands on the sixteenth when Grant, after overcoming errors by his subordinates and an abortive breakout by the garrison, forced his enemy to surrender unconditionally. The coup made the victor's name a household word throughout the Union. Only 3,200 troops avoided Grant's clutches, including 700 cavalrymen under a hard-bitten colonel from Tennessee, Nathan Bedford Forrest, who fled to safety through the icy backwaters of the Cumberland.[10]

Grant's string of victories had far-reaching effects, the most sweeping being the virtual abandonment of both Kentucky and Tennessee to the Union and the destruction of what was left of Johnston's line. The remaining defenders flew through Tennessee into northern Mississippi, re-forming near the rail center of Corinth. There Johnston organized what would become an army of 45,000 and began planning to respond to Grant's offensive. The latter's command, which began to gather along the lower Tennessee at Pittsburg Landing, only twenty miles north of Corinth, had swollen to 40,000 by late March, and nearly as many reinforcements were on the way from Union-occupied Nashville under Maj. Gen. Don Carlos Buell. Johnston realized that if his command were to survive he must take a calculated risk and strike quickly at Grant's camps.[11]

The effect of the loss of Henry and Donelson was felt as far south as Mobile and Pensacola. Braxton Bragg saw the necessity of augmenting Johnston; he had written to Secretary of War Benjamin about it even before word of Donelson's fall reached the Gulf Coast. Fearing that Confederate forces in the West were scattered too widely to achieve anything of substance either offensively or defensively, Bragg warned Benjamin that "important strategic points only should be held. All means not necessary to secure these should be concentrated for a heavy blow upon the enemy where we can best assail him." Bragg cited New Orleans, Mobile, and Pensacola as worthy of continued defense; he recommended abandoning the rest of Florida and all of Texas and shifting their resources to Kentucky, which he viewed as the key to the Confederate heartland.[12]

Bragg's assessment of affairs did not tally with that of the Confederate War Department, which considered the Bluegrass State a lost cause, at least for the near term. But because Jefferson Davis and his war secretary believed Tennessee eminently recoverable, they gave careful attention to Bragg's call for a concentration somewhere in the Confederate interior. Within hours of receiving his suggestions, Benjamin informed him of "a change in our whole plan of campaign" in the western theater. Bragg was to abandon Pensacola and the other Florida ports. He would leave a small garrison inside Forts Gaines and Morgan, which commanded the entrance to Mobile Bay. With the rest of his available force he was to report at once to Johnston at Corinth. Benjamin explained that thousands of troops would move to northern Mississippi from New Orleans, the Atlantic coast of Florida, and other outlying posts.[13]

Bragg's contribution to Johnston's so-called Army of the Mississippi would total three brigades. One was commanded by Brig. Gen. Adley H. Gladden, a fifty-year-old Mexican War hero from South Carolina. In late January Bragg had summoned Gladden from Pensacola to Mobile to replace Leroy Walker in command of the four Alabama regiments that included Wheeler's well-drilled and recently armed outfit. Bragg, who continued to regard Walker as unfit for field duty, shunted him off to Montgomery to oversee the training of recruits. When even this duty proved to be beyond Walker's abilities, the well-dressed brigadier found himself transferred to a minor command in northern Alabama. Realizing he would never have the opportunity to prove himself as a soldier, Walker resigned his commission at the close of March and thereafter devoted himself to political and judicial affairs.[14]

According to John Du Bose, Gladden's brigade consisted of the 18th, 19th, 22nd, and 23rd Alabama Infantry, as well as a light artillery battery organized in Tuscaloosa and a cavalry company from Dallas County, Alabama. Along with the other brigades under Bragg, Gladden's left Mobile in late February and, after a long and much-interrupted journey mostly by train and partly on foot, reached Jackson, Tennessee, fifty-some miles north of Corinth, in the first week of March. There the advance elements of the Army of the Mississippi were gathering under the supervision of Johnston's senior subordinate, Gen. Pierre G. T. Beauregard, a Louisiana Creole who had pounded Fort Sumter into submission and had played a prominent role at Manassas.

Soon after Bragg's arrival at Jackson, Gladden's troops underwent a reorganization. Colonel Wheeler's regiment was removed from the command and placed in a provisional brigade that also included the 25th Alabama Infantry, the 1st Alabama Battalion, and a battery of Alabama and Florida artillery. As senior officer in this organization, Wheeler was designated an acting brigadier general to command it. It was a heady honor for a young and untried colonel, but Wheeler accepted the promotion with quiet confidence and a determination to succeed.

In response to orders, his new command assumed an advanced position near the farming village of Monterey, midway between Corinth and Pittsburg Landing, where it could sound a warning if Grant moved closer to Johnston's staging area. The acting brigadier recalled that in his new venue, "I reconnoitered close up to the Federal lines, captured prisoners from the enemy's pickets, and gained information of their position and the general conformation of the country."[15]

On March 10, a detachment of the division of Brig. Gen. William Tecumseh Sherman, one of the forces that had recently augmented Grant, advanced on Monterey. The Federals drove Wheeler's pickets back on their main line, where they made a stand along with the rest of their brigade. The determination with which the command held its position so impressed the attackers that after probing for nonexistent weak points they returned to camp on the Tennessee, presumably ignorant of the extent of the build-up at Corinth.[16]

Wheeler remained an acting brigadier until the last day in March, when another force of similar size replaced his on outpost duty. Upon rejoining the main army, he found himself in charge only of his regiment. Despite the coolheaded leadership he had displayed at Monterey, he lacked the seniority to retain the larger command.

He returned to the army as it prepared to break camp with the intention of giving battle to Grant. A week earlier, Johnston himself had reached Corinth to confer with Beauregard and other subordinates. Within days, the army leader had reorganized his enlarged command, dividing it into four corps. These he assigned to Bragg; Maj. Gen. Leonidas Polk, a West Pointer who had joined the Episcopal Church and had become Missionary Bishop of the Southwest before returning to uniform in 1861; Maj. Gen. Hardee, whose tactics had helped train almost every regiment in Johnston's army; and Maj. Gen. John C. Breckinridge, a former vice president of the United States and an unsuccessful candidate in the 1860 presidential race.[17]

Following Johnston's reorganization, Wheeler's Alabamians were in the brigade of Brig. Gen. John King Jackson. A thirty-four-year-old Georgian—a native, like Wheeler, of Augusta—Jackson lacked military experience but enjoyed the confidence of Johnston, who had empowered him to organize the first troops to reach Mississippi. In addition to Wheeler's outfit, Jackson's brigade comprised the 17th Alabama, under Lt. Col. Robert C. Fariss; the 18th Alabama of Col. Eli S. Shorter; Col. John C. Moore's 2nd Texas Infantry; and Capt. I. P. Girardey's Georgia battery.[18]

Like every other element of the Army of the Mississippi, Jackson's command—with the exception of Wheeler's regiment, which had under its belt that brief encounter against Sherman—had little knowledge of battle. Like their equally raw comrades in the ranks, however, Jackson's troops entertained no doubt they would acquit themselves honorably in defense of their states, their nation, and their cause.

Their highest-ranking superior shared their belief. By April 2, Johnston had penned the orders that would govern the march to Pittsburg Landing as well as a motivational address to be read aloud to the army on the march. The latter conveyed his conviction that "with the resolution and discipline and valor becoming men fighting for all worth living or dying for, you cannot but march to a decisive victory over the agrarian mercenaries sent to subjugate you and despoil you of your liberties, your property and your honor. . . . The eyes and hopes of eight millions of people rest upon you; you are expected to show yourselves worthy of your lineage, worthy of the women of the South, whose noble devotion in this war has never been exceeded in any time. With such incentive to brave deeds and with the trust that God is with us, your general will lead you confidently to the combat—assured of success."[19]

——— ——— ——— ———

Begun on April 3, the movement aimed at Grant's camps on the Tennessee proceeded over lowlands that had been turned into a "saturated sponge" by recent torrents and which slowed the army to a crawl on the first day out. Johnston attempted to speed things up the next day, when Hardee's corps led the column, followed by Bragg's, then Polk's, and with Breckinridge's reserve corps bringing up the rear. Despite the mud and the "drooping skies," the column made better progress, although it lost some of its strength. The green troops were not used to hard and continuous marching; dozens dropped out of the ranks to rest sore feet and relieve parched throats.[20]

As the straggling increased the march slowed again, causing the army leader much concern. Sometime on the fifth, as his regiment neared the Tennessee line, Colonel Wheeler found Johnston, surrounded by staff officers and couriers, sitting his horse on the side of the road, alternately studying the passing troops and scowling at his pocket-watch. At one point, he was heard to exclaim, "This is not war, it is puerile!" Spurring to the head of Bragg's column, Johnston found it had been brought almost to a standstill by the mismanaged supply train in its front. Angrily he sent the wagons to the roadside and ordered Bragg to pick up the pace.[21]

By late on the fifth, Johnston's advance echelon was within striking distance of the enemy, but it had arrived too late to begin an offensive. The twenty-three-mile march from Corinth, which Johnston had expected to consume a single day, had taken two and a half. Joining his superior at the head of the column, General Beauregard, a conservative soldier who feared precipitate action more than defeat, told Johnston that the Yankees must have detected the errant advance and prepared to receive it; he urged a return to Corinth, where the army should dig in and await Grant's attack. Johnston rejected the suggestion, declaring that he would assault the Federals were they a million strong.[22]

Throughout that night, the army waited in fragile silence, steeling itself for the attack and hoping beyond hope that the Yankees were less vigilant than Beauregard feared. Few rations were available to the hungry soldiers; as Du Bose observed, "the rain had melted the bread in the haversacks and none could be found" in the wagons.[23]

As his weary, famished troops snatched at sleep, Johnston put the final touches to his battle plan. Early the next morning, his troops would attack in three waves. Hardee's two divisions at the forefront of the column would advance first. Bragg's two divisions, 400 yards to the rear, would follow, backed by Polk's smaller command (three brigades), 800 yards farther back. The three brigades of Breckinridge's command, immediately behind Polk, would go in once the fight had been joined and where Johnston believed they would do the most good. He intended that Hardee strike the Union center and right while Bragg, supported by Polk, attacked Grant's left, pushing it back across Snake Creek to the banks of the Tennessee River. So sure was Johnston that his plan would succeed that he promised his staff they would be watering their horses in the Tennessee before another evening.

At first, his confidence appeared to be well placed. Fighting began along the Union right-center at about 5 AM on April 6 when opposing pickets collided in the morning mist. Minutes later, the better part of Hardee's corps swept forward to engage the division of Brig. Gen. Benjamin F. Prentiss. At first outnumbered but then reinforced, Prentiss's men held Hardee's troops at bay for almost three hours. Around eight o'clock, Johnston finally committed Bragg's command. It advanced not only against Prentiss but also farther east toward the position of Col. David Stuart's brigade of Illinois and Ohio infantry. The division of Brig. Gen. Jones M. Withers formed the right flank of Bragg's offensive. Jackson's brigade held the center of Withers's line, with Gladden's brigade (now led by Col. Zachariah Deas, Gladden having fallen mortally wounded) on Jackson's left and the brigade of Brig. Gen. James R. Chalmers on his right.

With Bragg's support, Hardee broke Prentiss's line, then began to drive in Sherman's division, which hugged the Union right near a log chapel known as Shiloh Church. The attackers overran Sherman's camps, which they looted of rations, arms, ammunition, and equipment. Well before noon, it appeared that Johnston's surprise assault had carried the day. Grant, however, rushed to the battlefield from his headquarters at Savannah, ten miles away—he had been breakfasting when the shooting started. Upon arriving he fed in reinforcements to stabilize his embattled line. Under his supervision, Prentiss and Sherman reformed their battered columns two miles in rear of the positions they had held when first attacked.[24]

As many as a dozen assaults by Hardee and Bragg—whose lines became inextricably entangled when crossing the broken terrain between the armies—proved necessary to carry Prentiss's new position, which embattled attackers later dubbed the "Hornet's Nest." Despite the unceasing pressure, which included a barrage laid down by sixty Confederate cannons, Prentiss's 2,200 men held their ground for several hours.[25]

Bragg's soldiers not only supported Hardee against Grant's right flank but shifted eastward toward the Tennessee. Beginning at about 10 AM, aided by two of Polk's brigades and later by Breckinridge's reserves, Bragg aimed his attack at the Union left. Despite valiant efforts to hold on, the defenders under Brig. Gen. S. A. Hurlbut and Stuart were compelled to give ground—at first stubbornly and reluctantly, then with alacrity and in some confusion. John Du Bose described the scene in his characteristic prose: "Grapple followed grapple and retreat. . . . The pursuing Confederates re-formed their lines and fought again and again, forcing their brave foe back to the river, foot by foot." In this sector, as on the opposite flank, "that weird song, never heard before, the rebel yell, broke upon the air. It was the cry of defiance from men who stood between the invader and their homes amidst the forest and on the prairies."[26]

Among those fighting for hearth and home were the Alabamians and Texans of Jackson's brigade, most of whom had the opportunity to take part not only in the attacks on the Hornet's Nest but also in the critical assault against the Union left. The brigade saw limited involvement in the first of these actions but acquitted itself well. In the later struggle, however, the brigade became fragmented and scattered, so much so that in a postwar account published in the *Southern Historical Society Papers* Joseph Wheeler claimed that late in the fight "command of the brigade devolved upon me." This was not literally true, for Jackson remained in titular command throughout the fight. But Wheeler's regiment was the only element of the brigade to maintain cohesion from first to last, a tribute to his leadership and the discipline he had instilled in his officers and men. Detachments of the other regiments under Jackson, which had become separated from the body of the brigade, rallied around the 19th and fought with it for the balance of the day.[27]

Jackson's men were in the second column of attack on Prentiss's original position, which had come unhinged by the time the brigade was sent in. Even so, as Wheeler stated in his official report of the battle, when his outfit advanced several of its men "were wounded by the scattering shots" of the retreating enemy. Along with other elements of Withers's division, Jackson's men pursued the dislodged Federals beyond their hastily abandoned encampment. Wheeler reported that his men halted in front of a second encampment some distance in rear of the first. In company with the 2nd Texas and Girardey's battery, the 19th was detached from the brigade and sent a mile or more to the right, where it confronted Stuart's Westerners. As the units moved into position, General Johnston himself called Wheeler, who had come into the fight on horseback, to his side. Wheeler galloped up, saluted, and received the army commander's order to assault the camp of the only intact force in its front, the 55th Illinois of Stuart's brigade.[28]

Under a covering fire by Captain Girardey, whose guns had unlimbered on a bluff overlooking the enemy flank, Wheeler led his men into their first charge of the war. To the multi-throated accompaniment of "that weird song," the still-raw recruits followed their little colonel through a brushy ravine that shielded them from enemy fire, then up the forward slope of a steep hill that provided no cover at all. In his report Wheeler boasted that the task assigned him "was performed by the regiment, under a heavy fire from a screened foe, with rapidity, regularity and cool gallantry. But little resistance was offered after reaching the camps, as the enemy fled . . . about two hundred yards from the camp."[29]

Reaching the cluster of abandoned tents, the regiment was halted by order of Johnston. Dismounting from his charger, Wheeler had the men lie prone while Girardey's gunners "fired over our heads sufficiently to shake their [new] line." After a few minutes of uneasy waiting, Wheeler got everyone to his feet and led the 19th toward the point where the Illinoisans were attempting to rally. "The regiment was moved forward rapidly," he wrote, "driving the enemy before it and dislodging him from every position where he attempted to make a stand, taking several prisoners and killing and wounding a large number."[30]

By their energetic advance, the Alabamians turned Stuart's right flank and compelled what remained of his brigade to withdraw to the top of a foliage-choked ridge along the river. By now exhausted by their exertions, Wheeler's men stepped aside as Chalmers's brigade reached the scene and assumed the burden of driving the Yankees from what looked like their final position. It proved to be a daunting task. Under a blizzard of rifle balls, Chalmers pushed to the base of the ridge but failed to evict the occupants from its summit.

By now Sidney Johnston had left this sector of the battlefield, having galloped to the center of his line, accompanied by his staff. There, at about 2:30 PM, while waxing enthusiastic about the progress of the fight, his booted foot stopped a minié ball. At first the injury appeared more painful than serious, but undetected blood loss caused Johnston's death within a couple of hours. His successor, Beauregard, never as sanguine of victory as his fallen superior, would make a half-hearted attempt to complete the victory before changing his mind and ordering a halt to offensive operations.[31]

Unaware of the shifting prospects of its army, shortly before four o'clock Wheeler's regiment—apparently at General Withers's order—countermarched from the scene of its triumphal charge to reengage Prentiss's brigade. The latter had fled the Hornet's Nest in favor of holding a sunken lane near the main road to Pittsburg Landing. The shift of position carried Wheeler's men through a woodlot that had been set afire by sparks from artillery shells and which exposed the column to a deadly cannonade. The movement ended with the 19th, which had suffered several casualties en route, forming a battle line in the left rear of Chalmers's embattled command. "I was met here," Wheeler recalled, "by General Chalmers, who told me his brigade was worn out and overpowered by superior numbers."[32]

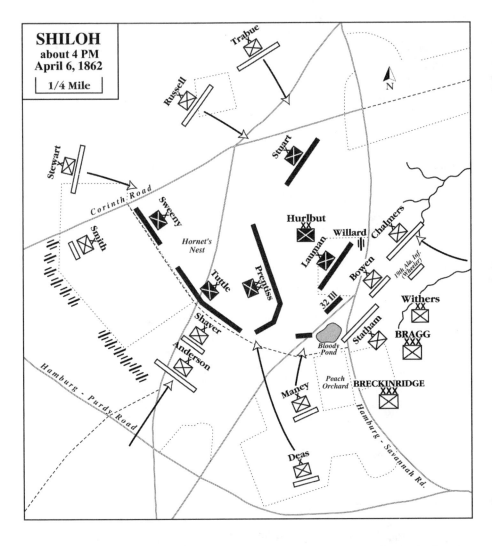

Wheeler saw at once that his assistance was imperative, so he deployed the 19th for its second attack of the day. When it surged forward it achieved what Chalmers's entire brigade had been unable to accomplish. Bayonets fixed, the regiment tore into a body of infantry covering Prentiss's eastern flank, principally the brigade of Col. Jacob G. Lauman. The Yankee line broke almost at first contact, its men turning to the rear and running. "We advanced," Wheeler observed, "about two hundred yards, the enemy having retreated . . . to another hill, where they were reinforced and in great measure secured from our fire."[33]

His regiment's second successful charge would produce a string of superlatives from Wheeler's pen—prose descriptive not only of the 19th Alabama but its commander as well: "The regiment here exhibited an example of cool, heroic courage which would do honor to soldiers of long experience in battle.

Subjected as they were to a deadly fire of artillery and a cross fire of infantry, they stood their ground with firmness and delivered their fire rapidly, but with cool deliberation and with good effect."[34]

But he and his men were not done. When a Union force on the west side of the enemy-held ridge began to enfilade Wheeler's left flank with musketry, he coolly obliqued the regiment a few yards to the rear. In that more defensible position, the men unleashed a volley that quickly silenced the enemy. Wheeler would claim that in so doing his outfit made a pivotal contribution to Prentiss's decision to surrender what remained of his division, one of the defining events of the battle. He conceded that his opponents had fought long and stubbornly until "cut off and isolated, [when] they made a desperate charge in an effort to escape, driving everything before them until met by my brigade, which they fought with desperation until they saw that surrender was inevitable."[35]

———— ————

On this note, Wheeler's long and frenzied day appeared to draw to a satisfying close. By order of General Jackson or his superior, Withers, the 19th took custody of about 3,000 prisoners, many of them Prentiss's troops. Wheeler claimed that General Bragg personally instructed him to conduct the POWs to Corinth but revoked the order when he protested, opining that his regiment might be needed in its present position. According to Wheeler, Bragg then passed the duty to Shorter's 18th Alabama. Relieved of this onerous burden, Wheeler "promptly formed the rest of the brigade into line, replenished ammunition and moved forward toward the river."[36]

Whether he knew it or not, he was leading his command into danger, for Grant had massed dozens of cannons along the river near Pittsburg Landing, and two gunboats were on hand in the Tennessee to defend that rallying point with long-range firepower. If at first ignorant of what he was facing, Wheeler became aware of it soon enough. En route to the river his troops, in common with those of Chalmers, moving on their right, "met a warm fire, mostly from artillery, and when near the river, suffered some from the gunboats." Even so, Wheeler pushed ahead until at about 6 PM he reached the crest of a rise "some 300 yards in advance of our general line, most of which was still at the foot of the ridge." At Jackson's or Withers's order, he began to lead his men down the rear slope and into the vine-entangled ravine that separated them from the disorganized mass of Union troops huddling on the riverbank. Before reaching the enemy, however, Wheeler glanced to the rear and saw to his open-mouthed surprise that Chalmers's men were falling back. Soon Wheeler was ordered to march in the same direction. He obeyed with great reluctance.[37]

As they withdrew, many of his men expressed dismay that their final offensive had come to a premature end. They believed—as their commander doubtless did—that another hour of fighting, perhaps less, would have routed

Grant's army, driving it into the Tennessee. But their opinion counted for naught; Beauregard, influenced by Johnston's demise, gathering darkness, and reports that Grant had been reinforced, was unwilling to carry the fight to its conclusion. Although he had already announced to his superiors in Richmond "a complete victory," the hesitant Creole realized that his troops had been almost as disorganized by their success as Grant's men had by their overthrow and retreat. Already 8,000 Confederates had been killed or wounded while hundreds of others had straggled to the rear—and still others continued to loot the camps they had captured early in the fight. Beauregard doubted that those who remained on the field were enough to finish the job that had begun so impressively. That work could wait until morning, following a night of rest. As he later admitted in a rare display of candor and introspection, he was absolutely certain that Grant had been backed into a corner from which he could not escape.[38]

But he was deluding himself. Heavy rains and incessant shelling denied his men the sleep they needed; by morning many had been reduced to a state of nervous exhaustion. Then, too, during the night Grant was reinforced not only by one of his own detached divisions (commanded by Brig. Gen. Lew Wallace, future author of *Ben-Hur*) but also by two-thirds of Buell's army, which crossed the river to Pittsburg Landing via steamboat. By the soggy dawn of April 7, Grant was prepared to take the offensive. Not long after sunup, thousands of Federal troops attacked out of their compact lodgment along the river. They fanned out westward and southward toward the positions of their weary enemy, many of whom were unprepared to withstand an assault.[39]

On the 19th Alabama's front, the fighting resumed at about 4 AM when word reached General Withers that a blue-clad column in full battle array—it proved to be Brig. Gen. William Nelson's division of Buell's army—was moving in his direction. Withers hastily formed a line of battle near the point to which his men had withdrawn the previous evening. The right flank of this line was occupied by Chalmers's battered but intact brigade, with what remained of Jackson's still-scattered command farther to the left, astride the so-called Purdy-Hamburg Road. Jackson himself was nowhere to be found, having assumed command of three leaderless regiments attached to other brigades in Bragg's corps. In his own account, written for the Southern Historical Society, Wheeler left no doubt about who commanded in the absence of his superior. At Withers's order, he led the entire brigade when it went forward to meet Nelson's advance.[40]

Unlike the assaults of the previous day, this one, which Wheeler led on foot, was abruptly checked by Nelson's larger force. Forced to fall back after suffering heavily, Wheeler's troops held their new position against mounting pressure for perhaps an hour. Then the Yankees advanced, and Wheeler's command retreated yet again, this time falling back on Withers's main body.

Under a misty rain and a torrent of musketry, the Confederates dug in and staved off further efforts to dislodge them. Twice the blue phalanx pulled back, perhaps to replenish ammunition. Wheeler took advantage of the second withdrawal, snatching up a regimental flag and leading his brigade to the top of a hill from which Nelson's men already had been driven. Suddenly the more numerous Federals advanced and regained the lost eminence. They could not, however, break Wheeler's hold on his own position, which lay within rifle shot of Nelson's line, especially after he was reinforced by regiments from Missouri and Louisiana.[41]

The see-saw contest went on until midafternoon, the soldiers of Nelson and Withers alternatively gaining and losing the advantage. Farther to the left, however, the fresher, more numerous Federals were dislodging critical sectors of Beauregard's line. Just after three o'clock and for the second time in two days, Withers received orders to break contact and withdraw. Within minutes his division was moving as a body several hundred yards to the rear. There it was held relatively idle for perhaps an hour while the army commenced a full-scale withdrawal.

During the retrograde, Wheeler's brigade was assigned a post of honor, that of rear guard. The position entailed great risk, and would be especially dangerous if Grant pursued closely. "Fortunately," Wheeler recalled, "the enemy . . . showed no disposition to advance, and the firing was at long range and without much effect." Jackson's erstwhile command sparred with the enemy only intermittently and at great distance. By nightfall, with the once exultant and now weary and demoralized Army of the Mississippi well on its way to Corinth, the fighting ceased altogether. The first major engagement in the western theater was history.[42]

— — — —

For driving the enemy from successive positions on April 6 and holding his ground against heavy odds for much of the seventh, Colonel Joseph Wheeler was commended by several superiors including Bragg, Withers, and Chalmers. Certainly he was entitled to credit for his handling of the 19th Alabama and, later, the remnants of Jackson's brigade. However, he appears to have decided over time that his conduct was deserving of even greater recognition. In his *Southern Historical Society Papers* article, he exaggerated his role in the fight and claimed honors not strictly his due. He contended that for the better part of both days of combat he commanded not only his regiment but every other component of Jackson's brigade. Yet Jackson would maintain that Wheeler stepped in to replace him only after the first day's fighting had ended. And in his afteraction account of the battle, Wheeler admitted that when Jackson went missing General Withers assumed command of the brigade and attached it to Chalmers's command. As senior officer, Chalmers would have led the combined force. Historians fail to assign Wheeler brigade command on either day of the battle. The author of a recent study of Shiloh complicates the issue by claiming that on

April 7 what remained of Jackson's command was led by Colonel Moore of the 2nd Texas.[43]

In his article, Wheeler made other claims that cannot be verified. Some strain credulity, including his alleged remonstrance to General Bragg for ordering him to go to the rear at the height of the battle. Many were nothing more than attempts to elevate his own stature and magnify the contributions of his command to a critically important battle. Why he felt the need to do so is difficult to understand, for, clearly, he and his regiment had performed stoutly on both days of the fight, to their everlasting credit. Wheeler, however, would never be content to allow the facts to speak for themselves.

If he was driven by a compulsion to exaggerate and fancify in order to strengthen his claims to success, he was by no means alone—every Civil War commander, in recounting his participation in battle, resorted at some point to self-serving fiction. But Wheeler could always be counted on to exceed the norm. He would embellish the record whenever reality failed to produce the impression of himself that he wished to convey to his superiors.

3

BLUEGRASS BOUND

With amazing swiftness, the Army of the Mississippi had gone from the precipice of victory to the valley floor of defeat and demoralization. By the morning of the eighth, as the bitter and sullen Confederates withdrew from the field of lost opportunities, Braxton Bragg, from the midst of the retreat column near Monterey, notified Beauregard that "our condition is horrible. Troops utterly disorganized and demoralized. Road almost impassable. No provisions and no forage; consequently everything is feeble."[1]

The state of the army was bad enough; an even greater concern was the specter of enemy pursuit. Should the retreat column be attacked short of its prepared positions at Corinth, it might disintegrate. "If we are pursued by a vigorous force," Bragg warned Beauregard, "we will lose all in the rear. The whole road presents the scene of a rout, and no mortal power could restrain it." Bragg's fears infected his superior to the point that the following day Beauregard wired the War Office begging that reinforcements be dispatched at once from Georgia and the Carolinas. Those positions the Confederacy "could afford to lose for a while," whereas if Beauregard's army—now reduced to 35,000 effectives—was overwhelmed, "we lose the Mississippi Valley and probably our cause."[2]

Not everyone on the roads to northern Mississippi gave way to gloom and panic. Throughout the eighth, the rear of the retreat column, which included dozens of ambulances crammed with the wounded and disabled, was in the capable hands of John Breckinridge. At the head of a column composed of 1,200 infantry and four light cannons, with cavalry units guarding his flanks, the erstwhile presidential candidate was prepared to take on any force that ventured his way, holding it at bay until the army could make good its escape. Rumor had several regiments of Yankee infantry, supported by 500 cavalrymen, hot on Breckinridge's heels, but as of midafternoon on the eighth "we have gathered things up pretty well to this point. I am getting forward stragglers, sick, and wounded as fast as possible."[3]

The determination Breckinridge conveyed was somewhat diluted by his concern that "my troops are worn-out, and I don't think can be relied on after the first volley." The general himself was approaching exhaustion, and by the morning of the ninth was ill, writing Beauregard that he was almost unfit for duty. Fortunately, help was at hand, in the person of Joseph Wheeler. By nine-thirty that morning, the commander of the 19th Alabama Infantry had reached Breckinridge's side along the familiar outskirts of Monterey. Although battle casualties and straggling had reduced his regiment to no more than one hundred officers and men, Wheeler, Breckinridge reported, was strong enough "to take charge of any troops sent on" toward Monterey. It can be surmised that reports of Wheeler's performance in the recent battle recommended him for such an important mission.[4]

Wheeler's job as commander of the "demi brigade" assigned him for the operation—eventually 400 infantry and nearly 200 cavalry—was an arduous one, especially given the mud through which his men sloshed while casting their eyes ever rearward. It turned out, however, to be a much less dangerous task than anticipated. As Ulysses S. Grant noted in a dispatch to his departmental commander, Maj. Gen. Henry Wager Halleck, the combined Union forces were "much too fatigued from two days' hard fighting and exposure in the open air in a drenching rain during the intervening night to pursue immediately." By some point on April 8, however, a pursuit column, consisting of two infantry brigades, was organized and placed under William T. Sherman. Sherman plodded southward in the Rebels' wake for about six miles but failed to overtake Wheeler.[5]

The following day cavalry alone resumed the pursuit, and on the morning of the twelfth this small force encountered Wheeler's rearmost pickets a short distance above Monterey. Through field glasses Wheeler estimated the enemy force at about 200, a figure that did not frighten him. As he reported laconically, "I ordered all available mounted men to the front, and the enemy retired after some circuitous movements." After this, Wheeler's force, as also Beauregard's army in its entirety, was home free on the road to Corinth.[6]

———

Back at the support base he and Sidney Johnston had departed on the third, Beauregard, despite suffering from a debilitating illness whose onset predated Shiloh, tried to bind up his army's wounds while preparing it for a renewal of campaigning. The job was made tougher by the air of "gloom and sadness" that pervaded the Corinth area, a symptom of the army's growing demoralization. One of Beauregard's artillerymen found the town and its environs "as quiet as if the whole country around was one church. The loss of friends, and the horrible scenes which they had just witnessed, together with their almost miraculous escape, seemed to quiet every one. Neither drum [n]or fife could be heard" for a week or more after the army's return.[7]

The uneasy silence bothered Beauregard less than the knowledge that Grant—who had been superseded at Pittsburg Landing by his superior, Halleck— would bestir himself at some point and invade northern Mississippi. The Confederate commander could not know that Halleck would defer a full-scale pursuit until the following month. But whenever he advanced, Halleck would not find the hero of Fort Sumter and Manassas hunkered down in a town devoid of natural defenses and adequate stores of ordnance, equipment, and rations. By late May, with Halleck and Grant moving slowly in his direction, Beauregard decided to evacuate Corinth as soon as he completed reorganizing his army and assimilating 30,000 recently arrived reinforcements under Maj. Gens. Earl Van Dorn and Sterling Price—troops whose slow and cautious transfer from Arkansas had kept them from joining Johnston before Shiloh.[8]

To buy the time he needed to withdraw in the direction of Tupelo, Beauregard detailed a number of raiding parties, placed them under able officers, and sent them toward the enemy. They were to strike and harass Halleck's column, slowing its progress by inflicting enough casualties to induce caution. In essence, the mission was a reprise of Wheeler's rearguard duty, but on a larger scale. Wheeler was a logical choice to head one of these parties, for he had proven himself worthy of heavy responsibility and the command of large numbers of troops. On May 10, he had led detachments of his regiment and other elements of Withers's division in driving the Yankees from a strategic position near Farmington, Mississippi, a few miles east of Corinth. By month's end, Withers had assigned Wheeler a brigade of infantry encompassing, in addition to his own men, the 22nd, 25th, and 26th Alabama, plus the six-gun battery of Capt. Felix H. Robertson. The latter, a twenty-three-year-old Texan, was an energetic and multitalented officer who would serve Wheeler many times, and in many capacities, over the next three years.[9]

On the evening of May 28, as Beauregard put final touches to his evacuation, Wheeler, accompanied by a detachment of his brigade perhaps 350 strong, started north. His assigned route returned him to Monterey, where he had already twice engaged the enemy to good effect. Nearing the town early the next morning, he linked up with 200 Mississippians under a Lt. Col. Mills who had been picketing the vicinity and skirmishing with enemy patrols. Wheeler discovered that one such patrol, whose strength exceeded Mills's force, had driven its pickets about half a mile away. The Yankees had occupied the vacated ground, which included a swamp so deep and so heavily wooded that Mills had been unable to regain the position despite several attempts.

A quick survey of the situation convinced Wheeler that he had the manpower to succeed where his colleague had failed. As he had at Shiloh, he drew upon the lessons he had gleaned from his West Point textbooks, especially Professor Dennis Hart Mahan's seminal *Treatise on Advanced-Guard, Out-Post, and Detachment Service of Troops*. In conformance with Mahan's principles, he sent forward a line of skirmishers to draw the Federals' fire, thus gaining an understanding of their position and strength. Then he strove to flank the enemy out of their swampy venue before it could be made impregnable. He moved Mills's Mississippians, as well as a small body of cavalry just up from Corinth under Col. James H. Clanton, to the left of the road to Monterey.

Under cover of their fire and the shelling of Robertson's cannons, Wheeler led his own force forward and toward the left. As soon as he gained a vantage point from which to strike, he shouted out the order to charge and the line swept forward, he out in front on his warhorse. Ordered not to fire until within effective rifle-range of the enemy, his men at first unleashed only the now-familiar Rebel Yell. As at Shiloh, the tremulous wailing had an effect. Well before the attackers slowed and began to discharge their shoulder-arms, the enemy abandoned their post and ran for their lives through the swamp. Several fell once the attackers began to deliver a volley; other fugitives were bowled over by canister from Robertson's guns. Wheeler calculated that seventy Federals became *hors de combat* before the fighting ceased.

Not content to inflict casualties, he continued the pursuit until halted by wide and swift-moving Bridge Creek. His orders from Beauregard called on him to go no farther so long as the enemy stayed on the far side of the stream. To ensure this, Wheeler grouped his riflemen into skirmish lines and had them pepper the "less advantageous position" their enemy had taken up. To these units he soon added Mills's and Clanton's men. The combined force ensured that the enemy remained so far off it could not observe, let alone disrupt, Beauregard's pullout from Corinth.[10]

In later years, when he had the opportunity to read Union reports of the engagement, Wheeler was surprised and amused to learn that his opponents had greatly overestimated the strength of his command. The miscalculation may have been an honest mistake or an attempt to explain their precipitate retreat. Either way, the Yankees had given an unintended compliment to Wheeler's leadership and the caliber of his brigade.

His skirmishers remained in position well into the evening of the twenty-ninth, by which time the better part of Beauregard's army was on its weary way to Tupelo. At an opportune time, Wheeler disengaged and fell in with the rear of Beauregard's main column. No sooner had he done so than he found himself hotly engaged with a much stronger foe. Near Tishomic Creek, about four miles south of Corinth, a body of Union cavalry struck the shank of the column, forcing Wheeler to turn about and fight, enabling his comrades to lengthen their head start.

The ground on which Wheeler chose to fight was, as he recalled after the war, "a low swampy wooded expanse" leading to a bridge over the creek via a narrow road that had been corduroyed (shored up with split logs). Forewarned of the bluecoats' approach, he placed his men in creekside woods, unlimbered Robertson's battery, and positioned its guns to sweep the road. Presently, the Yankees came "thundering down the corduroy road. When within fifty yards of the bridge, a section of twelve pound[er]s, Napoleon guns, and the Infantry opened fire, throwing the entire mass of charging Cavalry into confusion, some seeking safety in the swamps, and others flying to the rear with all possible alacrity." Thus checked, the pursuers caused neither Wheeler nor Beauregard additional trouble beyond intermittent, long-distance harassment.[11]

Once again Colonel Wheeler had performed effectively in field command, for which he would win new plaudits. As he had in his Shiloh report, he bestowed praise of his own, describing his men's conduct as "commendable, subjected as they were to a heavy fire of both artillery and infantry, from a foe secreted by the density of undergrowth. They advanced steadily, not using their arms until they were ordered, when they fired with good effect. . . . Officers and soldiers all did well." Success had come, however, at substantial cost to such a small force—six men killed outright, ten others severely wounded, some of whom would succumb in later days.[12]

Toward evening on the thirtieth, having repulsed several limited efforts to drive him from the river, Wheeler was ordered to rejoin Beauregard's rear guard. For the next several days he helped protect the southward passage of the army, which was facilitated by elaborate ruses to make the Yankees believe that Corinth was still held in force, including the mounting of "Quaker guns"—logs shaped and positioned to give the impression, at long distance, of heavy artillery. Although aided by this "masterpiece of trickery," Wheeler's covering job was often frustrating, sometimes dangerous, and always taxing—but he performed it well. His reputation for ably protecting the route of retreat continued to grow. He hoped, however, that he would not have many occasions to display such prowess.[13]

———

The Army of the Mississippi found life at Tupelo, where it arrived on June 2, a great improvement over its cheerless station below the Tennessee border. Here natural defenses such as swamps and commanding ridges were abundant, the water source was purer, and railroad-borne supplies were more accessible. These advantages gave Beauregard hope that the army's strength would be so fully restored that it could soon bear another confrontation with the troops of Halleck, Grant, and Buell.

If Beauregard's men appeared to flourish in their new venue, their commander did not. The illness Beauregard had contracted before Shiloh had worsened—now he was afflicted by a throat infection so severe it threatened his ability to command. He was hurting in other ways as well. His ability to lead had been compromised by his retreats from Shiloh and Corinth, which had opened to his enemy a communication link between Paducah, Kentucky, and Chattanooga, Tennessee. Then, too, his reputation had been weakened, perhaps fatally, by an acrimonious dispute with Jefferson Davis and other Confederate officials over Beauregard's failure to keep Richmond informed of his plans and the condition of his command. On June 20, three days after Beauregard left Tupelo on what he expected to be a brief sick leave, Davis, who had lost confidence in the Creole, relieved him from command and gave his job to Braxton Bragg.[14]

Bragg was a dour ascetic whose gloomy disposition, martinet's ways, and preoccupation with minutiae caused him endless problems in interpersonal relations. Yet he was a competent strategist and had a clear vision of how to revive the spirits of his newly acquired command. By anyone's standards he was also an effective organizer and drillmaster. One of his artillerymen observed that "a thorough reorganization of the whole army took place" within a month of Bragg's promotion, "and constant drill was our daily avocation. The health of the whole army improved materially."[15]

Bragg used his authority as a department commander to create subdivisions to be headed by subordinates whom he preferred not to command directly. He assigned General Van Dorn and his 14,000 troops to the District of the Mississippi, with responsibility for defending Vicksburg, the most important Confederate stronghold on the Mississippi. Meanwhile, the 11,000 troops under General Price joined the District of the Tennessee, where they were assigned to halt any enemy advance across northern Mississippi. This left the Army of the Mississippi with 31,000 effectives. Bragg temporarily assigned them to General Hardee, with General Polk as second-in-command.[16]

Not surprisingly, it was the army at Tupelo that received Bragg's immediate attention. He was convinced that the Army of the Mississippi would accomplish nothing of substance in its present position. Strong though they appeared, the defenses of Tupelo would not withstand an attack by the forces under Halleck, which numbered more than 100,000 officers and men. Nor could the army profit by retiring north and offering battle. To solidify morale, Bragg would have to come up with another idea for regaining the offensive, one that would not conflict with his concomitant responsibility to protect a wide corridor of the Confederacy. An advance into West Tennessee, for instance, would open Alabama and Georgia to enemy invasion. If, instead, he crossed the river into Middle Tennessee, he would be placing his finite resources between the heavier armies under Grant and Buell.

A third option was available to Bragg, described after the war by Joseph Wheeler: "A rapid march through Alabama to Chattanooga would save that city [from an expected advance by Buell], protect Georgia from invasion, and open the way into Tennessee and Kentucky." This movement had special appeal because numerous military and political officials exiled from the Bluegrass State wished to see their homeland relieved of Yankee occupation. It was widely believed that if a Confederate army entered Kentucky, thousands of her sons would flock to its banner.[17]

One of the most vocal proponents of Bragg's transfer to Chattanooga was Maj. Gen. Edmund Kirby Smith, commander of the Department of East Tennessee. One of the Confederacy's earliest heroes (known in some circles as "the Blücher of Manassas"), Smith had since been exiled to what he considered an inferior command in the West. With only 15,000 troops he was responsible for defending a vast fiefdom that included North Carolina west of the Blue Ridge as well as a portion of northern Georgia. The transplanted Virginian was convinced that only Bragg had the manpower to keep Buell from seizing Chattanooga, one of the strongholds of Smith's department. The loss of that communications hub would deal a body blow not only to Smith but to the Southern nation as a whole. It would sever the rail artery that connected Confederate forces in Virginia and the West, while opening a path of invasion to Atlanta, the industrial center of the Deep South. It might also cause the loss of arsenals in Georgia that supplied both Bragg and Smith with arms and ammunition.[18]

Smith had an additional reason for seeking Bragg's assistance. Although it was his job to defend Chattanooga, the Virginian was even more interested in driving an 8,500-man detachment of Buell's army under Brig. Gen. George W. Morgan out of Cumberland Gap, a strategic gorge that straddled the Tennessee-Kentucky line. Once he disposed of Morgan, Smith would be free to roam through the Bluegrass State, capturing outposts and seizing supplies all the way to the Ohio River. He believed these objectives unattainable, however, unless Bragg took position at or near Chattanooga, where he could safeguard his colleague's rear and line of communications.

The Richmond authorities were responsive to, but not enthusiastic about, Smith's project. By late June, Robert E. Lee's Army of Northern Virginia was driving twice as many invaders—George B. McClellan's Army of the Potomac—from the gates of the Confederate capital, and government officials were focused on that effort. A distracted Jefferson Davis and his new secretary of war, George Randolph, merely asked Bragg to assist Smith as best he could. Bragg, aware that his superiors prized interdepartmental cooperation, took steps to satisfy them as early as June 27, when he ordered one of his infantry divisions to Chattanooga.[19]

Over the next four weeks, it became clear that Buell's Army of the Ohio also had designs on Chattanooga. As was his custom, however, it took Buell much time to get moving in that direction. As early as June 11, Halleck had ordered his subordinate to invade East Tennessee. Buell made a ponderous effort to obey by recalling and grouping his scattered forces in northern Alabama and Middle Tennessee, a process delayed by inadequate transportation. The need to repair or improve the roads and rail lines over which his troops must travel prevented Buell from making substantial progress until mid-July.[20]

Protecting those communications proved to be a Herculean task. Early in July, John Hunt Morgan began his storied career as a cavalry raider by leading 800 horsemen against several objectives in lower Kentucky, including the principal supply line to Cumberland Gap. His troopers captured a half million dollars worth of stores at one place alone. An even greater blow to Buell's communications fell on July 13, when Col. Nathan Bedford Forrest, at the head of a 1,000-man force, struck the supply base at Murfreesboro, in Middle Tennessee. With remarkable speed, Forrest captured a Yankee force equal to his own, then confiscated or destroyed supplies worth almost a million dollars. His work unfinished, Forrest headed east toward the Union stronghold of Nashville via other fortified points that fell into his hands, including McMinnville and Lebanon. After destroying bridges and culverts south of the Tennessee capital, the raiding leader bypassed Nashville, returning to home base after outdistancing numerous pursuers.[21]

Beset by so many difficulties in his rear, Buell, who had crossed the Tennessee River from Alabama on July 4, was not in a position to threaten Chattanooga until two weeks after that. On the nineteenth, Kirby Smith notified Bragg that "Buell with his whole force is opposite Chattanooga, which he is momentarily expected to attack." The Virginian asked that the balance of the Army of the Mississippi hasten to the threatened point.

Bragg had already concluded that he would move against the rear of Buell's army. On the twenty-first he notified Richmond that he would do so from Chattanooga—at once. That advance would constitute the opening act of a long, turgid, and sometimes bathetic drama known as the Perryville Campaign.[22]

———— ————

Even before deciding to enter East Tennessee, Bragg devised stratagems to deceive those Yankees close to Tupelo into thinking he was going to move much farther west. At an early stage he enlisted the help of Colonel Wheeler, who responded with energy and imagination. On the morning of July 11, the outposts of Wheeler's 19th Alabama near Guntown, north of Tupelo, received a flag-of-truce party from inside the enemy's lines. In company with his second-in-command, Lt. Col. E. D. Tracy, and two other officers including an emissary from General Bragg's headquarters, Wheeler greeted Col. Philip Henry Sheridan of the 2nd Michigan Cavalry (a future infantry division commander, and later a cavalry corps commander in Virginia), as well as Col. Robert O. Selfridge, a cavalry staff officer. After exchanging pleasantries, the two parties engaged in a lengthy parlay. Its subject remains unknown, although it probably concerned the exchange of prisoners or the escort of citizens caught between the lines. Colonel Selfridge noted that Sheridan and he were treated with utmost courtesy by their hosts, "who received our dispatches, and with whom we exchanged newspapers and discussed in the most friendly manner the various topics of the day."[23]

During the confab, Selfridge picked up several bits of information that the Confederates appeared to drop incautiously. These included the interesting "fact" that the army at Tupelo, which "numbers from 70,000 to 75,000 strong," intended to remain in its present position "until the maturing and gathering of the present corn crop" provided it with marching rations. Then and only then would the Confederates relocate—and when they did, they would head north toward the railhead at Holly Springs. Wheeler and his colleagues interspersed enough verifiable information—including Bragg's replacement of Beauregard and the latter's much-criticized retreat from Shiloh—to make the rest of their careful deception appear plausible.[24]

Whether or not the ruse had strategic effects, the meeting displayed Wheeler's admirable slyness. Surely Bragg's representative on the scene, Capt. T. M. Lenoir, informed his superior of the colonel's well-orchestrated attempt to further Bragg's diversionary effort. Coming on the heels of Wheeler's recent success in the field, this performance would have added to his stature in the eyes of his army commander, who by now must have repented the pique he had displayed over Wheeler's leap from lieutenant to colonel.

A reward was not slow in coming. Seven days after his meeting with Sheridan and Selfridge, Wheeler was ordered to take command of the cavalry brigade of the Army of the Mississippi. He relieved General Chalmers, who after transferring from infantry service following Shiloh had been disabled by illness. This assignment made Wheeler an acting brigadier general and hinted that the promotion would become permanent in due course. There was logic behind the assignment, for although Wheeler had been commanding infantry for the better part of a year, his prewar training and experience had been in the mounted ranks. Even so, the appointment surprised many observers, who considered Wheeler too young for so lofty a position. Some ascribed Bragg's move to favoritism toward a fellow West Pointer.

The assignment required Wheeler to sever his relationship with the regiment with which he had been so long and intimately involved. As it was, he barely had time to bid officers and enlisted men farewell before turning the 19th Alabama over to Lieutenant Colonel Tracy and departing for his new headquarters just outside Tupelo.[25]

———— ———— ———— ————

From the outset, Wheeler's new command posed problems. As one of his subordinates wrote, "the Colonel had first to find his cavalry for it was scattered over a front extending from Ripley, Miss., to the Alabama state line." The primary difficulty was that under Chalmers the brigade—whose horses had seen hard service after Shiloh, especially during the retreat from Corinth to Tupelo—had relocated to a quiet sector of Mississippi where it could more readily obtain provender. Wheeler immediately ordered the far-flung detachments to concentrate in the vicinity of Holly Springs, on the Mississippi Central about sixty miles northwest of Tupelo.[26]

Holly Springs would serve as a convenient jumping-off point for a mission assigned Wheeler by army headquarters. To feed Bragg's appetite for diversionary movements, he was to move into West Tennessee as if his brigade were the vanguard of a full-scale advance in that direction. Wheeler's initial destinations were the villages of Grand Junction and Bolivar. The ambitious colonel, however, had his sights set even farther north—he hoped to attack and then loot Buell's supply depot at the rail junction at Jackson.

Before making contact with his officers and men, Wheeler pored over regimental returns until he gained a fair understanding of the forces at his disposal. A fair understanding is all that can be arrived at today, for documents relating to the size and composition of his brigade are fragmentary and incomplete. It appears that, as originally constituted, the command consisted of five regiments: the 1st Tennessee under Col. William Hicks ("Red") Jackson, the 1st Mississippi of Col. R. A. Pinson, the 2nd Arkansas Cavalry, commanded by Col. W. F. Slemons, Col. James Hagan's 3rd Alabama, and Lt. Col. W. B. Wade's 8th Confederate Cavalry, a regular army unit recruited mainly in Alabama and Tennessee.

Previously these outfits and been assigned to General Price's District of the Tennessee, but upon Wheeler's promotion Bragg had transferred them to the Army of the Mississippi, which would need mobile support during the coming movement. Their assignment to Wheeler left Price with an understrength cavalry brigade under Brig. Gen. Frank C. Armstrong. Price, himself about to advance toward Corinth—now under enemy occupation—in cooperation with Van Dorn, feared that the regiments lost to Wheeler left him with too little mounted support. He appealed to Bragg, only to be told that it was "impossible to spare you more cavalry than already given."[27]

Each of Wheeler's units had a paper strength of 1,000 officers and troopers, but because detachments were widely dispersed on a variety of missions the brigadier-to-be found at his immediate disposal only about one-fourth of this total. It was a disconcerting situation, but there was no help for it—he had been given an important mission by Bragg and he had to carry it out with the resources at hand.

On or about July 22 he left Tupelo in the company of a small escort and a coterie of recently acquired staff officers. Arriving at Holly Springs, he reported to the local commander, Brig. Gen. John B. Villepigue, explained his mission, and secured his colleague's support and cooperation. Over the next few days, Wheeler grouped and inspected the detachments that reported to him at irregular intervals, while gaining a nodding acquaintance with their leaders.[28]

He found the units to be composed of promising material. Many officers and men were veterans not only of Shiloh but of the various skirmishes and engagements that preceded and followed the great battle, and they looked capable of withstanding hard campaigning. Their horses were a different matter; despite Chalmers's best efforts, the animals continued to look overworked and underfed, and some appeared close to breaking down. Presumably, before leaving Holly Springs a certain number were exchanged for the few remounts available in Villepigue's domain.

Wheeler was also dismayed by the wide variety of weapons the troopers toted. Few wielded carbines; fewer still had sabers, which appeared to be the exclusive possession of the officers. The majority of the enlisted force carried long-range rifles, principally English-made Enfields; these would prove difficult to shoot, and all but impossible to reload, on horseback. An appalling number carried inappropriate or obsolete arms such as shotguns and hunting rifles, including flintlocks. From the first, Wheeler thought of these horsemen not as cavalry but as mounted riflemen, members of the arm of the military in which he had won his spurs and which he preferred to all other branches of the service.

Through arduous and sometimes frustrating labor, by the twenty-fifth Wheeler had grouped about 1,000 members of Wade's, Pinson's, and Slemons's regiments in and around Holly Springs. That morning he led them out of the depot village toward the Tennessee border. He planned to threaten the outpost at Bolivar, burn the railroad trestles between that village and Jackson, then destroy the stores stockpiled at Jackson, including hundreds of bales of cotton the Yankees had confiscated from local factors for resale in the North.[29]

It was an ambitious project—perhaps overly so, which might explain why it fell short of its assigned objectives. In his biography of Wheeler, John Dyer ascribes the failure to Villepigue's untimely recall of the Mississippi infantry units he had loaned Wheeler for the mission. In reality, the brigadier ordered the return only of Jackson's detachment of cavalry. Wheeler had intended to use his attached infantry to attack the garrison at Grand Junction, a few miles below Bolivar, and to mangle railroad track in that vicinity. Upon approaching Grand Junction, however, scouts reported that the Federals had evacuated two days earlier. It was Wheeler who ordered the foot soldiers to return to Holly Springs "as soon as they had created the impression that a general advance of our forces was intended in the direction of West Tennessee." The Mississippians accomplished their mission, not only deceiving Union observers as to their destination but also destroying 200 bales of cotton found piled around Grand Junction.[30]

Left with 500 riders after Jackson's detaching, Wheeler cut loose from his infantry comrades and moved directly on Bolivar. En route, he attacked a small outpost near Middleburg, "capturing prisoners, horses, arms, wagons, and 300 bales of cotton." Upon approaching Bolivar, his skirmishers—presumably fighting on foot—drove in enemy pickets. The skirmishers "so thoroughly shut them in [the village] as to enable us to send out a large number of squads of men" to confiscate supplies and incinerate more cotton. During the course of the mission, Wheeler's troops consigned to the flames no fewer than 3,000 bales of that valuable commodity.[31]

These acts of destruction did not exhaust Wheeler's accomplishments. Before he could push on from Bolivar he received orders to rejoin Bragg's army, the advance echelon of which had reached Chattanooga by troop train via Mobile, Alabama, and Atlanta, Georgia, on July 29. The peremptory recall forced him to relinquish his hope of attacking the state capital. However, before turning his raiding column about and starting homeward, Wheeler dispatched one of his troopers, posing as a deserter, inside the lines at Bolivar. As instructed, the man informed the local commander that a force several times the size of Wheeler's was advancing on him.

Wheeler's ruse was so effective that the alarmed officer begged for help from one of Grant's senior subordinates, Maj. Gen. John A. McClernand. McClernand reinforced Bolivar with troops from Corinth, Jackson, and other garrisons. The transfer of defenders from the Jackson area enabled two of Wheeler's detachments to wreck neighboring railroad bridges and cut the local telegraph line for "a considerable distance."[32]

Although reluctant to abort the mission, Wheeler—as he would demonstrate time and again in future campaigning—was highly responsive to given orders. Properly skeptical of reports that masses of angry pursuers were forming in his rear, he pointed his 500 riders southward. By the evening of August 1 they were back at Holly Springs, where Wheeler penned an after-action report detailing the expedition's achievements. As he had done after Shiloh, he leavened his operational narrative with dollops of praise and commendation. "With but 500 cavalry, much worn and jaded by previous service and privation," he wrote, "we penetrated some 70 miles behind the enemy's lines, destroyed the railroad bridges in his rear, and met him in eight separate engagements, in all of which . . . he was thoroughly defeated, many of his horses and men being killed, wounded, or taken prisoners."[33]

If the document boasted more than its share of hyperbole and contained questionable claims as to the extent of McClernand's reaction to the deserter's story, it was accurate in its essentials. Braxton Bragg, himself prone to exaggerated descriptions of feats performed and obstacles overcome, would enjoy reading it, and that was what counted.

———— ————

On the last day of July, as Wheeler's raiders returned to Tupelo, Kirby Smith left his headquarters at Knoxville to meet with Bragg at Chattanooga, there to plan a cooperative movement through Middle Tennessee into Kentucky. During the two-day conference, the generals adopted a broad strategy of "mutual support and effective cooperation." Their forces would operate independently of each other until each had attained its immediate objective—for Smith, the defeat of the occupants of Cumberland Gap; for Bragg, the running to earth of Buell's Army of the Ohio.[34]

Whatever they accomplished, the conferees failed to fashion a timetable for joining in defeating Buell and expelling him from Tennessee. Nor did they reach an agreement on the long-term objectives of the coming campaign. Jefferson Davis preferred that his generals combine to defeat Buell before pushing on to the Bluegrass, but Bragg and—especially—Smith, did not see the efficacy of this. Within days of the Chattanooga meeting, the latter was seeking Richmond's approval, instead, of an independent thrust into Kentucky without reference to Buell. At the same time, the duplicitous Virginian assured his senior associate that he would not act unilaterally. He would move against Kentucky only in cooperation with the Army of the Mississippi and only after receiving the go-ahead from Bragg.[35]

If Smith effectively backed away from his previously stated intentions, Bragg soon followed suit. Within a week of assuring Smith that he would boldly confront Buell—who had finally left northern Alabama for Tennessee—Bragg hedged his bets. Even without Smith's support he might cut off and defeat Buell in the open, but it seemed doubtful that if the Union commander fortified Nashville, as Bragg suspected he would, he could be driven out with the 27,000 troops Bragg retained in the wake of the reinforcements he had sent to Smith.

Not until late August did Bragg's supply wagons make the long overland trek from Mississippi to East Tennessee; by then the Louisianan had decided to bypass Buell entirely as he marched through central Kentucky. He would move north via Sparta, Tennessee, and Albany, Danville, and Harrodsburg, Kentucky, with the objective of linking with Smith at or near Lexington. From there—assuming a slow or nonexistent pursuit by Buell—Bragg would forge north to the state capital, Frankfort, where he intended to install a Confederate government headed by Kentucky's exiled lieutenant governor, Richard C. Hawes. That done, he could move in a number of directions, any of them guaranteed to strike fear into the hearts of the enemy on both sides of the Ohio.

Continuing north offered the best opportunity not only to discomfit the Yankees but also to win personal and professional notability. Although he did not commit himself to the objective, Bragg envisioned operating against heavily populated communities such as Louisville and Cincinnati. By occupying the former and threatening the latter, he and his troops would become heroes in the eyes of the Southern public even if they failed to bring Buell to battle.[36]

The campaign to liberate Kentucky got under way on August 13, when Smith's cavalry under Col. John Scott (which included John Morgan's men) began a cautious advance from Knoxville toward Cumberland Gap. Bragg remained in and near Chattanooga for another two weeks, securing logistical support and calling in outlying detachments. During this period, he also attended to organizational details. On the fifteenth he divided his infantry into two wings, each consisting of two divisions. Polk was given command of the right wing, Hardee the left. When Bragg's movement began, two cavalry brigades would cover the flanks of the army, which would march north in two columns—Polk's wing on the east and Hardee's on the west, in closer proximity to the assumed location of the enemy. One of the mounted forces would be led by Bedford Forrest, who since his Murfreesboro raid had been threatening Nashville and other strongholds in Middle Tennessee. The untutored Tennessean—a natural-born cavalryman—would join Bragg's army on the march.[37]

The second cavalry force would consist of three of the regiments recently assigned to Wheeler. The several units the colonel had commanded on
the Bolivar expedition had been removed from his authority, at least temporarily. Some had been reassigned to Van Dorn and Price; others, including the
veteran outfits of Hagan and Wade, had been tendered to Maj. Gen. Samuel
Jones, commanding at Chattanooga. In place of these units, on August 26 Wheeler
was assigned three others: the 1st Alabama under Col. William Wirt Allen, the
3rd Georgia under Col. Martin J. Crawford, and a company-size force of Alabama partisan rangers under Capt. Lemuel G. Mead.

Wheeler could not have been pleased by the exchange. Allen's regiment
was well disciplined and well officered, but Crawford and his men were not
deemed to be dependable and Mead's unit was too small and of too independent
a mindset to do Wheeler much good. Even so, during the operation that lay
ahead Wheeler would acquire a number of other units that would serve him
faithfully and well on a provisional basis. The first of these, Col. J. Warren
Grigsby's 1st Kentucky (only six companies strong), reported to him just before
the army cast loose from Tennessee.[38]

On the twenty-sixth, Bragg sent a small force under Brig. Gen. Samuel
Bell Maxey across the Tennessee to drive some of Buell's troops out of Bridgeport, Alabama, as well as from nearby Battle Creek. The occupation secured the
crossing sites that Hardee's and Polk's wings used two days later. Before that
crossing, early on the twenty-eighth ("a bright and beautiful morning," as he
described it), Wheeler forded the Tennessee at the head of Allen's and Grigsby's
regiments and moved into position to screen Hardee's infantry and artillery. The
following day the acting brigadier was ordered to neutralize the Union outpost
at Altamont, two days' ride ahead. Throughout the twenty-eighth, Wheeler led
his demibrigade across steep and treacherous Walden's Ridge in the Cumberland
Plateau. On the north side of the rocky shelf, he moved through the Sequatchie
Valley, then northwestward via the Therman Road.[39]

This first leg of the invasion was a memorable experience. Years later
Wheeler vividly recalled the "zigzag ascent" he and his men had to make "up the
steep, crooked and rugged path half hidden by green leaves which covered the
mountain side." Despite the tough going, the travelers retained enough stamina
to put up a good fight when they reached Altamont on the morning of the
thirtieth. They drove in a force of foot soldiers that had been picketing the
camps of Maj. Gen. Alexander M. McCook's division and pursued them as far as
their bivouac, which they attacked, killing or wounding at least four of the enemy. Wheeler's small command created so much havoc that General Buell believed the assault had been conducted by a substantial portion of Hardee's column. Evidently, Wheeler's men had fought so effectively on foot that they had
given the impression of being infantry. In response to the attack, Buell withdrew
to Murfreesboro not only McCook's division but also other portions of his scattered army.[40]

After McCook decamped, a gratified Wheeler retraced his steps to the Sequatchie Valley. Once there he reestablished contact with Hardee, then set a northwestwardly course, one that would enable him to guard the column's flank closely. On the morning of September 7, after three or four days on the march, his advance guard reached the bustling village of Carthage. This day Wheeler was ordered to send Allen's regiment to report at Bragg's headquarters; he was compensated for the loss with the addition of the 3rd Georgia and later a 200-man detachment of the 9th Tennessee Cavalry under Col. J. D. Bennett.[41]

At frequent points during the march, Wheeler detached to monitor enemy movements farther west, while also wrecking sections of Buell's main supply artery, the Louisville & Nashville Railroad, and downing the telegraph lines that paralleled the tracks. He performed his many missions with customary thoroughness. A Tennessee officer who observed the cavalry leader for the first time was impressed by what he saw: "He was throwing every obstacle possible to be conceived [of], in the way of the enemy's march to check and hinder his progress—Every bridge, however small or insignificant, on the road, was destroyed and the track torn up" for miles around.[42]

On the eleventh, having crossed into Kentucky—a feat that energized and gratified his entire command—Wheeler added a touch of boldness to his persona by laying a trap for Brig. Gen. Thomas L. Crittenden's 5th Division, Army of the Ohio. Like many another of Buell's subordinates, Crittenden had reacted to reports of Bragg's advance by marching up the right-of-way of the L & N toward Bowling Green. He had gotten as far as the village of Woodburn, where he had gone into bivouac. Getting wind of Wheeler's proximity and unable to judge the size of his force, the Union leader countermarched to avoid contact with it. His faintheartedness deprived Wheeler of captures beyond the one officer and several privates his advance guard cut off from the rear of Crittenden's column.

It was probably well for Wheeler that he did not encounter Crittenden in battle, for the cavalry had gotten so far afield of Hardee's column as to be beyond quick support. Apprehending his vulnerability, Wheeler recalled his forwardmost units and turned east. As he marched, he discovered that a sizable detachment of Crittenden's division—both infantry and cavalry—was pursuing him. Instead of shrinking from the challenge, Wheeler embraced it. Dangling a portion of his force in the enemy's face, Wheeler again attempted to lure his adversary into a trap. He was disappointed when Crittenden's innate caution prompted him to retreat after a brief and perfunctory engagement.[43]

A second, potentially bloodier and more disastrous, clash on the same ground was barely averted. While Wheeler opposed Crittenden, the head of Forrest's brigade—which had joined Bragg's army at Sparta, Tennessee, on September 3—neared the scene of the confrontation with Crittenden from the southeast. Not expecting to meet Confederate cavalry in that vicinity, Forrest mistook

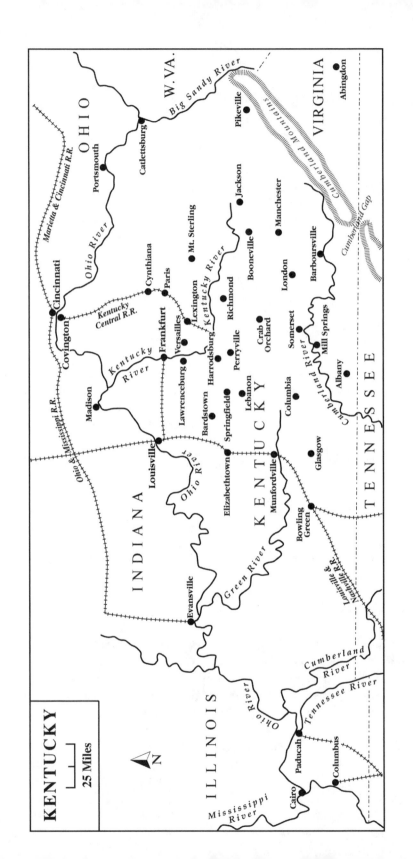

Wheeler's horsemen for Buell's. The Tennessean had just given the order for one of his units, the 8th Texas ("Terry's Rangers") to charge the left flank of Wheeler's command when the regiment's lieutenant colonel correctly identified the troops in his front and called off the attack.

The near-clash of friendly forces appears to have created some friction between the commanders, who came into close contact here for the first time. Forrest's earliest biographers assert that when the 8th Texas arrived it found Wheeler's troopers "falling back helter skelter and in much confusion." When confronted by the Texans, Wheeler's men were thrown into "even greater disorder." In the months and years to come, Wheeler and Forrest would forge an uneasy relationship; this fact may have influenced the authors—who had written their book with the close cooperation of their subject—to denigrate Wheeler by portraying his command as less than steadfast. Wheeler had grounds for believing the same to be true of Forrest, who after identifying Wheeler's cavalry declined to support it against Crittenden, quickly departing to rejoin Bragg. In his report of the confused fight at Woodburn, Wheeler showed admirable restraint when describing Forrest's withdrawal: "Finding he could not engage the enemy to advantage, he retired toward Glasgow."[44]

When he reported at army headquarters, Forrest, now a brigadier general, undoubtedly expected to command the mounted arm of the Army of the Mississippi. Largely because of the way Bragg perceived him, however, Forrest was disappointed. Bragg admired Forrest's leadership and tactical skill and he appreciated the contributions the Tennessean had made to Confederate fortunes in the West. But while he viewed Forrest and his men as good fighters, he considered them poor soldiers. To Bragg's way of thinking, Forrest was basically a partisan leader, effective at scouting and raiding but neither physically nor psychologically equipped to handle the mundane duties inherent in close support of the main army. Bragg also believed that Forrest, a self-taught warrior, was fatally limited by his lack of a West Point education. Thus, when he assigned Forrest's brigade to Polk's wing, Bragg made no reference to Forrest's rank or seniority, as if he was Wheeler's equal, not his superior.[45]

Forrest retained his new command for less than a fortnight. For a time he performed capably, especially when he operated well in advance of Polk's infantry. On September 16, his troopers intercepted Yankees trying to escape the outpost at Munfordville, which lay in Polk's path. Forrest thus played a role in forcing the eventual surrender of the garrison. In later days, however—just as Bragg had anticipated—he proved unable or unwilling to subordinate himself to Polk. He protested that his men and horses were too broken down to carry out the bishop-general's orders, which involved not only guarding the flanks of the right wing but also breaking the railroad between Elizabethtown and Louisville. On September 25, after Forrest's latest complaint, Bragg called him to army headquarters. He ordered the brigadier to turn over his command to his senior subordinate, Col. John Austin Wharton of the 8th Texas, preparatory to its assimilation into Wheeler's command.[46]

Bragg gave Forrest a new mission that would forever separate him from his original command. He was to return to Middle Tennessee, where his popularity would help him recruit and organize another brigade. Forrest was authorized to raise six regiments, two of cavalry and four of infantry, with which he was to "operate against the enemy wherever found, but especially at Nashville, Clarksville, &c., cutting off supplies, capturing trains, and harassing them in all ways practicable."[47]

These were responsibilities Bragg thought Forrest best equipped to handle. Wheeler he believed capable of other duties of greater importance to an army in the field. With his West Point education (his dismal classroom performance notwithstanding) and his prewar mounted experience, the Georgian was better suited to take orders from his superiors, cooperate with infantry and artillery forces, and closely support the main body. Bragg looked for competence in his subordinates but also for the ability to salute smartly and do as they were told. Free-thinkers with an independent bent—even brilliant ones such as Forrest—had no place in Bragg's military world. From now on he would rely on Joe Wheeler, who through a combination of hard work and quiet competence had made himself indispensable to his army and its commander.

4

PRAISE AND PROMOTION

While Bragg's main army closed up on Munfordville, Wheeler continued to keep an eye on enemy forces in the vicinity of Bowling Green. On September 13 he established an outpost at Merry Oaks, midway between Bowling Green and Glasgow, before moving closer to Bowling Green via Oakland Station on the L & N. That night he discovered a Union infantry division, supported by a sizable body of horsemen, crossing the Green River on the northward-running turnpike between Glasgow and Cave City. This sighting, combined with the detection of a wagon train 2,000 vehicles long that appeared ready to cross the stream, suggested a general movement in the direction of Louisville. Wheeler, however, was uncertain whether the advancing troops were members of Buell's main army or the occupants of local outposts.[1]

Whatever its origin, the enemy force should have concerned Bragg, but when word of its movement was relayed to his headquarters he conveyed disinterest. He appeared to believe that Buell would not move far from Bowling Green before turning west and detouring around the Army of the Mississippi in order to reach Louisville without giving battle. Bragg remained convinced that he could beat his opponent to Ohio and that time remained to link up with Smith. The latter was basking in the aftermath of his August 30 capture of Richmond, Kentucky, a coup that had yielded almost 4,000 prisoners. From Richmond, Smith had advanced to Lexington—almost ninety miles northeast of Munfordville—where he remained. If the gap between his force and Bragg's could be bridged and the combined force moved against Louisville, it could strike Buell's army a heavy, perhaps a decisive, blow short of its apparent destination.[2]

A united effort against Buell called for quick action, but at the critical juncture Bragg was delayed by events seemingly beyond his control. For one thing, the capture of Munfordville—which Bragg believed he must achieve before moving against Buell—proved to be a slow and difficult matter. Instead of quickly carrying the 11,000-man garrison, he was forced to lay siege to it. The Yankees held out until the seventeenth—the same day Robert E. Lee's invasion of Maryland reached high tide with his strategic defeat at Antietam. Bragg spent the following day inspecting the captured works—his first trophies of the campaign— as well as resting his hard-marching soldiers and thanking the Almighty for His role in the outcome.[3]

On the eighteenth, the departmental commander sent a staff officer to Lexington to ask Smith to send his supply trains, followed by his entire command, to Bardstown, forty-some miles northeast of Munfordville. Bragg's own troops were to start for Bardstown the next morning. But at almost the last minute, Bragg postponed the movement. Soon after daylight on the seventeenth, a Yankee force of unknown identity and strength had pressed Wheeler so vigorously that he had been forced to devote his full attention to parrying the blow. While he was thus diverted, another column slipped around his flank on the road to Louisville. The elusive Yankees drove off detachments Wheeler had stationed at Merry Oaks under Col. John F. Lay of the 6th Confederate Cavalry.

When Wheeler caught up with the enemy column, he found it too strong to contend with except at long range. Weary from days of marching, scouting, and fighting, and frustrated by his scouts' lack of vigilance, late in the day he withdrew his main force to Glasgow, where he collected outlying detachments and brought up the brigade's supply wagons. All these he led to Munfordville, where he joined Bragg at 8 AM on the eighteenth.[4]

After receiving Wheeler's account of the previous day's misfortunes, Bragg began to fear that Buell, instead of bypassing his opponent on a circuitous course to Louisville, was marching toward Munfordville with the intention of attacking him. It was now that Bragg suspended the march on Bardstown. At the same time, he ordered Wheeler to reestablish contact with the enemy, whose directional heading he was to determine and whose intentions he was to divine. The peremptory assignment could be construed as a rebuke to Wheeler's faulty leadership. The acting brigadier vowed to make amends, and quickly.

Minutes after leaving Bragg's side, Wheeler was galloping westward under a steady rain at the head of a force that now included Allen's and Hagan's regiments as well as two horse artillery pieces under Lt. S. G. Hanley. Reaching his objective, he spent the balance of the eighteenth scouting around Cave City, where his advance sparred with a growing number of bluecoats. The news he relayed to army headquarters—that the enemy was concentrating heavily in his front as if in preparation for a full-scale offensive—prompted Bragg to call in Forrest from Elizabethtown and to prepare to defend his position, including the fortifications that had fallen to him on the seventeenth.[5]

At first, Bragg appeared confident of handling Buell. When Wheeler returned to army headquarters early on the nineteenth he found his superior "anxious for a fight," "never more determined or more confident" of success. But Bragg's self-confidence was an ephemeral thing; it usually gave way to self-doubt, and it did in this instance. As John Hunt Morgan's brother-in-law, Col. Basil W. Duke, later observed, "Here was the first exhibition of that vacillation, that fatal irresolution, which was to wither the bright hopes his promises and his previous action had aroused."[6]

Uncertain that Wheeler's reports reflected reality, on the nineteenth Bragg dispatched an infantry division under Maj. Gen. Solomon Bolivar Buckner to reconnoiter the cave country. When Buckner sent back a report that the Yankees appeared content to spar with Wheeler's men, Bragg decided that Buell was not coming his way after all, at least not in force. Then Bragg reasoned that if he did not need to hunker down and await the enemy, he still had time to link up with Smith. Soon Bragg had regained his determination to move to Bardstown. Early the next morning he started his supply trains in that direction, and by midday his foot soldiers were trudging up the Bardstown turnpike.[7]

As the army moved out, Wheeler, still in close contact with Federals of all arms, took on the task of protecting the withdrawal from Munfordville. "Our front was kept unchanged," he wrote, "and every effort made to prevent the enemy from learning our movements." His job was aided by the arrival, late on the twentieth, of Bedford Forrest's brigade, now led by Colonel Wharton. The lanky, tawny-skinned Texan was an ambitious officer with a streak of stubbornness that in time would harm his relationship with Wheeler, his senior by date of commission. On the present occasion, however, he would perform creditably in a subordinate role, although disappointed to learn that Wheeler intended to place him in a reserve position in the rear.[8]

On the early afternoon on the twentieth the Federals advanced in strength sufficient to shove Wheeler's brigade to within four miles of Green River. Then, and again later in the day, by which time Wheeler had crossed his and Wharton's troops to the north side of the river, the enemy attempted to outflank him on the right. Both times they were thwarted by dismounted detachments of the 1st Alabama, 1st Kentucky, and 3rd Georgia, supported in front by the two horse artillery pieces and in the rear by Wharton's reserves. For their steadfastness, Wheeler's men suffered several casualties, the highest ranking being Wirt Allen's second-in-command, Lt. Col. T. B. Brown, who died during a "handsome charge" on "the enemy's dense lines of infantry."[9]

The fighting tapered off after the Yankees managed to bull their way across Green River. It resumed early the next morning, the twenty-first, when Wheeler broke contact and began to retire to the Bardstown Pike, Wharton's men leading the way. About noon the enemy's cavalry, in advance of their main force, caught up with Wheeler's brigade, and the fighting resumed. It lasted until dark, when the Yankees pulled back and went into bivouac.

With Bragg well on his way to Bardstown, Wheeler was ordered to join Hardee near Hodgensville (the birthplace of Abraham Lincoln), about twenty-five miles farther south. Late on the twenty-first he started out with the better part of his command, Wharton's troopers again in the advance. He left behind enough scouts to keep tabs on the enemy as they fell back and regained the road to Louisville. The scouts, said Wheeler, "counted the regiments, batteries, and wagons which passed, a report of which was sent to headquarters."[10]

Wheeler's men were at Hodgensville at the appointed time. They remained there until the twenty-seventh, alternately resting and reconnoitering. By then Wharton's brigade had marched to Bardstown. Wheeler followed with his entire force minus only Crawford's Georgians, who by Bragg's order were left in a blocking position near the hamlet of New Haven. Two days later, to Wheeler's regret—though perhaps not to his surprise—Buell's troops overawed the 3rd Georgia at New Haven. Surrounding the regiment, they forced its 250 officers and men to surrender without firing a shot. For showing neither vigilance nor resistance, Crawford was court-martialed, and in December he was convicted of gross negligence.[11]

Bragg, with the advance echelon of the main army, had reached Bardstown on the twenty-second. He had selected that point as a rendezvous with Smith because of its location midway between Munfordville and Lexington. Upon arriving, however, Bragg found no sign of the Virginian and his command. A waiting courier informed Bragg that Smith had decided he dare not abandon his present position, the presumed objective of George W. Morgan, whose Federals had only recently evacuated Cumberland Gap. Ostensibly, Smith's intention in advancing from Knoxville had been to rout Morgan, but he had failed to do more than pin his opponent to his mountain position.

Smith was not the only high-ranking officer unable or unwilling to carry out his part of the invasion. Others on whom Bragg had counted for support had failed to deliver. These included Van Dorn and Price, who, after Bragg left Chattanooga, violated their orders by attacking Grant's lines in West Tennessee and northern Mississippi. The result was a severe repulse at Iuka; both generals would soon suffer a second, larger defeat at Corinth. Still another potential source of reinforcement for Bragg, the division of John Breckinridge, had been delayed en route to Kentucky by orders to support Van Dorn.[12]

If Bragg was chagrined by his lack of cooperation he was plainly upset by the failure of Kentuckians to join his ranks in substantial numbers. On October 4, having accompanied one of his detachments to Frankfort, Bragg installed Richard Hawes as governor of Confederate Kentucky. The army leader must have wondered how long this regime would endure given the apparent unwillingness of Hawes's fellow Kentuckians to throw off the yoke of Union oppression.

Yet another, more troubling concern was Bragg's inability to deny his enemy access to Louisville. Two days after Bragg reached Bardstown, Buell marched into the port city at the head of his Army of the Ohio. What the Union leader intended next was anyone's guess, but the prospects were ominous.[13]

— — — —

To keep watch over the Yankees in and around Louisville, on the twenty-seventh Wheeler's horsemen took up a position at Boston, a few miles east of the Union citadel. From Boston southwestward as far as Elizabethtown Wheeler's mounted riflemen reconnoitered, occasionally tangling with outlying detachments of Buell's command. By October 4, when he was recalled to Bardstown to guard the left wing of the Army of the Mississippi, Wheeler had informed General Polk—now commanding in the absence of Bragg, who had gone to Lexington to confer with Smith—that the Federals were advancing from Louisville toward Frankfort, with the apparent intent of giving battle. The intelligence was faulty—the movement toward the capital was a feint—but it was relayed on the second to Bragg, who ordered Polk to move north to Bloomfield and strike Buell in the flank and rear. Bragg wished Kirby Smith to move against Buell at the same time. But when other evidence convinced Bragg that the advance toward Frankfort was a blind, he ordered Polk to withhold his movement.

Bragg's strong-willed subordinate had other ideas. Basing his actions on reports that had Buell moving in force against his current position at Bardstown, Polk decided to withdraw the army to Danville, almost forty miles to the east. The resulting fallback prompted the evacuation of Frankfort only hours after Hawes's oath-taking. By the time Bragg, now hastening to join Polk, countermanded the latter's order, the army's left wing under Hardee had reached Perryville, immediately south of Danville. Hardee had halted there in response to reports that water fit to drink could be found in the bed of Doctor's Fork, potable water being a precious commodity during this summer of severe drought. By October 7, one of Buell's columns had drawn to within striking distance of the same location, and a battle was imminent.[14]

Wheeler's horsemen had made the journey from Bardstown to Perryville in company with Hardee's wing, whose flanks and rear the cavalry had been assigned to protect. On October 4, near the village of Glenville, part of Buell's advance had overtaken Wheeler's command, the rear portion of which it tried to cut off. To prevent this, Wheeler, who was riding with his main body farther east, led a detachment back to Glenville where he rescued some pickets on the verge of being surrounded. Having remained outside Glenville for the night, Wheeler's detachment, including the nearly captured pickets, had to detour around another body of bluecoats that had interposed between it and the rest of the cavalry. After reuniting with the main body, Wheeler led the way to Springfield, due west of Perryville, where he observed and reported Buell's advance.[15]

The reconnaissance ended abruptly on the morning of the sixth, when a strong enemy force of all arms—part of Maj. Gen. Charles C. Gilbert's corps of Buell's army—appeared east of Springfield and advanced on Wheeler. For a time the cavalry held its ground on the outskirts of the village, fighting dismounted from behind fences and stone walls. Shortly before noon, as more and more of Gilbert's men reached the scene and became engaged, Wheeler remounted his brigade and had it fall back, slowly and in good order—a process he would repeat on many later fields to good effect.

Wheeler's retrograde covered about three miles. At that point he halted the command, dismounted it, and staked out a defensive perimeter on high ground. From here his men held back the Union cavalry of Capt. Ebenezer Gay, supported in the rear by Brig. Gen. James B. Steedman's infantry brigade. A two-hour standoff closed with Wheeler's men falling back to avoid encircle-ment. Yet another stand two miles closer to Perryville along Little Beech Fork ended the same way. Concerned that this latest position did not afford sufficient cover, Wheeler abandoned the creek line but only after he had repulsed an attack by Gay's horsemen. Night came on soon afterward, enabling Wheeler to boast that throughout the day he had limited Gilbert's forward progress to four miles.

That night Wheeler concealed his men in woods east of Little Beech Fork. Early on the morning of the seventh, Gilbert's column, Gay's troopers in the van, resumed its drive toward Perryville, now six miles to the east. Wheeler's brigade fell back before it until, one mile from the town, the colonel located "a very favorable position" that would facilitate another delaying action. At the base of Brown's Hill, which the Yankees had to approach via a long, narrow ravine, Wheeler deployed most of his men afoot, while a mounted squadron waited behind the hill for an opportunity to attack. Atop the high ground, he unlimbered the six-pounder smoothbores of Hanley's battery, which he shielded from enemy view behind piles of corn stacks and fence rails.[16]

At about nine o'clock, Gay's horsemen reached Brown's Hill and began to exchange rifle- and carbine-fire with the Confederates. After almost an hour of indecisive skirmishing an impatient Gay ordered his lead regiment, the 9th Kentucky, to deliver a saber charge—with disastrous results. Wheeler permitted the attackers to come on until well within rifle and canister range, whereupon his men opened "upon them with excellent effect, thoroughly stampeding their entire front." However, "so effectual and unexpected was this stampede of so large a force of cavalry, artillery, and a portion of their infantry that our cavalry could not be placed in a position to charge them in time to accomplish all that could be desired." He committed his mounted squadron anyway; the troopers "succeeded in capturing 1 officer and 8 men, together with about 50 stand of superior arms, and great numbers of blankets, saddle bags, &c., which they had thrown away in their flight." Once the Yankees were beyond pursuit, Wheeler recalled his men to their original position, where they stood ready for additional fighting, either offensive or defensive.[17]

Though his cavalry had been checked, Gilbert's foot troops had yet to see action. Shortly before noon, a sizable body of infantry came up in rear of Gay's re-formed ranks. The forwardmost brigade, its movements directed by General Buell himself and backed by a rifled battery that exchanged fire with

Hanley's smoothbores, advanced confidently on Wheeler. Outgunned and outpositioned, Wheeler, at about 1 PM, fell back to the fringes of Perryville. Here he found himself within supporting range of infantry comrades, members of the brigade of Brig. Gen. St. John Liddell, one of Hardee's favorite subordinates. At the foot of Peters's Hill, a crescent-shaped eminence that commanded the surrounding area, Wheeler halted to fashion another ambuscade, one, however, that Gay's pursuing horsemen detected and avoided.

Just before sundown, Gilbert's lead division, that of Brig. Gen. Robert B. Mitchell, challenged Wheeler, only to be brought to a sudden halt by the firing of dismounted troopers and artillerists deployed along the western slope of Peters's Hill. As the Yankees reeled backward, Wheeler ordered detachments of Allen's and Hagan's regiments, supported by a few companies of the 1st Kentucky, to charge. The resulting attack, made to the accompaniment of the Rebel Yell, pierced the Union line and sent its troops whirling to the rear. Screaming at the top of their lungs, Alabamians and Kentuckians galloped out the Springfield-Perryville Road, dispatching luckless Yankees with pistol and sword and making prisoners of more than a few.

At first Wheeler was delighted by the effects of the charge. His mood changed abruptly, however, when his opponents showed that they too could spring an ambush. As Allen's and Hagan's riders pounded down the pike, concealed members of Mitchell's command bobbed up from roadside cornfields and dosed the column with a murderous volley of musketry. Numerous horses went down in the road, throwing their riders head over heels. Their comrades beat a wild retreat to Peters's Hill, every man for himself. Relieved to find that most of the men reached safety and reluctant to press his luck any further, Wheeler withdrew his command to Perryville in gathering darkness.

The fight Wheeler's brigade had put up over the past several days had proved its ability to fight effectively both on foot and in the saddle. It also testified to the discipline its leader, despite his brief tenure, had instilled in the command. Historians, however, would question the necessity of so much combat involvement, especially on the seventh. The previous evening, Hardee, at Perryville, had ordered Wheeler to break contact with Buell and fall back upon his infantry supports, telling him that if the enemy "wishes to fight, let him come on."[18]

What Hardee wanted from the cavalry was timely information about Union movements. He suspected, as he informed Wheeler, that the enemy's horsemen were attempting to outflank him and get in his rear. Wheeler knew this to be untrue but apparently he failed to tell Hardee, doubtless because he was too busy engaging Yankee infantry and cavalry. The author of the definitive study of mounted operations during the Perryville Campaign calls this lapse "evidence of the Confederate generals' failure to use their cavalry properly. In this case, Hardee should have pressed Wheeler on the matter of intelligence—intelligence that was so vital to the Confederate armies at this time."[19]

A lack of information also affected Bragg, who came to believe that the pending confrontation with Buell would take place not at Perryville but almost thirty miles to the northeast, near Versailles, or farther north at Frankfort where one of Buell's columns had been pressing Smith's command. For lack of hard information on enemy movements and intentions, Bragg believed that Smith was confronted by Buell's main body. Not until late on the seventh, in response to reports from Hardee that the enemy was only two miles from his position and coming on fast, did Bragg begin to concentrate the army at Perryville. At 5:40 PM he ordered Polk, with the main body near Harrodsburg, five miles northeast of Perryville (where Bragg had halted Polk's retreat from Bardstown), to go to Hardee's support. Upon arriving, Polk was to "give the enemy battle immediately, rout him, and then move to our support at Versailles."[20]

Once again, one of Bragg's subordinates substituted his own judgment for that of his superior. When Bragg joined Polk and Hardee on the field of battle at 9:30 on the morning of the eighth, he found that Polk had withheld an attack in favor of assuming a "defensive-offensive" posture. He had formed the 15,000 troops within his reach in a concave line of battle facing west against the Yankees who had pressured Wheeler and Hardee the previous day. Infantry, supported closely by artillery, held most of this line, with cavalry massed on its flanks. Wharton's brigade—which in response to Polk's orders had been picketing far from Perryville, near Lebanon and Danville, and had not reached Perryville until the evening of October 7—had been placed on the far right of the army. Polk had stationed Wheeler's horsemen on the left flank. After about 10 AM the latter found themselves confronted by a substantial component of Maj. Gen. George H. Thomas's II Corps—the infantry division of Thomas L. Crittenden, with which Wheeler had tangled fiercely three weeks ago, just after entering Kentucky.[21]

The fighting did not begin in earnest until early in the afternoon, when Gilbert's column pressed Hardee's position. The infantry division of Brig. Gen. Phil Sheridan—the erstwhile cavalry colonel whom Wheeler had attempted to deceive during a flag-of-truce conference at Guntown, Mississippi—delivered the initial assault. Hardee responded with a strong counterattack, and the battle soon became general.

John Dyer contends that the part played by Wheeler's brigade in the fighting on the eighth "was of little importance." Other historians claim that throughout the day Wheeler's mounted riflemen, backed by their two cannons, kept Crittenden off balance and confused, so that he made a negligible contribution to Buell's battle plan. Moreover, Polk's faulty dispositions had permitted Thomas's corps to overlap the Confederate left, leaving the flank vulnerable to a turning movement; that none occurred appears to be a tribute to the stubborn resistance offered by Wheeler's 1,200-man command throughout the day.[22]

For his part, Wheeler claimed much for his brigade during this, the only major action fought on Kentucky soil. At approximately 10 AM his pickets on the road between Lebanon and Perryville were driven in by a "large body of cavalry," the 1st Kentucky and 7th Pennsylvania. Mounted men pressed up the road, supported on either side by dismounted carbineers. Undoubtedly Wheeler would have moved to neutralize this threat of his own volition, but Polk, learning of the advance, ordered him to clear the road. In response, "we charged the enemy," Wheeler reported, "throwing their entire force of cavalry into confusion and putting it to flight." He added that "we pursued them at full charge for 2 miles, capturing many prisoners and horses in single combat and driving the remaining [troops] under cover of their masses of infantry. The enemy also fled terror-stricken from a battery placed in advance of their general line and left it at our disposal."[23]

Wheeler described this charge, made by a single column consisting of detachments from Allen's and Hagan's Alabamians, as "one of the most brilliant of the campaign." Upon their return, however, Wheeler found his position threatened by forces so large "we were prevented [from] making any farther advance. I therefore withdrew a short distance and again deployed our line, engaging the enemy with both cavalry and artillery until night, and prevented this large force [whose size he estimated as two divisions] from taking any other part in the contest of that day."[24]

Wheeler's claim of arresting the progress of enemy forces many times his size was taken at face value by his superiors, several of whom—chief among them, Braxton Bragg—praised the tenacity and skill of the colonel's valiant 1,200. Latter-day historians offer a less laudatory assessment of Wheeler's contributions to what ended—despite 3,400 Confederate troops being rendered *hors de combat*—as a limited tactical success for the Army of the Mississippi but something less than a clear-cut victory. A recent chronicler of the engagement, Kenneth W. Noe, contends that Wheeler's feats this day have been exaggerated: "Little evidence exists that Crittenden's men were fooled by Wheeler, or even took much notice of him. Buell's orders and the strained communications between Buell and Thomas did more to keep II Corps out of the battle. . . . Those factors probably would have held the corps in position Wheeler or no Wheeler."[25]

In a larger sense, Wheeler's determination to occupy Crittenden's attention may have hurt rather than aided his army. As was true of his attempts to slow Gilbert's advance toward Perryville, this day he had been more concerned with fighting than in intelligence gathering and dissemination. He himself lacked critical information about the enemy. Until midafternoon on the eighth he had believed his men opposed only by mounted Yankees; not until about three o'clock was he able to inform Bragg that a large force of all arms was confronting him on the Lebanon Pike—and when he did report the fact he did so in vague and general terms, not in a decisive rendering of facts that might have enabled Bragg to adjust and refine his plan of battle. As Noe asserts, "the Battle of Perryville might have been quite different had Bragg known that an unbloodied Federal corps waited to the south[west of Perryville]. And Bragg should have known—it was Wheeler's job to tell him."[26]

On the other hand, had Wheeler's men not skirmished so stubbornly and charged so boldly, the battle might have turned sharply and quickly in Buell's favor. As Noe admits, absent Wheeler's opposition the cavalry attached to Thomas's wing, under Brig. Gen. Edward M. McCook, "would have been free to ride straight into Perryville and provide *their* commanders with more accurate information. Had they done so, they would have found a wide-open Confederate flank ripe for a II Corps attack. The entire battle, indeed the course of the war in the West, might have changed."[27]

— — — —

However debatable Wheeler's contribution on October 8, the value of his contribution to his army in the immediate aftermath of the battle is undeniable. This service began on the evening after the battle, when Bragg met with his ranking subordinates to ponder the army's next move. Having driven the troops on Buell's left flank more than mile from their initial positions, and having held the rest of the Army of the Ohio in place, Bragg appeared to hold the initiative when darkness ended the day's fighting.

His soldiers sensed that, should the battle resume the next morning, they would clear the field of the enemy—most appeared to hunger for the opportunity to do so. But Bragg, whose earlier confidence had been diluted by his natural tendency toward self-doubt and excess caution, decided he could fight no further until he made contact with Kirby Smith. Thus, at about midnight, after petitioning the latter to join him at Harrodsburg, he recalled his army to its prebattle positions. Early on the ninth he broke contact with his hard-pressed enemy and put his men in column on the road to Harrodsburg.

Logically enough, Bragg tabbed Wheeler's horsemen to facilitate the retreat by holding back the enemy until the infantry and artillery could clear the field. Wheeler was specifically instructed to prevent a pursuit by Buell on the road to Danville. He disposed of his regiments and cannons accordingly; but not until several hours after Bragg's disappointed troops began to move off for Harrodsburg did the enemy show signs of pursuing. As Wheeler wrote after the war, "it was fully 10 o'clock when, standing on the edge of the town [Perryville], I saw the advance of the skirmish line of Buell's army." The bluecoats moved so slowly that Wheeler easily kept between them and Bragg's main army. Even when Bragg halted eight miles from the evacuated battlefield, prepared to fight, the Yankees showed no inclination to accept the challenge.[28]

For two days the retreat proceeded without interruption. Over that period, Wheeler took several blows from the cavalry spearheading Buell's lethargic pursuit, but he easily parried them. Even as he deflected the thrusts, he kept scouts posted along the road to Harrodsburg. On the tenth, these observers informed him that a portion of the enemy column was diverging toward Danville. After relaying the news to Bragg, Wheeler galloped there at the head of his brigade.

The following morning, infantry under Col. William B. Hazen, supported by a light battery and the 1st Kentucky (Union) Cavalry, advanced on the town. Hazen encountered Wheeler's command "drawn up in line of battle at the Fair Grounds, 1 mile from Danville, with cavalry and artillery. The latter opened without effect upon the skirmishers, who, pushing forward persistently, had no difficulty in driving the enemy through the town." The force Hazen drove consisted primarily of Wade's 8th Confederate, which only that morning had rejoined Wheeler for the first time since Bragg's army left Chattanooga. Despite his command's precipitate withdrawal, Wheeler fell back only a short distance from Danville, where he remained, as if defiantly, until the evening of the twelfth. At that time, as per orders, he crossed Dick's River and fell back to Camp Dick Robinson, a rendezvous for Union troops established in August 1861.[29]

It was at Camp Dick Robinson that Wheeler received extremely welcome news: Bragg had elevated him to command every cavalry unit in the Army of the Mississippi. Attaining this, the highest position anyone in his arm could aspire to, must have been a heady experience for an officer who had just turned twenty-six, especially one who had comported himself so poorly in his West Point studies, including cavalry tactics. The assignment must have been especially gratifying given the more highly celebrated cavalry officers who were available to serve Bragg. The assignment suggested that the soldier of ability and competence, who scrupulously obeyed given orders, adapted quickly to fluctuating situations, and gave the fullest amount of attention and energy to his assigned duties, might outpace the brilliant scholar and textbook-bound theoretician.

Wheeler's promotion did not greatly alter his relations with his ranking subordinate, John Wharton, whose brigade—which now consisted of the 4th Kentucky, 8th Texas, and three companies of the 1st Kentucky—Wheeler had been directing, on the basis of seniority, whenever Wharton's and his own command came within supporting distance. The difference was that from now on Wheeler could give Wharton orders wherever the latter was stationed.

Wharton's units were not the only recent additions to Wheeler's sphere of authority. By mid-October, his own brigade had expanded by taking in various regiments and battalions that had become available over the past six weeks. That command now consisted of the 1st and 3rd Alabama, the 2nd and 3rd Georgia, and the 6th Confederate, as well as the balance of the 1st Kentucky. It appears that even after Wheeler began operating as Bragg's chief of cavalry he retained direct command of the brigade—when he was apart from it leadership probably passed to the senior regimental leader, Wirt Allen.[30]

By naming Wheeler chief of cavalry, Bragg put him directly in line for promotion to brigadier general. On November 4 he would follow up his action by formally requesting of Adj. Gen. Samuel Cooper in Richmond the appointment of both Wheeler and Wharton to be brigadiers, "positions they so justly deserve, and are so competent to fill." As he had shown while at Pensacola, Bragg was a stickler for rank and seniority. The dates of their commissioning as colonels would ensure that Wheeler remained senior to Wharton. The War Department acted quickly to grant Bragg's request; Wheeler's appointment dated from October 30, Wharton's from November 10.[31]

By all indications, Wheeler's assignment and promotion had come about logically, given that the only cavalry officer senior to him, Forrest, was no longer with the army. Even so, Bragg's action emphasized the trust he had placed in the callow Georgian. So did the praise that Bragg had consistently bestowed on Wheeler throughout the campaign. The most recent tribute had come late on the thirteenth, in response to Wheeler's report that Buell's army had turned toward Danville. The army leader informed Wheeler that "the information you send is very important. It is just what I needed and I thank you for it. This information leaves no doubt as to the proper course for me to pursue." He closed by ordering Wheeler to "hold the enemy firmly until tomorrow."[32]

——— —— ——

Until this point, Wheeler, in common with many of his colleagues, had expected the army to renew the fight in Kentucky, especially since Bragg, having reached Harrodsburg, had finally linked up with Smith. Presently, however, it became evident that Bragg believed his "proper course" was to leave the state. Many considerations had led him to this conclusion. In his present position his army had access to few supplies and fewer recruits, and he feared that autumnal rains would wash out southward-leading roads, making a deferred withdrawal hazardous if not impossible. Then, too, Bragg was disturbed by reports that Buell was soon to be heavily reinforced, and he was distressed by the recently received news of Van Dorn's and Price's defeat at Corinth. Under these circumstances, he perceived that the fate of the Confederacy rested on his returning his army intact to its base of operations and supply in East Tennessee.[33]

Some historians believe that in abandoning the strong line he and Smith had built at Harrodsburg, Bragg lost an opportunity to salvage victory and redeem himself for his precipitate withdrawal from Perryville. Among the Confederate high command, Smith, Polk, and Hardee felt this way, and Smith told Bragg so in plain terms. Even Bragg's opponent was taken aback when the Army of the Mississippi withdrew to Bryantsville on the evening of the tenth. Buell suspected that, rather than retreating, Bragg was maneuvering in hopes of catching him in a trap. The Union commander could not believe his enemy would end his invasion of Kentucky without giving battle at least once more.[34]

From Bryantsville on the thirteenth Bragg started his and Smith's troops toward Cumberland Gap. At the outset of the march, Wheeler's troopers helped their comrades in the other arms destroy whatever supplies could not be carried off, thus denying them to Buell. Then, as the withdrawal got well under way,

Wheeler divided his newly enlarged command to better shoulder the many responsibilities thrust upon it—guarding the rear and flanks of the moving column, corralling stragglers, arresting deserters, and escorting the supply wagons that accompanied the army.

The slowly moving vehicles demanded a great deal of time and energy while provoking frustration bordering on exasperation. As Wheeler was to write, "the large trains of captured stores made the progress of our infantry very slow, and the corps commanders sent frequent admonitions to me urging the importance of persistent resistance to Buell's advance. In crossing Big Hill, and at other points, the trains hardly averaged five miles a day."[35]

When not protecting the vehicles whose contents—rations, forage, and other supplies confiscated from Unionist enclaves in Kentucky—gave Bragg's invasion some semblance of accomplishment, Wheeler's cavalry fanned out to cover the army's flanks and rear. Once the last of his infantry and artillery comrades had passed, Wheeler's troopers littered the roads—especially after dark—with felled trees, fence rails, and anything else that might obstruct the slowly pursuing enemy. John Dyer speculates that "Wheeler's tree felling was something new and unexpected in the war, for it evoked no little comment from the Federal officers." Several of them cited it when testifying before a postcampaign military commission inquiring into various aspects of Buell's generalship, one of which was referred to in the commission's report as "Permitting the Rebels to Escape Without Loss from Kentucky."[36]

Then and later, Wheeler's resourcefulness also provoked comment from observers in gray. Maj. Baxter Smith, commander of a Tennessee battalion in Wharton's brigade, remarked after the war that the new cavalry commander "particularly distinguished himself" by his "untiring and sleepless" efforts to delay and discomfit the Yankees to the rear. Smith was equally impressed by personal qualities he observed in Wheeler: "[I] found him to be a thorough soldier & as gentle as a woman, and as courteous as a cavalier of an older time." Wheeler's courage was testified to by the fact that he "could generally be found with the rear guard, as the enemy advanced, seeing personally that nothing was omitted [that was] necessary to check the enemy's advance." Smith was likewise pleased to discover that Wheeler's "habits were strictly temperate, and he usually laid down to sleep at night, with his men in bivouac."[37]

The withdrawal, initially organized in one long, unwieldy column, became bifurcated when the combined forces reached Lancaster, Kentucky, about sixteen miles southeast of Danville, on the fourteenth. From that point on, Wheeler had to split his force to cover the diverging columns of Bragg and Smith. Almost as soon as the latter began to go his own way, he expressed a fear of being overtaken by Buell, whom he would have to confront unsupported for an indefinite time. In something close to panic, Smith informed Bragg that he had "little hope" of getting through to Tennessee with his trains and artillery intact; both had turned off the main road onto a "circuitous route" that left them vulnerable to pursuit and capture. Responding to his superior's concern, Wheeler is supposed to have given assurance that the cavalry would do its job and Smith would have "to abandon nothing." If he indeed offered this pledge, he made good on it. Not a single wagon or cannon fell into Buell's hands during the retreat, which the enemy ceased to press after October 22.[38]

During those thirteen days between the commencement of Bragg's retreat and the end of the enemy's pursuit, the troopers under Wheeler's command clashed time and again with pursuing troops of all arms, over one five-day period fighting twenty-six rear-guard engagements. The spirited encounters occurred at Danville and Stanford on the fourteenth; two days later near Mount Vernon, Rocky Hill, and other points north of Rockcastle River; at Mershon's Cross Roads and Hazel Patch on the eighteenth; and at Pittman's Cross Roads, near London, Kentucky, on the nineteenth.

On some of these occasions, heavier and better-positioned enemy forces compelled Wheeler to give ground and, occasionally, beat a quick retreat to avoid encirclement. More often than not, however, the Confederates fought stubbornly and when forced to withdraw, did so grudgingly. When opportunity presented itself, they would rally and counterattack, delaying Buell and making him cautious and wary. This fight-and-fall-back strategy, a major feature of mounted infantry operations first displayed on the movement into Kentucky, was never more effectively practiced than on this retreat (although Dyer overreaches when describing Wheeler as the originator of mounted infantry tactics). In fact, by the time the army finally halted its retrograde, Wheeler's command had virtually perfected the technique.

The effective job Wheeler had turned in during the retreat did not go unnoticed. On the nineteenth, Bragg's adjutant general informed him that his boss considered the cavalry's service "particularly gratifying, and supports the reputation you have already won for high soldierly qualities." The following day, General Smith added his gratitude and congratulations, and promised to make his feelings known to the authorities in Richmond. The uniformly laudatory response made Wheeler dare to aspire to rank and authority even higher than that so recently conferred upon him.[39]

5

DEFENDING IN FRONT, ATTACKING IN REAR

The retreat of Bragg's and Smith's forces through Kentucky to East Tennessee had been a nightmare for all involved, but especially for the foot soldiers. By the time the Confederates reached safe haven on the south side of the Cumberland plateau at Morristown, they were, as historian Thomas L. Connelly observes, "on the verge of sheer physical collapse." The troops had experienced "incredible suffering—a two-hundred-mile march across rocky, muddy roads in bad weather. Many troops were barefoot and had only tattered scraps of clothing. They subsisted on parched corn and drank polluted water from roadside pools where dead livestock lay."[1]

The ordeal of Bragg's cavalry had been somewhat less severe. While probably as poorly shod as their infantry comrades, at least the troopers could ride homeward. Moreover, their mobility enabled them to forage off local corn cribs, chicken coops, and smoke-houses—a practice that would grow more widespread as the war progressed, eroding discipline and promoting straggling and desertion in a way that would cause grief not only to the victims of such behavior but to Wheeler and his subordinates, as well. Perhaps the greatest difference in the moods of the two service arms was that while Bragg's foot soldiers had been demoralized by an abortive invasion and a defeat snatched from the jaws of victory, their mounted comrades left Kentucky buoyed by the knowledge that they had skillfully protected the army from even greater disaster.

If they had not always performed brilliantly before and during the battle of October 8, Wheeler's troopers had earned their pay during the return trip. They had fended off repeated efforts by a stronger and better-equipped enemy flushed with victory to waylay the Confederates short of their home base in the mountains. A word of official thanks for a job well done seemed in order. On the twenty-third, from his temporary headquarters at Cumberland Gap, Wheeler issued a proclamation commending his troopers for their soldierly bearing, endurance, and combat prowess. General Orders Number 3, grandly addressed to the "Cavalry Corps, Army of the Mississippi" and read by staff officers to assembled units, lauded the command's "gallantry in action . . . [and] cheerful endurance of sufferings from hunger, fatigue, and exposure. . . . For nearly two months, you have scarcely for a moment been without the range of the enemy's musketry. In more than twenty pitched fights, many of which lasted throughout the day, you have successfully combated largely superior numbers of the enemy's troops of all arms. . . . In this continual series of combats and brilliant charges many gallant officers and brave men have fallen. We mourn their loss; we commend their valor. Let us emulate their soldierly virtues."[2]

If Bragg's weary, footsore soldiers longed for a protracted respite, they were doomed to disappointment. On October 27, less than a week after reaching Morristown, they were packed aboard the cars of the East Tennessee Railroad for a long and jouncing ride to Chattanooga. From that mountain-enclosed stronghold the troops were borne along the banks of the Tennessee River to Bridgeport, Alabama. Crossing the river by ferryboat, they boarded another train that would carry them to Murfreesboro. While their infantry comrades rode the rails, Wheeler's and Wharton's brigades made the trip from Bridgeport overland, as did most of Bragg's artillery.

Bragg's radical change of base was owing to his belief that Middle Tennessee offered geographical advantages that would enable him to contend successfully with the Union army that had also departed Kentucky for the Volunteer State. Any supplies he could not gather in that bountiful region he could obtain via the Western & Atlantic Railroad, which linked his army to its supply depots at Chattanooga and farther south. From Murfreesboro Bragg could also develop a project dear to him as well as to other Confederate military and political officials—the recapture of Nashville.[3]

Bragg's apparently hasty decision to transfer his base of operations to a location so far from Chattanooga prompted Jefferson Davis to call him to Richmond in the last days of October to discuss his plans for the Army of the Mississippi. The several-day conference in the Confederate capital predated a month-long series of command and organizational changes within and without the army. After Bragg returned to Tennessee, Smith and Polk, who in the aftermath of the Kentucky campaign had severely criticized his generalship, were also called to Davis's side for an interview. Although neither general attempted to mask his antipathy toward Bragg, the president, by appealing to their patriotism and goodwill, persuaded them to serve Bragg as faithfully as possible. Upon their return to the army, Polk resumed command of his corps and Smith not only sent two divisions from his command to Bragg but also agreed to accompany them and subordinate himself to Bragg's authority. Davis was so appreciative of their support that he promoted both of them—as he also did Hardee, another vocal critic of Bragg—to lieutenant general, only one rank below their common superior.

Kirby Smith's tenure as a corps commander under Bragg lasted only a few weeks. In mid-December, as part of a raft of other organizational changes, the War Department shunted one of Smith's divisions to Vicksburg, headquarters of Lt. Gen. John C. Pemberton's recently created Department of Mississippi and East Louisiana. The transfer left Smith with so small a command that it was soon abolished, and its erstwhile leader returned to his old headquarters at Knoxville. He remained there until the following February when, at the urging of President Davis, he went west to head the Confederate Trans-Mississippi Department.[4]

Another geographical command came into existence in late November when Davis belatedly decided that the various lines of military authority in the western theater required centralized control. After perusing a short list of candidates that included the otherwise occupied Robert E. Lee (whose Army of Northern Virginia had recently returned to its namesake state after ending its invasion of Maryland) and the imperious and erratic P. G. T. Beauregard, Davis finally selected for the position of theater commander Joseph E. Johnston, who had led the Army of Northern Virginia from First Manassas until last May 31, when he was disabled by wounds during the Battle of Seven Pines. From headquarters at or near Chattanooga, Johnston would supervise a vast fiefdom encompassing territory and resources from the Blue Ridge Mountains of North Carolina to the Mississippi River. Those resources included the widely separated forces of Bragg, Smith, Pemberton, and Brig. Gen. John H. Forney, who headed the District of the Gulf, headquartered at Mobile.[5]

Of the many administrative changes that swept the western armies in this autumn of 1863, only one appeared to generate little or no controversy. On November 20, Braxton Bragg renamed his command to emphasize its connection with its primary area of operations. As he observed in the concluding section of General Orders No. 151, "with the remembrance of Richmond, Munfordville, and Perryville so fresh in our minds, let us make a name for the now Army of Tennessee as enviable as those enjoyed by the armies of Kentucky and the Mississippi."[6]

— — — —

Upon his return from Richmond, Bragg established his headquarters at Tullahoma, thirty-five miles south of Murfreesboro. One of his first actions was to reorganize his mounted arm into five brigades, all of which answered to Wheeler. Three of these he considered "regular" cavalry—those commanded by Wheeler, Wharton, and Brig. Gen. John Pegram, erstwhile chief of staff to Kirby Smith. Pegram's undersized command, consisting of the 1st Georgia and 1st Louisiana Cavalry, had come over from the Army of Kentucky; during the Kentucky campaign it had been commanded by Col. John Scott. The other components of

Bragg's mounted arm—Forrest's new brigade, which consisted of the 4th, 8th, and 9th Tennessee and the 4th Alabama Cavalry, and John Hunt Morgan's 2nd, 7th, 8th, and 11th Kentucky—Bragg thought of as partisan units that operated effectively only when serving apart from the main army and especially when raiding inside Union territory.[7]

In accordance with his somewhat jaundiced view of Forrest and Morgan, Bragg ensured that during the fall of 1862 and into the following winter, both commanders spent a lot of time in the enemy's rear, harassing his outposts and cutting his communications. Early in December he sent Forrest on an expedition through West Tennessee in hopes of checking an advance by Ulysses S. Grant in the direction of Vicksburg. On his journey of destruction, Forrest sacked dozens of supply depots and captured hundreds of soldiers at Lexington, Trenton, Humboldt, and Union City, while demolishing many miles of track on the strategic Mobile & Ohio Railroad.[8]

Forrest's raid had long-range repercussions, especially as it was remotely coordinated with an expedition into the rear of Grant's army by Earl Van Dorn, who after his defeat at Corinth had retained a command in Mississippi, but only under the close supervision of Pemberton. On December 20, Van Dorn, leading 3,500 horsemen, descended on the supply hub Grant had established at a railroad center familiar to Wheeler—Holly Springs. After neutralizing the local garrison, Van Dorn destroyed not only Mississippi Central trackage but also a vast amount of military stores. The dual strikes of Forrest and Van Dorn so deprived Grant of critical resources that he aborted his overland advance against Pemberton and retraced his steps to the Tennessee border.[9]

Ten days after Forrest launched his expedition and five days after Van Dorn set out for Holly Springs, Bragg sent Morgan—fresh from routing a Union encampment at Hartsville, Tennessee, and more recently, from marrying nineteen-year-old Mattie Ready of Murfreesboro—on another raid into Kentucky. This, Morgan's most ambitious and audacious enterprise to date, was intended to disrupt the communications of the erstwhile Army of the Ohio, now known as the Army of the Cumberland. Don Carlos Buell's mismanaged fight at Perryville, combined with his half-hearted pursuit of the retreating Rebels, had cost him his job. At the end of October he had been replaced by Maj. Gen. William S. Rosecrans, a former subordinate of Grant whom the Lincoln administration viewed as a slow mover but a powerful and skillful fighter once committed to the offensive.

From December 21 to early January 1863, Morgan's "alligator riders" visited such old stamping grounds as Glasgow, Bardstown, Campbellsville, Burkesville, and Smithville, where they overpowered enemy garrisons, rendered unserviceable two million dollars in Union property including lengthy sections of the Louisville & Nashville Railroad, and eluded columns of enraged pursuers. The success of these forays, which seriously hampered two Union armies, seemed to validate Bragg's (and probably Wheeler's) assessment of both officers as partisans first, cavalrymen second.[10]

Some time in late November or December, Wheeler's sphere of authority again expanded. As had been the case with Forrest's old command, three more units that had once been assigned to the Army of Kentucky—originally parts of a brigade led by Col. Benjamin Allston and subsequently by John Pegram—were divided between Wheeler's and Wharton's brigades. Shortly afterward, yet another former component of Smith's command—a demibrigade, no more than 600 strong—transferred intact to the Army of Tennessee. Comprised of detachments of the 3rd, 5th, and 6th Kentucky, it was headed by Brig. Gen. Abraham Buford, a former dragoon officer and horse breeder from divided Kentucky, two of whose cousins were Union generals.[11]

— — — —

Joseph Wheeler, the wreathed stars of a general officer now adorning his collar, reported to Murfreesboro at the head of his own brigade on November 13. When he did so, Breckinridge's Army of Middle Tennessee, which Bragg had sent ahead to occupy Murfreesboro along with Forrest's new, partially organized brigade, was the only Confederate force of any size in the area of operations Bragg had designated for his army. Wharton's and Pegram's brigades were accompanying the main army, which was still en route from Chattanooga and would not reach Wheeler's station till late in the month. Buford's small brigade, at Bragg's order, was scouting well east of Wheeler's headquarters in the neighborhood of McMinnville.

In the absence of these resources, Breckinridge urged Wheeler to add Forrest's new command to the picket lines he had established south and east of Nashville. But no sooner did Wheeler move to comply than Bragg ordered him to complete the organization of that command so that it might accompany Forrest on his excursion into West Tennessee. Now Bragg suggested that Wheeler assume temporary command of Morgan's brigade, which had reached the Murfreesboro region after returning from its successful outing in Kentucky. It is not known whether Wheeler adopted this expedient, but if he assimilated Morgan's brigade he relinquished it as soon as Morgan secured Bragg's permission to attack Hartsville.[12]

Wheeler's need for the maximum number of horsemen grew geometrically as the 74,000 troops that had been Buell's began to pour into the Nashville area. By mid-November, three weeks after Rosecrans took command of this force, Wheeler's pickets were skirmishing with Yankee patrols on a daily basis. But holding back Rosecrans's cavalry was not Wheeler's only—or even his primary—mission. Exaggerated reports had led Bragg to the erroneous conclusion that Rosecrans's position was precarious because of steep declines in his commissary stores. Another mistaken belief was that Morgan's raids on the Louisville & Nashville Railroad early in the Kentucky Campaign had seriously hampered his opponent's ability to replenish those dwindling coffers. Bragg intended that further damage be done in the near future—enough, perhaps, to force an evacuation of Nashville.[13]

Bragg expected Wheeler's "regular" cavalry to contribute to this campaign, if only by preventing Rosecrans from tapping alternative sources of supply. As the Confederate commander informed Jefferson Davis by wire on November 24, "my infantry and artillery is concentrating in three corps at Murfreesboro, and on the turnpikes leading thereto, on the right and left, within supporting distance, and ready for any move. The three regular cavalry brigades are in front of the advanced infantry, and always in sight of the enemy, giving me daily information. He [Rosecrans] is thus kept from foraging this side of the Cumberland."[14]

In addition to keeping an eye on the growing number of outposts dotting the roads from Nashville and looking for ways to limit Union resupply, Wheeler was forced to attend to a myriad of more mundane tasks. Much of his time was consumed in completing the organizing, arming, and equipping of Forrest's Tennesseans and Alabamians and sending them on to Spencer's Springs, the jumping-off point for Forrest's upcoming raid. Wheeler also had to assimilate the most recent additions to his own command, including the 51st Alabama Mounted Infantry of Col. John Tyler Morgan.

Wheeler had also been saddled with recommending promotions to fill vacancies in the officer ranks. As Bragg informed him, "when any doubt exists as to their capacity or conduct," Wheeler was to establish examining boards to review the qualifications of subordinates with a view to retiring those judged unqualified, incompetent, or disabled. Wheeler was also charged with recruiting some of his battalions up to regimental strength, while scouring the Murfreesboro area for deserters and other absentees. When apprehended, such men were to be punished "according to the degree of their offense."[15]

As if these duties did not sufficiently occupy him, Wheeler assumed the lead in enforcing Bragg's General Orders No. 146, issued on November 15, which prohibited the "consumption of grain by distillation within the limits of this department." Local stills were to be shut down and their stores of grain and whiskey were to be seized and turned over to the army's commissariat. When not engaged in these and other special duties, Wheeler tried to find the time to inspect and drill his units. Most of them had not practiced the manual of arms—critical to maintaining operational proficiency—since the start of the Perryville Campaign.[16]

Although behind-the-lines activities demanded so much of his attention, Wheeler's primary responsibility was to command at the front, fifteen miles in advance of Bragg's main body. Through November and into December he traveled almost continuously from one forward location to another, with special emphasis on the outposts at Franklin, directly south of Nashville; at La Vergne, midway between Nashville and Murfreesboro; and along the line of the Nashville & Chattanooga. At each point he received reports from his scouts, interrogated prisoners, and conducted personal reconnaissances, sometimes accompanied by only a few staff officers.

The job regularly exposed him to enemy fire. On or about November 27, Wheeler barely escaped death when a scouting party he was accompanying near La Vergne attracted a Yankee shell. The round killed one of his aides, a Captain Rudd, as well as Wheeler's horse, while peppering the general's leg with shrapnel. Rudd thus became the first of fifteen members of Wheeler's staff to lose their lives in battle at the general's side. Almost as many horses would be shot from under Wheeler over the next two and a half years.

Such statistics indicate how often Wheeler put himself and those near him in harm's way—the habit of an officer who believed in always leading from the front. He did not believe in going to the rear unless wholly disabled. On this occasion, as another staff officer observed, "notwithstanding the intense pain from which he was suffering," Wheeler appropriated another steed "and remained on the field until he had driven the enemy away." When reports of the episode reached army headquarters, Bragg issued his cavalry chief a mild reproof: "You expose yourself too recklessly in affairs of this character."[17]

Through most of December, Wheeler's pickets and skirmishers engaged patrols out of Nashville, often with their general on hand to supervise. They did a creditable job of disrupting the operations of Rosecrans's commissariat; on the sixth, a detachment of the 51st Alabama cut off a forage train returning to the Union stronghold. Twelve wagons pulled by sixty-two mules and guarded by thirty infantrymen fell into the Alabamians' hands. Three days later, supported by some infantrymen and a light battery, Wheeler boldly attacked the head of a brigade-size column of infantry near La Vergne, taking several prisoners and thrusting the main force back into Nashville. And on or about the sixteenth, a detachment of Terry's Texas Rangers cut off a reserve picket post on the turnpike between Murfreesboro and Nashville. A Texan reported that six Yankees were killed "and about 40 taken prisoners, with their fine repeating rifles, horses, saddles, etc." He considered the raid "a brilliant little exploit."[18]

These small but stirring successes buoyed the morale not only of Wheeler's troopers but of Bragg's entire army, as did intelligence of victories in other theaters. On the seventeenth, one of Wharton's men, whose command was observing enemy movements north of Murfreesboro, relayed to his wife news from Fredericksburg, Virginia, where four days earlier Lee had decisively defeated Ambrose Burnside's Army of the Potomac. Exaggerating only slightly, the man crowed that the Yankees "lost 15000 killed & wounded—ours much less. . . . I think, love, the signs of the times quite favorable to a speedy peace. . . ." A comrade in Wheeler's brigade agreed that in the light of Lee's victory "things look hopeful for us" while the people of the North were experiencing "a feeling near akin to despair. . . . [U]nless the greatest success attends their arms in the West, all is lost and the [Union] cause had better be given up."[19]

Perhaps in time even the Federals in Nashville would come to see things this way. Although they continued to stage attacks on Bragg's lines—on the twelfth they struck one of Wharton's detachments at Franklin with vigor, causing it to withdraw with substantial loss—by mid-December Braxton Bragg permitted himself to believe that Rosecrans might evacuate, leaving the state capital open for occupation. On the twentieth he ordered his cavalry commander to "press forward your line in order to ascertain the true condition of things." Wheeler, although less hopeful than his superior that the enemy would turn around and leave, drove in Rosecrans's pickets on the Nashville Pike, taking prisoners whom he questioned and confiscating or destroying many stores. From what Wheeler could learn, the Yankees were gearing up for a general movement. Although the nature of that movement remained unknown, Wheeler doubted that it would be a retrograde. He was aware that Rosecrans had been sent to Nashville not merely to occupy Bragg's attention but to drive his army out of Tennessee.[20]

Wheeler's view of things was validated on the day after Bragg's soldiers celebrated Christmas in their bitterly cold camps along Stones River. At about 6 AM on the twenty-sixth, some 60,000 Union infantry advanced southward and eastward in three columns, their front and flanks screened by the 4,200 cavalry of Maj. Gen. David S. Stanley. Obviously "Old Rosey" intended to force a climactic confrontation.

As the enemy advance got under way, Wheeler's brigade occupied a position along the Nashville Pike and adjacent Stewart's Creek. A strong line of vedettes (mounted pickets) covered the position, which stretched from a point east of Stones River to as far west as the Nashville suburb of Brentwood. As Wheeler later noted, his outposts reached as far forward as ten miles from the capital, "the posts of the pickets and grand guards being at favorable positions on the avenues of approach and at points varying from 300 to 1,000 yards in rear of the line of vedettes." Wharton's larger brigade, whose picket line ran from Nolensville toward Franklin, connected with the left flank of Wheeler's. In that position Wharton had been attacked on Christmas morning by cavalry backed by foot soldiers, causing the Texan to fight to hold his line "from sunrise until dark"—a harbinger of the larger movement now under way.[21]

Meanwhile, Pegram's little brigade picketed the countryside on Wheeler's right, covering the approach to Lebanon. When reports of the enemy's advance reached him, Bragg moved infantry to within supporting distance of the cavalry. Brig. Gen. George Maney's brigade came up to augment Wheeler's brigade; the brigade of Brig. Gen. Sterling Wood marched to Triune, within range of Wharton's position; and Col. John Q. Loomis's brigade took position beside and behind Pegram.[22]

After alerting Bragg, Wheeler ordered up his entire brigade while instructing Wharton and Pegram to reinforce their lines. When the body of his command, under Wirt Allen, reached him, he guided it to a point two miles northwest of La Vergne. He dismounted hundreds of its troopers, who scrambled to form a battle line covering the turnpike and the crossings of Hurricane Creek. Behind the cavalry's line Wheeler unlimbered a recently acquired battery of Arkansas horse artillery.

Presently, Wheeler's men made contact with the advance guard of Rosecrans's left wing under Wheeler's old Kentucky Campaign opponent, Thomas L. Crittenden. Stanley's horsemen, screening Crittenden's foot troops, advanced briskly and confidently until they encountered Wheeler's well-formed line, which blocked access to the Hurricane Creek fords. Stanley engaged Wheeler with mounted and dismounted units as well as with a battery of his own. The result was a half-hour standoff that ended only after Brig. Gen. John M. Palmer's Union infantry reached the field and advanced simultaneously against Wheeler's front and flanks. At Wheeler's order, his men relinquished their positions, but with defiant deliberation. As they withdrew, Palmer forced his way across the creek. Evening came on, however, before he could advance farther. He was forced to halt short of La Vergne, which Wheeler's horsemen and Maney's foot soldiers occupied throughout the night.[23]

Although his most advanced infantry had moved at a moment's notice to confront the enemy, Bragg required time to mass the balance of his army and deploy it properly. To buy that time, he perforce turned to his cavalry commander. When the fighting along the Nashville Pike ceased on the twenty-sixth, Wheeler galloped to Murfreesboro to attend a council of war called by Bragg. As soon as he reached army headquarters Bragg asked him how long he could hold Rosecrans's troops north of Stones River. Conflicting accounts cloud Wheeler's reply. The version set down by Wheeler's early biographer, Du Bose, has him answering, "about four days, general," while Hardee, who overhears him, exclaims, "They will run right over you!" In *Campaigns of Wheeler and His Cavalry*—published in 1899 as edited by William Carey Dodson but almost all of which was written by Wheeler himself—the cavalry leader replies, "two or three days," prompting Hardee and Polk to pronounce such a feat "an impossibility."[24]

Whatever Wheeler actually promised, he made good on his word. Over the next three or four days his brigade exploited to the fullest the fight-with-draw-fight maneuver it had virtually perfected during the Kentucky Campaign. Not only were Crittenden's cavalry and infantry limited to a glacial pace but Wheeler's men took a heavy toll of them. As their leader boasted in his after-action report, they spent the entire time "killing and wounding large numbers, [while] meeting but very slight losses ourselves."[25]

At times, the clashes could be quite spirited. On the twenty-seventh Wharton's men near Triune absorbed a mounted attack by Union cavalry attached to the Union right wing under Alexander McCook. Stiffened as it was by infantry support, the assault, which took place under a cold and steady rain, forced Wharton's men, in company with Wood's foot soldiers, to retire across Nelson's Creek. They did so with the same grudging reluctance Wheeler's brigade had displayed the previous day. The chaplain of Terry's Texas Rangers, who often observed the war from the front lines, wrote that "it was now the evident policy of our Generals to draw the enemy on and mass our troops at Murfreesboro. Hence our skirmishing and falling back." He called the twenty-seventh "a day of constant vigilance and fighting." It ended with the men of Wharton and Wood in flight south but not in a panic. When McCook's pursuit bogged down on the muddy terrain, the Rebel cavalry and infantry reached safety via the turnpike to Eagleville.[26]

The following day, as Wood's infantry continued its withdrawal to Murfreesboro, part of Wharton's command fell back to the village of Salem while another detachment ranged all the way to Eagleville. The latter force kept McCook's column under such close observation that Wharton assuaged Bragg's concern that the Federals might outflank him—instead, he reported, they appeared to be heading toward a collision with the main body of the Army of Tennessee. Meanwhile, throughout the twenty-eighth Wheeler's brigade came under heavy but sporadic pressure. Crittenden remained on the left bank of Stewart's Creek while the corps of McCook and George H. Thomas (the latter facing Pegram's brigade on Wheeler's right) reached the positions Rosecrans had assigned them to. It was well for Wheeler that the Federals moved so deliberately, for the cavalry in their path was without support, Bragg having recalled all infantry units to the rear.

The Yankees confronting Wheeler resumed their advance early on the twenty-ninth, minus a cavalry screen. Blasting away with the cannons he had placed atop a ridge overlooking Stewart's Creek, Crittenden attempted to pry Wheeler's skirmishers from heavy cover on the other side of the stream. Wheeler replied with shells from his battery of Arkansas horse artillery, commanded by Capt. J. H. Wiggins, but failed to prevent some infantrymen from wading across the creek, gaining the right bank, and pushing south for a mile and a half, forcing another Rebel retreat. At that point the Federals drew up on the banks of Overall Creek, less than a mile from Bragg's infantry line northwest of Murfreesboro. No longer harassed by Wheeler, Crittenden's men deployed for battle, ready to add their weight to the impending clash of arms.

Wheeler's primary task—to delay the Yankees till Bragg's army could form to receive them—had been completed. He guided his men across a Stones River ford, and, as evening approached, moved out the Lebanon Pike toward Bragg's far right, which was anchored by Breckinridge's division of Polk's corps. Wheeler deployed his troopers almost a mile in front of Breckinridge's line. He connected with the left flank of Pegram's brigade, which Bragg had withdrawn from Thomas's front early that afternoon. Pegram also had formed in advance of Breckinridge's line but well to the east of the Lebanon Pike. On the opposite end of the Army's position, Wharton's large brigade, having withdrawn in the face of McCook's advance, was guarding the front, flank, and rear of Hardee's corps. For the first time since occupying the Murfreesboro vicinity, Bragg's army was intact, in battle formation, and prepared to fight.[27]

Soon after reaching his assigned position, Wheeler, accompanied by some staff officers, rode out to the country home that housed army headquarters to report his return. Upon his arrival he was greeted not only by Bragg but also by Polk, Hardee, and their staffs. After exchanging salutes all around, Wheeler found himself "almost overcome with embarrassment" when Bragg, in a gesture uncharacteristically warm, clasped his hand and exclaimed within earshot of the other subordinates, "General Wheeler, you have not only accomplished what Generals Polk and Hardee said was impossible, but very much more. Your work is done, and we will now take the enemy in hand and see by the grace of God what we can do with him."[28]

Historians have followed Bragg's lead in giving Wheeler credit for a difficult mission well and faithfully performed. One chronicler of the Murfreesboro Campaign, Edwin C. Bearss, deviates from the norm by arguing persuasively that Rosecrans's strategy of deliberate concentration and the foul weather that had transformed country roads into quagmires were more responsible for the deliberate pace of the Federal advance than the intervention of Wheeler, Wharton, and Pegram (the latter having rendered negligible service between the twenty-sixth and twenty-ninth). As Bearss puts it, "at no time during the Army of the Cumberland's approach march did the resistance of the Confederate cavalry prevent any of Rosecrans' units from reaching its assigned objective. 'General Mud' succeeded where Bragg's weakened cavalry force could not."[29]

——— ——— ——— ———

Wheeler's troopers were tired, wet, and cold from their recent exertions, but more hard work was in the offing. Close to midnight on December 29–30, Bragg ordered the cavalry to pass around the Union left by a circuitous route. The objective was to overtake and waylay supply trains traveling between Nashville and the rear of the Army of the Cumberland. A heavy blow to his communications might distract and discomfit Rosecrans at a critical time, facilitating the attack Bragg planned to launch against his right flank. Wheeler was instructed to conduct the mission with the four regiments and two battalions of his own brigade plus Wiggins's battery. Lt. Col. James E. Carter's 1st Tennessee Cavalry, which had not served under Wheeler since the Bolivar expedition, was a late addition to the strike force.[30]

Wheeler started out in the sodden murk of early morning, trotting north

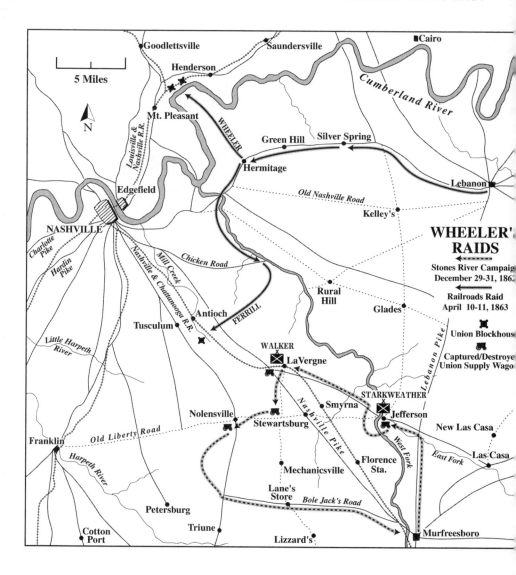

along the turnpike to Jefferson. "The rain was falling," recalled an officer in the 8th Confederate, "and the darkness so dense that a man could not see the comrade riding at his side." By daylight, now inside enemy lines, the column neared Jefferson, which Wheeler's scouts reported to be in enemy hands. Wheeler had been ordered to cut communications, not fight a pitched battle, and so he detoured around the town along a country trail south of the turnpike. A few minutes of travel brought the head of his line to a ford near Neal's Mill, where the pike crossed Stones River.[31]

On the far side, the column veered north until it again approached the turnpike, along which the scouts sighted a supply train, sixty or so wagons long, moving toward Jefferson from the west. The train was lugging the baggage and provisions of Col. John C. Starkweather's infantry brigade, a part of Thomas's wing. "We attacked vigorously," Wheeler reported, "[and] drove off the guards," of which there had been few, then swarmed over the wagons, setting fire to many and disabling others by shooting down their teams or capturing their drivers. A few escapees rushed word of the attack to Starkweather at Jefferson, who promptly ordered two of his outfits, the 21st Wisconsin and 79th Pennsylvania, to drive off the raiders. Instead, they were driven back by Wheeler's dismounted riflemen. And when Starkweather sent a picked force of fifty men to take the raiders in flank, Wheeler's scouts detected its approach in time to thwart it.[32]

Falling back in haste, the flanking party joined the rest of Starkweather's command in throwing up a line of works opposite Wheeler's front. Unable to drive off the Federals, even with well-placed shells from Wiggins's guns, Wheeler ordered his men to clear out. Their job was done—the four-hour fight had cost Starkweather twenty wagons and between fifty and ninety of his men, taken prisoner (estimates of the total number vary widely). But Wheeler's greatest feat was the attention his strike forced Rosecrans to devote to his trains, which caused him to hold Starkweather in place, guarding against future strikes, instead of committing his veteran troops to the battle that commenced the next morning.

Decamping the Jefferson vicinity, Wheeler led his men northwestward toward La Vergne, on the railroad between Nashville and Murfreesboro. En route, his advance guard snatched up two foraging parties. Wheeler, however, was hunting bigger game. He found it shortly after noon in the fields outside La Vergne: the reserve supply column of McCook's corps. Although larger than the train Wheeler had set upon near Jefferson, it was just as lightly defended. After splitting his force into three detachments, Wheeler attacked the wagons from as many directions. "We dashed in," wrote one trooper, "four or five regiments, at full speed, fired a few shots and we had possession of an army train of over three hundred wagons, richly laden with quartermaster's and commissary stores." Many of these were quickly appropriated for the use and pleasure of their captors, but almost one million dollars worth of stores and provisions went up in smoke when dozens of wagons were put to the torch.[33]

Aware that he was operating well inside enemy lines, Wheeler did not tarry at La Vergne. As the wagons burned, he guided his column southwestward in the direction of Rock Spring and Nolensville via what one raider called "a liberal application of the spur for two hours." Before his rear guard could clear the area, however, an Ohio infantry brigade under Col. Moses B. Walker, another element of Thomas's corps, hurried up from Stewartsboro and opened on the Rebels with its rifles as well as with an attached battery. Walker had arrived too late, however, to do more than spur the tag end of Wheeler's column into flight. The colonel briefly pursued Wheeler's main body but, not surprisingly, failed to overtake it. Recalling his men, Walker determined to occupy the La

Vergne vicinity in case other Rebel raiders came his way. His stationary posture ensured that his soldiers, as well as Starkweather's, would contribute nothing to Rosecrans's battle strategy. While the effects of these brigades' noninvolvement in the battle then raging across Stones River cannot be determined with any degree of precision, their absence must have handicapped Rosecrans to some extent, especially as he had intended that they spearhead the assault he was to launch against his enemy's right—a mirror image of Bragg's battle plan.[34]

At their next port of call, Rock Spring, northwest of Stewartsburg, Wheeler's raiders overtook a third wagon train, which they easily captured, rifled, and burned, while paroling their captured guards. Then it was on to Nolensville, about three miles farther west, where the gray column encountered yet another train of mule-drawn vehicles ripe for the taking. Like Wheeler's other prizes, most of the wagons carried rations and forage, but baggage wagons and ambulances also fell to the raiders when they attacked "like a tornado" and overpowered the guard. Wheeler discovered the vehicles to be bulging with an assortment of spoils including many appropriated from local secessionists: "Corn, bed clothing, house furniture, eggs, poultry, butter, etc., etc." As he helped himself to these treasures, one raider calculated that "our achievements for the day summed up [to] 500 wagons, 600 prisoners and many mules."[35]

While Wheeler's provost marshals issued parole papers to this latest haul of POWs, the raiding column bivouacked in fields five miles southeast of Nolensville. Soon everyone was slumbering in the glow of the burning wagons. At about two o'clock the next morning, the last day of 1862, Wheeler got them back on the road, which veered briefly in the direction of Franklin before resuming its southward arc. Just above Triune, Wheeler led the men east along the Bole Jack Road to Wilkinson's Cross Roads, where they contacted the pickets of Wharton's brigade on the Confederate left. Thus ended a journey that had carried Wheeler and his 2,000 men completely around their enemy and had gained them a vast array of spoils.

———   ———   ———   ———

When Wheeler returned to his army, he found a major battle in progress. Preliminary actions had flared throughout the previous day when Bragg's foot soldiers moved into attack positions, screened by Wharton's horsemen. Just after dawn on the thirty-first, as Wheeler pushed east along Bole Jack Road, Hardee's corps, supported closely by Wharton's riders, had inaugurated the fighting with a vicious assault against McCook's wing. The move came early enough to beat Rosecrans to the punch and force him to recall the troops he had sent to strike Bragg's right. Hardee's foot soldiers drove several Union brigades out of position while Wharton's men attacked, routed, and pursued a brigade of Union horsemen. By nine-thirty the Union right was collapsing and its survivors were fleeing north to stake out a new line roughly parallel to the Franklin Pike. Over the next three hours elements of Rosecrans's center and left also fell back to this position, which they extended and strengthened. They had disengaged following a valiant counterattack by comrades under Wheeler's flag-of-truce visitor, Philip Sheridan.[36]

Wheeler's troopers entered the battle soon after making contact with Wharton's pickets. Wheeler issued orders not only to his and Wharton's brigades but also to the demibrigade of Abraham Buford, which, at Bragg's order, had marched at daybreak to Wilkinson's Cross Roads from its most recent station at Rover, eighteen miles southwest of Murfreesboro. All three commands were to wreak further damage on supply columns along the turnpike from Nashville to Murfreesboro, Wharton by operating on the east side of Overall Creek, Wheeler and Buford, along the west bank.

After sending Wharton's troopers on their way, Wheeler pushed north, Buford's fresh brigade in the vanguard. The column forded Overall Creek, then advanced on the Nashville Pike. Just short of that thoroughfare Buford's Kentuckians ran into the vanguard of Thomas's command, supported by David Stanley's cavalry and a light battery that had unlimbered on the east side of the creek. When they drew near the enemy position, Buford's troopers were blasted with shell and canister, suffering several casualties. Despite enjoying the support of Wharton on his right, Wheeler grew concerned that he lacked the strength to take on a large portion of the main enemy force, which had yet to crumple under the weight of Hardee's offensive. When Wharton's advance failed to hit home as envisioned, Wheeler retreated to Wilkinson's Cross Roads, where Wharton's men joined him.[37]

Neither brigade remained in this relatively tranquil area for long. After blunting Wharton's assault, Stanley's Federals advanced across Overall Creek and took up a position adjacent to a woodside chapel known as Asbury Church. Alerted to the movement by his scouts, Wheeler feared that in his new position Stanley could turn Bragg's left, move into the Rebel rear, and create the kind of havoc that Wheeler himself had produced behind Rosecrans's lines. Wheeler acted quickly to preempt such a movement. Soon he was leading his own and Buford's brigades, by way of both banks of Overall Creek, to Asbury Church. Arriving there at about 4 PM, he confronted Stanley's force, which appeared ready to meet him. An advance by two of Stanley's regiments brought the head of Wheeler's command to a halt, but Buford's Kentuckians charged over the stream and forced units on Stanley's flank to give way. His line suddenly compromised, Stanley withdrew toward the Nashville Pike.

Wheeler led the two brigades in a cautious pursuit that eventually brought them to Stanley's new position behind a wooded ridge adjacent to the pike. With daylight fading, Wheeler prepared a two-rank assault on the enemy center as well as a flanking movement against Stanley's left. Before the deployment was complete, Stanley sent detachments of three of his regiments down the ridge in a saber charge. The attack caught Wheeler's flanking force by surprise and sent it to the rear in consternation and confusion. Soon after the attack hit home, Stanley's senior subordinate, Col. Robert H. G. Minty, battered other sections of Wheeler's line with a force of both mounted and dismounted troopers. Wheeler was both surprised and alarmed when the Yankees flooded over his position and sent many of his units into headlong retreat. By a strenuous effort he managed to restore order in the ranks, but by then the darkness was nearly total, precluding any counterattack. Convinced that the Federals no longer posed a threat to the army's rear, Wheeler returned his brigades to Wilkinson's Cross Roads, where he bivouacked for the night.[38]

———— ———— ———— ————

Reporting by courier to army headquarters, Wheeler learned that Bragg had been largely successful throughout the day just ended. By dint of strength and determination, his army had thrust Rosecrans's troops north and east of the main battlefield, where they were clinging to a V-shaped salient fronted by a tangled woodland straddling both the Nashville Pike and the Chattanooga & Nashville Railroad. Largely because Rosecrans had massed his artillery in that sector, he had thrown back a series of attacks that finally ceased after dark.

Given his adversary's narrow front and tenuous hold on the turnpike, the principal retreat route to Nashville, Bragg fully expected to drive him from the field come morning. In fact, he half-expected Rosecrans to retreat before sunrise. Yet the dawning of New Year's Day 1863 found the Army of the Cumberland holding the position into which Bragg had hammered it. Instead of administering a *coup de grace*, the Confederate commander rested his army throughout the day, content to engage the Yankees in long-range skirmishing and artillery exchanges.[39]

While the infantry caught its breath, the cavalry was again put in motion. Perturbed by Rosecrans's stubbornness, Bragg hoped to force him into retreat. His chosen method was another strike against the supply lines in his enemy's rear. This time, as Wheeler learned during an early morning conference at army headquarters, the task would be assigned to all three of the army's brigades of horse.

After breaking up its frigid bivouac, Wheeler concentrated his far-flung command near Wilkinson's Cross Roads. There he briefed Wharton, Buford, and their senior subordinates on the objectives of the mission. Preliminaries attended to, he led the combined force north from the crossroads toward the point where Stewart's Creek crossed the Nashville Turnpike, which he hoped would prove to be a lightly guarded route to the Union rear. But he was disappointed, for when he reached the crossing he found the surrounding countryside alive with vigilant Yankees manning strategically placed outposts. Unable to force a crossing, Wheeler decided to move farther west in the direction of La Vergne, scene of his recent triumph. He gingerly broke contact with the outpost troops and circled toward the south, before heading north toward his new objective.

The revised route paid dividends—his troopers met no interference short of the Nashville Pike. Approaching the thoroughfare within striking distance of La Vergne, Wheeler's scouts sent back word that yet another supply convoy was in sight. Moving ponderously toward Nashville, the train consisted of perhaps 300 vehicles—baggage and supply wagons as well as ambulances carrying soldiers wounded in the previous day's fight. Hoping to waylay not only these spoils but any others remaining in La Vergne, Wheeler led Buford's brigade as well as his own toward the train, while dispatching Wharton's to attack the railroad village.

Only the main column accomplished something of value. Wharton's attack on the garrison at La Vergne went awry when the Yankees took up a formidable position inside a cedar brake. Sheltered by the thicket, they withstood repeated attacks by the 4th Tennessee and 1st Confederate regiments and the 14th Alabama Battalion. Stymied at every turn, Wharton broke off the fight and withdrew, having suffered several times as many casualties as his inaccessible opponents.[40]

While his subordinate was finding frustration and defeat, Wheeler overhauled a thirty-wagon section at the rear of the train moving up the turnpike. Under his personal supervision, his advance guard attacked the mounted portion of the convoy and after sharp but brief fighting chased it away. This feat forced the surrender of the wagon guard, a couple of companies of an Indiana infantry regiment. After burning the wagons that had fallen so easily into his hands, Wheeler led his and Buford's brigades westward, hoping to overtake the rest of the supply column.

A march of several miles at a rapid clip brought the head of the raiding force into contact with a large body of cavalry under another of Stanley's brigade commanders, Col. Louis Zahm, which had been escorting the forward section of the immense train. Wheeler ordered his advance echelon to hold the Yankees in place while he guided the main body westward in the hope of overtaking the rest of the supply column. It was an ambitious plan—perhaps too much so—for Zahm defeated it by refusing to be pinned down. After fending off Wheeler's advance, the Federals raced along the pike until they closed up with the rear of the train, from which they refused to be driven by a series of small-unit attacks.

Hoping by some stratagem to interpose between Zahm and the train, Wheeler kept up a pursuit for several miles toward Nashville. By midmorning, having found no opportunity to attack, he recklessly struck at the rear of the train as it rounded a bend in the road, only to find Zahm's troopers waiting, dismounted, behind prepared positions. Probably against his better judgment, Wheeler pressed the attack, which failed miserably. A second assault met an overwhelming repulse when Zahm counterattacked at close to his full strength. Having destroyed barely a half-dozen wagons, all of which had broken down and stalled, Wheeler called a retreat, thereby ensuring that the greater part of the train would reach Nashville intact. His accomplishments this day fail to match the claims he made in his after-action report, including the assertion that he had "captured and destroyed a large number of wagons and stores," while also seizing and carrying off an artillery piece.[41]

Moving beyond range of Zahm's troopers, Wheeler collected his scattered ranks and led them south of La Vergne, where he rendezvoused with Wharton's tired, hurting command. Through the balance of the day the reunited force remained comparatively idle. Toward evening, however, Wheeler was met by a courier from army headquarters bearing an order for him to return to Wilkinson's Cross Roads. By 2 AM on January 2 his raiders had reached Overall Creek, along both sides of which they dismounted and sought sleep within sight of infantry comrades along the army's left flank.

Later that morning, the battle that had broken off after dark on the thirty-first resumed with full fury. The cavalry, however, took little part in it. By now Wheeler had reported in person to Bragg, to whom he described the strenuous labor his troopers had performed over the past twenty-four hours. Perhaps he hinted that they and their mounts could use more than a few hours' respite; whether prompted or not, Bragg ordered Wheeler to rest his men and feed his animals through the balance of the day. Most of the command enjoyed an uninterrupted and much-appreciated break, although late that afternoon Bragg moved a part of Wharton's brigade across Stones River to back up the army's right, where the majority of the renewed fighting would occur.[42]

The second day of battle did not go as Bragg had expected. Instead of being uprooted and prodded into headlong flight, Rosecrans crossed the river with one of General Crittenden's divisions. A late-afternoon offensive by John Breckinridge forced Crittenden back across the stream with heavy losses. But then the impulsive Kentuckian, giving way to momentum and adrenalin, advanced into the path of massed artillery, which broke his column to pieces. The barrage unleashed by Rosecrans's sixty guns, combined with a counterattack by fresh Union troops, chased Breckinridge's survivors back to their starting point, leaving high carnage in their wake and spreading uncertainty among Breckinridge's troops. Would Bragg on the third make a new attempt to pry his opponent from his apparently formidable position, or would he make the same decision he had reached on the night of his near-triumph at Perryville? Joe Wheeler could not say which course his superior would take, though he probably suspected that Bragg would fight no more on the fields and ridges around Murfreesboro. If so, he was correct.[43]

6

TARGETING SHIPS, FORTS, AND TRAINS

*T*hough his army had been mauled on December 31, Rosecrans had remained on the field that night and the next, defiantly ready to accept a renewal of battle. Bragg, after the shattering of his right wing on January 2, initially appeared to emulate his opponent's tenacity. To a suggestion by Leonidas Polk early on the third that the army had been fought out and should withdraw, Bragg replied, "We shall maintain our position at every hazard." Only a few hours after breathing defiance, however, the ever-vacillating commander began to consider retreating to Shelbyville. He was concerned about his grievous losses—almost 30 percent of the troops engaged—and he was alert to rumors that even as his army reeled from blood loss, his enemy was being revived by the timely arrival of reinforcements.[1]

Bragg's cavalry leader was partly to blame for his anxiety. Wheeler, who had yet to perfect the art of intelligence interpretation and analysis, had reported that Rosecrans, early on the third, was gaining accessions from Nashville. While the report was true, Wheeler failed to ascertain—or failed to tell Bragg—that the reinforcements amounted to a single infantry brigade escorting a supply column. A gravely concerned Bragg huddled with his corps commanders late on the morning of the third, and when Hardee as well as Polk advised retreat, he agreed.[2]

The withdrawal got under way before noon under a heavy downpour. First to hit the roads were the army's supply wagons, followed by the infantry. As on so many past occasions, Wheeler's horsemen were assigned the task of securing the retreat by covering the army's flanks and rear while also preempting enemy pursuit by aggressively skirmishing.

Wheeler had only recently returned to the army following yet another raid on enemy communications ordered by Bragg. At 9 PM on the second, as the fighting between the main armies began to die down, the brigadier led his own and Buford's brigades northwestward from Wilkinson's Cross Roads. Some time after midnight, he allowed travel-weary men and horses to rest before resuming the march at daybreak on the third. After capturing a foraging party at Antioch Church, the column spent the balance of the morning heading back to the Nashville Pike in search of additional supply trains en route to or from the Tennessee capital.

The advance guard made contact with just such a prize—Wheeler called it a "large ordnance train"—at Cox's Hill, seven miles southeast of Nashville. The ninety-five wagons, en route from Nashville to the front, were guarded by eight companies of infantry and a detachment of Zahm's cavalry. Attacking with his own brigade, Wheeler chased away the troopers covering the right flank of the train and cut off and destroyed a number of vehicles. His success, however, was short-lived, for the rest of Zahm's troopers galloped up and drove away the wagon-burners, while the foot soldiers—whose strength Wheeler later magnified into three times the size of his own force—dug in atop a commanding rise from which they blasted their adversaries into retreat.

After this, his second repulse by train guards in two days, Wheeler withdrew to Antioch Church. A courier from Bragg met him there, ordering him back to the main army. It was now that Wheeler learned of his superior's intent to abandon the battlefield for points south. By 4 AM on the fourth, when the cavalry made contact with Bragg's left flank near Overall Creek, the army had retired below Stones River. Wheeler not only kept his two brigades north of the stream for the next five hours, he put them in bivouac and allowed them additional rest. In the meantime, the main army started for Shelbyville, Polk's troops by the turnpike that connected that town with Murfreesboro, Hardee's men via the Manchester Pike. The hard-fighting horsemen of John Wharton screened Polk's withdrawal, while Pegram's brigade, which had seen relatively little action since the thirty-first, covered the rear and flanks of Hardee's column.

Wheeler awakened his people shortly before 9 AM and led them across Stones River and into the streets of now-abandoned Murfreesboro. If he expected to be challenged by the enemy in his rear, the slow, cautious advance of Rosecrans's army disabused him of this idea. Not until 3 PM did the first Yankees—infantry and artillery—come into view on the north side of the stream. The skirmishing that broke out lasted until after dark, when the bluecoats unexpectedly left the riverbank. They caused no further trouble to the cavalry, whose pickets, Wheeler reported, "were unmolested during the night."[3]

Anticipating renewed pressure come morning, Wheeler withdrew from Murfreesboro at daylight on the fifth and marched about three miles south of the town, his brigade by the Manchester Pike, Buford's via the direct route to Shelbyville. At about 1 PM Rosecrans, having occupied Murfreesboro, advanced a strong force south of the town, including the horsemen under David Stanley. After sizing up the opposition, Rosecrans's cavalry commander led a charge at the forefront of the 4th Regulars (the prewar 2nd United States Cavalry) that scattered Wheeler's advance guard and forced the main portion of his command to withdraw another half mile or so.

The withdrawal took the Confederates across Lytle Creek, on the south side of which Wheeler dismounted substantial portions of both brigades and unlimbered Wiggins's battery. He placed the combined force behind roadside fences shielded from early detection by a ridge. At about three o'clock Union infantry, supported by Stanley's horsemen and some artillery, advanced unsuspectingly toward this formidable position. When they got to within 250 yards of his line, Wheeler opened on them, as did Wiggins's gunners, firing above the heads of the dismounted men. For half an hour or more the fighting raged; it ended in a general advance that forced Wheeler to retire to a point five miles from Murfreesboro. There, near the hamlet of Bellbuckle and the mountain gap of the same name, he took up a stronger position than before. There, too, he united with Pegram's brigade, which had preceded his own down the turnpike. Wheeler's line of defense appeared so formidable that when Stanley came up to it in advance of the pursuit force, he feared to attack until his comrades caught up to him.

Close to sundown, when Yankee artillery came on the scene, Stanley's troopers stepped aside and allowed the guns to carry on the fight. They spent the last hour of sunlight dueling with Wiggins's battery—a contest that ended with Wheeler and Pegram withdrawing another mile or so to the south. At this point, as Wheeler reported, the Federals "turned off and left the field." Evidently they believed they had shoved their adversaries far enough down the pike to neutralize any threat to Rosecrans's occupation of Murfreesboro and its environs. So ended the campaign that the Confederates would refer to as Murfreesboro and the Yankees would name for the river that flowed west of that battle-scarred village.[4]

———

With his position at Bellbuckle secure, Wheeler totaled up his most recent casualties; a half-dozen of his men had been wounded during the past two days including two of his most valuable staff officers, Lts. William E. Wales and Elisha S. Burford. When these are added to the toll that had accrued since December 30, the losses of the cavalry under Wheeler's authority (exclusive of Pegram's brigade, which submitted no casualty report) amount to seven officers and thirty-six enlisted men killed, twenty-five officers and 178 men wounded, and eight officers and 195 men missing or captured, for a grand total of 449—approximately 11 percent of its present-for-duty strength. This was an especially high figure for cavalry, which normally did not suffer losses on a par with infantry units.[5]

The grim statistics indicated how often Wheeler's troopers had been exposed to close-up fighting, whether skirmishing with the enemy's advance or raiding behind his lines. In the main, Wheeler's people had performed admirably in both roles, although their greatest success had occurred when fighting and falling back. That tactic had greatly delayed Rosecrans's advance from Nashville—so much so that by the time the Yankees reached Stones River the Army of Tennessee was fully prepared to meet them. The advantage thus given Bragg at the outset of the battle ought to have helped him to win it.

The rough and broken terrain along both of Bragg's flanks limited opportunities for mounted operations, so Bragg had made the proper decision in sending Wheeler against enemy supply lines rather than chaining him to the front during the two days of carnage outside Murfreesboro. However, of the several raids Wheeler had led against Rosecrans's supply columns, only the first, which had targeted wagons at four widely spaced points, had achieved material success. And this was not so much due to the physical damage the Rebels inflicted, substantial though it was, as to its influence on Rosecrans's strategy as reflected in his withholding from combat of two veteran brigades of infantry. If the damage done to Rosecrans's trains failed to cripple his army as Bragg had hoped, it did elevate the morale of Wheeler's men while also supplying them with goods not available from their own quartermaster and commissary officers. Some of the achievements Wheeler cited in his operational reports may have been exaggerations, but it is undeniable that his troopers served effectively throughout the campaign in a variety of tactical roles.[6]

That effectiveness is thrown into high relief by the uneven performance of those mounted units that served beyond the reach of Wheeler's control for long periods of the campaign. While the brigades of Wheeler and Buford were doing damage in the enemy's rear, those of Wharton and Pegram remained on the field of battle, guarding Bragg's flanks and rear, gathering intelligence that would shape the army leader's plans, and occasionally engaging enemy cavalry and even infantry. On the first day of the fighting, Wharton ably supported Hardee's near-overwhelming offensive, relentlessly pursuing the retreating foe, but he had failed to seize key points on the battlefield and had been forced to relinquish those lesser positions he did occupy. On the other flank of the army, Pegram's men had performed poorly, perhaps validating the view of some observers that the Virginian's abilities did not warrant his sudden elevation from staff officer to combat commander.[7]

Pegram had failed to commit fully his brigade on either day of the battle, while his feeble efforts at intelligence gathering may well have killed Bragg's hope of an outright victory on December 31. Pegram, who had been instructed to monitor the Stones River fords in his front, that morning reported the crossing of one of Rosecrans's divisions and the imminent advance of a second. He did not, however, detect the recall of both commands in the wake of Hardee's offensive. John Breckinridge, whose division was to have followed up Hardee's success, refused to commit more than one brigade for fear the rest would be savaged by the Yankees who supposedly remained on his side of the river. The single brigade failed to accomplish what Breckinridge's entire command might have, and a golden opportunity turned to dross.[8]

Wheeler's performance during the eleven days between Rosecrans's advance from Nashville and the securing of Bragg's withdrawal to Shelbyville received prominent mention in Bragg's official report of the campaign. In fact, the army leader lauded both Wheeler and Wharton as "eminently distinguished throughout the campaign, as they had been for a month previous in many successive conflicts with the enemy. Under their skillful and gallant lead the reputation of our cavalry has been justly enhanced."[9]

This was heady praise indeed, especially for an officer like Joe Wheeler, barely twenty-six years old and only six months into Confederate cavalry service. And yet, while greatly pleased by the kind of commendation that gratified his need for recognition and reward, he accepted it in the composed, reserved manner that was another of his defining characteristics.

———————

Like the rest of the army, Wheeler's officers and men were surprised and disappointed by Bragg's latest retreat. Many troopers tried to convince themselves that their leader knew what he was doing. "We are at a loss to know why Bragg retreated on Sunday," one wrote philosophically in a letter home, "but suppose he had good reasons—that he is a great General none can deny & history will no doubt clear up all mysteries." A less-forgiving comrade complained to his parents that "I can't understand why Bragg retreated from Murfreesboro— he had the Yanks completely whip[p]ed, and if he had followed them up, they could not have made another stand between here and Nashville, and there we could have starved them out—Instead of that we are in full retreat for Miss[issippi]—I suppose."[10]

In actuality, Wheeler's people were about to head north, not south. Desiring to finish a job well begun, Bragg, from his new headquarters southeast of Shelbyville, determined to send every available cavalryman against Rosecrans's communication lines, especially those north, south, and west of Nashville. On the seventh, he ordered Wheeler to embark on this operation "with such cavalry as he can take, including all of Morgan's command," the latter having returned to the army following his "Christmas Raid" inside Kentucky. Later Forrest's command would also come under Wheeler's authority.[11]

Whether or not Bragg or Wheeler perceived it at the time, numerous factors militated against the success of a prolonged campaign in the Union rear. As William Carey Dodson noted, by January 8, the starting date of the raid, the weather had turned "bitter cold, and rain, snow or sleet was falling almost incessantly. The command was without tents, and many of the men [were] thinly clad, which caused them to suffer intensely. Under these conditions they had been fighting daily, almost hourly, for the past fortnight. Notwithstanding this,

General Wheeler collected about 600 men, and amid snow and ice commenced the march."[12]

The exact composition of Wheeler's force cannot be determined. It did include a large detachment of the 8th Confederate Cavalry under Colonel Wade, as well as three light cannons. The compact size of the column would enhance mobility, and enough raiding veterans were included to give hope that it would accomplish something substantial.

Initially, the expeditionary force made for the scene of Wheeler's recent depredations, the roads that linked Murfreesboro and Nashville. There it overtook and lay waste to a few supply trains, each composed of several wagons. At the same time, patrols attacked the Nashville & Chattanooga, wrecking as much track as crowbar- and axe-wielding raiders with fingers benumbed by cold weather could manage. Eight miles below Nashville, where the tracks crossed Mill Creek, a raiding party under one of Morgan's most resourceful subordinates, Capt. Richard McCann of the 9th Kentucky, destroyed an engine and a train of cars, then demolished a trestle that was a conduit between Rosecrans's army and its base of supply to the north.[13]

From the railroad Wheeler marched west by northwest, heading for Ashland Landing on the north bank of the Cumberland River. There stores of all kinds that had been shipped downriver from Louisville had been stored pending their transfer by wagon to Nashville and Murfreesboro. Bragg continued to believe that the Yankees were perilously short of rations and forage; he expected Wheeler to make that shortage still more acute.

On the twelfth the raiders reached Clarksville, on the south bank of the river that had become one of Rosecrans's chief avenues of supply. Here Wheeler divided his force to strike simultaneously from divergent points. While he and the main body remained near the landing at Clarksville, Colonel Wade, with his regiment and one gun, marched upstream to Harpeth Shoals. Upon his departure, Wheeler dismounted most of his men and deployed them behind trees along the riverbank while emplacing his two artillery pieces on a foliage-shielded bluff. Then he waited for night to fall.

At about eight o'clock on that dark and frigid evening, the supply steamer *Charter*, escorting a troop transport, approached the landing, unaware of pending danger. At Wheeler's signal, the cannons opened on both ships. The fire was accurate enough to force the vessels to heave to, surrender, and permit their assailants to board them. As one of Wheeler's officers reported, "the soldiers aboard and crews were paroled and both boats with their rich cargoes burned to the water's edge."[14]

Meanwhile, Colonel Wade was enjoying even greater success at the same game. On the morning of the thirteenth a shell from the six-pounder cannon he had placed on the bluffs overlooking Harpeth Shoals tore through the cabin of the steamer *Trio*, which had come downriver from Louisville. She quickly headed for shore. Her cargo, however, turned out to be convalescent soldiers who had been wounded in the recent battle. Before the patients could be unloaded and paroled, two other steamers hove into view from the north. Wade's men, dismounted and concealed behind good cover, peppered the pilothouse and deck of the *Hastings* with rifle fire. She, too, proved to be loaded with wounded Federals. The surgeon in charge of the ship initially refused Wade's surrender demand, but additional volleys of musketry persuaded him to reconsider.[15]

As *Hastings* made for shore, her companion vessel, the *Parthenia*, attempted to escape by coming about until a shell from Wade's 6-pounder sliced through her port side. The colonel and several of his officers boarded the surrendered ships and helped themselves to the spoils of war. The "gang of drunken rebels," as an Ohio chaplain aboard the *Hastings* called them, relieved the passengers of their "blankets, rations, medicines, and in many instances their clothing; robbed the officers of their side-arms, overcoats, hats, &c.; the boat of all her freight, stores, and money, and her officers of their personal property." Afterward, Wade's men burned and sank *Parthenia* and *Trio*. The *Hastings* was permitted to convey her suffering cargo to Louisville.[16]

As the ships burned, Wade's men were surprised by the sudden appearance of a wooden gunboat, the *Slidell*, which approached the landing with port guns firing. She raked the occupied bluff with a broadside that by some miracle inflicted no casualties. Wade's riflemen and cannoneers immediately replied, inflicting so much damage on the little warship that within minutes she rounded to shore, where her twenty-two-man crew became prisoners.

While Wade and his "horse marines" had been defeating the U.S. Navy, Wheeler, back at Clarksville, was faring less well against two other gunboats that had churned upriver to shell his position. Against their armor-plated sides the light guns and rifles of Wheeler's command made little impression. Hoping that reinforcements would turn the tide, the brigadier twice summoned Wade to his side, but the colonel ignored him until the *Slidell* had burned to the water line. By the time he joined Wheeler at Clarksville, night had come on, snow was falling, and the ironclad had withdrawn, having inflicted minimal damage ashore.[17]

On the fourteenth, the reunited force marched south to confront a fleet of transports that had tied up on the river below Harpeth Shoals. Bereft of gunboat support, their crews beat a hasty retreat after reducing their draught by tossing overboard ordnance, commissary, and quartermaster's stores. Wheeler himself could not have done a better job of denying Rosecrans resupply. Even so, the expeditionary leader was not content with his success thus far. Later in the day a large detachment from his column—some on horseback, some aboard ferry boats—braved the "angry torrent, much swollen by recent rains" to cross to the north side of the Cumberland. Once on dry ground they made for the landing at Ashland, whose small garrison they quickly overawed. In a short time, several acres worth of military stores were afire.[18]

By the fifteenth, the expeditionary force—its mission well and thoroughly accomplished—was heading back to Bragg's army. Their recent exertions were fresh in the men's minds, and they would remain so for a long time. Many years later an officer of the 8th Confederate Cavalry vividly recalled details of the raid, including spending bone-numbing hours in the saddle, splashing through "ice cold and pommel deep" streams, and trying to sleep in freezing temperatures. The expedition, he wrote, had been "filled with as many hardships and as much physical suffering as ever fell to a cavalry command" on a raid. The only solace came from captured rations including the "sustaining grog recovered from the burned steamers."[19]

Rewards less tangible but no less warming to the soul awaited Wheeler's return to army headquarters. On January 23, a resolution was offered in the lower house of the Confederate Congress that led to the adoption of a resolution praising "the bold and daring attack of General Wheeler and his command upon the enemy on Cumberland river," and offering the formal Thanks of Congress. Another gesture of commendation and recompense, this one extended to Wheeler himself, preceded the action of Congress by six days. On January 17—the day a detachment of Wheeler's force under Maj. D. W. Holman captured yet another steamer on the Cumberland—Braxton Bragg, having been kept informed by courier of the expedition's daily progress, petitioned the War Department to approve Wheeler's promotion for gallantry in action. On January 22, the promotion took effect. It made Bragg's cavalry leader the youngest major general in Confederate service.[20]

———   ———

Wheeler's increased rank gave him effective command of every cavalry unit in Middle Tennessee. This included Forrest's new brigade, which was resting and reequipping after its raid into the western reaches of the state. Forrest's main body was stationed at and near Columbia. There it protected Bragg's army against attack by the Franklin-based Yankees who made up part of the left wing of the Army of the Cumberland.

Bragg believed that at least a portion of Forrest's command should be made available for further operations against Union shipping on the Cumberland. During the fortnight following the raid of January 8–15, Bragg and Wheeler had fleshed out the details of this project, aimed at a long-term, if not a permanent, interruption of enemy river commerce. On January 26 Forrest was ordered to take 800 of his men and join Wheeler on the Cumberland near Dover and adjacent Fort Donelson, which had been in Union hands since falling to Grant almost one year ago. Wheeler's own force, which consisted of Wharton's brigade, approximately 2,000 strong, and some light guns, moved out in advance of Forrest's 800. On February 2 the latter overtook the larger column fifteen miles from Dover.[21]

Forrest found his newly appointed superior in a foul mood. Wheeler and Wharton and their men had ridden for hours into the teeth of a howling wind to reach the Cumberland, only to find it empty of shipping. The raid to Clarksville, Harpeth Shoals, and Ashland had generated so much publicity that Rosecrans, as Wheeler learned, had "determined not to send any more boats either up or down the river while we remained in position to interrupt their passage. The scarcity of forage made it impossible for me to remain long on the other side of the river, and all the ferryboats above Dover had been destroyed. I accordingly had but the alternative to remain idle or attack the force at Dover." That fortified town was garrisoned by 600 troops under Col. Abner C. Harding— a detachment of an Illinois infantry regiment, a company of Iowa cavalry, and four 12-pounder rifles.[22]

Wheeler was not the only discontented general on the Cumberland. The order that had assigned a large number of his troopers to another man—a younger one, at that—rankled Forrest. He was also upset that he had been ordered on expedition on such short notice that he had lacked the time to outfit his command fully for the march. His discontent was evident in his vocal opposition to Wheeler's plan to attack Dover. The Tennessean argued that the operation "did not promise results in any wise commensurate with inevitable losses, and possible hazard of serious disaster" would follow an attack by cavalry against well-defended fortifications. When he failed to dissuade Wheeler, Forrest asked at least two of his subordinates, "If I am killed in this fight, will you see justice is done by me by officially stating that I protested against the attack, and that I am not willing to be held responsible for any disaster that may result?"[23]

Whether Forrest spoke in this articulate manner or, as seems more likely, in the homespun words he favored, he believed he had put his feelings on record. He was wrong: later Wheeler would contend that he and Forrest had agreed that "nothing could be lost by attack upon the garrison," which "we had good reason to believe . . . could be easily captured." Whatever the result of their conference, Wheeler had Wharton's and Forrest's brigades approach Dover by separate routes that converged almost within artillery-range of the fort. Both commands were in position to strike by two o'clock on the bone-chilling afternoon of February 3.[24]

After placing his six field pieces on an elevation that appeared to command Dover, Wheeler ordered Forrest's men into position east and southeast of the town, where they faced an array of earthworks, redoubts, and rifle pits. Wharton's troopers he deployed on the southwestern edge of Dover. Wheeler later reported that he had instructed both commands to attack on foot. Yet as soon as he left Forrest to take up a central position from which to observe the assault, his unwilling subordinate misinterpreted a shift of position by some of Harding's troops as a prelude to evacuation. To exploit the advantage thus given him, Forrest mounted a large portion of his force and led it in a charge.

The outcome was predictable: from behind its strong works, the garrison shattered Forrest's column, bowling over galloping horses and throwing their riders onto the frost-covered earth. Among those painfully unhorsed was Forrest himself. After failing to make headway in any direction, he angrily ordered a retreat to a ridge parallel to the works in his front, where the artillery attached to his command took over the fight. By then almost one-fourth of his men had fallen to rifle- and cannon-fire.

Although caught off guard by Forrest's premature offensive, Wharton's brigade attacked afoot as ordered and achieved limited success. At first, the Yankees in its front gave ground with surprising alacrity. "We drove them back to town and into their earthworks," one of the Texan's troopers recalled, "but we were losing so many men, we concluded that it was going to cost more" than the effort was worth. At this point, Wharton's men encountered opposition from an unexpected quarter: "The gun-boats coming up commenced a perilous shelling of the woods, so we retired leaving our dead on the field and our wounded in the neighboring houses all of whom fell into the enemy's hands." The trooper concluded that "it was a rash and senseless fight for us for we could not have held the place an hour had we taken it, as it was under the guns of the gun-boats. . . . Since the fight none of the Genls seem to take the credit of the affair and try to saddle it on the other but as Wheeler ranked Forrest and Wharton he has to shoulder the glory."[25]

In fact, although Wheeler refused to admit the attack had accomplished nothing (in his report of the affair he claimed to have captured numerous prisoners and one cannon and to have sunk a river steamer laden with supplies), he accepted responsibility for Forrest's and Wharton's repulse. This he attributed mainly to an inadequate ammunition supply—an excuse that appears to validate at least one of Forrest's objections to the mission. Wheeler also conceded the validity of another of Forrest's charges—that the enemy's position was unassailable. After the attack was called off, Forrest joined him in concluding that "they were too strongly posted to continue the attack any further."[26]

Some time after 8 PM, Harding's guns having ceased firing, Wheeler mounted both brigades and pulled out of Dover. They remained just beyond cannon-range until the next morning, when, alarmed by reports that 5,000 reinforcements from Fort Henry and elsewhere were gathering in his rear, Wheeler decided to retreat to a point below Duck River where he could refit in safety. He did so by crossing the entire force at Centreville.

When laying out a bivouac about four miles from Dover, Wheeler appropriated a farmhouse for his headquarters. At a kitchen table he sat tallying up his losses in preparation for compiling a report of the debacle. He finally arrived at an estimate so low as to invite incredulity—fewer than 100 casualties, all told. He knew full well that Wharton's brigade, which had suffered less heavily than Forrest's, had absorbed almost that many. The actual total was closer to 300 killed, wounded, and missing.[27]

For help in preparing his narrative of operations, he called his brigade leaders to his headquarters and interviewed them. When Wharton made mention of the heavy casualties on his command, Wheeler contradicted him. At that point Forrest, who had been straining mightily to hold his emotions in check, bounded from his chair, hovered above his diminutive superior, and blurted out, "General Wheeler, you know I was against this attack. I said all I could and should against it—and now—say what you like, do what you like, nothing'll bring back my brave fellows lying dead or wounded and freezing around that fort tonight. You know I mean no disrespect . . . but you've got to put one thing in that report to Bragg: tell him I'll be in my coffin before I'll fight again under your command!"[28]

Having thus unburdened himself, Forrest let his temper cool. He apologized for the outburst and even offered his sword should Wheeler choose to take it—and thus his command—from him. After a moment or two, Wheeler calmly replied that he alone bore responsibility for making the attack and would accept the consequences. In so saying, he chose to overlook not only Forrest's act of insubordination but also his failure to obey Wheeler's instructions to attack Dover afoot and in coordination with Wharton.[29]

The hostile confrontation would have lasting consequences for Confederate cavalry organization and operations. Wishing to placate the fiery Tennessean, Braxton Bragg ensured that whenever Forrest operated closely with the Army of Tennessee, he and Wheeler would serve miles apart from one another, on opposite ends of the army, whenever possible. A permanent separation would follow. Shortly before the attack on Dover, Joseph E. Johnston had merged Van Dorn's command, 6,000 strong, into the Army of Tennessee. In coming weeks Bragg would reorganize his mounted arm by dividing it between Van Dorn and Wheeler. Forrest would serve under Van Dorn.

Bragg's choice of cavalry commanders made much sense. The Dover affair notwithstanding, Wheeler was clearly a talented soldier. And although Van Dorn had proved to be a poor army commander, his Holly Springs raid had confirmed his ability as a cavalry leader. He certainly had the experience such a position required. Before the war Van Dorn, like Wheeler, had been a cavalry officer—and also, incidentally, an inveterate rake, a reputation he continued to cultivate. Despite their sometimes clashing personalities, Forrest would remain Van Dorn's senior subordinate up to the time of the latter's death—at the hands of an outraged husband—in early May 1863.[30]

Forrest would succeed his murdered superior but would command Van Dorn's corps for only four months before another acrimonious exchange with a superior officer would result in his banishment from the Army of Tennessee. Late in September 1863, following a verbal altercation with Braxton Bragg more hostile than his run-ins with Wheeler, Forrest would leave the Army of Tennessee to assume an independent command elsewhere in the vast western theater. He would not return to the army named for his native state for more than a year.

Although Forrest's and Wheeler's paths were fated to cross again in this war, they would never again serve together in the true sense of the term. Despite Forrest's protestations of respect for his erstwhile superior, after Dover he refused to trust Wheeler's judgment or leadership. Try as he might, he could not banish from his mind the image of a snow-covered riverbank littered with the bodies of soldiers dead of their wounds or from exposure to the pitiless cold of a winter's night in Middle Tennessee.

— — — —

As soon as it returned to the army, which was now holding a line that ran from Shelbyville to Wartrace, thirty miles to the west, Wheeler's command resumed the job of guarding the flanks and rear of its infantry and artillery comrades and observing enemy movements on the side of a mountainous shelf that ran between the lines. Perhaps as a result of the numerous recent attacks on his communications, General Rosecrans showed no inclination to advance beyond that natural divide. Throughout the winter and into the spring Halleck and Lincoln prodded their subordinate to get off dead center and at least threaten strategic Chattanooga. Yet Old Rosey seemed determined to uphold his reputation as one who moved against the enemy only when good and ready; and he would not be ready until certain organizational and resource deficiencies were corrected. For one thing, he believed his mounted arm was so weak that he could not cope with the annoying and costly depredations of Wheeler, Forrest, and Morgan. As he complained to Halleck, "I must have cavalry or mounted infantry. . . . With mounted infantry I can drive the rebel cavalry to the wall. . . . Not so now."[31]

For his part, Wheeler was less concerned with the size of his command than with the need to make it more efficient. Held relatively idle by winter weather, he used the respite to inspect and drill his regiments and battalions, paying special attention to a recent influx of raw recruits. His primary instructional tool was a three-volume manual of his own composition, *A Revised System of Cavalry Tactics, for the Use of the Cavalry and Mounted Infantry, C. S. A.,* which was published early in the year by a Mobile, Alabama, printing company. Despite its title, the work offered a tactical system that fit the peculiar needs of the mounted riflemen who predominated in Wheeler's ranks.

The most notable feature of the work was its promotion of a single-rank formation for horsemen on the offensive in contrast to the double-rank system advocated by every cavalry manual published by the U.S. War Department since 1841. Wheeler believed the single rank would concentrate the shock force of a charging column, reduce the disorder inspired by a two-rank assault, and enable troopers more quickly to re-form after a charge. Another feature was Wheeler's use of flanking squadrons, which he believed added staying power to an assault while preventing the enemy from judging whether he was being attacked by one line or two.[32]

Wheeler's preference for a single-rank assault was hardly an innovation. *The Trooper's Manual,* compiled in 1861 by Col. J. Lucius Davis of the 10th Virginia, the primary tactics manual of J. E. B. Stuart's cavalry, also endorsed the single rank. So did the manual—also published in 1861—that Brig. Gen. Philip St. George Cooke developed for the United States cavalry. But Wheeler's work placed an even greater emphasis on this formation than either of those earlier texts. Moreover, it tailored its system to the preferred weapons of mounted infantry: rifles and pistols, in contrast to the sabers and carbines wielded by the more traditional horse soldiers who predominated in the eastern armies. By and large, Wheeler's manual succeeded in its stated purpose of meeting "the vital need for some system of cavalry tactics which would insure uniformity among the heterogeneous elements of mounted divisions calling themselves cavalry."[33]

When not disseminating or implementing his tactical theories, Wheeler devoted much time and attention to organizational matters. Three weeks after returning from the Dover mission, his command was increased to division strength; it consisted of his old brigade, now commanded by Colonel Hagan, and the brigades of Wharton and Morgan. Buford's Kentuckians had been transferred to Forrest's command, now part of Van Dorn's division, while Pegram's recently enlarged brigade had been reassigned to the Department of East Tennessee.

Hot on the heels of this expansion came another. Because recruits continued to swell the ranks of the army's mounted arm even in winter, Bragg announced in mid-March that "the cavalry division[s] of this command having become so large, will be hereafter designated as corps, and will be known by the names of their respective commanders, viz.: Van Dorn's and Wheeler's." Within the new table of organization, Wheeler's command embraced two divisions, each of two brigades. The first division eventually would consist of the 7th Alabama, the 2nd, 3rd, and 4th Georgia, the 3rd Kentucky, the 4th Tennessee, the 8th and 11th Texas, and the 3rd Confederate Cavalry, all under John Wharton. The second division comprised the 1st, 3rd, 4th, and 51st Alabama and the 1st and 8th Confederate regiments and was assigned to Brig. Gen. William Thompson Martin, a native Kentuckian who had spent the first year and a half of the war in Virginia as one of J. E. B. Stuart's subordinates. A talented organizer and tactician, the newly minted brigadier seemed poised to continue his successful career in his new sphere of operations. Like Forrest, however, Martin had an independent streak that would contribute to a friction-laden relationship with Wheeler.[34]

———— ————

Regardless of the weather, Wheeler juggled a variety of front-line duties. He supervised a cordon of pickets and scouts well in advance of Bragg's army, one that eventually stretched from Columbia, southwest of Nashville, to McMinnville, along the upper Cumberland plateau, a distance of seventy miles. Virtually every day during the winter and into the spring of 1863, the members of this force stabbed at Rosecrans's outposts or his supply lines to Nashville. A typical report of operations against these targets, submitted by General Wharton early in March, consisted of one sentence: "I attack them every day."[35]

Wheeler was not interested only in short-range, hit-and-run missions; he favored more strategic strikes well beyond Rosecrans's lines. In March, for example, he proposed to Bragg that his command "might make a successful raid into Kentucky. By preparing some boats we could . . . be in Louisville in five days, and if necessary be back to this point in ten days more. We could bring out a great quantity of provisions and other stores." The cautious Bragg disapproved the project for fear that Rosecrans might take advantage of Wheeler's absence by advancing from Murfreesboro. Bragg tried to soften the blow by praising Wheeler's recent efforts "to discipline and regulate your command."[36]

In addition to planning operations of his own, Wheeler stood ready to support Van Dorn and Forrest, who occasionally attacked outposts as deep inside enemy territory as the suburbs of Nashville. These attacks increased dramatically in number when spring-like weather returned to Middle Tennessee, and they invited retaliation. On March 4, two Federal brigades, one each of infantry and cavalry, reconnoitered toward Van Dorn's outpost at Columbia and his headquarters at Spring Hill. That day and the next the intelligence-gatherers were accosted by a force twice their size. Van Dorn, with the divisions of Forrest and now–Brig. Gen. William Jackson, supported by a detachment of Martin's division on loan from Wheeler, challenged the enemy force at Thompson's Station, nine miles south of Franklin on the railroad to Decatur. Surrounding their quarry, they forced the cavalry portion of it to retreat, then tore into the infantry, killing or wounding 400 Yankees and capturing 1,200 others.[37]

Three weeks after this brilliant affair, Forrest struck again. This time he crossed the Harpeth River above Franklin and ripped up the railroad near Brentwood Station. The following day, at the head of Frank Armstrong's brigade, he advanced on an enemy outpost in the same vicinity, drove off its pickets, surrounded the post, and forced 520 members of its garrison to surrender. Forrest capped his triumph by seizing a stockade that guarded a railroad bridge over the Little Harpeth River a mile and a half south of Brentwood. There he received the surrender of another 300 Yankees.[38]

As April came in, Van Dorn and Forrest continued their harassment of enemy units between Nashville and Franklin. Perhaps inspired by their boldness or envious of the publicity they garnered, Wheeler plotted an expedition of his own that would strike farther north and east. His chosen targets were the two railroads that sustained the Army of the Cumberland in the field: the Louisville & Nashville, by which it received supplies from the north, and the Nashville & Chattanooga, which hauled those supplies to the front. Although both lines had been attacked more than once by John Hunt Morgan, they had not been targeted simultaneously. Wheeler planned to do so, waylaying trains approaching Nashville from both north and south.

On April 7, with his plan approved by army headquarters, Wheeler set out on a mission that for drama and spectacle would rival anything Van Dorn and Forrest had accomplished. Leaving the balance of his command in General

Martin's hands, he rode toward Nashville accompanied by the 1,900 troopers of Wharton's division and a battery under Lt. Arthur Pice. By the morning of the ninth he had reached Lebanon, thirty miles east of the Union stronghold. There, for the first time since his command had been enlarged, Wheeler was joined on expedition by Morgan's men—a 600-man detachment under Colonel Duke. Unwilling to share the glory of the upcoming operation, Wheeler planned to restrict Duke's men to a rear-guard role while his own troopers attacked the rail lines.[39]

On the morning of the tenth, Wheeler led his column out the Nashville Pike toward the cotton plantation of Andrew Jackson, ten miles closer to Nashville. Within sight of the Hermitage, Jackson's stately Greek Revival mansion, Wheeler split his force. Duke's command he left behind to secure the rear; Wharton's brigade he led northwestward toward the L & N. Meanwhile, Lt. Col. Steven C. Ferrill's 8th Texas turned south toward the N & C with orders "to cross Stone's River, attack the railroad trains, and do any other good in his power, and return to Lebanon."[40]

After parting ways with Ferrill, Wheeler proceeded along a narrow road to a point about nine miles from Nashville. He was aiming for the south bank of the Cumberland River, where he intended to bombard passing trains with Pice's battery. To reach the river, however, he had to interpose between well-guarded blockhouses that had been constructed to protect the railroad against just such an expedition as his. By dismounting two of Wharton's regiments, sending their men "creeping up to the bank," and hand-dragging Pice's guns to water's edge, Wheeler escaped detection by Yankees almost near enough to reach out and touch him.[41]

For two hours Wheeler's men lay in wait under "the strictest silence." Their patience was rewarded when a locomotive hauling eighteen cars loaded with cavalry horses and beef cattle approached on a bluff running along the north side of the river. At Wheeler's signal, Pice's battery, which had unlimbered 300 yards from the tracks, opened with gratifying effect. "The first three shots," Wheeler announced, "broke open the boiler and stopped the train, and a few volleys from a dismounted regiment drove off the guard." While some of Wharton's men engaged the occupants of the blockhouses, Wheeler attempted to cross the river and take possession of the train, but failed through his inability to locate a suitable ford.

Pice's guns, meanwhile, continued to blast away, reducing the locomotive to ruins in less than half an hour. The shelling made casualties of only two guards but killed most of the train's equine and bovine passengers. When convinced that the blockhouses had been neutralized, Wheeler called in his detachments, mounted and limbered up, and headed back to Lebanon, his lone casualty a wounded enlisted man.[42]

While Wheeler had been demolishing his train, Colonel Ferrill had been similarly occupied. After striking the Nashville & Chattanooga near Antioch

Station, nine miles east of Nashville, Wheeler's subordinate had his men tear up just enough rails to stop a speeding train. Then Ferrill, whose force included no artillery, placed his dismounted troopers behind cover at a bend in the track. They had barely finished getting into position when a train of several cars filled with civilian and military passengers and several dozen guards chugged and hissed into view. The train came on, one Texan recalled, "unconscious of any danger. 40 or 50 of the guards were standing or sitting on the top of the Cars. Below they seemed to be full of passengers. Just as the Engineer saw the broken track and whistled on the breaks, we fired, some at the guard on top and the rest at the windows and platforms. They returned the fire in an instant and jumping out and rallying behind the Cars were about to make us a stubborn fight, when the old Col[onel] ordered a charge, and down the bank we rushed with a yell, which made them take to an open field. Some of us chased them across it into the woods killing several."[43]

Ferrill would claim that his men dispatched upwards of 100 Yankees (Wheeler lowered the estimate to thirty, while surviving Federals maintained that only sixteen of their comrades had been killed or wounded). Seventy guards and passengers had been captured, including three members of General Rosecrans's staff. The attackers also liberated forty Confederates who had been on their way to prison in Nashville. After destroying the train, breaking the track for a considerable distance, and paroling most of the Yankees, Ferrill rode homeward, his saddlebags filled with thousands of dollars, the contents of an Adams Express safe found aboard the train.

By the early hours of April 11, Wheeler and Wharton had reached the outskirts of Lebanon, where they rejoined Basil Duke. After sunup the combined units passed through the village on their homeward jaunt. They failed to rendezvous with Ferrill, but couriers brought them word of his success. Therefore, by the time Wheeler reoccupied his old post on the Shelbyville-Wartrace line, he had the satisfaction of knowing that his two-pronged assault on Rosecrans's railroads had been, literally and figuratively, a smashing triumph. He could not know that this would be the last truly successful raid he would ever lead.[44]

7

AT LONG LAST, VICTORY

*T*ired of being raided right, left, and rear by Wheeler, Forrest, and Morgan, General Rosecrans planned an expedition of his own inside enemy lines. His objective was the section of the Western & Atlantic that ran through Rome, Georgia. If enough damage were done to that critical supply line, Bragg would have to withdraw from Murfreesboro by moving east toward Chattanooga or south into Georgia. Either way, Rosecrans would have forced his opponent out of Middle Tennessee at minimal cost to himself.

Unfortunately, Rosecrans assigned the expedition not to Stanley's cavalry but to a brigade of mule-mounted infantrymen under Col. Abel D. Streight. Despite having a head start, Streight was overtaken short of Rome on May 2 by a smaller but more combative force of horsemen under Bedford Forrest, Bragg's choice of a pursuit leader in Wheeler's absence from the army. Through a combination of gumption and guile, Forrest forced Streight to surrender his 2,000-man "Mule Brigade."[1]

Rosecrans's initial venture into raiding may have been a flop, but Ulysses S. Grant enjoyed great success with an expedition launched a week after Streight got under way. Beginning on April 17, as Grant's army prepared to descend upon Vicksburg, 1,700 conventionally mounted troopers under Col. Benjamin H. Grierson rode the length of Mississippi, destroying railroad track, rolling stock, and supply depots. Grierson not only outsmarted numerous pursuers, but so distracted General Pemberton that he failed to obstruct Grant's April 30 landing at Bruinsburg, within striking range of the Confederate citadel. That event effectively doomed Vicksburg to capture or surrender.[2]

Joe Wheeler knew little of Streight's failure and Grierson's success until he rejoined his army after his own raid. As he settled into the daily routine of observing and reporting on Yankee movements, he basked for a time in the glow of his exploits outside Nashville. He even began to accept social invitations. On one occasion he dined with his staff at the home of a prominent citizen of Beersheba Springs, south of McMinnville. Another guest, literary maven Lucy French, noted in her diary that Wheeler, whom she found "scarcely much taller than myself—dark eyes and hair—black whiskers—a round head—good forehead," was at his most gracious and gentlemanly. He seemed pleased with the local military situation; when another guest mentioned townspeople's fears that a major battle was imminent Wheeler remarked that "he was only fearful that Rosecrans would not come out and fight." Mrs. French expressed delight at sharing a table with such a distinguished soldier, although "some think his attacking Fort Donelson with cavalry was not very judicious."[3]

Shortly before starting on his railroads raid Wheeler had learned that his subordinate John Hunt Morgan, with a large portion of the division that guarded the far right near McMinnville, had attacked a Yankee scouting party near Milton and had been repulsed at a heavy cost in casualties. The defeat suggested that the partisan leader was no longer the master of his enemy. Wheeler wondered whether Morgan had been promoted beyond his ability or whether his command had grown too large for him to handle.[4]

His doubts were reinforced when, a fortnight after the debacle at Milton, a body of Stanley's cavalry overran some of Morgan's camps near Liberty and scattered their demoralized occupants. Colonel Duke stemmed the rout but could not re-form the men. This second defeat seemed to confirm what many observers believed: that Morgan's career had been in a downward spiral ever since his marriage to Mattie Ready. As the editor of a Unionist newspaper in Nashville put it, "the fair Delilah . . . has shorn him of his locks."[5]

Morgan's reputation suffered further on April 19 when Union horsemen raided his headquarters and forced him, along with many of his men, into a disgraceful retreat.[5] This incident troubled Morgan's close friend William J. Hardee. Trying to account for the Kentuckian's decline, Hardee passed along a rumor (one that Virginia French had also heard) that the famous raider could not get along with Wheeler and disliked having to report to him. Whether Wheeler himself heard the story is unknown; but early in May he relieved Morgan's command from duty on the right flank and replaced it with Wharton's division. He sent Morgan to central Kentucky, where a camp had been established for him in a quiet region so that he could rest and refit his command. There, too, perhaps, he could recover the self-confidence he appeared to have lost at the hands of a suddenly active and audacious enemy.[6]

Morgan remained in his "dead camp" until the end of May. By then he had begun to plan an operation that would recoup the prestige he and his once-invincible horsemen appeared to have lost. Early in June he sought Wheeler's permission to lead his entire command in a raid on Louisville, whose once-formidable garrison had been greatly reduced. The project appealed to Morgan's superior, who had advocated something similar three months earlier but failed to win Bragg's consent. This time the army leader granted half of what was sought. With

Wheeler's approval he authorized Morgan to cross the Cumberland into southern Kentucky, but with only 1,500 men and a few guns. Bragg expected Morgan to seize provisions including beef on the hoof, damage Louisville's "public works, &c." as well as sections of the L & N, and return promptly. He also saw another potential benefit in the mission, for he clung to the delusion that stories of Morgan's cavaliers rampaging through their home state would persuade patriotic Kentuckians to accompany them to Tennessee and join Bragg's army.[7]

Unknown to either of his superiors, Morgan determined to take with him upwards of 2,500 men; moreover, he had no intention of halting at the banks of the Ohio River. He was determined to cross that stream and raid through Indiana and Ohio. An expedition so deep inside Union territory would outshine anything achieved by Grierson and other contenders for preeminence in raiding.

As was often the case, Morgan's grandiose plans did not survive the rigors of field campaigning. At the outset, however, his effort to bring the war into the front yards of the North's citizenry achieved gratifying success. On July 2, he led two brigades west from Burkesville, Kentucky, then across the rain-swollen Cumberland aboard rafts and barges. Above the river his hard-bitten riders swatted aside local Yankees, although they also suffered heavily when attacking outposts along the Green River. After damaging stretches of the Louisville & Nashville, the raiders crossed into Ohio. For the next three weeks they inflicted damage indiscriminately on private and public property while keeping ahead of a small army of pursuers.

Finally overtaken near Buffington Island, Ohio, Morgan lost 700 men in a vicious firefight (he was already missing several hundred others, who had straggled from or deserted his column, a testimony to his poor record as a disciplinarian). Along with 364 of his remaining troops, the general surrendered near Salineville on July 26, ending what would become the war's longest raid. Along with Basil Duke and other subordinates, Morgan was incarcerated in the state penitentiary at Columbus, from which he staged a characteristically daring escape five months later. But even before he returned to Tennessee, his effective contributions to the Confederacy had ended. His life ended, also, the following September, when Federal troops surrounded him and some of his men near Greenville and he made the mistake of trying to fight his way out.[8]

The prolonged estrangement of Morgan's men meant a substantial loss of manpower to Wheeler's command. This loss came on the heels of another that had taken place in May when, in response to Grant's and Grierson's movements, General Johnston transferred Breckinridge's division from Middle Tennessee to the defense of soon-to-be-besieged Vicksburg. Most of the cavalry that the late Earl Van Dorn had commanded—formed into a division under Red Jackson—either accompanied or followed Breckinridge. The transfer reduced Forrest's command, to which Jackson's men had been assigned, to a single division under Frank Armstrong.

Many in the Army of Tennessee regarded the transfer of so many troops as dangerous folly; they would merely swell the ranks of Grant's captives once Vicksburg fell to him. Johnston himself felt the same but was constrained to act as he did by orders from Richmond. Short-term results were clear. Before the transfers and Morgan's raid, Bragg's army reported almost 16,000 cavalry available for duty; by late June the number was less than 9,000.[9]

A related concern was the general perception that Rosecrans, for all his apparent lethargy, would not remain inactive much longer. Wheeler, as he had indicated when dining at Beersheba Springs, for a time professed to believe otherwise. By mid-June, however, he had learned from scouting reports, newspaper accounts, prisoner interrogations, and other sources that Old Rosey was under great pressure from Washington to force a showdown with Bragg. The latter's rationale for ordering only half of Morgan's command to participate in the Louisville mission was that every horseman was needed to detect and oppose an imminent advance on Tullahoma.

The only good news to circulate through the army came from Virginia, where Lee had dispatched the latest in a long series of incompetent opponents— "Fighting Joe" Hooker, whom the Confederate hero had confounded, bedazzled, and then pummeled into submission near Chancellorsville, a woodland clearing west of Fredericksburg. Lee's triumph, however, had come at a fearful cost: his brilliant subordinate, Stonewall Jackson, had fallen mortally wounded. The brightest lights of the Confederacy seemed to be winking out, one after another.[10]

———   ———

The long-anticipated advance of the Army of the Cumberland began on the morning of June 23 as three columns of infantry, screened by horsemen, moved south from Murfreesboro with the intention of maneuvering Bragg's army out of Middle Tennessee. The advance coincided with major operations under way elsewhere in the war-torn nation—the final phase of Grant's investment of Vicksburg; the tightening of the siege lines outside Port Hudson, Louisiana, the only other outpost on the Mississippi still in Rebel hands; and the concentration of two-thirds of the Army of Northern Virginia on the south bank of the Potomac as Lee's second invasion of the North neared high tide.

Of these several major events, the one of greatest interest to the Army of Tennessee was, of course, the one unfolding in its front. Reduced to its essentials, Rosecrans's strategy comprised a movement against his enemy's left flank via the Triune and Shelbyville pikes—a powerful offensive aimed at occupying the gaps in the mountains that separated the armies—and a deceptive advance toward Bragg's right near Manchester. Rosecrans calculated that his opponent would interpret the latter as a feint, prompting him to strengthen the fortified post at Shelbyville. By doing so he would weaken his right, where the topography was less rugged than anywhere else in the area of operations, offering the invaders an easier passage. Once lightly opposed, Rosecrans would convert the seeming feint into a major thrust that would carry him into the Confederate rear via a crossing of the Elk River. In that sector he could sever Bragg's communications with Chattanooga and block his line of southward retreat.

Rosecrans's strategy was so well conceived and so artfully executed that the Tullahoma Campaign became one of the most brilliant turning movements of the war, especially notable for its success in attaining results at a small cost in casualties. Only the rains that drenched Middle Tennessee for several days after Rosecrans moved out spared Bragg's army from total ruin. The downpour converted sandy roads into earthen sponges, preventing men, horses, wagons, and artillery from making the kind of progress required by a plan predicated on exact timing.[11]

A major factor in Rosecrans's success was the completeness of his deception. Bragg was cozened into leaving all but undefended the route taken by the critical maneuver element of his opponent's army. And it was to Joe Wheeler's lasting discredit that he was fooled to such an extent that for days he sent army headquarters erroneous, conflicting, and incomplete reports of enemy movements and intentions. The upshot was that Bragg's ability to react effectively to a fast-moving, ever-changing situation was almost fatally compromised.

Wheeler's error-marred performance actually began more than two weeks before Rosecrans advanced. On June 6 Bragg, fearing his adversary might move at any time, had ordered his cavalry chief to concentrate his force and prepare it for combat. In doing so, Wheeler had massed along his army's left. He moved some of Wharton's men westward from their post on the right and augmented Forrest's reduced command at Spring Hill with almost 1,000 of Martin's troopers under Martin himself. Statements attributable to Wheeler, published in *Campaigns of Wheeler and His Cavalry*, indicate that Bragg had placed Martin's men in front of the left flank in preparation for yet another strike at the supply trains in the Union rear. Historians, however, fault Wheeler for allocating too few resources to defending the center and right of his army's line, especially that sector from Hoover's Gap eastward.

One day before Rosecrans advanced Wheeler compounded his faulty dispositions by transferring more of Wharton's men from the right and center toward Shelbyville. This shift uncovered the mountain gaps Rosecrans was anxious to seize. Now the critical sector between Liberty and Hoover's Gaps was held by a single brigade, and only one of its regiments, the 1st Kentucky, was in position to block access to Hoover's Gap, the more strategic of the two defiles.[12]

The flaws in Wheeler's unit alignment became evident early on the twenty-fourth, when Rosecrans moved simultaneously against Shelbyville and the gaps. Even as Wheeler galloped westward in the rain to supervise defensive actions on the left, heavy columns of infantry approached Hoover's, spearheaded by a unit whose capabilities Wheeler ought to have fully appreciated—five regiments of mounted infantry under Col. John T. Wilder, an element of George H.

Thomas's army corps. Wilder's 2,000 men, veteran fighters all, were armed with seven-shot Spencer repeaters whose rapidity of fire had caused the command to be dubbed the "Lightning Brigade."

Sweeping its few defenders from the mouth of the gap, Wilder's men galloped along the length of the defile and emerged from its southern end. Almost four miles from the point of their attack, the horsemen were finally halted by one of Hardee's infantry brigades under Brig. Gen. William B. Bate. Bate's late arrival was due to Wheeler's failure to rush word of the Union advance to the rest of the army. Bate attempted desperately to gain possession of the gap, but his repeated attacks were beaten back by the extraordinary firepower of the Federals. After losing almost a quarter of his men, Bate fell back, conceding possession of the gap to the enemy.[13]

Over the next two days, Thomas's infantry and artillery debouched from Hoover's Gap and pushed south while Crittenden's corps, despite slow going over wretched roads, moved on Thomas's left toward Manchester. Farther east, the corps of Maj. Gens. Alexander McCook and Gordon Granger, supported closely by Stanley's cavalry, confronted Polk's foot soldiers at Shelbyville and Hardee's between Wartrace and Tullahoma. Wheeler rushed as many troopers as he could spare to Polk's front north of Shelbyville, where they tangled with Yankees of all arms at such points as Middletown, Unionville, Rover, and Eagleville.

Wheeler should have been suspicious that most of the opposition in this sector was coming from Stanley's cavalry, but he appears to have taken little notice. In his *Campaigns* book, he claimed to have "argued" with Bragg that unless the army's right was shored up the enemy "would throw his left wing upon our line of retreat to Chattanooga." But this view appears to have been a product of hindsight, for the record indicates that, rather than Wheeler alerting his superiors to this danger to the army, the opposite is true. In a rather sharply worded message late in the afternoon of the twenty-ninth, the army's chief of staff, Brig. Gen. W. W. Mackall, directed Wheeler's attention to the right flank: "General Bragg urges you to ascertain where their left rests to-night, what kind of force, and so to observe it during the night." Mackall wished to hear reports of any movement in that sector "hour to hour, or, better, the moment it occurs." Fifteen minutes later the chief of staff repeated his demand for information on enemy movements opposite the flank and added pointedly, "Try to get it soon and accurate."[14]

One reason for the vexation on display at army headquarters was that over the previous two days Bragg had accepted Wheeler's appraisal of Shelbyville as Rosecrans's primary objective. Acting on this assessment, on the morning of the twenty-sixth the army leader ordered Polk to cut through Guy's Gap, between Shelbyville and Murfreesboro, and strike the west flank of the Yankee force that had pushed through Liberty Gap and was driving back Hardee's corps. Later that day, Bragg was shocked to learn that another body of the enemy had materialized at Manchester as if poised to turn his right. Wheeler's scouts should have provided a warning, but the small force of horsemen remaining in that sector had been cut off from contact with the main army.[15]

A harassed Bragg cancelled Polk's advance and ordered the entire army back to the entrenched position at Tullahoma. One imagines that he spoke through clenched teeth as he directed his mounted leader to cover the retreat of the infantry and guard the army's trains. Those tasks Wheeler performed with conspicuous ability. Though the wagons struggled south over what he called "a single and very bad road," they made it safely to Tullahoma. As the vehicles rolled on, Wheeler ordered Martin's division and Forrest's command to fall back to Shelbyville, which they should reach by evening. Wharton was instructed to resist as stiffly as possible the advance against Bragg's right, although he was to do so from Wartrace, well to the north and west of Manchester.[16]

Martin's force, some 900 sabers, "after a severe march, in a drenching rain, which had damaged his ammunition, and most of his guns," reached Shelbyville on the morning of June 27. At once it occupied the works above the town. The deployment was completed just as the head of Granger's column, screened by Stanley's horse soldiers, approached on the turnpike from Murfreesboro.

Joining Martin behind the local defenses, Wheeler learned to his chagrin that on the way there 200 of his subordinate's men had been surrounded and captured by Granger's advance. A second detachment, 600 strong, which Martin had stationed on his right in advance of the works above Shelbyville, fled the area to avoid being cut off by another fast-moving Union force. That left only 600 troopers in position to oppose Granger and Stanley. Wheeler immediately assumed command of this force. Believing it too small to hold the Shelbyville defenses, he had it fall back into the town itself. He would make a stand on the north side of Duck River until Forrest's men, on the roads to the north and west, reinforced him.[17]

Wheeler was proposing a risky move, for with Polk and Hardee concentrating their troops around Tullahoma, he was opposing by himself a force too massive to hold back for long. The river at his back was deep and fast-moving, offering no escape should he be pressed on all sides, as seemed entirely likely. But his determination to hold the town was strengthened when Forrest, still a few miles off, begged him to remain "until I arrive, or I will be cut off, as the Shelbyville bridge is my only means of crossing Duck River." According to Wheeler, the courier bearing this message also conveyed a pledge that his commander would attack the west flank of the force in Wheeler's front, something the latter believed could be easily accomplished "by taking a short cut by a crossroad, three miles shorter than by [the direct road to] Shelbyville."[18]

If Forrest made such a promise, he did not keep it or make use of the escape route he claimed was absolutely essential to the safety of his command. By early afternoon, Wheeler's hold on the town was loosening under repeated assaults on the barricades his men had thrown up in the streets of Shelbyville. By his claim, his troopers repulsed three separate attacks, after which the bluecoats spread out on all sides with the intention of surrounding Wheeler's force and cutting it off from the river.

Eventually Wheeler decided that his efforts in Forrest's behalf were for naught, that his subordinate was not coming. He was correct: Forrest and his command had escaped across the river via a hidden ford several miles below the town. His options reduced to one, Wheeler ordered everyone remaining with him to make his way, as best he could, across the stream. While officers and men withdrew, he stayed behind, accompanied by a small escort, blasting away at the nearest bluecoats. By the time the greater part of his command had crossed, the human cordon around Shelbyville was virtually airtight.

Perhaps too late, Wheeler turned toward the bridge. Cutting through a startled mass of Yankees aiming to block his only route of retreat, he raced toward the structure only to find it in the possession of Stanley's horsemen. Fearful that if not checked the cavalry would pursue Bragg's wagon train—the rear portion of which could still be seen trundling south—Wheeler managed to add to his escort sixty troopers who had failed to heed his every-man-for-himself injunction and lead them against the enemy. The unexpected assault succeeded in "driving them back into the town in utter confusion, opening the road for the escape of [the] command, and placing the wagon train out of danger." In a brief time, however, Stanley's men rallied and counterattacked, forcing Wheeler and his escort to fight desperately to thrust them back.[19]

Wheeler's heroics bought his army some time, but eventually it ran out. A new horde of would-be captors massed in his rear, blocking his path to the bridge, and all but thirteen of his escort had been cut down by pistol or saber. The prudent course would have been surrender—instead, with a shout that might have come from a leather-lunged six-footer, Wheeler led the survivors to a rise fifteen to twenty feet above Duck River. Without hesitating, he plunged headlong into a stream "swollen to a mighty torrent" by the recent rains. Horse and rider struck the water with a tremendous thud and sank, rock-like, toward the bottom before bobbing wildly to the surface, shaken but unhurt. Each of the gallant thirteen followed Wheeler's lead, slamming into the water and cutting through it until able to clamber up the opposite bank. Once on dry ground they followed Wheeler as he spurred toward the rear of their army, now well into its fourth full-scale retreat of the war.[20]

——— ——— ———

Initially Bragg intended to make a stand at Tullahoma. He was emboldened by the successful concentration of his army as well as by reports that Rosecrans's attempt to destroy the all-important bridge over Elk River—an effort spearheaded by Wilder's mounted infantry—had been thwarted. The army leader maintained his resolve through the midafternoon of June 29 but it did not survive a subsequent meeting with Polk and Hardee, who gave their superior conflicting opinions as to whether the army should retreat farther. Late the next day, a nervous Bragg learned that Rosecrans was massing around Manchester, threatening the Confederate rear. That night, the Army of Tennessee crossed the Elk River near Decherd and Winchester and resumed its southward journey.[21]

The retreat took the army farther than anyone could have imagined. On July 1, following another war council, Bragg ordered the abandonment of Middle Tennessee. His new route carried his soldiers eastward in the direction of the stronghold of Chattanooga, the only place where Bragg would feel safe from pursuit. The first stop was the mountain village of Cowan, where the army formed a line of battle in case Rosecrans moved quickly to the attack. When he did not, Bragg crossed his army over Sewanee Mountain, site of the University of the South, an institution Bishop Polk had helped found in 1856 and over which he hoped to preside some day. Late that afternoon, the withdrawal came to a conclusion on the outskirts of Chattanooga.[22]

At every stage of the retreat, Wheeler's and Forrest's horsemen had done their best to hold back the enemy while also protecting the army's flanks and trains. The troopers had played a major role in keeping the Elk River bridge out of Wilder's clutches, and as soon as the army was on the south side of the stream Wheeler made sure the span was thoroughly dismantled. When crossing Sewanee Mountain, Wheeler's rear guard fended off blow after blow from Stanley's troopers and their infantry supports.

In contrast to his practice of the first hectic days of the campaign, when he had sent infrequent dispatches, Wheeler kept Bragg closely informed of his activities throughout the retreat. On July 1 he sent a typically pithy report of the fighting that spilled across the grounds of Polk's unfinished academy: "The enemy are engaging us warmly at this point. Our men are maintaining their ground bravely." Two days later, as the army continued its crossing of Sewanee, he reported that his hard-pressed troopers were obstructing the roads with dislodged boulders and felled trees. The enemy's harassment continued for another two days, Wheeler's men parrying every thrust, all of which he meticulously reported in hopes of easing Bragg's evident anxiety. Finally, on July 4, with his infantry and artillery comrades safely ensconced around Chattanooga, Wheeler could boast that the Federals, who had once again been thrown back, "show no disposition to pursue any farther."[23]

The retreat had taken a heavy physical toll of the army, especially its mounted arm. A member of the 8th Texas remarked that from the time it departed Tullahoma, the cavalry had been "in the saddle and wet to the skin by the rain." A Tennessean complained that by the time it reached Chattanooga "our Company was nearly broke down. We have slept 4 hours in 5 days and nights."[24]

The withdrawal had also strained the army's emotional strength, although most of the rank-and-file refused to give way to gloom or defeatism. In a letter written on July 7, a tired and wet Texan told his father, "Now just glance at your map and see what an ample and delicious slice of Tenn[essee] we have given up. . . . Bragg will be censured much for this move but there was no alternative for him. And the manner in which he brought off his army, stores, waggons, &c, &c deserves the highest commendation." A comrade in the 51st Alabama admitted that "our soldiers generally are much discouraged at the situation of affairs but I think it will wear off & they will fight more desperately than they ever have done. We have a great deal to discourage us but I feel like we will come out all right."[25]

Such men would have been forgiven had they succumbed to despair. Within days of reaching their mountain sanctuary, they received word of a series of defeats to Confederate forces on other fronts. On July 3, the decisive repulse of an attack against the center of the Union line south of Gettysburg, Pennsylvania, forever to be known as Pickett's Charge, had effectively ended Robert E. Lee's final invasion of the North. The following day General Pemberton surrendered his starving garrison to the army that had besieged Vicksburg for the previous forty-seven days. And on July 7, the outpost at Port Hudson, isolated by Vicksburg's fall, succumbed to a less well-mounted siege. Port Hudson's capitulation enabled Abraham Lincoln to exult that "the Father of Waters runs unvexed to the sea." Although the soldiers of the Army of Tennessee would not have known it at the time, this demoralizing combination of events presaged the ultimate downfall of the Southern nation and the end of its experiment in rebellion.

———— ———— ———— ————

For six weeks after reaching Chattanooga, Bragg's army waited for Rosecrans to move against it. Throughout that anxious period, Wheeler's cavalry guarded the army's front and supply lines while almost continuously scouting toward Yankee-occupied Tullahoma. Martin's division guarded the extended left flank of the army, picketing the Tennessee River from Chattanooga southwestward as far as Decatur, Alabama. At Decatur, it connected with the pickets of Col. Philip D. Roddey, one of Forrest's erstwhile subordinates whose brigade had been placed temporarily under Wheeler. The rest of Wheeler's corps was beyond his immediate reach. By August 2, Wharton's division had been sent south to the countryside around Rome, Georgia, there to guard the upper reaches of the Western & Atlantic, the line that Colonel Streight had strained to reach and damage. At the suggestion of Wheeler, who had established himself at Gadsden, Alabama, additional steps were taken to defend the western flank of the railroad, which the cavalry had the responsibility of guarding. Blockhouses were constructed beside bridges and elsewhere along the tracks, while precut lumber was stockpiled in case the stockades failed to prevent raiders from damaging the line.[26]

On the army's right, Forrest's troopers patrolled northward from Chattanooga toward Kingston, Tennessee. For two months after the army's fallback to Chattanooga, the command comprised only Frank Armstrong's division. In early September, however, it returned to a corps organization with the addition of a division under John Pegram. For the previous several months Pegram's cavalry had been a part of the Department of East Tennessee. On August 6, that department was transformed into a corps under Simon Bolivar Buckner and assigned to Bragg.[27]

Despite the good service Wheeler had rendered during the retreat to the mountains, his dyspeptic superior saw fit to reprimand him more than once in the weeks that followed. On July 17, Bragg faulted Wheeler for reporting inaccuracies. These probably related to the number of officers and men present for duty, figures that Wheeler had a habit of inflating. When Wheeler failed to correct the mistakes, Bragg sent him a second, more pointed, reminder. On July 30, Bragg blamed his cavalry chief for unspecified offenses committed by two of his units near Cherokee Springs, which, according to reports, were "doing some harm and no good" in their present locale.[28]

Bragg may have had grounds for complaint on administrative issues, but he himself was responsible for a more serious error: the poor positioning of the cavalry. Although the army commander feared an attack by Rosecrans, he doubted it would come before the culmination of a separate campaign in East Tennessee. Ambrose E. Burnside, who after Fredericksburg had lost command of the Army of the Potomac, had been sent west at the head of the IX Army Corps. By mid-August Burnside, from his headquarters on the upper Cumberland River, was planning to seize and occupy strategic Knoxville. After a raid by his cavalry that destroyed a strategic bridge over the Holston River south of Knoxville, he began his advance on the city, the defense of which had been entrusted to Buckner prior to his transfer to Bragg's army at Chattanooga.

Suspecting that if Knoxville fell Rosecrans would join forces with Burnside before advancing on Chattanooga, Bragg neglected Wheeler's sector and devoted an inordinate amount of attention to the flank that Forrest was picketing. The extended line that Martin's division occupied—which had undoubtedly been laid out by Bragg— extended so far west of Chattanooga that its pickets would have difficulty detecting an enemy advancing from Tullahoma, especially one that used multiple routes.[29]

In addition to being too thinly stretched, Martin's pickets appear to have been lacking in vigilance, which was Wheeler's fault as well as his subordinate's. Early in August Bragg's inspector general had reported riding from Lookout Mountain southwest of Chattanooga into the city without being challenged by a single picket. Almost three weeks later the same officer, having completed an inspection of Wheeler's corps, informed army headquarters that its condition was quite poor, although he did not specify any deficiencies.[30]

If the inspection report was accurate, Wheeler's command chose an unpropitious time to relax its vigilance. On August 15, Rosecrans finally advanced on Chattanooga; at the same time, Burnside moved from the Cumberland

River toward Knoxville. By the twentieth Rosecrans had crossed the mountains to Stevenson and Bridgeport; the following day he reached the Tennessee River within striking range of Bragg's city. One day later, Union artillery began to shell the defenses of the Army of Tennessee. Bragg reacted by hunkering down inside his works and preparing to assimilate reinforcements—not only Buckner's troops from Knoxville but also a 9,000-man force sent from Mississippi by Joe Johnston. The additions would give Bragg enough foot soldiers to man four corps, which he assigned to Polk, Buckner, Daniel Harvey Hill, and William H. T. Walker. (In July Hardee, thoroughly disgusted with Bragg's leadership, had transferred to the Army of Mississippi.)

When word of Rosecrans's advance reached him, Wheeler called in his outlying pickets and prepared to assume the age-old mission of delaying the enemy. This time, the mission appeared impossible. By September 4 Rosecrans had gotten his entire army over the river below Chattanooga and was prepared to push through the mountains to block Bragg's path of retreat. On the sixth, Bragg swallowed hard and made plans to abandon the city and fall back across the Georgia line. He expected to concentrate in the vicinity of La Fayette on West Chickamauga Creek, twenty-six miles south of Chattanooga. There he could strike at Rosecrans's several columns as they emerged through the mountain gaps.[31]

When Bragg made his move, it would be at the head of an army even larger than the one he now commanded. On the day Bragg evacuated Chattanooga, Jefferson Davis made a decision in Richmond that, besides affecting Bragg's encounter with Rosecrans, would powerfully influence the course of the war in the West. In the wake of the repeated urgings of Robert E. Lee's senior subordinate, the Confederate president had agreed to send most of James Longstreet's corps by rail to northern Georgia. Initially it was proposed that Lee himself command the detachment, but on September 9, when the troops began to leave army headquarters at Orange Court House, the ambitious Longstreet—whom some observers believed lusted after Bragg's command—was at their head.

The lengthy journey was made even longer by overburdened engines, a shortage of passenger and platform cars, worn and broken track, and a detour around East Tennessee caused by Burnside's recent occupation of Knoxville. Even so, by the seventeenth the vanguard of Longstreet's force—the divisions of Maj. Gens. John Bell Hood and Lafayette McLaws plus a small contingent of cavalry and a battalion of light artillery—had linked with Bragg's army. The much-maligned Military Railroad had come through for the Army of Tennessee.

By now Bragg had ended his retreat and gone over to the offensive. By turning back toward Chattanooga, he hoped to interpose between his pursuers and the city he had given up to them. Rosecrans's army was hastening south and east in three columns, confident that its enemy was in full and disorderly flight toward Atlanta. Already Bragg had attempted to exploit this rashness by ambushing a large segment of Thomas's corps as it emerged from McLemore's Cove, a cul-de-sac in the valley between Lookout and Pigeon mountains. The vacillation of a couple of division leaders had ruined Bragg's strategy, permitting Thomas to escape the trap. But now, on September 18, from a concealed position in the heavily wooded country east of Chickamauga Creek, Bragg was again in a position to surprise his slowly concentrating and less-than-vigilant foe.[32]

Since the evacuation of Chattanooga Wheeler's horsemen, despite their weakened condition, had shouldered a heavy workload effectively and without complaint. After vacating their picket posts, they had secured the army's withdrawal to La Fayette. By retarding Rosecrans's three-directional pursuit, they had enabled Bragg to concentrate his forces for a surprise strike (the botched ambush at McLemore's Cove had not been their fault). And they had tracked the movements of the Yankee columns so adroitly that Wheeler had correctly estimated the immediate objective of each.

Throughout the fallback to Chickamauga Creek, the cavalry had failed to carry out only one assignment. So anxious was Bragg to gain information on Rosecrans's positions and intentions that at the outset of the withdrawal from Chattanooga he had ordered Wheeler, "even at the sacrifice of troops," to attack and drive in Rosecrans's pickets, taking prisoners who could be interrogated. The order required Wheeler to find a path over Lookout Mountain into Wills's Valley. On September 4–5, he dutifully entered the valley but sent forward only a small party to gather intelligence. Wheeler's action enabled him to acquire the intelligence Bragg needed without the heavy casualties that would have resulted had he attacked the head of the Yankee column then entering the valley from the other side. Some historians fault Wheeler's judgment in this instance; others, such as John Dyer, believe that he acted with commendable prudence: "Every pass [in Wills's Valley] was strongly picketed by enemy cavalry, and even if Wheeler had succeeded in forcing an entrance his retreat could have been shut off by the simple process of closing the gap behind him. As a result, Wheeler, who made a fetish of obeying orders, disobeyed one."[33]

As the armies moved toward a confrontation along Chickamauga Creek, Bragg drew in his cavalry. Forrest's corps guarded the army's right flank east of the stream, while Wheeler took up a position from which to protect the left, or southern, flank. Early on the eighteenth he was at Owen's Ford, two miles below the hamlet of Crawfish Springs, observing the movements of the southernmost component of Rosecrans's six-mile-long line: Maj. Gen. James S. Negley's division of Thomas's corps. Wheeler and his troopers, like most of the forces in their sector, saw little action this day. Bragg had ordered a dawn assault against the Union left, but his plans miscarried through the interplay of several factors, including the resistance of Rosecrans's cavalry, now under Brig. Gen. Robert B. Mitchell. Shortly before 5 PM one of Polk's divisions finally fought its way across the creek, but too late to unhinge Crittenden's corps as Bragg had intended.[34]

Wheeler remained at and near Owen's Ford throughout the nineteenth, the first full day of battle. That day began when a division from Thomas's corps—

which, having shifted position, now formed the Union left—encountered Forrest's dismounted horsemen and drove them back until it struck two infantry divisions in the cavalry's rear. Throughout the morning and afternoon, attacks and counterattacks swept across the upper reaches of the creek. Bragg's resources this day included the first three of Longstreet's brigades to reach the field, although Longstreet himself failed to reach army headquarters until near midnight. In his absence, Hood, holding the left-center of Bragg's line, drove back the Yankees opposite him, while on his right Maj. Gen. Alexander P. Stewart's division momentarily pierced the Union line and gained possession of the strategic road to La Fayette.[35]

The fighting on the nineteenth, while heavy and at times frenzied, was also piecemeal and spasmodic, almost chaotic. On the Confederate side of the field, little appeared to have been accomplished, although thousands of lives had been sacrificed in a desperate search for a breakthrough. A golden opportunity was lost late in the day when Bragg failed to exploit a two-mile gap that had opened between Crittenden's and Thomas's positions. Commenting darkly on the quality of the fighting, D. H. Hill, whose infantry corps occupied a position on Wheeler's right, described it as the jabs "of the amateur boxer, and not the crushing blows of the trained pugilist."[36]

As had been the case on the eighteenth, those Confederates on the left saw relatively little action, although exposed to "the far-away thunder of artillery [that] told the story of the hard fighting that was going on where the infantry were at work." This was generally true of Wheeler's position at Owen's Ford, although at some point he crossed the river and skirmished briskly with the foot soldiers along Negley's lower flank. In fact, Wheeler claimed to have "warmly assailed" a force that formed across his front, "dividing the column and driving the enemy in confusion in both directions." For his part, Negley reported engaging in skirmishing at many points but failed to identify the forces he opposed.

Although Wheeler received generally good grades for his leadership this day, a dissenting voice came from Chaplain Robert F. Bunting, of the 8th Texas. Placed in an exposed position enfiladed by dismounted cavalry supporting Negley, the Texas Rangers lost heavily in both men and horses before being allowed to move out of range. Wheeler, Bunting claimed, was "responsible for the failure, for instead of sending us alone to that position, his whole force should have been thrown across the creek and hurled upon the enemy, and they could have easily been routed. It is evident we have too many commanders and not enough of system."[37]

———— ———— ———— ————

The combat on Sunday, September 20, was not nearly as indecisive as its predecessor. With most of Longstreet's men now on hand, Bragg assigned their general to command the army's left flank, while Polk supervised operations of the right. At about 9:30 AM the battle resumed with an attack against the north end of Rosecrans's line, one that swept gradually south through the day. Longstreet's assault did not get under way until just before noon but once in motion it achieved dramatic success. In attempting to strengthen that part of his line under heavy fire, Rosecrans mistakenly withdrew a division from the center of his line and failed to fill the gap thus created. By happenstance, this was the sector that Longstreet struck at the head of eight brigades arranged in three lines. Passing through the gap, the attackers drove simultaneously north and south, sweeping everyone and everything from their path. The Union right disintegrated under the force of the unexpected thrust; even Rosecrans's headquarters was overrun, forcing him and his staff to flee toward Chattanooga. Only the upper portion of the Union line, held stubbornly by Thomas and reinforced at a critical time, remained intact under a terrific pounding. By four-thirty, however, Thomas was withdrawing in the direction of Rossville.[38]

On the Confederate left, Wheeler's men, who had recrossed the creek to the south, saw action throughout the day. Apparently, however, they did not become heavily engaged until late morning, when the cavalry supporting Negley moved away from Wheeler and closer to the center of the fighting. Wheeler responded by moving Wharton's and Martin's divisions about a mile and a half upriver to Glass's Mill. Here they came in contact with Edward M. McCook's cavalry division, which Wheeler's scouts had observed moving toward Crawfish Springs from the southwest. "We had hardly reached this spot," recalled teen-aged trooper John Allan Wyeth of the 51st Alabama, when "a lively fight was precipitated. One of our batteries went immediately into action just in front of our position, and we were posted to guard it. The federal guns about five hundred yards away soon got the range and threw a lot of shrapnel, which kept us on the anxious seat for fully an hour."[39]

As he noted in his report of the battle, as soon as he encountered McCook's troopers Wheeler "dismounted all my available force, crossed, and warmly assailed the enemy, hoping that we might draw troops from this sector and thus create a diversion." He was able to accomplish more than this, for the dismounted Yankees suddenly saddled up and fell back on that part of Rosecrans's line then being crushed by Longstreet. Wheeler drove his enemy as far as Crawfish Springs, taking forty prisoners "besides the wounded."[40]

From Crawfish Springs Wheeler returned to the creek at Lee and Gordon's Mills, almost two and a half miles north of his position of that morning. Here, at about three o'clock, he pitched into the nearest Union force of unknown identity—probably stragglers dislodged from Rosecrans's left. Not surprisingly, after a brief struggle the Yankees "commenced retreating in confusion. We followed as rapidly as possible, capturing about 1,000 prisoners, 20 wagons, and a large amount of arms and ordnance stores."[41]

Pressing deep inside what had been the enemy's main line of battle, by sunset Wheeler had captured "five large hospitals, with a considerable supply of medicines, camp equipage, and a great number of wounded prisoners, besides over 100 surgeons." John Wyeth's company was one of the units detailed to collect discarded weapons and equipment useful to Wheeler's command. "The dead Federals were scattered everywhere," the youngster recalled, "in some places very thick. I counted seven who had fallen in one pile, and I recall but one that had not been stripped of all outer clothing."[42]

The amount of debris in the Union rear and of the spoils taken by Wheeler's men revealed how badly the Yankees had been whipped and how effectively the Army of Tennessee had performed under Braxton Bragg. The logical question, which must have crossed Wheeler's mind at some point even as he prepared to press toward Chattanooga, was, having gained the victory, what would Bragg do with it?

8

WAR CHILD

*H*istorian Stanley F. Horn observes that "a victory not recognized is almost as profitless as a victory not gained." This adage held true at Chickamauga, for Braxton Bragg, who had never experienced a major victory, did not recognize it when he saw it, and so, ignoring widespread reports of the panicky retreat of his enemy, for many hours after the fight ceased he refused to acknowledge that his army had prevailed and that he needed to do something to secure and extend his triumph. Later, when he realized the size of his soldiers' accomplishment, he claimed that they had been too exhausted by their recent exertions to pursue Rosecrans's fugitives.

When he finally ordered a northward advance, Bragg directed his army, not across the Tennessee River and into the rear of the beaten Yankees, but toward Chattanooga, as if he expected to march unmolested through its streets to the huzzahs of the citizenry. Longstreet would always insist that on the day after the fight he urged upon his superior a more ambitious course and that Bragg had agreed not only to a rapid pursuit but also to a turning movement north of Chattanooga—only to give way to his own timidity and uncertainty and change his mind.[1]

This is not to say that Bragg lacked good reasons for moving cautiously. His army was almost out of rations, the result of the poorly maintained rail line to Atlanta. It also lacked the pontoon trains critical to crossing the Tennessee in force. Then, too, its losses over the past two days—nearly 18,000 had been killed, wounded, or captured—militated against a movement toward the rear of a sizeable enemy, even one demoralized by defeat and the loss of almost as many officers and men.[2]

Even so, anger and disappointment were manifest when Bragg's troops discovered they would not follow up their hard-won success. Some refused to believe it. On the twenty-first, Bedford Forrest and 400 of his best men harassed the Union rear guard near Rossville. From a commanding vantage point, Forrest saw thousands of Federals streaming off through Lookout Valley, supply wagons strung out behind, "evacuating as hard as they can go." He rushed word to his immediate superior, General Polk, and advised that "we ought to press forward as rapidly as possible."[3]

But no forward movement—at least not a rapid one—took place. Bragg had adopted a safer course: he would mount a siege that would starve his opponent out of Chattanooga just as Grant had starved Vicksburg into submission. The army's reaction to his decision was swift and sharp: officers and men throughout the ranks set up a cry of complaint and condemnation. Many termed Bragg's refusal to pursue not merely a blunder but a sign of moral infirmity.

Bragg's decision led to a rebellion within the ranks of his senior subordinates. After attending a September 26 "indignation meeting," Polk detailed his criticisms in a personal letter to President Davis, while Longstreet wrote in similar terms to Robert E. Lee and the new secretary of war, James Seddon. In his missive to Seddon, Longstreet predicted that "nothing but the hand of God can save us or help us as long as we have our present commander."[4]

A single gathering being insufficient to air all high-level grievances, a second, held on October 4, produced a remarkable "round robin" petition that enumerated Bragg's errors and failures and called for his immediate ouster. The paper was sent to Davis, who upon reading it made preparations to visit the army in hopes of adjudicating the interpersonal wrangling that was threatening to bring it down.

But when he arrived at Bragg's headquarters on October 9, the president only exacerbated the situation with his remarkable clumsiness. Davis's approach to problem solving was indelicate and direct. He called on four of Bragg's most senior generals to state, in Bragg's presence, whether they believed their superior fit to command the army. Each of the respondents delivered a scathing critique of Bragg's generalship and recommended his removal. This highly unusual truth-telling session may have cleared the air but it failed to produce a consensus on the army's next course of action. Some of Bragg's generals opted for a decisive forward movement, others for a more circumspect advance. But when days of rain turned every road between army headquarters and Chattanooga into soup, all thought of an offensive was given up. The only recourse was to besiege Rosecrans's army into surrender—Bragg's preference all along.

Another baleful result of Davis's visit was that Bragg was authorized to fire or at least temporarily transfer several of his high-ranking critics, including Polk, Hill, and Maj. Gen. Thomas C. Hindman. Eventually, each man left the army on his own terms (although Polk would return eight months later). Even with their departure, the interpersonal problems that had infected Bragg's command for so long would continue to fester.[5]

One of the few senior officers who refused to give in to the prevailing discontent and condemn his commander for numerous sins of commission and omission was Bragg's chief of cavalry, who had not attended either the protest meetings or the chest-baring session chaired by Davis. Several times over the previous months and more than once during the recent campaign, Bragg had faulted Wheeler for mistakes in judgment as well as tactical errors. Even so, Wheeler continued to respect his superior and trust his instincts.

His support of Bragg stemmed from his gratitude for the favors the man had done him. The Louisianan had been responsible for Wheeler's meteoric rise in the mounted arm, promoting him over the heads of senior officers with more illustrious reputations. Such solicitude engendered loyalty, which for Wheeler was more than an abstract concept or a temporary expedient—it was the linchpin of institutional stability, especially in the military. Then, too, Wheeler disapproved of the grumbling and backbiting that ran rampant in the upper levels of the army, and he despised disgruntled subordinates who sought to undermine and obstruct their superiors. Such behavior could have nothing less than a deleterious effect on organizational cohesion and morale. The Army of Tennessee had too many enemies outside its ranks to tolerate malcontents, agitators, and fomenters of dissent.

Acting on these convictions, Wheeler quietly and conscientiously attended to his duties in the wake of the critical but unfinished victory at Chickamauga. On September 21, when his immediate superior, Longstreet, ordered him to scout the enemy's most recent positions, Wheeler mulled over his earlier instructions from Bragg to collect abandoned equipage, round up stragglers, and secure the immediate area of operations. Determined to comply with both sets of orders, he assigned 500 men to reconnoiter forward and two regiments to police the battlefield.

Some time that morning, his priorities shifted in the direction of following the foe. Wheeler had detected "a heavy dust in Chattanooga Valley, which appeared to indicate a movement from Chattanooga along the foot of Lookout Mountain toward McLemore's Cove." He immediately assembled the 1,700 members of his command not engaged in other duties and started for the valley. After progressing only a few miles he came upon the force that had raised the telltale clouds. After driving it toward Chattanooga, he turned west and moved to McLemore's Cove. En route the head of his column bumped into a skirmish line manned by dismounted cavalry in advance of a large body of foot soldiers and artillerymen and a line of supply vehicles. The prolonged struggle that ensued ended with Wheeler striking simultaneously at the column's front and flanks. When the enemy began to waver, "we charged in line and also in column on the road, driving him in confusion." The running fight continued for some miles, the Yankees several times halting in hopes of rallying but each time resuming the retreat. By day's end Wheeler had bagged 400 prisoners, eighteen stands of colors, and ninety wagons "loaded with valuable baggage."[6]

The following morning, he turned back toward Chattanooga under orders to "press the enemy hotly and vigorously as long as he remains this side of the river." Late in the day, new orders called for him to press his pursuit on the other side of the Tennessee in remote cooperation with Forrest's cavalry. Early on the afternoon of the twenty-third, before Wheeler could comply, he was directed instead to ascend Lookout Mountain and sweep the summit free of pickets and skirmishers. As he did, he passed through the hilltop village of Summertown, which he reached at sundown. Before darkness descended, his scouts detected a regiment-size force of Federals ensconced behind mountaintop breastworks. With a portion of his 100-man advance guard, Wheeler lashed the front of this position with rifle-fire while the rest of his command charged on foot against both flanks. The demoralized defenders abandoned their works almost at first contact, leaving behind rifles, knapsacks, overcoats, and cooking utensils—"also their supper, already cooked."[7]

After permitting his troopers to finish a meal that would have been a crime to waste, Wheeler was met by a courier from army headquarters. The orders the man carried called on Wheeler to turn over the position he had taken to infantry comrades and report with his entire command at Chickamauga Station on the railroad east of Chattanooga. When he reached that depot early on the twenty-fourth, he found additional instructions waiting for him. He was to join Forrest, who had moved up the Chattanooga-Knoxville railroad to the village of Charleston. But when Wheeler arrived at the appointed place, he learned that the Tennessean had pushed farther north in pursuit of a body of Burnside's cavalry operating in the Cedar Springs–Athens vicinity. Forrest chased the Yankees to Philadelphia, more than twenty-five miles north of Charleston, before retracing his steps and joining Wheeler.[8]

Bragg had ordered the cavalry leaders to ford the Tennessee, cross Walden's Ridge, and enter the Sequatchie Valley, Wheeler's base of operations at the outset of the Perryville Campaign. In the Sequatchie they were to "press the enemy, [and] intercept and break up all his lines of communication and retreat." Bragg hoped that they would inflict enough damage to Rosecrans's line of supply to doom his army inside Chattanooga.[9]

By now the siege of that city was well under way. Below Chattanooga Bragg had established a six-mile-long line stretching eastward from the foot of Lookout Mountain to Missionary Ridge (the latter eminence was a long, rugged spur of the former) and from there northward to the confluence of Chickamauga Creek and the Tennessee River. By commanding the railroad to Bridgeport, Alabama, this line denied Rosecrans direct access to his supply base at Nashville, forcing him to rely on a single, fragile supply route sixty miles in length that ran through the Sequatchie. Convoyed wagons had to clamber up steep ridges and along narrow roads to haul provisions from the railhead at Stevenson to a garrison already reduced to subsisting on half-rations.[10]

Wheeler, who had both the experience and the temperament for this sort of work, looked forward to the interdiction mission. Yet he was wary of having Forrest, for the first time since the botched attack on Dover, serving under him as Bragg appeared to contemplate. On the twenty-eighth, Bragg instructed Forrest to make his entire command available to Wheeler for the duration of the raid. He worded the order so ambiguously, however, that Forrest believed he was being stripped of his command. He had heard that Bragg had criticized his recent pursuit of Burnside's cavalry, and he interpreted the order as both rebuke and punishment. Infuriated by what he considered a spiteful slap at his leadership, Forrest sent his superior a heated letter of protest and then confronted him at army headquarters. During the encounter he denounced Bragg's "cowardly and contemptible persecution of me," which Forrest dated from Shiloh. "You may as well not issue any more orders to me," the cavalryman snapped, "for I will not obey them."[11]

Before Bragg could explain himself, Forrest stalked off, seething with rage. He went looking for President Davis, who was still visiting the army and from whom he correctly expected a sympathetic hearing. Realizing that Forrest could never again serve under Bragg but wishing to retain his services, Davis agreed to provide him with a new command in West Tennessee.

Forrest would prosper in his new realm, which would serve as a stepping-stone to departmental command and promotion to lieutenant general. One year hence, he would agree to serve again in the Army of Tennessee. But the assignment would be a temporary one, and Forrest would answer to someone other than Braxton Bragg.[12]

—— —— —— ——

Before his blow-up with Bragg, Forrest had tried to exclude his command from the Sequatchie Valley expedition on the grounds that the men and their mounts had been too weakened by their recent labors to provide Wheeler effective support. When on the afternoon of September 30 he rendezvoused with his colleague's troopers at Cotton Port on the south bank of the Tennessee between Chattanooga and Knoxville, Wheeler concurred with Forrest's reasoning. With extreme reluctance the latter had furnished three brigades for the mission, mostly from Frank Armstrong's division. Armstrong, however, following the lead of his superior, begged off the mission, and Wheeler assigned his men to a new subordinate, Brig. Gen. Henry B. Davidson. Joining Davidson in inspecting the leased brigades, Wheeler found them to be "mere skeletons, scarcely averaging 500 effective men each. These were badly armed, had but a small supply of ammunition, and their horses were in horrible condition. . . . The men were worn out, and without rations."[13]

The situation was deplorable, but there was no help for it. Wheeler himself, as well as both of his division commanders, had protested this mission, coming as it did in the wake of unending days of riding and fighting, but Bragg had been adamant that it go forward. Bragg realized that he had made a most unpopular move in attempting to starve out Chattanooga; now he had to make good on his gamble.

That evening, following a futile effort to resupply and remount his own and Forrest's troopers, Wheeler led the combined force—almost 4,000 officers and men and six artillery pieces from Wiggins's battery and the Tennessee battery of Capt. B. F. White Jr.—across the river. The crossing was made without concerted opposition from the Federal cavalry that patrolled the west bank of the Tennessee under Brig. Gen. George Crook. Evidently Crook had no desire to take on such a sizeable column, even a tired, poorly armed, and badly equipped one. The brigadier did, however, alert his immediate superior, General Mitchell, and Rosecrans's headquarters to the crossing, ensuring that, as soon as outlying detachments could be called in, the raiding column would be followed and attacked.[14]

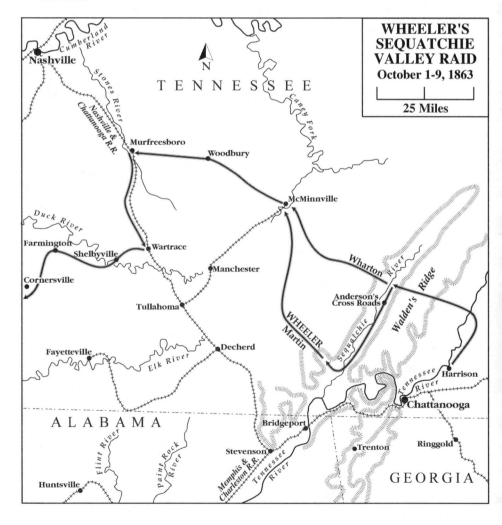

For the first several days of the expedition, Wheeler and his men had things very much their own way. On the evening of October 1, having spent the day further organizing his heterogeneous command, Wheeler led the way toward the massive wall of rock and soil known as Walden's Ridge, the boundary of the valley in which Wheeler's scouts already had sighted columns of Yankee wagons groaning under full loads of supplies. Not long after the march got under way, a sudden, hard rain came down, turning the few roads in that area into beds of mire. One result was that it was late on the second when the van of the raiding column reached the summit of the ridge, 1,500 feet above the surrounding terrain.

That night, as campfires blazed across the mountaintop, Wheeler called a meeting of his division and brigade leaders. He announced that Rosecrans's wagon train had been located six miles inside Sequatchie Valley, trundling south toward Anderson's Cross Roads. He declared that the train would be overtaken the following day—but only by a third of Wheeler's command. Wheeler would go after it along with Martin's 1,500 troopers and a few hundred of Forrest's men. Meanwhile, Wharton, with his single brigade and the greater portion of Davidson's force, would move through the valley to McMinnville, where reserve supplies had been stored for the relief of Chattanooga. Wheeler added, with a touch of theatricality, that not long after the larger column captured the depot he would join it at McMinnville "if I am alive."[15]

Most of his subordinates approved the plan either overtly or tacitly, but General Wharton loudly voiced his opposition. Given the widely dispersed but numerous Yankee cavalry known to be prowling the valley, a division of manpower such as Wheeler had in mind posed too many risks. After some conversation—and perhaps a heated argument—Wheeler carried his point and Wharton fell silent. But that he had spoken out against the plan, and with such vehemence, told Wheeler that the ambitious Texan was chafing under his subordinate status. Clearly Wharton believed that his long and faithful service entitled him to leadership of a mission of this importance and he resented being denied participation in its most critical and dramatic phase, the capture and destruction of the supply train.[16]

On the morning of October 3, the columns parted ways. Before dawn, Wheeler and Martin headed south across the mountaintop; six hours later, the disgruntled Wharton descended the ridge and started cross-country toward McMinnville. Both forces were heading toward the successful accomplishment of their assigned missions—and toward a near-disastrous rendezvous with Rosecrans's cavalry.

Wheeler and Martin were the first to overtake their quarry, a detached thirty-two-wagon section of an immense supply train, each wagon pulled by six mules. Leaving behind enough men to overtake the vehicles and overawe their guard, Wheeler continued across the top of Walden's Ridge to Anderson's Cross

Roads. A few miles farther on he and his men beheld what one trooper called "the richest scene that the eye of a cavalryman can behold. Along the side of the mountain hundreds of large Federal wagons were standing, with their big white covers on them, like so many African elephants, solemn in their stately grandeur. They had been rushed up there by the teamsters and abandoned." The situation seemed too good to be true. "This was too rich a bonanza to be left without an escort; and in a few minutes the rifles sounded from the mountain sides, indicating that we would have to do some fighting for such booty."[17]

As volley after volley of small-arms fire echoed through the valley, Wheeler hurled portions of his column at the cavalry and infantry escorting the train and who were now using the parked wagons as cover. Wheeler's first attack, made by two regiments of John Tyler Morgan's brigade, was repulsed, but a second assault struck home. One participant, the callow Alabamian John Allen Wyeth, recalled that "as soon as our line could be formed, we rode forward at full speed, and receiving a volley at close quarters, were successful in riding over and capturing the entire escort within a few minutes." That escort proved to be so large—nearly 1,200 officers and men—that its capture alone appeared to validate Wheeler's mission.[18]

More importantly, the pursuers had seized a train variously estimated to have between 800 and 1,800 vehicles. The balance of the day was devoted to denying their contents to the enemy. Troopers brandishing torches galloped the length of the ten-mile-long column, setting fire to the canvas tops of the wagons. Other raiders performed the less exhilarating duty of dispatching the mule teams with pistol and saber. Still others—a substantial number, it would seem—defied the prohibition of Wheeler and his officers by breaking into the wagons and carting off whatever tempted their taste buds or tickled their fancy—everything from boxes of crackers and cans of milk and dehydrated vegetables to items of tack and military and civilian apparel. Trooper Wyeth helped himself to the contents of one vehicle only to be told loudly and vehemently to "get out of that wagon!" The source of this order turned out to be General Wheeler himself. The youngster obeyed and thereafter enjoyed "the honor of riding side by side with my commander for some distance further among the captured wagons. As he turned back, he ordered the small squadron that was in advance, to go on until the last wagon had been destroyed, which order was fully executed."[19]

——— ——— ———

While Rosecrans's vehicles burned and their teams lay dead or dying in their traces, Wharton's column completed its trek to McMinnville. Its leader expected to have to fight his way into the town, probably at the loss of many lives, but he worried for naught. When presented with a capitulation demand, the local commander, Maj. Michael L. Patterson (son-in-law of Tennessee Provisional Governor Andrew Johnson), surrendered the post and its 587-man garrison without firing a shot. The surprised and gratified raiders took possession of Patterson's depot, whereupon they perpetrated, in the words of the distraught major, "the most brutal outrages on the part of the rebels, ever known in any civilized war in America or elsewhere." The Rebels not only burned a vast array of quartermaster's and commissary stores but helped themselves to the belongings of Patterson's troops, robbing them of boots, gloves, headgear, outerwear, and a vast array of personal items—billfolds, pocket watches, even finger rings. Local citizens—conceivably including Southern sympathizers—suffered the same fate as the luckless garrison.[20]

Here was yet another sign of the lack of discipline that had come to characterize Wheeler's command. As the general himself had demonstrated by reproving Wyeth, he was adamantly opposed to the appropriation of goods earmarked for destruction in pursuance of orders, and especially to the theft of personal belongings. But Wheeler lacked the ability—perhaps the stature, the persona—to enforce his views on his men, many of whom were becoming more skillful and brazen in their theft of private property, especially that belonging to POWs and civilians.

Wheeler and his triumphant troopers crossed the Cumberland Mountains and reached McMinnville early on October 4. They spent the rest of the day helping comrades complete the demolition of the depot, which included a locomotive, several cars, and a railroad trestle. By the morning of the fifth, the last torch had been applied and the last item of military value had been appropriated by sanctioned or unsanctioned means. The reunited expeditionary force left the burning ruins behind as it followed Wheeler northwestward toward Woodbury and Murfreesboro. Crossing Stones River, a stream that brought back vivid memories of a winter's battle, Wheeler made a demonstration against Murfreesboro, capturing a stockade at the railroad bridge and paroling its fifty-two defenders.

After destroying tracks and ties on the Nashville & Chattanooga for three miles below the bridge, he turned the column south toward Christiana and Fosterville. Through the day and well into the next his men wrecked every railroad bridge between Murfreesboro and Wartrace. On the sixth, they veered west toward Shelbyville—the scene of Wheeler's desperate leap into the Duck River—where their advance guard destroyed yet another supply depot, one considerably smaller than the one at McMinnville. Near nightfall Wheeler put his tired but exhilarated troopers into bivouac a few miles north of Farmington.[21]

Despite the fact that Yankee cavalry had sparred with Wharton's column on the road to McMinnville as well as with the reunited command on the road to Murfreesboro, Wheeler must have felt secure in this pleasant locale, for he appears not to have posted sentinels at strategic points. This was a major omission, as he learned early on the seventh, when Crook's division of cavalry, mounted infantry—including the Lightning Brigade of Colonel Wilder—and horse artillery trained their sights on the raiders' riverside nook. Thanks to the apparent failure of General Davidson—whose command Wheeler had stationed along the banks of Duck River in advance of the rest of the command—to spread a timely alarm, the Yankees took their enemy almost completely unawares. "The first intimation that we had of the presence of the enemy," wrote one of Forrest's men, "was when cannon balls came crashing through the timber and we could hear the firing of our men and the enemy out on the pike, half a mile off."[22]

Wheeler cobbled together a defensive line, but a part of it crumbled when General Davidson, instead of falling back on the main force in response to Wheeler's order, moved south to Farmington. Crook concentrated his firepower against Davidson's isolated force, shattering it and sending its fragments staggering off in retreat. One of Davidson's subordinates, Col. George B. Hodge, tried to stem the rout but found the troopers in the path of Crook's assault racing in every direction, "wild and frantic with panic." Oblivious to Hodge's command to halt, they threw themselves into the saddle and "rode over my command like madmen." An unusually candid Wheeler noted in his after-action report that while most of his men gallantly met the attack, "others acted shamefully."[23]

Wheeler rushed Martin's division, trailed by Wharton's, to Davidson's assistance. He shelled the attackers with Wiggins's and White's batteries, but Crook's horse artillerymen got their range almost immediately and put some of their guns out of action. Before the day ended, the graycoats had left behind four disabled cannons (Wheeler would claim three) to be captured. Undaunted by his losses, Wheeler whipped five of Martin's regiments into position in rear of Davidson's dissolving line. Martin's veterans absorbed the attack, halting the Federal advance at least temporarily.

Wheeler would report that Martin's men repulsed the enemy so decisively as to dispel any further threat to his command; in reality, only the coming of night saved the raiders from annihilation. Under the cover of darkness, Wheeler was able to disengage and turn southwestward toward home. Abandoning not only his guns but also many of the wagons whose capture had given the raid an aura of success, the general led his battered ranks toward the safety of the Tennessee River. The retreat had a frantic, every-man-for-himself quality that dampened the spirit of officers and men who a few hours earlier had believed this journey at a glorious close.

Only when he reached the river near Decatur, Alabama, on the eighth was Wheeler safe from possible attack by Crook or other elements of General Mitchell's corps. After crossing near Muscle Shoals, he put his exhausted troopers into bivouac and toted up the results of his latest excursion through the enemy's country. He determined that his men had burned, disabled, or otherwise rendered unserviceable more than 1,000 supply wagons while ravaging one large supply depot and several smaller ones. Such accomplishments ought to have ensured the collapse of Rosecrans's army through privation and want, thus rendering the expedition a strategic success despite its tactical failures at the end.[24]

But it was not to be. Alarmed officials in Washington reacted swiftly and decisively to Rosecrans's battlefield defeat and his army's incarceration in Chattanooga. Only five days after Chickamauga two infantry corps, detached from Maj. Gen. George Gordon Meade's Army of the Potomac, began to entrain for Tennessee via northern Alabama. A week later—the day Wheeler climbed Walden's Ridge prior to descending into the Sequatchie—the first wave of reinforcements, under Meade's predecessor in army command, Joe Hooker, was arriving within marching distance of Chattanooga. By then, too, General-in-Chief Halleck had ordered Grant to send to Memphis all of his available forces. These latter additions—four divisions under Sherman—reached Chattanooga by mid-November. Grant preceded Sherman to Tennessee; en route, he was named commander of the newly created Military Division of the Mississippi, a vast fiefdom encompassing the Army of the Cumberland—command of which Grant took from Rosecrans and gave to the "Rock of Chickamauga," George Thomas—as well as Sherman's Army of the Tennessee and the Army of the Ohio, command of which would eventually go to Maj. Gen. John M. Schofield.[25]

Even before Sherman arrived, Grant moved to lift the siege that had driven the occupants of Chattanooga to the brink of starvation. With the assistance of his chief engineer, Brig. Gen. William Farrar Smith, and the support of elements of Thomas's and Hooker's commands, the department leader established and secured a supply line that ran from Brown's Ferry on the Tennessee River to Chattanooga via a route beyond the reach of Bragg's artillery in Lookout Valley.

When the so-called "Cracker Line" opened to supply traffic in the last days of October, Wheeler's raid lost its strategic significance. It became chiefly notable for the hundreds of casualties his command had suffered because of its loping pace through Middle Tennessee and its commander's cavalier attitude toward enemy pursuit. Although the mission had been undertaken against Wheeler's better judgment and executed by troopers borne down by weeks of almost uninterrupted riding and fighting, as its leader he bore primary responsibility for its almost ruinous outcome. Once again, poor tactical decisions, a lack of vigilance, and a tendency to underestimate a powerful opponent had combined to call into question Wheeler's fitness to command in independent operations.[26]

Even so, the general derived a lasting benefit from the raid. Soon after he crossed the Tennessee to safety, he sought permission from the owner of a plantation near Courtland to encamp men and horses on his estate. Col. Richard Jones readily agreed, and the command snoozed away the night in the fields surrounding an elegant manor house known as Caledonia. The following morning Wheeler was receiving casualty reports from his subordinates when his host paid a courtesy call at his headquarters.

Wheeler found that Colonel Jones was accompanied by his pretty, nineteen-year-old daughter Daniella, widow of Benjamin Sherrod, owner of neighboring Pond Spring. The teenager had inherited the 1,800-acre estate after the death of her elderly husband but had returned to live at Caledonia. That morning, Mrs. Sherrod had expressed to one of Wheeler's men an interest in seeing his famous commander. The trooper had replied with a chuckle, "Well, madam, you won't see a great deal of him when you do." When presented to the general, however, Daniella was impressed less by his stature—or the lack of it—than by the sadness she saw in his eyes and the compassion she heard in his voice as he read the names of officers and men killed, wounded, or missing on the expedition.[27]

Wheeler was no ladies' man, but he knew beauty and grace when he saw it, and he appears to have been smitten from the moment he took Daniella's hand. He would correspond with Mrs. Sherrod through the remainder of the war, and when it ended he would return to Courtland to ask again for her hand, this time in marriage.

——— ——— ——— ———

Wheeler and his raiders remained in northwestern Alabama for nearly three weeks. The respite was providential, for the troopers of Wharton, Martin, and Forrest were in no shape to resume active operations on short notice. Their most critical deficiency was horseflesh. The extended stint of rear-guard duty in an area lightly touched by the hand of war enabled them to augment their stock. At least the men were well protected against the autumn winds then blowing through the Tennessee Valley. One trooper cheerfully enumerated what he and his comrades had saved from the flames that engulfed the captured supply wagons: "Blankets Boots hats pants Coats, Overcoats and in fact every other article necessary for winter wear."[28]

On October 12, while at Courtland, Wheeler compiled his first report of the raid—he would write a second, longer report two and a half weeks later, after returning to the army, perhaps because the first had been among a file of headquarters papers captured by a Union scouting party near Trenton, Tennessee. Like most of his previous postcampaign writings, neither report should be considered a historical document. In both he played up his destruction of enemy property and played down his defeats, ascribing the manhandling of his command along the Duck River to "a mistake by General Davidson's" (although his second report praised the "good conduct" of Davidson and the other subordinates Forrest had provided him). Wheeler claimed that the battle at Farmington had hurt the attackers more than it had their quarry; Wheeler had absorbed "less than one-fourth" of Crook's casualties. He reported the loss of two artillery pieces, which he blamed on fragile carriages. George H. Thomas, who forwarded the captured copy of Wheeler's initial report to the U.S. War Department, observed sarcastically that its author "forgets to mention the loss of four of his guns at Farmington. His report is probably equally truthful in other respects."[29]

Wheeler was justifiably critical—although only mildly so—of two colleagues who had been ordered to attack other sectors of Rosecrans's communications line in cooperation with his own efforts. Major Gen. Stephen Dill Lee, commander of cavalry in the wide-ranging Department of Mississippi, Alabama, West Tennessee, and East Louisiana, had neglected to strike objectives in the Tuscumbia, Alabama, area that might have diverted some of Wheeler's pursuers. The slow-moving Lee had not even crossed the Tennessee by the time Wheeler's expedition ended. A smaller force with whom Lee was to have cooperated, Philip D. Roddey's Alabama brigade, had crossed the river in remote support of Wheeler but had withdrawn after encountering slight resistance. If Wheeler had failed to attain his every assigned objective, at least he had exerted himself to complete his mission and had conscientiously shouldered his responsibilities.[30]

However immodest and inaccurate, Wheeler's second report pleased its core audience. Two days after he forwarded it to army headquarters, Bragg's adjutant general informed Wheeler that "His Excellency President Davis has been here and read your report. He requested the general commanding to make known to you and your command his satisfaction and appreciation of your services."[31]

Wheeler's rosy report was intended for an official audience, but one of his aides ensured that an account of his boss's exploits would circulate throughout the civilian community. On October 10 Major Burford sent a lengthy review of "one of the most brilliant campaigns of the War" to an editor friend, who saw to its newspaper publication. Burford described as "immense" the destruction Wheeler had inflicted on Rosecrans's supply system and opined that it would force the Union commander to abandon Chattanooga.[32]

The major adorned his breathless account with several references to Wheeler as "the War Child," an appellation that may have originated with Burford himself. The publication of his narrative in the Tennessee press—and undoubtedly in other newspapers as well, since Southern prints regularly ran stories that had originated with their competitors—appears to have ensured a wide circulation for this poetic nickname, rendering it a close competitor to the older and more popular "Fightin' Joe."[33]

— — — —

Forrest's transfer from Tennessee left Wheeler in command of a single, enlarged corps of cavalry attached to Bragg's army. The expanded command, the organization of which was completed in late November, consisted of four divisions commanded by Generals Wharton, Martin, Armstrong, and Brig. Gen. John H. Kelly. Wharton's division was made up of a Texas, Arkansas, and North Carolina brigade led by Col. Thomas Harrison, as well as a Tennessee brigade that had been assigned to General Davidson in spite of Wheeler's recent criticisms. Martin's division comprised the Alabama brigade of now–Brig. Gen. J. T. Morgan and Col. Charles C. Crews's Georgia brigade.

Armstrong's division was divided into two brigades under Brig. Gen. William Y. C. Humes, whose conduct during the recent expedition had won

Wheeler's unalloyed approval, and the three Kentucky battalions of Col. C. H. Tyler. The division commanded by the twenty-three-year-old Kelly, the youngest general officer in the Confederacy—his appointment owed to a strong performance in infantry command at Chickamauga—consisted of four regular Confederate regiments under Colonel Wade, Wheeler's compatriot on the raid against Tennessee River shipping, and a Kentucky and Tennessee brigade led by J. Warren Grigsby. The corps also included four horse artillery batteries, three organized in Tennessee, the other in Arkansas.[34]

Several of these officers, notably Morgan, Humes, Crews, and Grigsby, owed their positions to their superior's influence with Braxton Bragg. Wheeler exploited that influence to meet his continuing need for able subordinates. "What we want," he informed Bragg during his respite at Courtland, "is officers," especially those able to shoulder brigade command. To this end, he strove—sometimes fruitfully, sometimes in vain—to persuade his superior to send him experienced cavalrymen currently detached from the corps, such as colonels A. A. Russell and Robert Houston Anderson, and such versatile infantry leaders as Arthur M. Manigault of South Carolina and Edward C. Walthall of Mississippi.

New commanders were welcome, for there was, or would soon be, room in the upper echelon of the cavalry. Upon returning from the Sequatchie Raid, General Wharton had gained permission to go to Richmond in hopes of securing a command of his own. His sometimes-volatile relationship with Wheeler, which had neared the boiling point at the outset of the expedition, was effectively at an end. Rumor had it that Wharton was seeking a transfer to the Trans-Mississippi Department, where he could serve in relative proximity to his home state. Wheeler, however, gave credence to another rumor: that the man was after his job. In December he informed Bragg that Wharton was still in Virginia, where he was bad-mouthing his commander to anyone who would listen, especially Texas politicos: "Gen'l W. is still hard at work to get command of the Cavalry of this army. He is aided by his friends in Richmond. It is astonishing to me how such falsifications could have been imposed upon the War Department. . . . Only the other day a gentleman received a private letter from Richmond which stated that . . . Genl. Wheeler would be relieved from his command."[35]

Wheeler intended to have a talk with his dissatisfied subordinate as soon as he rejoined the army. He believed Wharton "too discreet" to admit to his blatant politicking, "but his staff and other agents are getting very bold." With an almost audible sigh, he lamented that "such men should find it necessary to use such ungenerous means to injure the character of another for their own elevation." But even as he decried Wharton's tactics, Wheeler offered to share with Bragg some derogatory gossip about the man, and he admitted to having supplied high-ranking colleagues with "a few items" of information that put Wharton in a bad light, "as I felt it my duty to do so."[36]

On October 17, army headquarters ordered Wheeler to return to the army via Guntersville, Alabama. Within a few days the Decatur-Courtland vicinity was empty of horsemen. It was a sad bunch of troopers who departed the verdant fields along the Tennessee River where they had enjoyed their first respite beyond range of Yankee guns in many months. Their commander shared in the prevailing mood. Not only did he have to part company with his host— and his daughter—but he regretted giving up the social life he had enjoyed in the Courtland area. The general had become such a fixture at local balls and collations that he had inspired a dance tune, "Wheeler's Polka."[37]

Wheeler's orders sent him across the river to Cleveland, Tennessee, twenty-five miles east of Chattanooga. Initially he supposed he had been placed here to guard the extended right flank of Bragg's army, but he was quickly disabused of the notion. Bragg wished Wheeler, with the better part of his now-enlarged command, to join General Longstreet in a campaign to capture Burnside's isolated garrison at Knoxville. Bragg and President Davis, who was still traveling with the army, suspected that the reinforcements Grant had led to Chattanooga would soon attempt to break the Confederates' hold on Lookout Mountain and Missionary Ridge. Both men believed, however, that if he made haste, Longstreet could bag Burnside's garrison and return in time to help parry Grant's thrust.

Davis was the principal proponent of the Knoxville plan. He supported it mainly from a desire to satisfy Longstreet's almost insatiable hunger for independent command. Moreover, the president feared that if Longstreet continued to serve under Bragg, the enmity that had grown between them since Chickamauga would suddenly ignite. He was not certain the Army of Tennessee would survive the explosion.[38]

Planning for the expedition proceeded quickly if rather haphazardly. Not enough thought went into the logistical support of Longstreet's column, and its artillery arm proved deficient in horses and ammunition. Still, the force assigned to the operation appeared substantial enough to do its job. Longstreet would be accompanied by the troops he had brought with him from Virginia, the divisions of McLaws and Brig. Gen. Micah Jenkins (the latter's original commander, Hood, had lost a leg at Chickamauga), plus a brigade of Department of East Tennessee cavalry under Brig. Gen. John Stuart Williams. Later two brigades of horsemen from western Virginia under Brig. Gen. William E. Jones and Col. Milton J. Ferguson would also join Longstreet. Each of these brigades would serve independent of Wheeler's authority. Wheeler's command would be limited to Martin's division, the division of Frank Armstrong (this time accompanied by its commander), Harrison's brigade of Wharton's division, and elements of three batteries of horse artillery. Longstreet's force amounted to 14,000 infantry and 5,000 cavalry, about one-third of Bragg's effective strength.[39]

On November 4, Longstreet's infantry started by rail for Sweetwater Station, almost forty miles below Knoxville, followed six days later by the ill-prepared artillery. Having ridden cross-country, Wheeler's command rendezvoused with the foot soldiers at Sweetwater late on the eleventh. While his engineers scouted the best places to ford the Tennessee River—they would select a point near Loudon—Longstreet ordered Wheeler, with his main body, to sweep across the Little Tennessee and attack the outpost at Maryville, seventeen miles south of Knoxville.

Longstreet was not certain that Wheeler could pass the rain-swollen river should he find it strongly picketed. If unable to cross, he should make a diversion in favor of Longstreet's advance on Burnside's stronghold. Longstreet's concern, however, was misplaced. After dark on the thirteenth Wheeler pushed across the stream with one of Martin's brigades and one of Armstrong's. The crossing left Maryville—which, Wheeler discovered, was defended by a single regiment of cavalry—isolated and vulnerable. After token resistance, the garrison evacuated, scrambling to safety across Stock Creek.[40]

From Maryville Wheeler led the way north in accordance with his orders to take and hold, if possible, the southeastern heights of Knoxville. Crossing Little River, he discovered that he was driving before him detachments of cavalry from the commands of some of Kentucky's most celebrated Unionists, Brig. Gens. William P. Sanders and James M. Shackleford and Cols. Frank Wolford and Charles D. Pennebaker. "After a short fight," wrote one of Wheeler's aides, the Kentucky Tories "were driven for two miles, when, with a battery to assist them, they made a stand in a strong position beyond a creek which could not be crossed by horses, the enemy having destroyed the bridge."[41]

Undaunted, Wheeler dismounted a large portion of his command. He set up his artillery on the south side of the creek and sent his skirmishers across the turgid stream under cover of shell and canister. The first to cross kept the Federals at bay while a fatigue party worked feverishly to repair the bridge. Once the structure was restored, Armstrong's troopers attacked and uprooted the infantry, who fled across a pontoon bridge over the Holston River. Taking up the temporary span, they continued their flight until inside the works at Knoxville.[42]

While Wheeler was advancing against Maryville and points north, Longstreet crossed the Tennessee near Loudon on a pontoon bridge of his own. On the fifteenth, he engaged Burnside's advance echelon on the north bank and got the better of his opponents, who pulled back toward Knoxville. Longstreet, hoping to cut them off before they reached the safety of the garrison, staged an energetic but clumsy pursuit. He overtook his quarry at Lenoir's Station, eighteen miles from the city, but botched an attempt to bag it. He squandered a second chance at Campbell's Station, six miles closer to Knoxville. After the fiasco at Campbell's, the expeditionary commander watched in disgust as his enemy sprinted to safety inside the city whose defenses—earthworks protected by ditches, rifle-pits, and wood and wire entanglements—had been strengthened during the Confederates' mismanaged advance.[43]

After driving the Federals in his front across the Holston, Wheeler received a message from Longstreet urging him to join the main army in front of Knoxville "unless you are doing better service by moving along the enemy's flank than you could do here." Convinced that he could do no further good in his present position, Wheeler turned Martin's and Armstrong's men about and moved downriver.

He rejoined Longstreet on the seventeenth—just in time, it appeared, to support an all-out attack against Fort Sanders, a rectangular salient on the northwest corner of the enemy's defenses that appeared the key to Burnside's position. But eleventh-hour indecision over the best point of attack delayed the assault for several days. In the interim, Longstreet gave Wheeler another mission: he was to proceed to Kingston, on the lower bank of the Tennessee southwest of Knoxville, to drive away Union horsemen reported to be operating in that vicinity and whose presence prevented Kingston's use as a staging area for reinforcements en route from Bragg to Longstreet.[44]

Despite the bone-numbing weather and the frozen roads he would have to follow, early on November 22 Wheeler saluted smartly, rounded up his horsemen, and headed south. He started out in good order, but by the time he approached Kingston early the next morning his column had been depleted by an inordinate number of stragglers—yet another manifestation of the poor discipline of Wheeler's command. On numerous occasions Bedford Forrest had made equally fatiguing marches in even worse weather without losing nearly as many men, in spite of exhaustion and hypothermia among their ranks. This was because Forrest rode close herd on his troopers, who feared him more than they did the cold, the snow, or the enemy. None of Wheeler's men felt this way about their gentlemanly, soft-spoken commander, whom they disobeyed with impunity.

On the way to his objective Wheeler had heard that foot soldiers and cannoneers, as well as cavalry, occupied the Kingston area. Upon his arrival he found the report to be accurate; moreover, the garrison was alert and had assumed a defensive posture as if eager to engage Wheeler's depleted command. He was wise enough not to oblige his enemy. After some desultory skirmishing he called off the attack and withdrew over the same wretched roads and in the same foul weather that had plagued his march from Knoxville.[45]

When he returned to Longstreet's headquarters late that day, Wheeler learned that the long-delayed assault on Fort Sanders was still on hold. The extra time devoted to its planning went for naught. When finally launched before dawn on the twenty-ninth, it was defeated by clumsy execution as well as by the intricacy of Burnside's defenses, the tenacity of their occupants, and the ice-covered ground that hindered the attackers, among other factors. For a time Longstreet considered laying siege to Knoxville but he gave up the idea when, a few days after the failed assault, he learned that Grant had sent Sherman, with two corps, to relieve Burnside. The news persuaded Robert E. Lee's favorite subordinate to end his ill-starred expedition and withdraw from Knoxville.[46]

Although Wheeler's troopers had lent support to the assault on Fort Sanders, their commander had not been on hand to supervise them. Upon his return to Knoxville Longstreet had handed him a telegram from Bragg recalling him to Chattanooga "to assume command of the cavalry here." By late on the twenty-fourth, Wheeler had turned over his forces to General Martin and, accompanied by his staff, his escort, and some miscellaneous units detached from their parent organizations, was splashing through muddy, slushy roads leading south.[47]

As Wheeler rode, unpleasant thoughts crowded his mind. The peremptory tone of Bragg's summons suggested that something unexpected—something unfortunate—had happened to the Army of Tennessee. Wheeler's supposition was correct, but he did not know the half of it.

9

ESSENTIAL TO THE
EFFICIENCY OF THE CAVALRY

Wheeler's worst fears were confirmed well before he rejoined the Army of Tennessee at Ringgold, Georgia, on the Western & Atlantic fifteen miles southeast of Chattanooga, early on the afternoon of November 25. En route to that point where Bragg was attempting to rally his troops, Wheeler and his party were inundated by the sights and sounds of defeat and demoralization. They found themselves swept up in the general retreat, which proceeded in the direction of Dalton. What remained of Bragg's army would reach that village, another fifteen miles down the railroad, the following day.[1]

The process by which the army had lost its foothold on the high ground south of Chattanooga had begun on the twenty-third, when Grant acted on reports that Bragg had weakened his lines on Missionary Ridge by detaching and then augmenting Longstreet's force. Early that afternoon elements of Thomas's army had driven the Confederates from Orchard Knob, a ridge between the lines. The following day, Sherman's troops, who had arrived from Vicksburg three weeks earlier, crossed the Tennessee on pontoons and seized the northern extremity of Missionary Ridge. Hooker's column from the Army of the Potomac, aided by feints and supporting movements by other forces and shrouded in a thick fog that would give the day's fighting the name "Battle Above the Clouds," also advanced. The Potomac troops overwhelmed the Rebels holding the northern face of Lookout Mountain and drove them a considerable distance before enough Confederate reinforcements arrived to produce a stalemate.

On the twenty-fifth, with Bragg's hold on Missionary Ridge loosening, Grant launched a general assault. His soldiers' initial attacks against the flanks of the enemy line faltered; but late in the morning advances by supporting forces enabled Sherman to make headway against the south side of the ridge. Finally, near 4 PM, Grant hurled Thomas's army against Bragg's left flank at the base of the ridge. Failing to halt as ordered after capturing the first of three tiers of rifle pits, Thomas's men clambered up the steep slopes to the crest and drove its flabbergasted defenders into headlong retreat.

Thomas's precipitate advance surprised even Grant, who feared that it held hidden risks. Instead, by sundown, the crest had been secured, 2,000 Confederates had been taken prisoner, and nearly forty cannons had been seized—their crews had been unable to depress their pieces sufficiently to strike the Federals as they charged up the hill. Only the steadfastness of Maj. Gen. Patrick Cleburne's division, which despite unceasing pressure held onto a ridge 500 yards in rear of the initial battleground, prevented Grant from destroying the Army of Tennessee by cutting off its panic-stricken fragments.[2]

As soon as he reached Ringgold, Wheeler attempted to locate the forces he had left behind when departing Chattanooga for Knoxville: Davidson's brigade of Wharton's division and the two brigades of John Kelly. These units had become so scattered among the retreating columns that it took days to reunite them under his command. At first Wheeler was ordered to hold his advanced position near Tunnel Hill, where the tracks of the W & A passed through Chetoogetta Mountain, but by the twenty-ninth Bragg was considering sending him to rejoin Longstreet's command and escort it back it to the Army of Tennessee. This goal proved impossible, however, when the troops sent by Grant to relieve Knoxville interposed between the Confederate forces, compelling Longstreet to withdraw to upper East Tennessee. He would remain in that region until early spring, when he would lead the greater part of his expeditionary force back to Robert E. Lee.[3]

The end of November found the remnants of Bragg's beaten army safely ensconced in and near Dalton, a town encircled by the steep and rugged Cohutta Mountains. Bragg's left, or western, flank was shielded by equally steep and rugged Rocky Face Ridge, his right by the Conasauga River. Soon Wheeler's engineers and fatigue parties were laying out breastworks north of the town and south, toward Resaca on the Oostenaula River. Although aware of his enemy's disorganization, Grant was reluctant to attack these defenses. To turn the Army of Tennessee out of its new position would require a major effort based on long and careful planning.

In fact, it would be five months before any such effort was launched, and when it came Grant would be gone. By March 1864 he would be in Virginia, making his headquarters with the Army of the Potomac in his new role as general-in-chief of all United States forces. After his departure Sherman, his picked successor as commander of the Military Division of the Mississippi, would execute the grand strategy proposed by Grant before his promotion. Sherman's confrontation with the Army of Tennessee would be not an isolated movement but one of several simultaneous advances against Confederate forces east and west.[4]

When the campaign in the west got under way, Grant's most recent opponent would also be serving in Virginia—not in the field but behind a desk. On November 28, Braxton Bragg sent to Richmond a request to be relieved of his command. As he later told Adj. Gen. Cooper, "it will not do for me to remain." His army's rout at Lookout Mountain and Missionary Ridge, the last in a long series of defeats and disasters during his tenure, had been so devastating to the army's physical and mental health that even the self-delusive Bragg saw he could no longer command effectively. Even his staunch supporter Jefferson Davis was forced to agree.[5]

The same day Bragg sent in his resignation he relinquished the army to William J. Hardee, bade farewell to his staff and those few subordinates whose goodwill he retained (including Wheeler), and boarded an eastbound train. Word of his leave-taking produced predictable responses. A typical infantryman, writing soon afterward to his family, blamed his depression on "want of confidence in our Commanding General; but, happily for us, this objection has at last been removed." Many soldiers ascribed the defeats and loss of life that had brought about Bragg's downfall to flaws and failings in the general's character. Over time, other soldiers adopted a more charitable view of his leadership. After the war, one of Wheeler's enlisted men declared that although Bragg gave the strong impression of "a cold, austere officer and a thorough disciplinarian . . . no one ever doubted his bravery and patriotism. . . . His plans and orders for battle could not be excelled in their clocklike accuracy. . . . He was particularly unfortunate in the failure of his officers in obeying important orders."[6]

Given the humiliating circumstances of his departure, Bragg must have expected to be exiled to inactive duty or to a military backwater for the duration of the war. He was agreeably surprised to find himself installed in Richmond as military advisor to his patron and friend, Davis—the same post Robert E. Lee had held before called on to take command of the Army of Northern Virginia. Bragg's position was much more important than its innocuous title suggested, for it carried the power of a chief of staff, even that of an *ex officio* commander in chief. Through this appointment Bragg could not only salvage self-respect but could retaliate against those former subordinates whom he believed had done him dirt. In Richmond, he would also be in a position to reward those officers, such as Wheeler, who had remained loyal to him through thick and thin.[7]

Hardee served as Bragg's successor long enough to assign Wheeler a single major mission. The day after Christmas, the cavalry leader was relieved of covering the front of the army and ordered back toward Knoxville. Hardee's scouts had learned that Grant had dispatched a large supply column to relieve Burnside's garrison; Wheeler was to pursue, overtake, and destroy it in the manner of his recent depredations in the Sequatchie. He would do so with 1,200 members of General Kelly's command—fully three-quarters of the army's cavalry. (Wheeler's three other divisions, still detached under Longstreet, were on the brink of engaging a combined force of Grant's and Burnside's soldiers at Mossy Creek, southwest of Longstreet's current headquarters at Morristown, Tennessee. This engagement would rank as one of the more vicious fights in the western theater, but one destined to be little remembered except by those who took part in it. The long casualty list it produced ensured that when finally returned to Wheeler, those divisions would require reorganizing and recruiting.)[8]

Wheeler's talent for waylaying wagons deserted him on this, his latest assignment. Heading north from Dalton, he encountered the same severe weather that had assailed him during his operations around Knoxville. Chill winds and freezing temperatures combined with the poor quality of the few available roads to slow his pursuit, at some points, to a crawl. The result was his failure to overtake his quarry until the evening of the twenty-seventh, just as the train completed crossing the Hiawassie River to enter Charleston, a depot on the railroad between Chattanooga and Knoxville. As the rail line was guarded not only by cavalry but also by heavy detachments from Phil Sheridan's infantry division, Wheeler saw he would have to do some sharp fighting, and perhaps call on some luck, if he were to accomplish his mission.[9]

But he had no luck at all, and his troops fought poorly. Stabbing fitfully at the rear of the train, they cut off twenty of its guards but failed to bring the wagons to bay. An exasperated Wheeler then ordered Colonel Wade to charge the train at the head of a small brigade, his own 8th Confederate in the lead. The attack was barely under way when Wade was shot out of the saddle. Deprived of leadership, his men recoiled against the volleys of rifle fire unleashed by the guard. As the Rebels fell back, a well-concealed force of Yankee cavalry—part of Col. Eli Long's brigade of the Army of the Cumberland—broke cover and counterattacked. "The entire command," one of Wade's officers reported, "was thrown into confusion and retreat." A semiliterate enlisted man recalled that "the yankes . . . run rite in to our men with their pistols and sabers and shot and cut them with there sabers. . . . there was several of our boys lost there hats and nearly all of them lost there guns."[10]

Accompanied by his staff, his escort, and General Kelly, an ashen-faced Wheeler galloped into the midst of the fugitives, whom he unsuccessfully tried to rally. When his assailants fell back, he engaged them at long range but could find no opening for a renewed assault. Considering the effort a lost cause, he disengaged before Sheridan's foot soldiers could arrive and led his bruised and shaken command back to Dalton.

The repulse had been the product of many factors, including Wade's disabling, the substantial size and unusual combativeness of the train guard, the poor discipline of Wheeler's men, and their even poorer physical condition after an all-night march in brutal weather. Wheeler, however, chose to pin the defeat solely on Wade, with whom he had been on poor terms for almost a year. At his behest the colonel was court-martialed, but Wade was acquitted of the principal charges against him. Unwilling to rejoin Wheeler, he wangled a transfer to Forrest's cavalry in Mississippi. There, thanks to his single-minded quest to restore his reputation, he did "some brilliant service" under a commander less ill disposed toward him than Fightin' Joe.[11]

—— —— —— ——

As soon as he rejoined the army, Wheeler came under the command of Bragg's permanent successor—an officer who had not held a field command in nineteen months. This was Joseph E. Johnston, whom President Davis had persuaded to trade departmental duties for the Herculean task of reviving and reorganizing the command Bragg had led to disaster at Chattanooga.

Johnston's assignment had been a wrenching decision for Davis, who considered the prickly, egotistical Virginian a political opponent as well as a flawed strategist and tactician. During the fortnight following Bragg's resignation, however, the short list of replacement candidates had dwindled down to a mere handful, none of whom inspired Davis's confidence. In the main his decision, which he announced on December 18, reflected the counsel of Secretary of War Seddon, General Polk, and other influential political and military officials who believed that only Johnston could repair the damage Bragg had done to the principal Confederate army in the West.[12]

Johnston had accepted the assignment with a degree of reluctance that mirrored Davis's frame of mind in selecting him. Fearing that no force the size of Bragg's old command could defeat the three armies under Grant, Johnston relinquished his desk job with an almost audible sigh of resignation. Reaching Dalton two days after Christmas, he at once entered upon the duties of his position. Making the rounds of the army's expansive encampment, he made or renewed acquaintances with dozens of subordinates. These did not include Joe Wheeler, who did not return to Dalton until the last day of the year. When the cavalry leader reported, however, Johnston greeted him warmly and made no mention of the unfortunate raid on Charleston.

One of Wheeler's most notable attributes was his ability to get along with any superior regardless of the man's personality and managerial style. From their first meeting, he had no doubt that he could be a valuable subordinate to Johnston. His perception was that the man shared a number of character traits with his predecessor. Like Bragg, Johnston was inordinately proud of his talents and accomplishments (real and imagined), fiercely protective of his reputation, and jealous of his prerogatives. Over time, Johnston would also reveal himself to be stubborn, pedantic, temperamental, and secretive, as well as chronically discontented and pessimistic.

For the most part, Wheeler was able to overlook these flaws; moreover, he came to appreciate Johnston's strategic vision and tactical acuity. From the outset he was impressed, too, by his superior's native intelligence, sharp wit, and keen insight into human nature. He found that while occasionally sharp with, and condescending toward, his officers, Johnston was capable of displays of warmth, charm, even geniality, especially in the presence of enlisted men. Moreover, he affected an avuncular attitude toward noncommissioned officers and privates that gained him numerous admirers among the rank and file.[13]

Personally and politically, Johnston was a rival of Braxton Bragg's. As theater commander he had resisted pressure from Confederate officials to remove Bragg from the field. He had done so mainly for personal considerations, fearing that Bragg's relief would reflect poorly on the man who engineered it. In private, however, Johnston considered Bragg unfit to command an army in the field. Bragg was aware of Johnston's attitude and thoroughly resented it. In his new position at Jeff Davis's right hand, he would take his revenge by making it difficult if not impossible for his replacement to succeed where he himself had not.

The Johnston-Bragg rivalry threatened to place Wheeler—who was intent on maintaining cordial relations with both officers—in an unenviable position. The cavalry leader did his best to balance his loyalties. He strove to curry Bragg's goodwill through regular correspondence in which he maintained a deferential tone. Yet his own interests demanded that he give visible support to his immediate superior. His allegiance to Johnston was strengthened by the latter's efforts to promote Wheeler's ambitions by increasing and streamlining the mounted arm. Johnston avidly supported cavalry recruiting, especially that carried on in Tennessee and northern Alabama under the supervision of Brig. Gen. Gideon J. Pillow. In implementing an army-wide rehabilitation program, Johnston also saw to it that the cavalry got all the resources—remounts, equipment, and weapons—that Richmond could provide.[14]

Wheeler and his men appreciated the improvements in the supply system, especially when they were able to discard the antiquated and inadequate shoulder-arms many of them had long toted—shotguns, fowling-pieces, even flintlocks—for newly issued carbines. Over the winter of 1863–64, the short version of the British-made Enfield rifle, comparable in size and weight to most Union carbines, became available in sufficient quantity to make it the standard arm of Wheeler's command. New pistols were also received in some quantity, although the cavalry continued to lack the sabers that would make it a match for their sword-wielding opponents.[15]

One of the more visible features of Johnston's reforms was the emphasis he placed on training, which extended to all elements of the army. When not picketing or scouting, Wheeler's men were put through an instructional regimen not seen in the ranks since their earliest days in the field. Johnston also supported Wheeler's establishment of schools whose mission was to ensure that officers and men alike "would be properly instructed in cavalry tactics, including evolutions of the regiment and evolutions of the line." Wheeler was gratified when, on February 17, 1864, Johnston formally adopted his revised system of tactics for use throughout the army.[16]

Johnston's reforms and Wheeler's implementation of them paid handsome dividends. When the New Year, 1864, came in, the cavalry was in deplorable shape, suffering the lingering effects of its recent rout and retreat from Lookout Mountain. Almost every trooper was poorly clad and shod, indifferently mounted, ill equipped, and overworked. Less than three months later, the assistant quartermaster of the army, who had been harshly critical of the condition of the arm, made a "second very thorough inspection of the entire command of Major-General Wheeler" and found "a great change for the better in the general condition of the cavalry. The men are well clothed, and keep their camp in very good order, and their discipline indicates a spirit on the part of the officers to pay strict attention to the execution of orders." The effective strength of the command had increased since the last inspection, and the horses were well shod and groomed although suffering still from an army-wide scarcity of forage. Furthermore, "the command is rapidly improving in the drill; and when the weather permits, drills regularly twice a day" under Wheeler's personal supervision. The quartermaster found the cavalry's weaponry and ammunition to be "in as good order as could be expected," and he considered its transportation facilities adequate to its needs.[17]

The men themselves testified to the beneficial effects of Johnston's practices. As winter struggled to a close, an officer in the 8th Confederate Cavalry observed that "everything moved or was conducted with clock-work precision." The cavalry, in common with the rest of the army, felt it had been given a "new life" by a "commander in whom this army had full confidence. . . . Buoyant hope and confidence in ultimate victory animated every breast from teamsters to the General Staff."[18]

Only those troops encamped near Dalton shared in this revival of body and spirit. Throughout the winter and well into the spring, the three divisions under General Martin who remained with Longstreet's expeditionary force suffered privations and hardships greater than Johnston's main body had to endure. The East Tennessee winter was harsh and unrelenting, and the troopers could not escape it by huddling inside winterized tents and well-chinked cabins. One of Martin's subordinates recalled that "our clothing was worn and ragged. . . . Some were without shoes, very few had overcoats. We had to depend on foraging the country for supplies. Without wagons or tents, we marched and slept in the snow and rain. Our sufferings were almost beyond belief."[19]

Attuned to their plight, Wheeler was anxious to gather these men to him. He enlisted the help of higher headquarters; within a week of assuming command Johnston was importuning Richmond to authorize Martin's return. Not until mid-April, however, when Longstreet began his return march to Virginia, did the troopers Wheeler had left behind cross the mountains to Dalton. When they reached him, Wheeler was appalled by their pathetic condition. He immediately dispatched them down the railroad to Rome, whose supply depot would enable them to refit and rehabilitate as quickly as possible.[20]

Upon Martin's return, Wheeler reorganized his enlarged command. Even as Johnston regrouped the infantry into two corps under Hardee and Hood (the latter, recently promoted to lieutenant general, joined the army on February 4 after recuperating from the loss of his leg), Wheeler divided his command into three divisions under Martin, Kelly, and Humes. Martin's consisted of the five

Alabama regiments in the brigade of John T. Morgan and the five Georgia out-fits assigned to Brig. Gen. Alfred Iverson. Kelly's division comprised Wirt Allen's brigade of four regular Confederate regiments plus George Dibrell's four Ten-nessee regiments, recently a part of Longstreet's Department of East Tennessee. Humes's division, the largest of the three, contained another brigade that had recently served in Longstreet's department—two Texas regiments and one from Arkansas, led by Tom Harrison. The division also included five Tennessee regi-ments assigned to Col. George H. Ashby as well as a regiment and a battalion from Alabama under Col. Moses W. Hannon and J. Warren Grigsby's brigade of three Kentucky regiments, one independent squadron of Tennesseeans, and two separate battalions, one each from Kentucky and Tennessee. Wheeler's command also included eighteen pieces of horse artillery.[21]

Conspicuously absent from the order of battle was John A. Wharton, the bulk of whose command now resided in Humes's division. If the Texan had indeed sought to unseat Wheeler as the latter claimed, his intriguing had gone awry. Still, Wharton had gained a promotion to major general as well as a trans-fer to the army in Louisiana (he would serve in the Trans-Mississippi theater for the rest of the war). Wharton's gain was not Wheeler's loss, for the Army of Tennessee would not grieve over the disgruntled transferee.[22]

———— ———— ————

At the close of April 1864, Wheeler reported that his command, in-cluding absentees, numbered almost 19,000 officers and men, of whom only 10,058 were available for duty. This estimate and later manpower counts may have furnished the basis for John Dyer's claim that in the spring of 1864 Johnston's mounted arm outnumbered that of William T. Sherman. However, Wheeler's estimate was high, and deliberately so, for he consistently fudged manpower figures to make his command appear larger and more formidable than it was. It is unlikely that Wheeler, a notoriously poor administrator and record-keeper, had even a reasonably accurate idea of his numbers at this stage of the war.[23]

In fact, he was at a numerical disadvantage to his enemy. It is not likely that he mustered more than 9,000 effectives with which to begin the spring campaign. At this time, the three armies in Sherman's Military Division of the Mississippi, which totaled more than 100,000 troops of all arms, included some 12,500 cavalry available for duty. Even so, that Wheeler could mount and equip as many horsemen as he did short weeks after his command was nearly destroyed under Longstreet was testimony not only to his logistical and recruiting abilities but also to the strong and consistent support he received from his superior.[24]

Johnston championed not only Wheeler's cavalry, but Wheeler himself. Late in January, word reached Dalton that the cavalryman's promotion to major general, which had only recently come up for confirmation by the Confederate Senate, was in jeopardy. Members of the Texas delegation in Richmond were attempting to derail the process in order to place their favorite son, John Wharton, in command of Johnston's horsemen. Alabama's senators were seeking to block Wheeler's confirmation for other reasons. They condemned his transferral of mounted units out of the northern half of their state, which left that region, whose abundant crops and raw materials were valued by both armies, open to Union raids and perhaps to a full-scale invasion.[25]

The Alabamians' concern was heightened when, in the first days of February 1864, Sherman sent 25,000 troops of all arms from occupied Vicksburg on an extended raid into central Mississippi with orders to destroy railroads in and around Meridian. Seven thousand cavalry and twenty guns under Brig. Gen. William Sooy Smith were to advance from Memphis toward the same point. Though opposed by the two infantry divisions and two cavalry divisions of Leonidas Polk's Department of Mississippi and East Louisiana, Sherman succeeded in tearing up almost 100 miles of track and destroying a vast quantity of matériel. However, his cavalry raid ended in humiliating defeat thanks to the intervention of now–Major General Forrest, whose troopers bested Smith's much larger force at West Point and Okolona, Mississippi. Although one had gone awry, the twin offensives suggested the impunity with which an invader might menace the region supposedly abandoned through Wheeler's shortsighted policies.[26]

Wheeler's critics in Alabama did not confine their complaints to his military decision making, nor did they refrain from *ad hominem* commentary. They claimed that as a brigadier Wheeler had shown himself to be "successful, sober, industrious, and methodical . . . but when the field of his operations was enlarged, the draft on his intellect, which is one of mediocrity, became too heavy. He has signally failed to give satisfaction. More over, his person is small, and in his manner there is nothing manly and commanding. He evidently handles men awkwardly in battle." If unable to void his promotion, the senators intended to force his reappointment. The consequent loss of seniority "would place him in rank where, considering his youth and just claims, he should be, viz, behind Wharton and Martin and [S. D.] Lee and Forrest, either of whom is his superior in the field."[27]

Concerned by the growing opposition against Wheeler, Jefferson Davis petitioned Johnston to weigh in on the matter: "Your opinion . . . may be useful, and is desired." The army leader responded immediately and unequivocally, authorizing the president to let it be known that "I consider the confirmation of General Wheeler's nomination essential to the efficiency of the cavalry of this army." His words carried weight; following this ringing endorsement, the clamor against Wheeler began to abate and in due course his year-old promotion won the Senate's consent.[28]

— — — —

Wheeler showed his gratitude by supporting his superior, at least initially, in his extended war of words with Davis, Bragg, and Secretary of War Seddon over the strategy that should guide the Army of Tennessee through the winter and into the spring. Throughout that period, Johnston—mindful of his army's numerical and matériel deficiencies and convinced that when warm weather returned Sherman would advance against him in full force—was committed to remaining at Dalton and reacting to his opponent instead of taking the initiative. His strategic preference was for the defensive-offensive, which required a commander to act aggressively only when conversant with his enemy's strength, positions, and intentions, and called on him to strike a blow only when an opportunity clearly presented itself.

In sharp contrast, Davis and his military and civilian subordinates favored an early advance by the forces in Georgia and Tennessee. They feared that the enemy's spring offensive would focus on Robert E. Lee's army in Virginia; Grant's decision to accompany the Army of the Potomac during the next campaign seemed to confirm this view. To limit the forces brought to bear against Lee, Johnston should take the offensive, if only to prevent Sherman from reinforcing Grant and Meade.

Richmond believed the Army of Tennessee equal to this task, for during his brief stint in command General Hardee had compiled overly optimistic assessments of its condition, minimizing its deficiencies in artillery power, transportation, and troop strength (Hardee refused to concede that his 34,000 troops were opposed by three times as many Federals within striking distance of Dalton). Davis could also cite the inflated personnel returns submitted by Wheeler and some of his infantry colleagues as evidence that the army was strong enough to seize and maintain the offensive. The ambitious strategy that the president initially favored called for Johnston to evacuate Dalton, link with Longstreet south of Knoxville, and cross the Tennessee River and the Cumberland Mountains into Middle Tennessee. There, with the assistance of forces to be sent him under Polk and Beauregard that would swell his effective strength to around 60,000, Johnston should be able to seize Nashville from the Yankees.[29]

Johnston knew full well that such an undertaking was beyond his and Longstreet's capabilities. As historian Thomas Connelly has pointed out, in addition to the many other disadvantages under which he labored, Johnston's transportation system was so weak it could barely support the army in its fixed camp at Dalton; it could not hope to sustain anything approaching a full-scale offensive. Other considerations militated against adopting the government's strategy. In its winter camp in upper East Tennessee Longstreet's command was worse off than Johnston's. If, in its wretched condition, it tried to move south to cooperate with the Army of Tennessee it would be savaged by the heavily reinforced garrison at Knoxville. But Johnston's was a voice in the wilderness. Every argument he put forth, every objection he raised, no matter how forcefully stated, was airily dismissed by Davis and his underlings. Even a stream of emissaries from Richmond who confirmed the validity of Johnston's protests failed to convince the government of the impracticability of its blueprint for action.[30]

Frustrated and angry, Johnston called on his subordinates to buttress his arguments. He achieved indifferent success, in part because by the end of winter he had alienated many officers who had once been favorably disposed toward him. Those whose goodwill he retained but who remained loyal to his deposed predecessor refused to take his side. For his part, in public Wheeler made limited efforts to support his superior, while working behind his back to undercut him. In contrast to his assessments of his own command, Wheeler supplied his superior with reasonable estimates of Sherman's strength, gained from scouting reports, which Johnston relayed to the capital as evidence of the lopsided odds he faced even on the defensive. Wheeler also endorsed Johnston's claims of shortages of rations, forage, and wheeled transport—deficiencies that would hamstring any attempt to advance in force against Sherman.[31]

On the other hand, through his covert correspondence with Bragg Wheeler fueled Richmond's suspicion that Johnston was deliberately playing down his army's capabilities. Early in March 1864 the cavalry commander asserted that recent operations had revealed some weaknesses in Sherman's dispositions that Johnston could exploit if he was of a mind to. The following month he informed Bragg that if supplied with as few as 15,000 reinforcements, the army could fulfill Richmond's wishes for an invasion of East Tennessee without suffering crippling supply shortages. Throughout the campaign that lay ahead Wheeler would continue to counter his superior's arguments against an offensive, insisting that the army was stronger and more capable than Johnston admitted and that Sherman's numbers were steadily declining through attrition.[32]

Wheeler was not the only subordinate who through clandestine correspondence worked to subvert his commander's position with the government. Soon after joining the army at Dalton, General Hood also complained to Davis and Bragg about Johnston's unwillingness to challenge the enemy. Hood claimed that the Army of Tennessee was comparatively stronger and enjoyed higher morale than Sherman's hordes, whose strength he underestimated by at least 50,000. Hood also minimized the army's transportation problems. By his reckoning, only the addition of a few artillery horses was needed to put the command in peak operating condition.[33]

Wheeler also worked against his commander's interests in the wake of a controversy that exploded in the upper echelons of the army early in 1864. The day after New Year's General Cleburne, whose division had staged the heroic rear-guard action on November 25, read a paper he had authored to several high-ranking colleagues who had assembled to discuss the army's manpower problem. His solution was to enroll slaves into the ranks, those who served faithfully to be granted their freedom once the Confederacy prevailed. The Irish-born Cleburne did not share the marked white-supremacist attitudes of most of his colleagues; thus he was shocked by the firestorm his proposal ignited. While a number of high-ranking officers including Hardee, Hindman, and Wheeler's subordinate John Kelly signed a memorial in support of the proposal or in some other way signaled their approval of it, others, especially Maj. Gen. William H. T. Walker, denounced both the plan and its author in the harshest possible terms.[34]

Walker, who was outraged by the very idea of recruiting and arming slaves, chose to make a public issue of it. Not only did he personally solicit the views of many generals, he relayed them, along with copies of Cleburne's plan, to Richmond. Their receipt prompted Secretary Seddon to urge suppression of the documents, whose contents he considered "little appropriate for consideration in military circles" and whose public dissemination "can be productive only of discouragement, distraction, and dissention." Johnston, concerned by the ill feelings Cleburne's paper had provoked within his inner circle, was anxious to comply with Seddon's wish. Walker, however, continued to be vocal in his condemnation of the proposal. His reaction was shared by Joe Wheeler, whose strident outrage matched Walker's own. The indignant cavalry leader loudly proclaimed that had Cleburne broached such an inflammatory issue in Wheeler's home state, he would have been hanged on the spot.[35]

In the end, the controversy (which the government managed to keep out of the newspapers) guttered out despite Walker's and Wheeler's efforts to keep it aflame. The only long-range result of the *cause celebre* was the sharp downturn of Cleburne's career. Although he had forged a record of bravery and competence second to none at his level, on three occasions over the next several months he would be passed over for promotion to corps command. Conversely, as Thomas Connelly notes, "the strong defense of the status quo" by Wheeler, Walker, and other archconservatives "no doubt made the government more amenable to their views during the spring."[36]

———

Through the early part of the winter, Wheeler's outposts came into sharp but sporadic contact with Sherman's troops atop the heavily wooded ridges and in the mountain gorges northwest of Dalton. As early as the second week in January, skirmishing had become, in the words of one Texas trooper, "the order of the day." No major action took place until February 22, when a portion of Thomas's Army of the Cumberland—the largest of Sherman's three fighting forces—began to advance on Dalton from its base near Chattanooga. The movement was a demonstration in long-range support of the Meridian Expedition, but it had another objective as well: believing that Johnston had detached heavily to reinforce Polk, Sherman intended to scrutinize the Army of Tennessee for signs of weakness and faulty positioning.[37]

STATUE OF GEN. JOSEPH WHEELER
IN STATUARY HALL, U.S. CAPITOL,
DEDICATED MARCH 12, 1925

MAJ. GEN. JOSEPH WHEELER,
USA, 1898

BRIG. GEN. JOHN PEGRAM, CSA

JOSEPH WHEELER AS WEST
POINT CADET, 1859

MAJ. GEN. JOSEPH WHEELER,
CSA, CA. 1863

GEN. PIERRE G. T. BEAUREGARD,
CSA

MAJ. GEN. WILLIAM T. SHERMAN,
USA

LT. GEN. WADE HAMPTON,
CSA

Maj. Gen. George Stoneman,
USA

Lt. Gen. Ulysses S. Grant,
USA

GEN. EDMUND KIRBY SMITH,
CSA

GEN. BRAXTON BRAGG,
CSA

GEN. JOHN BELL HOOD,
CSA

LT. GEN. NATHAN BEDFORD
FORREST, CSA

BREVET MAJ. GEN. H. JUDSON
KILPATRICK, USA

BRIG. GEN. FRANK C.
ARMSTRONG, CSA

BRIG. GEN. ABRAHAM
BUFORD, CSA

BRIG. GEN. JAMES R.
CHALMERS, CSA

BRIG. GEN. SAMUEL W.
FERGUSON, CSA

BRIG. GEN. JOHN H. KELLY,
CSA

BRIG. GEN. LAWRENCE S. ROSS,
CSA

GEN. JOSEPH E. JOHNSTON,
CSA

TYPICAL CONFEDERATE CAVALRYMEN OF THE WESTERN THEATER

UNION-HELD BLOCKHOUSES

BRIG. GEN. JOHN HUNT
MORGAN, CSA

BRIG. GEN. WILLIAM H.
JACKSON, CSA

MAJ. GEN. JOHN A.
WHARTON, CSA

GEN. ALBERT SIDNEY
JOHNSTON, CSA

PRESIDENT WILLIAM
MCKINLEY

LEFT TO RIGHT: MAJ. GEN. JOSEPH WHEELER, MAJ. GEN. WILLIAM R. SHAFTER,
AND MAJ. GEN. NELSON A. MILES, 1898

Congressman and Mrs. Joseph Wheeler and their children, ca. 1895

The probing operation lasted three days. Federals of all arms pressed their opponents along Rocky Face Ridge. Some ranged toward Wheeler's headquarters at Tunnel Hill, the most extreme outpost on the Dalton defense line. They succeeded only in dislodging Wheeler's forwardmost pickets. Wheeler not only sent timely word of the advance to Johnston's headquarters but managed to regain lost positions even before infantry comrades came up to support him. Late on the twenty-fifth Thomas withdrew his troops ("mortified and disappointed at his utter failure," Wheeler insisted). At once Wheeler took up the pursuit, sniping at the Union rear and taking several prisoners. That Thomas—who erroneously believed he had forced Johnston to withdraw the forces sent to Mississippi—was willing to return to his original position did not detract from the sense of accomplishment the counterattack had given Wheeler's command. "Our losses were trifling," he claimed, "and the spirit of our army [was] improved, while the enemy suffered heavily in both spirits, men and material."[38]

Joe Johnston reacted differently to Thomas's probe. It seemed to confirm the belief—derived from Wheeler's daily intelligence reports—that when spring came Sherman intended to attack Dalton from the north and west via Mill Creek Gap and Crow Valley, striking toward the upper extremity of Rocky Face Ridge. This avenue of approach would expose what Johnston knew to be the weakest point on his defensive line.

Its position led Johnston to suspect that Thomas's command would spearhead the attack through Crow Valley. He doubted this would be the only offensive he would have to counter. It seemed likely that while Thomas advanced, the rest of the enemy would push south on the far side of the mountains with a view to circumventing his left flank and reaching the Confederate rear in the vicinity of Rome. By mid-April Johnston was sufficiently concerned by this prospect to take steps to shore up his rear echelon. Wheeler had ordered Martin's troopers to Rome not only to refit but also to help man local defenses then in process of being strengthened. Johnston took similar steps to bolster the works enclosing the railroad town of Resaca, midway between Dalton and Rome.[39]

Through the remainder of the winter Wheeler strained to keep his eye on the enemy while parrying Sherman's thrusts toward Tunnel Hill and elsewhere. Occasionally he made forays of his own toward the Union lines. On March 9, with 600 men, he crossed Taylor's Ridge, southwest of Dalton, and in the valley beyond attacked an outpost manned by unobservant Yankees, "capturing their camp, stores, equipage, and a number of prisoners with their horses and arms" although failing to seal off an escape route by which most of the garrison fled to safety.[40]

On the evening of April 3 Wheeler again penetrated deep inside enemy lines at the head of a small column, this time routing a regiment-sized force of pickets near Cleveland, Tennessee, and taking many spoils. Three weeks later he overran another outpost and came away with numerous prisoners. He found the tables turned when, on April 28, some Ohio troopers attacked and captured the hamlet adjacent to his headquarters at Tunnel Hill. The Yankees burned several dwellings and reportedly shot down thirteen members of the local garrison after they had surrendered. Wheeler counterattacked, killing a few, chasing the rest away, and vowing to avenge the murders. As one historian notes, the incident precipitated "a bitter enmity between the opposing cavalries, more bitter perhaps than between infantry unit or combatants in the eastern theater."[41]

— — — —

During the first week of May 1864, William T. Sherman proved his opponent correct. Johnston had failed to convince Jefferson Davis that the Union was capable of launching a continuous, simultaneous offensive on many fronts. But by the fourth of the month not only was Meade's Army of the Potomac moving to attack Robert E. Lee north of Richmond, smaller Union forces were advancing against the Confederate capital from the south, striking Confederate communications in West Virginia, and sweeping south through the Shenandoah Valley toward the rail center of Staunton. In the west, a small army was moving through Louisiana via the Red River, bent on invading Texas. And in southwestern Tennessee, all three of Sherman's armies were suddenly on the move toward Dalton and points west and south, with the great manufacturing, supply, and transportation center of Atlanta as a major objective. The multipronged strategy of Ulysses S. Grant had gotten off to a most promising start.

The first units to meet Sherman's advance were three of Wheeler's brigades—elements of the divisions of Humes and Kelly—that had been picketing their army's front and flanks along a line running from Ship's Gap on the west to the Conesauga on the east. By May 1–2 Wheeler's outposts near Ringgold Gap were skirmishing with Thomas's foot soldiers and the horsemen preceding them, members of the cavalry corps of Brig. Gen. Washington L. Elliott.

Within a few days the pressure on Wheeler's position became almost unbearable. By daylight on the seventh, he found himself confronting a battle line not less than one mile long. This line began on the west, where Thomas's old corps, commanded by Joe Hooker, passed through Nickajack Gap and took up a position facing Rocky Face Ridge. Then Maj. Gen. John M. Palmer's XIV Corps, which had come down from Ringgold, began to form on Hooker's left atop Tunnel Hill Ridge. To complete Thomas's line, before the morning was out the IV Corps of Maj. Gen. Oliver Otis Howard, which had pushed south from Cleveland, Tennessee, moved up to connect with Palmer's left across Crow Valley.[42]

These movements were formidable enough, but then Wheeler's scouts reported that the smallest of Sherman's armies, Schofield's Army of the Ohio (the XXIII Army Corps, formerly Ambrose Burnside's, supported by the four cavalry brigades of Maj. Gen. George Stoneman), had arrived from Knoxville and Cleveland to extend the Union line even farther to the east. Nor was this the extent of Wheeler's predicament. Major Gen. James B. McPherson's Army of the

Tennessee had been discovered passing along the west flank of Rocky Face Ridge, intent on circumventing the Confederate left and gaining the rear via one of two passes through Rocky Face—Mill Creek Gap or, farther south, Dug Gap.

Although he had long anticipated a flanking movement, Joe Johnston reacted sluggishly and inadequately to the mammoth offensive. After dark on the seventh he had Wheeler move a portion of Grigsby's brigade, followed hours later by its balance, to Dug Gap. He also ordered part of a small force of infantry, recently arrived at Resaca, to head toward the gaps from the south while the rest manned the newly constructed defenses at Resaca already held by Brig. Gen. James Cantey's foot brigade. Finally, he ordered Martin's cavalry to guard the Oostenuala River crossings northeast of Rome. Johnston, however, ignored the route that McPherson intended to take into the Rebel rear—through Snake Creek Gap to Resaca.[43]

Despite enjoying good cover—fighting mostly dismounted from behind rocks and trees—Wheeler's men were forced steadily south. They abandoned Tunnel Hill so precipitately that they failed to make good on their commander's promise that he would deny the enemy access to the 1,500-foot-long railroad tunnel by blowing it up. The error constituted, according to modern-day historians, "a major shortcoming of 'Fighting Joe's' Civil War career."[44]

By dark on May 7 Wheeler's command had taken refuge behind prepared defenses inside Mill Creek Gap where the army's infantry advance had come up and dug in. Wheeler was joined here the next day by the balance of Kelly's division, which had been relieved of temporary duty at Resaca. Through most of the eighth the troopers skirmished with portions of Thomas's and Schofield's commands, mainly to protect the Confederate right flank. Late in the afternoon, however, Grigsby's Kentuckians, fighting on foot, helped two regiments of foot solders repulse a determined effort against the other flank when a portion of Hooker's corps attempted to storm the heights adjacent to Dug Gap. The Federals were fully contained only after two of Pat Cleburne's brigades were sent to secure the threatened sector.

On May 9 Wheeler took on the troopers of Edward McCook's division of Elliott's corps. McCook attacked in an effort to turn the Confederate right via the road from Cleveland. His every attempt failed, thanks to an inspired defense by Allen's and Dibrell's brigades, assisted by the men of Wheeler's escort, the combined force being about one-fifth the size of McCook's command. When McCook began to fall back Wheeler counterattacked, "completely routing the enemy." Wheeler's effort was spearheaded by the 8th Texas Cavalry, whose conduct elicited effusive praise from numerous observers. "It don't hurt us though to be complimented," its commander informed his wife, "as we are *used to it.*"[45]

Pursuing McCook's men to Varnell's Station on the Western & Atlantic, Wheeler nabbed almost 100 prisoners including McCook's ranking subordinate, Col. Oscar H. La Grange. Supposedly the prisoner paid his captors the compliment of saying that had his own men fought as stoutly on this day as they had, he would have worn the brigadier's star his superior had promised him as a reward for a successful attack.[46]

About 10 AM on the ninth, as Wheeler was concentrating on blocking the Cleveland road, he received a communiqué from army headquarters directing him to guard every mountain pass below Dug Gap by which Sherman might gain access to Resaca and the Confederate rear. In his report of operations, Wheeler made no mention of having received this order or of detaching troops to Resaca of his own accord. The previous evening, however, he had sent Grigsby's brigade to the town from Dug Gap. Patrolling west of Resaca on the morning of the ninth, Grigsby unexpectedly encountered a column of Yankee infantry that proved to be the vanguard of McPherson's Army of the Tennessee, passing through Snake Creek Gap.

Grigsby labored to hold back the blue tide, but he was gradually forced backward. Eventually he joined his men to Cantey's foot soldiers behind the newly constructed works along the Oostenuala River. The defenses appeared so formidable, and Cantey and Grigsby held them so resolutely, that by sundown McPherson was withdrawing to the mouth of the gap as if cowed into retreat. By felicitous timing and good fortune, the Army of Tennessee had dodged a potentially fatal bullet. Johnston immediately dispatched portions of three divisions under Hood to secure the threatened sector. But once he learned of McPherson's withdrawal, Johnston, believing that Sherman's main effort would come farther north, halted the reinforcements at a point midway between Dalton and Resaca.[47]

While a large part of the army headed south, Wheeler spent the tenth and eleventh plying his favorite style of defensive warfare—fighting and falling back, harassing and slowing not only Elliott's and Stoneman's cavalry but also the thousands of infantrymen in their rear. Late on the eleventh, Johnston, who lacked a good idea of his enemy's positions and intentions, ordered his mounted leader to loop around the northern end of Rocky Face Ridge and assess the validity of reports, trickling in from the far flanks of the army, that blue-clad forces were continuing to move in the direction of Resaca. To comply, Wheeler piled into his nearest opponents, members of Stoneman's division, and drove them back to Rocky Face Ridge, "killing, wounding, and capturing fully 150 of the enemy," as he cheerfully proclaimed.[48]

Once Stoneman had been cleared from his path, Wheeler forged onward, expecting to encounter masses of Union infantry. He found, to his immense surprise, only two divisions in front of him. Where had the rest gone? Suddenly he was seized with the fear that he had been utterly deceived. The attacks he had been responding to over the past several days, apparently aimed at Johnston's center and right, had been feints. All but a fraction of Sherman's vast force had vacated the front, heading for Resaca via a wide envelopment to the west. The Army of Tennessee was in dire and imminent peril, and its cavalry commander appeared largely to blame.[49]

10

COUNTERMARCHING
THROUGH GEORGIA

Although Wheeler quickly passed the word that Sherman was hastening to Resaca, Johnston did not turn his army in that direction until early the next day, the thirteenth. To facilitate the disengagement, Wheeler's troopers replaced their infantry comrades in the works around Dalton, holding back the two divisions of Yankees that remained in the vicinity. By late morning, however, the pressure on his position was so strong that Wheeler was denuding the works and leading the way down the railroad to Tilton. When the body of his command departed, only Harrison's brigade was left to face, as one of its men claimed with permissible exaggeration, "an enemy over one hundred thousand strong. We disputed their right, and contended for every foot of ground they traveled."[1]

Wheeler's advance occupied Tilton in midafternoon. Joined there by an infantry brigade, its men frantically threw up breastworks. Behind these makeshift but serviceable defenses they held off the pursuing hordes for the balance of the day. They remained in position even after their left flank was partially turned, forcing Wheeler to "refuse" the rest of the line at a 90-degree angle to the east.[2]

Early on the fourteenth, by order of General Johnston, who had joined the main army in engaging McPherson's Federals atop a ridge west of Resaca, Wheeler abandoned the line he had held so firmly. At the head of John Kelly's division, he galloped south with the intention of developing Sherman's strength opposite Johnston's battle line. Predictably, he encountered heavy opposition—briefly, in fact, some of Kelly's men were shoved back inside the works they had vacated. Even so, Wheeler had gained intelligence of considerable value: the Federals facing Hood's corps, on the Confederate right, had been weakened by a shifting of troops to other parts of the field. Alerted to this fact, toward evening of the fourteenth Johnston had Hood attack the Union left. Hood's men penetrated so deeply into the enemy's midst as to end the threat to Resaca and lessen the possibility that the Army of Tennessee would be driven south of the Oostenaula in disorder and panic.[3]

Hood's assault was so successful that Johnston intended to renew it on the fifteenth. During the night, however, he learned by courier from Will Martin that Sherman was laying pontoons across the river at Lay's Ferry, beyond the Confederate left. The news prompted Johnston to end the first major confrontation of the campaign and cross the river on a pontoon bridge of his own. Many of Wheeler's troopers covered the operation from the north side, but while it was under way the War Child led Humes's division and Allen's brigade to the south bank, then turned in the direction of Calhoun. Near that village he encountered field hospitals—filled with wounded members of General Hardee's corps—under siege by some of Stoneman's cavalry. Wheeler attacked immediately, dislodging the enemy and following them closely for two miles. By the time the pursuit had ceased, he had taken forty prisoners and two stand of colors.[4]

By dawn of the sixteenth, the first enemy skirmishers were crossing the river in search of Johnston, who was passing down the railroad toward Adairsville, and Wheeler's men were lacing them with carbine- and rifle-fire. Late that morning Wheeler's men discovered and brought off intact a horseless battery of rifled guns, complete with caissons and limbers, inexplicably abandoned on the road from Calhoun. An officer of the 8th Confederate speculated that the cannons "had been sent up by rail for the use of the army and unloaded from the train by the roadside where we found them." Added to its discovery of Sherman's weakened position at Resaca, the rescue operation enabled Wheeler's command—now augmented by the return of Martin's division—to regain some of the reputation it had lost when fooled by Sherman's diversionary movement near Dalton.[5]

From behind a new line of field works, Wheeler's people sparred with the advancing Federals well into the afternoon of the seventeenth. Then, learning that his opponents were moving toward his rear, the cavalry leader withdrew to a prepared position a few miles south of Adairsville.

When leaving Calhoun, Wheeler made an enemy of an infantry officer who had been sent to support him. At Wheeler's order, young Col. James Cooper Nisbet placed his regiment, the 66th Georgia, on a hill alongside the railroad, thus filling a gap in the cavalry's picket line and protecting Wheeler's trains as they evacuated the area. When the rest of Wheeler's command vacated the position later in the day, he neglected to recall Nisbet's foot soldiers. The 66th Georgia held its position until nearly surrounded, when it was forced to fight its way out. In escaping near-encirclement, the regiment lost only one man—no thanks to Wheeler.

When Nisbet caught up with the diminutive cavalryman later in the day on the road to Adairsville, Wheeler told him that "I have another place in the line here for you." The colonel angrily replied that his men would assist Wheeler no longer unless they were supplied with horses aboard which they could flee if they had to, just as the cavalry did. When Wheeler refused the barbed request and ordered Nisbet to cooperate, the colonel told his second-in-command to resume the march until the 66th rejoined its brigade. Wheeler threatened to bring charges against the infantryman, whereupon Nisbet exploded, "You can prefer your charges and be damned! I will prefer counter charges against you for neglecting to send me an order to fall back when you withdrew." A chastened Wheeler made no reply and Nisbet marched on. Years later Nisbet recalled that "I was a hotheaded young fellow in those days. . . . General Wheeler thought I was inexperienced and tried a bluff. [But] I had seen nearly three years of actual service and more heavy fighting perhaps than he had, having been on the firing line oftener."[6]

——— ——— ———

After abandoning Calhoun, Johnston prepared to make a stand near Adairsville. The area appeared to be a good defensive position, flanked as it was by steep ridges. He had the manpower to make effective use of the terrain, for his army had been augmented by the advance echelon of Polk's command, just up from Mississippi—two infantry divisions and Red Jackson's three cavalry brigades. The addition of the Army of Mississippi gave Johnston a third corps and command of more than 60,000 soldiers. Even now, however, the army leader decided he was no match for Sherman unless he could fight on terrain even more conducive to defense than Adairsville offered. On the evening of the seventeenth he ordered a retreat toward Kingston, Cassville, and the Etowah River. Near Cassville the terrain was not only rugged but accessed by widely divergent roads that should spread Sherman's columns far apart. There Johnston might stage an effective ambush that would enable him to defeat his opponent in detail. His latest withdrawal, which began early on June 18, was covered by Wheeler's horsemen on the direct road to Cassville as well as on three adjacent roads. Farther north, Jackson's division screened that part of the army retreating in the direction of Kingston.[7]

At this point in the campaign, the command arrangement in the cavalry became a bit unwieldy. Because he had come to Johnston from another army, under normal circumstances Jackson operated independently of Wheeler's authority; only when their forces were grouped for joint operations would Wheeler command the whole. The arrangement allowed temporary transfers from one command to the other; on the present occasion, for example, Allen's brigade had been sent not only to support Jackson but to report to him.

Allen's detaching left Wheeler with Humes's division, now two brigades strong; Iverson's brigade of Martin's division; and Dibrell's and Hannon's brigades of Kelly's division (Hannon having recently been transferred from Humes's command). The single missing component was John T. Morgan's brigade, which appears to have been operating in the rear, perhaps because its leader had been charged with being drunk while on duty on May 14 and relieved of his command. (Subsequently, Wirt Allen, whose services Wheeler valued highly, would replace Morgan. When he did, Allen's old brigade would be assigned to Col.

Robert H. Anderson of the 5th Georgia.) Another recent change in the mounted ranks had begun with the arrival at Wheeler's headquarters of John Stuart "Cerro Gordo" Williams, whose nickname recalled a Mexican War engagement in which he had distinguished himself. Wheeler had assigned the newcomer, a native of Kentucky, to command Grigsby's brigade of Humes's division.[8]

Upon reaching Cassville on the nineteenth, Johnston informed his soldiers via published orders that their retreating days were over: "You will now turn and march to meet the advancing columns." But the devastating counterstroke that Johnston envisioned never materialized. The day began in a promising fashion, with Wheeler's cavalry and two horse artillery pieces assisting Hardee's corps in checking the advance of Thomas and McPherson toward the Confederate right and center via the road from Kingston. His preliminary movements having been successful, Johnston waited expectantly for Schofield's army to enter the fray farther to the left via the Adairsville road. He had deployed Hood's troops so as to take Schofield by surprise with an attack on his flank and rear. But at the critical hour Hood—whose carefully nurtured reputation was that of an aggressive fighter and inveterate risk-taker—withheld his blow when the rear of his own command was threatened by the unexpected appearance of a Union force of unknown size and uncertain composition. A frustrated Johnston promptly aborted the offensive. After falling back and regrouping, he decided to put his deferred plan into execution the next day. But Polk and Hood, who had begun to fear their positions were vulnerable to an enfilading fire from Sherman's artillery, talked him out of it and into another retreat, this one across the Etowah toward the mountain pass at Allatoona.[9]

Wheeler, of course, covered yet another withdrawal, one reminiscent of Braxton Bragg's retreat from Kentucky and abandonment of Tennessee. By 5 PM Johnston's army was digging in on the south side of the Etowah. The enemy, however, was slow to pursue, permitting the Confederates to remain in bivouac for some days, a respite sorely needed and greatly appreciated. For Wheeler's horsemen, however, the rest break was painfully brief. Late on the twenty-third, at Johnston's order, they recrossed the river and made for the rear of Sherman's army, located in the vicinity of Cassville. Wheeler would claim the mission was a reconnaissance, but Johnston would insist he instructed his cavalry leader to "avail himself of all opportunities to inflict harm upon the enemy, by breaking the railroad, and capturing or destroying trains and detachments."[10]

Accompanied by Kelly's and Humes's divisions, Wheeler moved northeastward around the enemy flank. En route, he learned that at Cass Station on the railroad an unknown quantity of enemy supplies had been stored. Envisioning another taking of spoils, he turned Kelly's division in that direction. Humes's men would follow after they wrecked a vital stretch of the railroad, preventing its use by Sherman.

Reaching the depot, Wheeler was cheered by the sight of an immense column of commissary and quartermaster's wagons—the first such prize to fall into his hands since his excursion into the Sequatchie Valley. After attacking and scattering their guards, he put Kelly's men to work overhauling the vehicles. Their contents set the captors to salivating. "The men had been fasting for some time," one recalled, "and were in fine condition to enjoy a feast. Canned fruits, vegetables and meats were found in profusion. It was regular 'hog-killing time' with the boys."[11]

Kelly ordered the captured wagons into motion, but they had barely cleared Cass Station when a roving band of Stoneman's cavalry reached the scene and attacked. The Yankees recaptured some of the spoils and made casualties of a few of Kelly's men. Just when things began to look bleak for the raiders, Humes's troopers reached the scene and plunged into the fray. As one Southern historian has written, "the ground was chewed up so often and so thoroughly by the heavy military traffic that the dust was eight inches deep and as fine as talcum powder. When collision was made at full charge the dust boiled up so thick that a horse couldn't be distinguished at arms length. The Confederates got off one volley from their pistols, then both sides mingled in the dust cloud stumbling and colliding on horseback with no way of knowing who was rubbing elbows and knees—friend or foe."[12]

The confused encounter ended with Stoneman in retreat and Wheeler bringing off more than 100 wagons along with almost as many prisoners. Some of the POWs made their escape, however, during a terrific thunderstorm that overtook the raiders before they could rejoin their army in its new position on the road to Dallas. The downpour—which marked the onset of seventeen days of rain—could not deter the troopers from feasting on the spoils they had seized in the enemy's rear. "Happily oblivious of past cares and trials," one Alabamian wrote, "we ate and drank to the fill thinking little of the morrow which however soon came on, freighted with new and greater privations."[13]

—— —— —— ——

Having relinquished his hold on Allatoona Pass—a position so formidable Sherman had refused to attack it—Johnston had moved to New Hope Church, twenty-six miles northwest of Atlanta. Sherman pursued, pushing across the Etowah and advancing in the direction of Powder Springs, below Dallas, in another attempt to pass the Confederate left flank. Like those that had preceded it, the effort failed signally. Reaching New Hope Church on the rainy morning of the twenty-fifth, Sherman found the Army of Tennessee ready to do battle, Johnston having detected the movement through the vigilance of the scouts Wheeler had left behind when heading for Cassville. Sherman, mistakenly believing he was facing only a portion of Johnston's army, threw Hooker's corps at the Confederate right and met a decisive repulse at the hands of A. P. Stewart's division of Hood's corps. The Federals would forever remember the scene of this terrible drubbing as the "Hell Hole."[14]

Wheeler's raiders rejoined the main army on the twenty-sixth. After sending the captured wagons to the army's quartermasters—a gesture that brought him a note of thanks from Johnston—Wheeler spent the next day guarding with 1,000 of his troopers Pat Cleburne's heavily entrenched division on the far Confederate right, focal point of another misguided attack by Sherman in the driving rain. During the fighting that broke out near Pickett's Mill—erroneously believed by Sherman to be the weakest, most exposed portion of his enemy's line—O. O. Howard's corps met a repulse as complete, and nearly as bloody, as Hooker had experienced two days earlier. Once again Sherman fell back to regroup and devise a new route to his ultimate destination, the Gate City of the South.[15]

The sweeping success of May 27 was not solely the work of Cleburne's infantry. The horse soldiers on his flank, fighting from inside the rifle pits they had carved out of the rocky soil along Pumpkinvine Creek, had given a spirited account of themselves throughout the day. By holding their ground under heavy and unremitting opposition, Wheeler's dismounted troopers had helped parry a thrust that, had it struck home, would have forced Johnston to abandon New Hope Church in haste and probably also in disorder.

By this point in the campaign, Wheeler's men had acquired a reputation for tactical versatility rivaled only by Phil Sheridan's cavalry of the Army of the Potomac. In the aftermath of Pickett's Mill the colonel of Terry's Texas Rangers observed that he and his comrades "have been digging ditches, building breastworks and lying in them for several weeks and the boys are already first-rate infantry." They had also proved themselves proficient in the more traditional roles of cavalry—raiding, scouting, reconnoitering. Even the enemy leader acknowledged the effectiveness of Wheeler's command in handling its myriad missions. In a May 22 letter to his wife, Sherman feared that his own horsemen were overmatched: "Our greatest danger is from cavalry, in which arm of service the enemy is superior to us in . . . quantity and quality, cutting our wagons or railroads." This was high praise indeed, especially considering its source.[16]

––––––

By the close of May, Wheeler's command had lost 73 men killed and nearly 350 wounded over the previous three weeks. The numbers were high for cavalry, which under normal circumstances saw limited front-line duty against foot troops, whose long-range arms accounted for the majority of battle casualties. The statistics testified to the frequency with which Wheeler's troopers had been committed to battle both on the offensive and on the defensive and served as an indicator of the intensity and duration of the action they had seen.[17]

Wheeler was proud of his troopers' record in close-quarters combat, but his preference had always been for those traditional roles and missions—especially protecting the head, flanks, and rear of the army on the march (more often, on the retreat), and conducting long-distance missions far from the main body. He had not always been successful at raiding, but he enjoyed the game, especially when his objective was a slow-moving supply train. Even during the present campaign, characterized as it had been by close and protracted contact with enemy forces of all arms, he had sought any opportunity to strike inside enemy lines. Not all of his efforts in this vein had been appropriately timed. On May 9, although locked in a running fight with McCook's Federals, he had answered Johnston's request for a scouting mission with a proposal to make a complete circuit of Sherman's army—a plan his superior quite properly rejected as too time-consuming.[18]

By late May, with nearly a month's experience in intense opposition to Sherman's invasion, Wheeler was envisioning a new opportunity to mount an operation in the Yankee rear. It had occurred to him as well as to many of his subordinates that the best way to disrupt Sherman's relentless advance on Atlanta was to strike decisively at the apparently vulnerable communications line that linked his armies to their supply hub in Middle Tennessee. Sudden, extensive damage to this elongated lifeline might cause Sherman's invasion to grind to a halt, just as Grant's advance on Vicksburg had halted when Earl Van Dorn attacked his supply base at Holly Springs.

The potential advantages of such a raid had not escaped Joe Johnston, who would soon come under pressure from Georgia political officials including Governor Joseph E. Brown to commit Wheeler's horsemen against Sherman's communications, an operation that if successful might spare their state from destruction and terror. Johnston, however, firmly believed he needed every cavalryman at his disposal to protect his flanks and front and provide it with timely intelligence. He could not spare even a small detachment to target the railroads in the enemy's rear. Instead, beginning in late May, he repeatedly urged Richmond to assign that task to Bedford Forrest, who not only had a record of consistent success at raiding but, in his present location in northern Mississippi, was spared the heavy opposition that Wheeler faced.

Unlike Johnston and Georgia's officials, Jefferson Davis had to think in terms of protecting the entire Confederate nation, not merely a single state. He could not bring himself to denude Mississippi of mounted defenders to administer what might prove to be a temporary check to Sherman's invasion. Even the short-term detaching of Forrest might have disastrous consequences—not only the overrunning of the Magnolia State, but perhaps a Yankee thrust into Alabama, whose farms, foundries, and access to the Gulf of Mexico were critical to the survival of the beleaguered Confederacy.[19]

The irresolvable clash of military and political interests meant that Forrest would not stray far from his base of operations near Tupelo. To ensure this, Sherman, at Grant's behest, would soon launch a series of expeditions into Forrest's bailiwick intended not only to immobilize him but to destroy his command. Each offensive would fall short of its mark and some—such as the one that

Forrest met and repulsed at Brice's Cross Roads, near Guntown, on June 10—would end in dramatic failure. Even so, they would keep him and his raiders occupied and off guard for much of the summer. Not until early autumn would Forrest be in a position to undertake the operations Sherman feared, and by then it would be too late to accomplish anything of lasting value. Forrest's raids would cause the invaders of Georgia headaches and hunger pangs, but they would not deter Sherman from attaining the objectives assigned to him at the outset of the campaign.[20]

The realities of the situation notwithstanding, throughout the spring and well into the summer, Wheeler petitioned the Richmond authorities, especially Bragg, to persuade Johnston to attack Sherman's railroads. "If my command or only a portion of it could be detached," he claimed, "I could promise good results. I could prevent my men from going into towns for plunder and could devote all my time to hard work on the line of Rail Road. I am certain I could materially change the aspect of the campaign."[21]

Wheeler's reference to pillaging pointed up a disciplinary problem that had long plagued his command and that appeared to worsen at every leg of the army's morale-sapping retreat through northern Georgia. In his postwar memoirs, Wheeler would claim that the image of his command as "an irresponsible horde of prowlers and pillagers, who roamed over the country committing outrages of all kinds upon the citizens" was overdrawn and inaccurate. In private, however, he admitted that some of his men were "miscreants who, under the protection of their country's uniform . . . committed wanton depredations upon the rights and property of citizens."[22]

Neither during nor after the conflict would Wheeler acknowledge the magnitude of the problem confronting him. By the end of May 1864, it had begun to threaten not only his command's effectiveness but also its good name. That threat would continue to grow until it reached alarming proportions during the latter half of the year and the early part of 1865.

——— ——— ———

For almost three weeks after Pickett's Mill, Wheeler's men spent the greater part of each day ensconced in rifle pits and behind breastworks, fighting dismounted in the manner of the infantrymen they had supported so closely on so many occasions. Both sides were nearly exhausted after their recent, almost incessant rounds of bloodletting, as well as partially immobilized by the continuing rains. For a time at least, they appeared willing to carry on the fight at long range. Observers began to detect the emergence of a pattern—the shift from a war of brisk maneuver to one of static defense from behind fortifications.

The new mode of warfare continued to produce bloodshed and hardship, but it also provided succor to troops who could be relieved from the front lines to seek rest in relatively safe sectors in the rear. On the last day of May an officer in Jackson's division, which guarded the army's left flank while Wheeler watched the right, cheerfully reported to his wife that "we are at rest. . . . all quiet along the lines—our horses unsaddled and also resting—an unusual thing for them." He added, unnecessarily, "We can appreciate it, I assure you." Wheeler used the respite not only to oversee the strengthening of his position by shovel and axe, but also to pen a lengthy report of his command's operations over the past three weeks. Not surprisingly, the document—rich in operational detail but replete with inaccuracies, evasions, and hyperbole—played up the cavalry's successes, downplayed its setbacks, and ignored its growing problems.[23]

On May 28 Johnston appeared willing to violate the status quo. Hopeful that a switch to the offensive would catch his opponent off guard, he positioned Hood's corps for a major attack on the Federal left. Once again, however, Hood, concerned about parallel shifts by units opposite him, failed to attack at the prescribed hour. His policy of judicious use of the counterattack again frustrated, on June 4 Johnston evacuated his position along Pumpkinvine Creek and marched his troops through the rain and mud to a point ten miles southeast of New Hope Church. Here his engineers laid out a line ten miles long, covering Lost and Pine Mountains. (Atop the latter eminence General Polk would be killed when struck by an artillery shell during a June 14 reconnaissance in company with Johnston.)[24]

The new position, which straddled the railroad, was so wide and deep that to defend it properly the army had to be stretched exceedingly thin. At first no infantry was available to man the sector east of the W & A, and it was held almost exclusively by dismounted cavalrymen, an undesirable situation that Johnston finally rectified by borrowing from Hood's corps. Before the transfer was completed, however, Wheeler's cavalry came under heavy attack. On June 9, Brig. Gen. Kenner Garrard's mounted division of the Army of the Cumberland, backed by two brigades of infantry, left its base at Ackworth, on the railroad, about eight miles north of the Confederate right, and drove in Wheeler's pickets. Continuing south, Garrard dislodged Martin's dismounted troopers from a succession of field-works. The seemingly inexorable push was finally halted near the rail depot of Big Shanty by dismounted troopers holding stronger defenses. Wheeler claimed that the Federals made two attempts to surmount the works. "Repulsed by a terrible fusillade" from Wheeler's main body, they grudgingly retired.[25]

To this point Joe Johnston had retained the trust and admiration of most of the army. As one of Red Jackson's officers put it in a June 9 letter, "I have as much confidence in him [as ever], and that confidence is well grounded because based upon his skill as a strategist." Yet that sentiment was sorely tested by the army leader's preference for retreating. After dark on June 19, he withdrew his troops from their most recent position and drew back to a more compact line anchored by natural cover. From here Johnston believed he could successfully strike his enemy or, even better, entice him to attack uphill against heavy works.

The most visible feature of the terrain on which the army settled was Kennesaw Mountain, a steeply sloped, boulder-strewn ridge two miles above Marietta.[26]

On June 20, Sherman ordered Garrard's cavalry to cross rain-swollen Noonday Creek and reconnoiter toward the Confederate right, which Wheeler's horsemen continued to cover. When the Federals had advanced about two miles beyond the creek, the Kentuckians of Cerro Gordo Williams, superbly supported by Anderson's brigade (Anderson would win promotion to brigadier general this day), slammed into the left flank of Minty's brigade. Caught unprepared, the hard-pressed Federals retreated in haste and disorder to the creek, where they were squeezed into a horseshoe-shaped pocket.

There followed some of the most spirited close-up combat ever experienced by the cavalries of the western theater. The strong showing of Wheeler's troopers gave evidence that his command, despite its mounted infantry image, was still a force when fighting in the saddle. Federals previously held on the north side of the creek crossed under fire and briefly repulsed Williams and Anderson—only to be taken in flank by large detachments of Martin's division, supported by Dibrell's Tennesseans. The accurate salvos of a battery that had accompanied Garrard and the firepower of Wilder's Lightning Brigade broke up this second offensive. Undeterred, Wheeler launched a third assault that drove back most of his opponents. When night came on, Wheeler, having accomplished his mission of protecting the Confederate right—albeit at the cost of several dozen casualties (roughly the same number as his men had inflicted on Garrard)—fell back to the army's main line. So ended what Joe Johnston would describe as "the most considerable cavalry affair of the campaign."[27]

———————

In the wake of the dramatic fight along Noonday Creek, the involvement of Wheeler's command in the June 27 battle of Kennesaw Mountain, which involved large portions of Johnston's army and took a grievous toll on Thomas's and McPherson's, must have appeared anticlimactic. Weary of attempting to outflank his enemy and prevented from doing so in any case by the bottomless roads, Sherman had lost patience with indirect assaults. This day, just as his opponent had hoped, he elected to attack uphill against the right and center of Johnston's heavily entrenched line.

The ill-considered offensive, conducted in 100-degree heat, wrested some works from the corps of Maj. Gen. William W. Loring, Polk's interim successor. As the attackers continued up the steep, rocky slope, however, a wall of musketry and cannon-fire fell on them with crushing force. During the lopsided struggle, which cost Sherman 3,000 casualties as against one-third as many for Johnston, Wheeler's men, fighting mostly afoot, provided effective but inconspicuous support to Brig. Gen. Winfield Scott Featherston's division, which bore the brunt of the attacks against Loring.[28]

Chastened by the results of his rashness and enabled to move more freely by the temporary cessation of the rain, Sherman returned to the strategy of flanking his adversary out of his prepared positions. Soon he was again threatening Johnston's line of supply, forcing the Confederate leader to fall back to the north bank of the Chattahoochee River, the last natural barrier between Sherman and Atlanta. Virtually by rote, Wheeler's men covered the right flank of their retreating comrades, Jackson's troopers the left.

This latest retrograde had a pronounced effect on the morale of Johnston's troops, many of whom had begun to question his Fabian tactics. The officer who had declared complete confidence in his army leader short weeks earlier now reported himself "in good spirits—though not so sanguine as I have been." He was not even certain that Johnston would make an effort to defend Atlanta.

Many other soldiers shared this man's concern, as did the authorities in Richmond. By the first week in July, even as they read Hood's and Wheeler's continuing denunciations of their superior's policies, Davis and other officials were asking Johnston for an unambiguous statement of his intentions. The stubborn Johnston refused to comply; to emissaries of the government he gave contradictory and evasive answers. Although he would claim that he had a plan to attack Sherman short of Atlanta, numerous critics—contemporaries of Johnston's and latter-day historians—would contend that he had no strategy to defend the city, nor perhaps had any intention of doing so. Johnston's secretiveness ratcheted up the tension in official Richmond, prompting Davis to warn him of the disaster that would befall the Confederacy should Georgia's metropolis be handed over to the enemy.[29]

The tension increased dramatically when Sherman's opponent failed to prevent him from crossing the Chattahoochee. On July 5 Johnston sent Wheeler's and Jackson's horsemen, reinforced by infantry, to observe and, if necessary, block the fords above and below the several railroad and foot bridges northwest of the city. But because most of the cavalry was dispatched to the downstream crossings, Wheeler was hard-pressed to guard the almost thirty-mile stretch of water that extended upstream beyond the Confederate right flank.

At one of these upper fords, near the mouth of Soap Creek, elements of Schofield's army fought their way across the river on the eighth. The next day, left with no alternative, Johnston began to cross his army to the south bank. His new plan was to make a stand along Peachtree Creek, in Atlanta's northern suburbs. This move cost Johnston—who over the previous three weeks had vowed to fight Sherman before reaching the Etowah River, then north of the Oostenaula, then along the Chattahoochee—the last vestiges of Jeff Davis's confidence.[30]

The axe fell two days after Braxton Bragg, whom Davis had dispatched to Georgia on a critical fact-finding mission, arrived in Atlanta. After interviewing Johnston, Hood, and other commanders, Davis's military advisor could not determine that the army leader "has any more plan for the future than he has had in the past." Late on the seventeenth, after Johnston failed to reply to an eleventh-hour request from Davis for details of his defensive strategy, he was relieved from command and Hood was appointed to succeed him.[31]

When the news spread through the army, now falling back to Peachtree Creek, it produced an almost palpable gloom and, in some quarters, a foreboding of disaster. One of Wheeler's troopers found his comrades "speechless, shaking their heads in answer to questions, as much as to say that a great mistake had been made, [and] predicting the most direful results." According to a member of Jackson's division, "it was the universal conviction of the army that Joseph E. Johnston was one of our greatest commanders . . . and that his removal was equal to the loss of one half of the army." For the same reason, Johnston's opponent, who had been frustrated by the man's deft maneuvering and hit-and-run tactics, responded cheerfully to the news of his relief. As Sherman wrote after the war, "at this critical moment the Confederate Government rendered us most valuable service. . . . I confess I was pleased at this change."[32]

The army seemed even more fearful of Hood's succession than of Johnston's departure. The one-legged general's reputation as an aggressive fighter (his willingness to abandon Cassville and New Hope Church notwithstanding) was troubling to soldiers who considered him rash and reckless with the lives of his men. Hood also lacked the good opinion of some of his inherited subordinates, including Generals Hardee and Stewart, the latter being Polk's permanent successor.

Joseph Wheeler, of course, expected to get along with the new commander; he would give the man the chance to prove himself less a gambler than a staunch fighter. In time, however, he would come to view Hood, a prewar cavalry officer, as lacking an understanding of how large bodies of horsemen could best be employed. More than once Wheeler would disobey the orders he received from his superior, believing them inappropriate to the situation or unnecessarily restrictive. On some occasions, his judgment would trump Hood's—at other times, it would not.

When Hood took the reins of command, Wheeler was opposing the advance of Sherman's legions toward Peachtree Creek. On July 18 Garrard's division—the cavalry directly opposite Wheeler's position—began a three-day raid east of Atlanta toward Covington and Stone Mountain. Its absence appeared to leave vulnerable the left flank of McPherson's army as it moved against the Peachtree Creek line. Early that day, Hardee's infantry and Wheeler's troopers, sharing space behind works thrown up on the north side of the stream, teamed in an effort to slow the Federals. By noon they had been forced to the south bank, but Wheeler's troopers had destroyed several bridges in retreating, for a time stranding the enemy on the north side. Hood was thus granted the time he needed to formulate a response to the Union advance. On the afternoon of the twentieth he launched a general offensive intended to drive every component of Sherman's army group across the creek.[33]

During that day's fighting, Wheeler's men supported the Rebel right—the corps formerly commanded by Hood and now temporarily led by Maj. Gen. Frank Cheatham, plus a large body of Georgia militiamen, which manned a line of works and rifle pits along the Decatur road. This day Wheeler had under his command only two divisions—Martin's (led by General Iverson, Martin having fallen ill) and Kelly's. Humes's men had been switched temporarily to the army's left flank. Their vacated position was held by a somewhat ragtag brigade of Alabamians and Mississippians on loan from Red Jackson and led by Brig. Gen. Samuel W. Ferguson. With this revamped force of 3,500 carbineers, Wheeler tried to parry a counterstroke made by McPherson's 25,000 Federals, apparently intent on turning Hood's right by crossing the tracks of the Georgia Railroad.[34]

Ferguson's presence weakened Wheeler's position. When McPherson advanced on the brigade, it suddenly gave way, its men running to the rear with no apparent intention of stopping. Wheeler hastened after them and by dint of strenuous effort reestablished Ferguson's line, which Hood reinforced with Cleburne's infantry, hurriedly shifted from the scene of action farther west. The Confederate right remained intact through the rest of the day.

Despite the satisfactory outcome, Hood's sortie had been a flat failure, thanks to delays in launching the initial attack, a lack of cooperation among the maneuver units, and the untimely move of Cleburne's division, which had deprived Hardee and Stewart, who made the main effort, of critical power. Hood's first offensive had cost his army almost 2,500 casualties, almost 1,000 more than Sherman suffered. It was a most inauspicious debut, one that appeared to validate Hood's reputation for risking too much and gaining too little.[35]

On the twenty-first, McPherson renewed his effort to break through on the right. At sunrise the Army of the Tennessee seized Bald Hill, a fortified rise two and a half miles east of Atlanta. During the offensive, Wheeler's troopers, who closely supported the foot soldiers defending Bald Hill, were attacked by two of McPherson's brigades. The Yankees concentrated against the works occupied by Ferguson's troopers, whose morale remained shaken by the previous day's difficulties. Again the brigade "gave way in some confusion," exposing the right flank to envelopment and Allen's brigade, on Ferguson's left, to possible destruction. Wheeler, initially fearing the worst, was relieved and heartened when the Alabamians, assisted by Iverson's brigade (today commanded by Colonel Crews of the 2nd Georgia) fought "brilliantly" to hold their ground. Although eventually forced from their position along with a large segment of Cleburne's command, Wheeler's brigades not only retired in good order but then suddenly halted, turned about, and hurled themselves at the enemy, screaming the Rebel Yell. Wide-eyed Federals squeezed off a single volley before fleeing, enabling their assailants to retake their lost position.[36]

The disgraceful performance of Ferguson's men notwithstanding, the fighting along Peachtree Creek gave Wheeler reason to feel good about the mettle of his combat-weary command. He was further cheered by its showing on the twenty-second when Hood launched his second sortie, his object to recapture ground lost two days before. This time he intended to use Stewart's corps to hold the greater part of Sherman's command north and northeast of Atlanta while Cheatham struck McPherson's army in front and Hardee attacked it in rear by means of a lengthy and tricky turning movement.

This promising but risky plan was defeated, like its predecessor, by a dismaying lack of coordination among the assault forces. On the morning of the twenty-second, after an all-night march around McPherson's eastern flank, Hardee struck what he thought was the Union rear. But in the dark he had failed to march far enough to clear the troops opposite him and hit McPherson's far left instead. Hardee's spirited attack inflicted numerous casualties—McPherson himself was shot dead at the height of the action—and it nearly drove a wedge between two Union corps. In the end, however, the timely arrival of reserves won the day for the Union. Attacks elsewhere along Sherman's line were also repulsed, ending the fight.[37]

Although Wheeler did not take part in the larger offensive, he more or less accomplished the mission Hardee had assigned him—to pass McPherson's flank, seize the supply depot at Decatur, and appropriate or destroy whatever he found there. The continuing absence of Wheeler's natural enemy, Garrard's division, enabled him to reach Decatur without opposition. Upon his arrival, however, he was greeted most unexpectedly by a division-size force of foot soldiers, well entrenched and protected by artillery. As if unconcerned, Wheeler unsaddled his lead regiments and moved to the attack—as per his orders—precisely at 1 PM. The Yankees countered by advancing two regiments of skirmishers. These were quickly dispersed by a combination of mounted and dismounted assaults from many angles.

As his troopers went forward, Wheeler rode from one column to another, exerting as much personal control over the fighting as humanly possible. He had done this on other fields, and the enemy remembered the tactic. After the war, one of Sherman's officers referred to Wheeler as "the only commander on either side who could be seen at five different places in a fight at the same time."[38]

The present effort was not an immediate success. "At first," Wheeler observed, "the galling fire made the most exposed portion of my line waver, but, quickly rallying, the onset was renewed, and with a triumphant shout the entire line of works was carried." He reported taking 200 prisoners, a rifled cannon, wagons, caissons, a large quantity of camp equipage, and hospital stores. Before he could pursue the escapees or inflict greater damage to the depot, however, General Hardee recalled him. Wheeler gathered up his men and led them to the position occupied by their infantry comrades. But they arrived too late—Hardee's corps had fought itself out, its offensive had been contained, and another battle had ended in something less than Confederate victory.[39]

———— ————

One pursuit may have been aborted, but a second was imminent. Reoccupying his former position on Hood's far right, Wheeler spent the next five days skirmishing with the now largely quiescent enemy. Early on the twenty-seventh, as Hood moved part of the army to the left in preparation for a third attempt at loosening Sherman's hold on Atlanta's northern environs, the cavalry replaced Hardee's people in the trenches along the Decatur road. In doing so Wheeler discovered that the army formerly commanded by James McPherson had broken contact and had fallen back north of the Georgia Railroad.

Soon after forwarding this information to army headquarters, Wheeler made an even more startling discovery: a large force of Garrard's division, which had rejoined Sherman, was passing around Hood's right flank toward Flat Rock on South River, fifteen miles southeast of Decatur. Its direction suggested a raid on the railroads—the Macon & Western and the Atlanta & West Point—by which the Army of Tennessee received rations and supplies from points south. Deducing that Garrard was heading for the depot at Jonesboro, eighteen miles below the city, Wheeler spent most of the day seeking authority to follow him. Reluctant to strip his flank, Hood did not extend permission until early evening, and even then he ordered Wheeler to remain with the army unless he believed it imperative to pursue with the greater part of his command.[40]

Wheeler was not about to miss an opportunity to strike at an enemy rampaging through his sector; so he made sure that all but a small portion of his corps was needed in pursuit. He spent hours removing the men from the trenches they had only recently occupied and reuniting them with their horses in the rear. As soon as his first brigade, Allen's, had been mounted, he sent it galloping toward Flat Rock. He remained behind long enough to put other units in motion. Finally, about nine o'clock, accompanied by staff and escort, he set out to overtake the Alabama brigade.

By hard riding, at daylight on the twenty-eighth he reached Flat Rock, where he found Allen exchanging shots with the Yankees, who had been brought to bay only minutes before. When the other, later-starting units reached him—they comprised elements of all three of his divisions including Humes's command, recently returned from supporting Red Jackson—Wheeler used them to surround Garrard's position along the banks of South River. To escape encirclement, Garrard's men suddenly abandoned the breastworks they had constructed and fled north toward Latimer's Corners. There they halted and dug in as if awaiting reinforcements.[41]

Wheeler pursued, brought Garrard's men to bay once more, and was about to launch one of his patented multidirectional assaults when a courier-borne message from Hood's chief of staff, Brig. Gen. Francis A. Shoup, informed him that Garrard's was not the only force running free in the Confederate rear. A second mounted column had been sighted moving around the army's right flank east of Garrard's route. Initially believed to be intent on destroying the Georgia Railroad, it had struck the line at Covington but had continued south in the direction of Macon. Wheeler would later learn that this body, led by George Stoneman, had been ordered to join Garrard in wrecking the Macon & Western. After completing this task, it was to reach and attack the notorious Andersonville prison camp, fifty miles below Macon. Stoneman, however, had decided to forgo the prosaic work of damaging rails and ties for the more dramatic task of liberating Union POWs. Unknown to Garrard, he was heading directly for Andersonville.[42]

Thus Wheeler had two targets—one in motion, the other temporarily stationary. Before he could decide how many troops to allot to each, he received another urgent communiqué from Shoup. Scouts had informed army headquarters that a third mounted force was galloping south of Atlanta, this one around the Confederate left. Commanded by General McCook, it appeared to be larger than either Garrard's or Stoneman's force. In fact it was larger, consisting as it did not only of McCook's own command but also of elements of the division of Brig. Gen. Lovell Rousseau. McCook's route suggested that he desired to cut the Atlanta & West Point or the Macon & Western—perhaps both. It seemed doubtful that Red Jackson, whose bailiwick McCook had invaded, could counter so large a force on his own.[43]

Wheeler was at a loss to counter all of these threats, especially considering that even after the last brigade to leave Atlanta joined him—Anderson's brigade was still straining to reach Latimer's Corners—he would be outnumbered by each of the enemy columns. Yet, should he fail to repulse any of the three, the most important city in the Deep South—perhaps in all the Confederacy—might be lost. He refused to imagine what that might lead to.

11

THE PURSUER AND
THE PURSUED

*A*s Wheeler pondered his seemingly impossible situation, most of the units that had gotten a late start from Atlanta reached his side. Conferring hastily with their commanders, he made a judicious allocation of resources based on the relative gravity of the threat posed by each enemy column. Because Garrard had backtracked from the Georgia Railroad and appeared confused and uncertain, Wheeler left only Dibrell's brigade, under General Kelly's command, to contend with him. Since Red Jackson was reported already in pursuit of McCook's force, Wheeler supported him with two brigades, Ashby's and Anderson's. As McCook appeared in a position to wreak the greatest amount of havoc on Hood's communications, Wheeler chose to lead this force in person, accompanied by the able and dependable General Humes. The balance of the command—Allen's, Crews's, and Williams's brigades, the latter temporarily led by Col. William C. P. Breckinridge of the 9th Kentucky, and the entire force by General Iverson— would head for Macon in hopes of overhauling Stoneman. All told, 10,000 Yankee raiders would be pursued by about 3,800 Confederates.[1]

Early in the afternoon of the twenty-ninth, the pursuit forces went their separate ways. The men of each entered upon the chase "like schoolboys in a game of base ball," as one put it. By hard riding, Wheeler, Humes, and Ashby reached Jonesboro by 4 PM, only to learn that McCook had hit the rail line six miles farther south at Lovejoy's Station. The 500-man column galloped in that direction, reaching Lovejoy's at dark. They found the enemy gone, at least a mile and a half of track torn up, and huge quantities of stores ablaze. It was later discovered that McCook had done comparable damage to the Atlanta & West Point while overtaking and destroying 1,000 supply wagons and nabbing 300 prisoners—all while parrying the thrusts of Frank Armstrong's brigade of Jackson's division. After McCook left Lovejoy's, Armstrong had managed to interpose between the enemy's main body and rear guard. Although eventually shoved aside, the brigadier continued to harass the Yankees, whose pace had begun to slow with the drag exerted by their prisoners and booty and by hours of nearly constant travel.[2]

At Lovejoy's Wheeler was met by a courier carrying a proposal by Jackson that the latter, with Brig. Gen. Lawrence S. Ross's brigade from Jackson's own division and Harrison's brigade, on loan from Wheeler, attempt to get ahead of the raiders while Wheeler—who had yet to be joined by Anderson—pressed McCook from the rear. Wheeler readily agreed and resumed the pursuit at a breakneck pace. Refusing to be stymied by a missing bridge over the Flint River, destroyed by McCook, he smoothly changed course in the direction of Fayetteville. Nine miles west of that town he caught up with the shank of the enemy column but found the Yankees slipping across Whitewater Creek on a bridge that was already afire.

Hopeful still of overtaking his prey, Wheeler put Ashby's engineers to work rebuilding the bridge, a task completed within an hour. "After crossing the bridge," he wrote, "I pressed on rapidly, in the extreme darkness encountering barricades every few hundred yards, the first intimation of the enemy being a volley from their small-arms." After delivering this welcome, the rear guard broke contact and raced to catch up with the main body. Wheeler followed, but more warily: he had built a career on fighting and falling back, but the enemy knew how to play the game as well.[3]

At daylight on the thirtieth Wheeler received a dispatch from Jackson informing him that McCook's weary riders had gone into bivouac at Shakerag, about seven miles west of Fayetteville. Despite the fatigue that his own men and their mounts were displaying, the pursuit leader picked up the pace, surging west "at full speed," as one of his men noted, "under a broiling sun." Within minutes Ashby's advance was overrunning a portion of the enemy's bivouac. Caught curiously unprepared, the sleep-befogged Yankees were driven from their temporary camp with a loss of forty dead, an unknown number wounded, and 200 prisoners. The chase was speedily resumed, Wheeler driving his quarry from point to point, drawing blood at every bend in the winding country road.[4]

Two miles from the Atlanta & West Point depot of Newnan, Wheeler made contact with a detachment of Jackson's command—the main body of Ross's brigade, plus a single regiment from Harrison's. Enabled by the added manpower to split his force, Wheeler sent Ashby's men galloping through Newnan to gain time on their quarry. The Yankees had bypassed the place by a detour to the south after finding it occupied by the dismounted cavalry of Brig. Gen. Philip D. Roddey (which had failed to support Wheeler on his Sequatchie Valley Raid), then en route to join Hood's army at Atlanta. With Ross's brigade, Wheeler kept close on McCook's heels.

Three miles beyond Newnan the hounds again caught up with the foxes. Although many of his men were dead tired, McCook had halted to give battle in the midst of a dense wood. Despite suspecting he would be outnumbered, perhaps ten-to-one, Wheeler dismounted most of Ross's men and led them toward the trees, while Ashby, who had gotten ahead of McCook, struck from the opposite direction. "I met with strong resistance at first," Wheeler reported, "but in a few moments the enemy gave way, when with a shout and a gallant charge, the entire line was thrown into confusion and commenced a disorderly retreat."[5]

But a number of Yankees refused to give way; some even counterattacked in a frantic effort to break free of encirclement. Shouting and shooting, an Iowa regiment swept around Ross's flank and took his dismounted line in rear, capturing many of his mounts. Without missing a beat, Wheeler had the brigade turn about, then led it in an assault that recovered almost every horse and captured many horse thieves. Only minutes later, McCook's men made another desperate attempt at a breakout. The blow they delivered staggered some of Ross's men and sent them reeling from the field. Again, however, Wheeler rallied the brigade, counterattacked, and threw the assailants back in turn.[6]

By now, the fighting had consumed almost two hours and both sides were nearing exhaustion. Wheeler was beginning to wonder if he would have to disengage when Anderson's brigade made its long-awaited appearance, followed shortly by General Roddey and 600 of his unhorsed troopers, who offered Wheeler their assistance. The reinforcements permitted Wheeler to advance in enough strength to shatter McCook's left flank and send those who had held it into headlong retreat. Coordinating his movements with Ashby's, Wheeler pursued and soon caught in a pincers two regiments of Yankees, "which surrendered in a body with all their artillery, wagons, and ambulances. The entire column was thrown into disorder, and a number of prisoners, arms, horses, and 2 stand of colors were captured in the pursuit that ensued."[7]

Those raiders with the best horses fled west over hill and dale. Wheeler chased them for four miles before he became convinced that no large organized force remained in his front. He had his buglers sound recall while permitting the comparatively fresh horsemen of Anderson to continue the chase in the direction of New River. Red Jackson, with the balance of his command, had also joined Wheeler, but with the fight all but ended he was detailed to escort Wheeler's 300 captives back to the scene of the most recent fighting, where he was to gather up arms and equipment abandoned by the skedaddlers.[8]

On his way to Covington on the Georgia Railroad, where he would place his sleep-deprived troopers into camp, Wheeler learned something of the fate of the other raiding parties. One had conceded failure and the other was about to meet disaster on a par with McCook, whose command had been so shot up, scattered, and demoralized that upon its return to Thomas's army it would have to be almost completely reconstituted. Garrard's men had marked time at Latimer's Corners until finally convinced that Stoneman was not coming to join them, whereupon, having accomplished nothing, they returned to their army via a wide circuit through Livonia and Stone Mountain. Meanwhile,

Stoneman's 2,200-man force was heading southeastward at a pace that kept it well ahead of Iverson and his pursuers. By the morning of June 30 it had advanced to within seven miles of Macon; there it was turned back by what one of Wheeler's men called "a few hundred old men and boys of [Governor] Joe Brown's militia," bolstered by some regular artillery units. Concerned by reports that doubled or tripled the 1,300 pursuers in his rear, Stoneman gave up all thought of reaching Andersonville and all hope of reaping the honors that would come to the prison's liberator. At first intent on circling east of Macon toward the state capital at Milledgeville, the Union leader withdrew the way he had come—a decision that delivered him into the hands of his enemy.[9]

On the morning of August 3, Stoneman's pursuers—today led by Colonel Crews, General Iverson having fallen sick—caught up to him near Sunshine Church, eight miles north of the village of Clinton. Crews's men built breastworks from behind which they repulsed repeated attacks by Stoneman's now-demoralized troopers. Over the next several hours, Crews extended his lines, until by early afternoon he had surrounded the bluecoats. Seeing no way out of the trap, Stoneman surrendered himself and the officers and men of one of his three brigades. Large portions of the other two, however, broke free of encirclement. Through a combination of wild riding and good luck both made it back to their lines outside Atlanta, but only after set upon and throttled by various pursuers.[10]

Surveying in later days these highly satisfying results—many of which had come about through his own energy and persistence—Wheeler would observe that "thus ended in most ignominious defeat and destruction the most stupendous cavalry operation of the war." Designed to win for him and his men the highest possible honors, this statement was a gross exaggeration even by Wheeler's standards. Yet his reasons for making it were both understandable and forgivable, as the laurels he sought were richly deserved. For the War Child and his worn-out but exuberant troopers, the devastating pursuit just ended would rank as the finest hour of their long, colorful, and eventful career.[11]

———   ———   ———   ———

Hood greeted his cavalry with words of praise and expressions of gratitude. Word of Wheeler's successful defense of the army's communications—the track the Yankees had torn up would be repaired in a matter of days—spread quickly through the ranks, raising hopes that Atlanta might yet be saved. The effect on morale was especially timely coming as it did on the heels of yet another failure by the main army. This had taken place on July 28 at Ezra Church, where a series of ill-considered attacks by Hood's permanent successor in corps command, S. D. Lee, had been repulsed with heavy loss. The outcome persuaded Hood, who had lost more than 12,000 men in three failed sorties over the past week, to go on the defensive and prepare to shield the city against assault. Little time remained to do so, however, for by the second week in August

Sherman's cannons were shelling downtown Atlanta as if in preparation for a major offensive.[12]

Hood's cavalry failed to gain the rest it needed. A few days after Wheeler had issued an address congratulating his troopers on "the energy and determined gallantry" they had recently displayed, the army leader ordered them on a raid of their own. Thanks to Wheeler's exertions, Sherman's cavalry was thought to be in such disarray that it could not counter a blow to its army's supply lines. Having exhausted his ability to assume the offensive, Hood was amenable to a long-range strike at the enemy's rear—something Joe Johnston had refused to order despite the urging of Georgia's officials. At the time Hood had faulted his superior for refusing to take a necessary risk—now he was in a position to validate his criticism.[13]

Hood was pinning his hopes on the theory that extended disruption of Sherman's logistical pipeline would force him to retreat or face starvation; either would enable the Army of Tennessee to survive another campaign. Therefore Hood directed Wheeler to destroy as much railroad track as he encountered between Atlanta and Chattanooga. He was then to cross the Tennessee River and fall upon the railroads that connected Sherman's armies with their rear supply base at Nashville. To ensure that the job was done thoroughly, when Wheeler turned for home he was to leave behind a 1,200-man demolition force (how the size of this force was arrived at remains a mystery). Finally, on his way back he was to break other railroads south of Chattanooga.

Here was a formidable set of objectives for men and horses still showing the effects of a lengthy pursuit of a fast-moving enemy. When they learned of the assignment, Wheeler's troopers agreed that they had not fully recovered from their recent exertions, yet many were enthusiastic about turning the tables on the enemy. As an enlisted man in the 10th Confederate Cavalry put it, "I hope we will be able to pay them back for all the raids they have made on us. If we can bee successful in getting in there rear and cut off there supplies it may bee the means of making them fall back from Atlanta."[14]

Although painfully aware of his command's debility, Wheeler expected to accomplish his ordained mission fully and in good season. Perhaps his recent, against-all-odds victory had given him an overly optimistic opinion of his troopers' capabilities. Perhaps, too, his successful pursuit of McCook, during which his decisions, not his superior's, had won the day made him believe he had earned the right to substitute his own strategy for Hood's, revising his timetable and itinerary based on his own instincts. The result would be a series of miscalculations the long-range effects of which would deeply tarnish the reputation he had so artfully burnished only days ago.[15]

On the morning of the tenth, Wheeler set out from Covington accompanied by no fewer than 4,500 officers and men drawn from the divisions of Humes, Kelly, and Martin (the latter just back from sick leave) and curved around the Union left flank northeast of Atlanta. Moving at a pace calculated to stymie

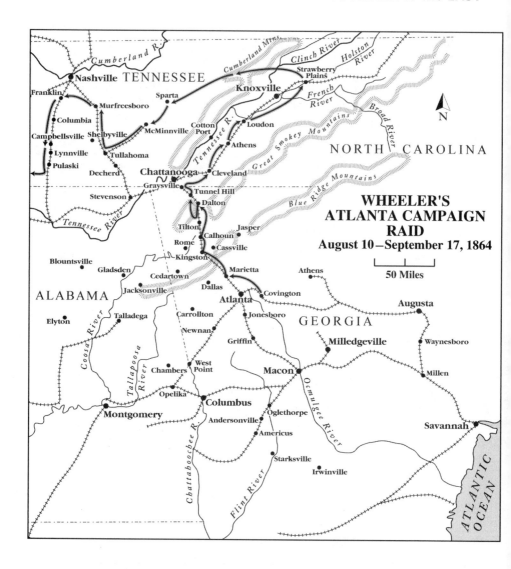

WHEELER'S
ATLANTA CAMPAIGN
RAID
August 10–September 17, 1864

50 Miles

pursuit but risky in light of his command's condition, the long column struck the railroad at Marietta, north of which the men began to dismantle the W & A. Near Cassville and Calhoun they tore up track easily enough, but intermittent rains, some of them quite heavy, prevented them from burning the ties they dislodged. Till now the raiders' expectations had been high, but at about this time they were given a glimpse of how temporary the damage they inflicted would prove to be. A Confederate regular recalled that the morning after his regiment uprooted track near Calhoun "we saw the enemy rebuilding [it] . . . faster than Wheeler's men . . . had been able to destroy it during the night."[16]

At Calhoun Wheeler made perhaps the most substantial contribution to the expedition when he corralled a cattle herd 1,700 strong. Hannon's brigade escorted the beeves all the way to Atlanta and into the hands of Hood's commissary officers. The army would eat well for weeks, but forage was in scarce supply everywhere. Upon leaving Calhoun, the raiders veered eastward into the countryside to seek hay, oats, and corn. After gathering up what little provender was available, they returned to the railroad at Dalton. At the abandoned winter camp of the Army of Tennessee troopers from Humes's and Kelly's divisions captured 200 members of the local garrison and helped themselves to the contents of a supply train parked nearby.[17]

This success was quickly followed by the first setback of the expedition. From Dalton, according to a previous arrangement, Wheeler headed south to a rendezvous with Martin's division, which he supposed was working its way north after overawing another garrison, this at Tilton. But Martin—who may have come off the sick rolls too soon—failed to appear at the rendezvous, causing Wheeler to fear "he had met with disaster or been prevented from joining me by some force of the enemy interposing between him and myself, all of which gave me much uneasiness." Later that day, however, he learned that Martin, without notifying him, had camped his troopers seven miles to the south, where they were hidden from view by a bend in the Coosa River.[18]

Wheeler was at first mystified, then enraged, by his subordinate's behavior. He reacted swiftly and sharply; convinced that "I could not expect any help from him, I as soon as possible placed him in arrest and sent him back to the army." He replaced Martin with General Iverson. His career ruined by this dereliction—the rationale for which was never disclosed—Martin would finish the war in command of a minor military district in northern Mississippi.[19]

After destroying the W & A on either side of Tilton along with a stockpile of stores, Wheeler was suddenly attacked by a roving force of railroad defenders under one of his opponents at Perryville, now—Maj. Gen. James B. Steedman. On this occasion, Wheeler claimed, the assailants lost more heavily than their victims. Unwilling to be diverted from his assigned mission, Wheeler held off Steedman with a part of his force and with the rest resumed the march. As he rode on, his advance guard wrecked additional sections of the railroad near its commander's old bailiwick, Tunnel Hill. Rumors made their way to Atlanta that Wheeler had destroyed the tunnel with explosives, but this was not the case. Why he neglected this second opportunity to deny Sherman's supply trains access to the tunnel defies analysis.

Wheeler lingered in the vicinity of Tunnel Hill until the twentieth, when he spurred north to attend to his remaining objectives. He left 200 picked men behind with orders "to strike the railroad every night at some five or six designated points." He later claimed that in his absence these wrecking crews succeeded in "running off" twenty trains and interrupting rail communication between Dalton and Atlanta for no less than two weeks.[20]

By now the raiders' mounts were suffering greatly from overwork and hunger, conditions that would only worsen given Wheeler's timetable and the picked-over condition of the country. Again Wheeler departed the railroad in search of more verdant regions, these north of the Tennessee. He had intended to cross the river near familiar old Cotton Port, but the recent rains had increased the water level by ten feet or more, making it impossible to ford anywhere below Kingston. Forging on, he sought to neutralize potential pursuers by making a show of force for the benefit of the Union outpost at Cleveland. With the Yankees there held in check, he crossed the Hiawassee, a Tennessee tributary, to Athens, capturing a large supply depot. At this point, for the first time on the expedition, many of Wheeler's men left the line of march to loot not only the homes of suspected Yankee sympathizers but also those of "good Southern people."[21]

Continuing upriver toward Loudon over some of the same ground he had crossed last December under Longstreet, the raiding leader searched for a point at which he could safely ford the Tennessee. The closer he got to Knoxville, the more frequent became the attacks on his flanks and rear delivered by regular Yankees and guerrilla bands. Parrying these jabs at the cost of a few casualties, he crossed the Little Tennessee and made haste for the next river barrier, the Holston. His frustration mounted when he discovered that stream too swollen to be forded at any point short of Knoxville.

Continuing up the riverbank despite growing opposition, he forded the French Broad River east of the Union stronghold, then, finally, the Holston. Turning west, he guided the column across the steep and rugged Cumberland Plateau, thus completing a nearly 200-mile detour from the point at which he had intended to cross the Tennessee. His orders had contemplated nothing so circuitous or so time-consuming as this unexpected deviation from his prescribed itinerary.[22]

The roundabout route was vexing enough, but Wheeler made a second miscalculation when nearing the Union outpost at Strawberry Plains, twenty-four miles northeast of Knoxville. En route to the Holston, Cerro Gordo Williams had sought permission to attack the post with 1,500 men from his own brigade and that of General Anderson (since its commander's wounding at Newnan, the latter command had been led by Brig. Gen. Felix H. Robertson, the twenty-five-year-old former chief of Wheeler's artillery). Williams also asked for four of the eight horse artillery pieces that had accompanied the expedition. After capturing the garrison and destroying an adjacent railroad bridge, the brigadier promised to make all haste to rejoin Wheeler on the march.

At first Wheeler refused the request, then reconsidered and gave his consent. This proved to be an unwise move, for his subordinate kept none of his promises. He found he could not capture Strawberry Plains, which was more heavily manned than he had supposed; he failed to wreck the bridge; and he proved unable to cross the rain-swollen Holston in time to overtake the main body, thus depriving Wheeler of one-third of his command for the balance of the expedition.[23]

To his credit, when finally able to ford, Williams rode hard and long to overtake his superior but was cut off from him by energetic pursuers. Near Murfreesboro, an exhausted Williams turned around and headed back to East Tennessee. From there he would move into southwestern Virginia to engage Yankee forces under Bvt. Maj. Gen. Stephen G. Burbridge.

In early October Wheeler, still fuming over Williams's dereliction, had him arrested and charged with conduct prejudicial of good order and military discipline. The case was referred to Adj. Gen. Cooper, who found Wheeler's charges "harsh and unusual" and set the accused free. Returning to his most recent post in the mountains of Virginia, Williams, much like William Martin, would complete his Confederate service far from the fields on which the war would be lost or won.[24]

After crossing into East Tennessee, Wheeler, with what remained of his command, revisited sites familiar from his Sequatchie expedition. His men seized and destroyed two trains of cars on the railroad between Chattanooga and Nashville, forced the evacuation of several outposts, and sacked supply depots including (once again) McMinnville. At this point, however, Wheeler's difficulties began to increase exponentially. The series of blockhouses that Sherman's chief engineer had established along the railroads below Nashville frustrated Wheeler's attempts to destroy strategic sections of track. As a member of the 5th Tennessee commented, whenever the Confederates showed themselves, "the Yanks . . . [would] run into their little forts which proved after trial to be bomb proof." Not only did these compact garrisons take a toll, so did bodies of infantry and cavalry that picked up the raiders' trail and bayed at their heels. On September 2, one of these forces of mixed arms, under General Rousseau (whose division had provided added strength to McCook's recent raid south of Atlanta), thudded into the head and flanks of the column. Although repulsed, Rousseau rallied the mounted portion of his command and continued to flay the raiders whenever opportunity arose.[25]

While passing through Middle Tennessee, Wheeler detached one of his smaller components—a regiment and a half under Colonel Dibrell—and sent it to attack a nearby outpost. Dibrell was then to proceed to his home region of Sparta, there to spend a few days recruiting his command to something closer to brigade strength, after which he was to rejoin Wheeler on the homeward leg of the raid. Dibrell captured the outpost, but his recruiting efforts came to an abrupt halt when Yankee cavalry attacked his rendezvous, cut him off from Wheeler, and prevented him from rejoining the expedition. Instead, the colonel wandered off to East Tennessee, where he located and fell in with General Williams. Neither command would be of additional use to Joe Wheeler and his rapidly shrinking force.[26]

Feeling increasingly vulnerable, Wheeler pushed on toward Nashville. After striking the Nashville & Chattanooga near Tullahoma, he turned north as if to attack the Tennessee capital. Some of his subordinates urged him do so, arguing that the city was guarded so lightly that it might fall at first contact. Although these officers did not come out and say so, the implication was that such a coup would rehabilitate Wheeler's faltering image as a raider. Their commander, who feared that to halt and plan an attack would prove fatal to his plans, refused to take the risk. He is reported to have told those who proposed the attack, "My troops were not given to me to make a name, but to do what I could for my country." Eight miles short of Nashville he veered west and headed for Franklin.[27]

The left turn proved unfortunate. Two and a half miles south of Franklin Wheeler stumbled into a battle with garrison troops in his front and Rousseau's cavalry toward the rear. One of the losses that resulted could not readily be overcome: the highly gifted General Kelly, mortally wounded while trying to obey Wheeler's order to capture a hill crowned by Yankee sharpshooters. A favorite of everyone who served with or under him, he would be lamented throughout the Army of Tennessee.[28]

Abruptly descending the railroad that connected Nashville to the Tennessee River, Wheeler staggered toward the Alabama border. With each passing mile, his column lost horses to exhaustion or starvation. And at virtually every village he entered or passed—Campbellsville, Lynnville, Pulaski—he was assaulted in front or rear, or both. He was left with little time to strike one of his primary objectives, the Alabama & Tennessee Railroad.

By the time he reached the border north of Stevenson, Alabama, his command was in tatters—so much so that most of his pursuers, believing they had emasculated the Confederate column, did not bother to finish the chase. On September 17 Wheeler halted—as he had eleven months before—near the town of Tuscumbia, to give exhausted men and animals a rest and to wait in vain for Williams and Dibrell to rejoin him.[29]

As soon as possible, he informed General Hood by telegraph of the results of his mission. On this occasion and later in his official report of the operation he engaged in what historians have called "an orgy of statistical self-congratulation." He admitted that the raid—the longest of his military career both in duration and distance covered—had been extended by high water, detours, jaded mounts, and dogged pursuers. Even so, he claimed to have inflicted on Sherman's supply lines damage that would take weeks to repair, severely hampering the armies opposing Hood. By way of additional accomplishments he cited the taking of 600 prisoners, 1,000 horses and mules, 200 supply wagons, and the cattle herd at Calhoun. These estimates appear reasonably accurate, but his claim to have brought back 800 absentees and to have added 2,000 recruits to the Confederate forces in the West bears no relation to reality.[30]

Although initially impressed by these supposed achievements, Hood came to dismiss them as so much window dressing. When he saw the condition of Wheeler's returning raiders he realized that whatever damage they had inflicted on Sherman did not compensate for the near-crippling losses they had suffered on their circuitous excursion through enemy country. In fact—as some of Wheeler's men had come to appreciate—the Yankees were able to replace in days and even hours those sections of track the raiders had ripped up, while making good the contents of the supply depots they had torched and looted. Damage this limited and temporary would never force Sherman to fall back from Atlanta for fear his soldiers would be driven to the brink of starvation.

In fact, the Federals would go forward to final victory. One result of Wheeler's overly extended journey was that it deprived his army of the services of half of its mounted arm at a critical juncture. For lack of mounted reconnaissance, Hood failed to detect another Union effort against the railroads south of Atlanta. From August 18 to 21 Brig. Gen. H. Judson Kilpatrick, a West Point classmate of Wheeler's who commanded a division of cavalry in the Army of the Cumberland, demolished rails and ties near Fairburn on the Atlanta & West Point and torched supplies at Jonesboro on the Macon & Western.[31]

The damage was repaired quickly enough, but a week later Hood's enemy totally disappeared from his front. Bereft of cavalry, Hood could only wonder if the siege of Atlanta had been lifted. He was slow to discover the truth—that Sherman had moved his armies around the west side of the city to strike the railroad at Jonesboro. The defeat of Hood's army at that place on the thirty-first made the Army of Tennessee's hold on Atlanta too tenuous. The following day Hood evacuated the city, and on September 2 the Federals took possession of it.[32]

The loss of the Gate City changed the course of the conflict. By late summer of 1864 the war to save the Union had met setbacks in every theater of operations. In the East, the campaign to take Richmond from below had fizzled out when Maj. Gen. Ben Butler's army allowed itself to be bottled up inside a peninsula between the James and Appomattox Rivers. Meanwhile, Maj. Gen. Franz Sigel's thrust through the Shenandoah Valley had been decisively repulsed at New Market. In Louisiana, Maj. Gen. N. P. Banks's invasion of Texas, which had gotten under way two months before the other operations unleashed by Grant, had met defeat through poor generalship, spirited opposition, a lack of support from cooperating forces, and low water on the Red River.[33]

Then, too, Grant's and Meade's campaign to entrap Lee's army inside the Richmond defenses, although productive of heavy casualties in the Virginia Wilderness (May 5–6), around Spotsylvania (May 7–20), on the North Anna River (May 23–27), and at Cold Harbor (June 1–12), had bogged down when the Army of the Potomac ran out of maneuvering room north of the enemy capital. Grant had been forced to move against Petersburg, the lightly guarded transportation center twenty-two miles to the south. Initial efforts to take the city, whose loss might have shut Lee's army off from supplies and reinforcements, were blunted by a small force of defenders under P. G. T. Beauregard. Finally Lee came down from Cold Harbor to secure the place and force Grant to besiege it. That operation, in effect since mid-June, had not been noticeably productive, although by slowly extending his lines around Petersburg Grant forced his opponent to stretch his defenses extremely thin.[34]

The disheartening failure to capture Petersburg and the glacial pace of the siege had combined with Sherman's prolonged campaign to darken the re-election prospects of Abraham Lincoln, who was supported by Republicans and prowar Democrats. Mainstream Democrats were now in the process of nominating George B. McClellan to oppose him on a platform that declared the war a costly failure and held out the promise of a negotiated peace. Aware that the people of the North had been borne down by a series of demoralizing reverses in the field, Lincoln had gone on record predicting his own defeat.[35]

The fall of Atlanta changed the prevailing mood almost overnight. Suddenly it became clear to anyone with a modicum of perceptivity that the Union armies had the resources, the know-how, and the will to win. Ultimate triumph no longer appeared a mirage on the arid horizon of the conflict. Added to small but dramatic victories that Gen. Phil Sheridan would gain in the Shenandoah Valley between mid-September and mid-October, the fall of the manufacturing and transportation center of the Deep South would ensure Lincoln's reelection, thus permitting the war to be won or lost on the field of battle, not at the polls.[36]

Atlanta's fall had a more immediate effect on the hearts and minds of Wheeler's cavalry. When they learned what had transpired in their absence from Hood, they saw that their recent exertions counted for nothing. As one trooper admitted in a letter home, "we whiped the yankes where ever we came in contact with them [and] we have tore up a great deal of railroad on our rout[e], but I am afraid it hant done much good [now] that we here that the yankeys have got atlanta." Outside observers were more blunt in their assessments of Wheeler's achievements. A Georgia militiaman put a heaping dose of sarcasm into his summary of the raid: "Wheeler made a mistake and went down into the Ga. [rail]road, captured Convers or burnt it up, recaptured Stone Mountain and burnt up the mountain, captured 6 head of beef cattle, killing one blind yearling, and returned to Hood and told him that the Yanks were ruined forever."[37]

————

Wheeler remained in northwest Alabama for almost two weeks, resting and refurbishing his command and hoping to restore the morale it had lost on the tortuous route from Covington to Tuscumbia. Only if he could see major improvements in his men's physical and psychological condition would he feel comfortable rejoining the army, which after abandoning Atlanta had moved to Palmetto Station, twenty-five miles to the southwest.

From the start, however, Wheeler seemed doomed to disappointment. On the twentieth, he was visited at Tuscumbia by Bedford Forrest and 4,500 of his men, then beginning a raid against Sherman's communications in northern Alabama and Middle Tennessee, an operation somehow designed to provide relief to Hood's fugitive army. Forrest was shocked and appalled at the condition of Wheeler's command, the effective strength of which he placed at between 500 and 1,000, in contrast to Wheeler's stated figure of 2,000. Many of the returnees, including more than a few of their officers, were openly bitter and dispirited; some appeared on the verge of mutiny.

Forrest found their commander just as depressed, if not more so. As he informed his immediate superior, Lt. Gen. Richard Taylor, commander of the Department of Alabama, Mississippi, and East Louisiana, Wheeler's command "is demoralized to such an extent that he expresses himself as disheartened, and that, having lost influence with the troops, and being unable to secure the aid and co-operation of his officers, he believes it to the interest of the service that he should be relieved from command."[38]

If Wheeler felt this way, he put on a brave face when writing that same day to General Hood. Apparently hoping for an opportunity to continue serving apart from the army, he suggested that what remained of his corps be added to Forrest's for the upcoming expedition, which was expected to consume ten or twelve days. The joint venture would not only take his men's mind off their woes, it would, by returning them to Tennessee, enable Wheeler to augment them through recruiting. If the request were denied, however, Wheeler would carry out, as soon as possible, the order to return to Georgia that General Shoup had sent him on August 31, had repeated one week later, and had repeated again on September 15.[39]

Wheeler's mood lightened, at least to a degree, when on the evening of the twenty-second he moved his corps east to Courtland. Over the next two days he visited the home of Colonel Jones and spent time in the company of his daughter. It is not known whether he pledged his troth to Mrs. Sherrod, but it appears that the emotions that had been stirring in him since their first meeting prompted some expression of his feelings toward the vivacious young widow. At any rate, Wheeler's spirits improved to the point that he gave up any thought of resigning his appointment.[40]

By the twenty-fourth he considered his command fit to march, if not to fight. Via Danville, Athens, and Stevenson, he returned it to northern Georgia. En route, in fulfillment of Hood's desire that he again damage the railroad south of Chattanooga, he did so at Dalton, where his men ripped up track for the second time in a month, as well as at Rome, where he terrorized the local garrison. But his days of operating far afield of Hood were almost over. At Dalton he received imperative orders to report at army headquarters, now located north of the Chattahoochee. He did so at Cedartown, about forty miles west of Marietta, on October 8. There he resumed his former mission of covering the army's flanks, rear, and supply trains as Hood continued his slow northward march.[41]

The movement away from Sherman initially confused Wheeler, but Hood assured the cavalryman he knew what he was doing. About one month earlier, Hood had begun to formulate a strategy to draw Sherman away from Atlanta while foiling his apparent intent to invade south Alabama. If Hood moved north, Sherman would have to follow. If Sherman attacked, he would have to do so on terrain favorable to the defenders. If Sherman turned south, instead, Hood could strike again at his rear and supply lines.

Two weeks before Wheeler rejoined Hood, President Davis had arrived from Richmond to confer with the army leader and help refine his new strategy. The two men decided that the army should attack the W & A in order to increase the likelihood that Sherman would pursue and give battle with a reduced force (he would have left a part of his army in Atlanta to handle occupation duty). Hood promised Davis that if Sherman ignored the threat to his rear, spurned a confrontation, and began to march eastward from Atlanta, as Davis feared, the Army of Tennessee would follow him all the way to the coast.[42]

Even before Wheeler rejoined him, however, Hood had changed his mind without informing Davis, who by then had departed for Augusta, Georgia, there to offer the peripatetic P. G. T. Beauregard command of a territorial division encompassing the armies of both Hood and Richard Taylor. Now the commander of the Army of Tennessee intended to march his 40,000 troops, including Wheeler's horsemen, to the Tennessee River. He proposed as much to Beauregard when he conferred for the first time with his new departmental commander. But within days of this conference, Hood recast his plans yet again. He vowed to cross the Tennessee, push north to Nashville, invade Kentucky, and reach the Ohio River within striking distance of Cincinnati. In essence, Hood was reviving the grandiose scheme that Bragg had failed to pull off two years ago.

When Beauregard learned of his subordinate's change of plans, he tried to persuade him to adhere to the strategy Davis had blessed. But Hood was so adamant about abandoning Georgia for Middle Tennessee that in the end Beauregard consented to it and so informed Richmond. The only concession he wrung from Hood was that Wheeler's cavalry was to be left in Georgia to operate against Sherman's supply lines and watch his movements. Rather than Wheeler, Hood could call not only on Red Jackson but on Forrest, who, after his current expedition, would attach himself to the Army of Tennessee for the first time in thirteen months.[43]

The directive for Wheeler to follow Sherman reached the cavalry leader on October 22. It may have produced mixed emotions. Wheeler would have enjoyed accompanying Hood on his exciting journey, but he prized the opportunity to continue operating apart from the main army. Wheeler's orders enjoined him to keep the railroad between Atlanta and Dalton "constantly cut, and should the enemy evacuate Atlanta, you must destroy all the road north of the Chattahoochee, and constantly concentrate toward your left." It was assumed that Wheeler would remain indefinitely beyond Hood's reach; nevertheless, he should be "prepared at any time to join the main body of the army." Until that time came, he would operate under the remote command of General Hardee, who now headed the Department of South Carolina, Georgia, and Florida.[44]

When these instructions reached him, Wheeler was near La Fayette, where Hood had sent him in response to reports that a Union column had been dispatched to pursue him up the line of the W & A. In fact, by this point Sherman had given up his half-heated pursuit of Hood, who, as Sherman wrote, "had an army capable of endangering at all times my communications, but unable to meet me in open fight. To follow him would simply amount to being decoyed away from Georgia, with little prospect of overtaking and overwhelming him." To counter the communications threat, Sherman had dispatched George Thomas to organize troops soon to be sent to him at Nashville. Those forces would include two corps and two separate divisions of infantry, plus all but one of Sherman's cavalry divisions. With his remaining resources—the XIV, XV, XVII, and XX Corps of infantry and Judson Kilpatrick's horsemen—Sherman would destroy the military capacity of Atlanta and the railroad to Chattanooga, then forge east through the heart of Georgia toward a variety of possible objectives on the Atlantic or Gulf coasts including, Savannah, Charleston, and Pensacola.[45]

On October 26 Wheeler performed his last service in support of Hood's departing army when he tangled at Goshen with elements of Sherman's advance. When the skirmishing ceased, the Yankees turned their back on the Army of Tennessee and returned to Atlanta. Once Wheeler understood what Sherman was up to, he knew he must follow him, not with any hope of stopping him—which, without substantial infantry support, would be impossible—but to impede his progress by striking his rear, flanks, and cavalry screen and by cutting off raiding forces and foraging parties, of which Wheeler suspected there would be many. To accomplish all this he would have to make do with a few thousand horsemen, the remnants of the divisions of Wirt Allen (consisting of the brigades of Anderson, Crews, and Hagan), Humes (Ashby's, Harrison's, and Dibrell's brigades, the latter having finally returned from East Tennessee), and Iverson (the brigades of Ferguson, Hannon, and Brig. Gen. Joseph H. Lewis, the last-named recently converted from infantry). Wheeler's horsemen would be supported by four batteries of light artillery.[46]

Almost all of these units had been decimated by the rigors of battle and raiding. The effects of attrition could be seen in the command's lack of proper rank. As John Du Bose observed, "At this point in the conflict, Brigadier-generals commanded divisions, colonels commanded brigades, captains commanded regiments, greatly to the regret and annoyance of General Wheeler, and against his persistent but vain protests to the War Department." Of greater import, the men these officers commanded were poorly clothed, armed, and mounted. Discipline was notably weak—in some cases, nonexistent—largely due to the loss of so many officers. With the exception of Lewis's men, most of whom were delighted to be riding to war after three years of pounding hard and muddy roads, the rank-and-file remained demoralized by the arduous, seemingly profitless service they had performed in north Georgia and Middle Tennessee.[47]

Wheeler began his almost single-handed opposition to Sherman on November 13 by returning to one of his old haunts, Jonesboro on the railroad to Macon. Three days later Sherman led his troops out of Atlanta, which had been reduced to a fire-gutted shell, and started eastward toward Milledgeville. His opponents were mystified and alarmed, however, when the right wing of his 60,000-man command—O. O. Howard's Army of the Tennessee (the XV and XVII Corps), preceded by Kilpatrick's troopers—turned in the direction of Macon. Unaware the movement was a feint, Wheeler galloped to the apparently threatened city at the head of his depleted corps. En route—at Griffin on the seventeenth, and Forsyth on the eighteenth and nineteenth—he tangled for the first time with Kilpatrick, whom he would come to revile as a scoundrel and marauder. ("Kill-Cavalry," who had been quoted as hoping to turn Georgia into a land of "chimneys without houses," had issued sulphur matches to his troopers, with which they were to burn everything in their path.)[48]

On the nineteenth, Wheeler sent Crews's brigade to Macon, where it joined Georgia militia under Maj. Gen. Howell Cobb, Iverson's cavalry division (which had been occupying the area for some time), and General Hardee. The latter, the ranking officer on the scene, advanced Crews and his men on the Milledgeville road, where they had a rather violent confrontation with Kilpatrick before falling back to Walnut Creek.[49]

That same day Wheeler, with the main body of his command, skirmished with XV Corps infantry in the direction Griswoldville on the Augusta & Savannah Railroad. The following evening, the twentieth, Wheeler rode hard to the depot village but arrived too late to prevent its occupation by Kilpatrick, whose troopers burned the town and mangled the railroad. Wheeler enjoyed a measure of revenge when, on the "smokey & foggy" morning of the twenty-first, he drove one of Kilpatrick's two brigades from its bivouac by feinting in front and attacking in rear with Terry's Texas Rangers. "The maneuver was made in gallant style," recalled an admiring Georgian, "and the Federal[s] completely routed, leaving twenty five dead upon the field." By riding hard, Wheeler attacked the same force the next day, adding sixty Yankees to his burgeoning haul of POWs.[50]

By the twenty-fourth it had become evident that Sherman was marching toward Milledgeville, bypassing Macon. Wheeler hastened his command eastward across the bridgeless Oconee River, which his men and their horses were forced to swim. He then occupied Sandersville, twenty-eight miles east of the Georgia capital. Despite his exertions, the head start the Yankees had gotten enabled them to reunite their divergent wings at Milledgeville without opposition.

They spent four days in the town, departing on the twenty-fifth. By then they had ransacked the place, paying special attention to the public buildings, including the chambers of the legislature—where some of Sherman's officers met in session and "passed" a law rescinding Georgia's ordinance of secession—and the state library, which was despoiled of hundreds of volumes.

Wheeler's men reached the town too late to prevent any of these depredations; still their arrival drew cheers and tears from the maltreated townspeople. One woman claimed that her heart "leaped for joy" at the sight of the gray troopers, who, it was obvious, had suffered, too. "A few ragged men came riding up and bowed and brandished their pistols, the tears streamed from our eyes—strong men wept—God bless our soldiers, our poor suffering soldiers."[51]

Upon exiting Milledgeville, Sherman moved Kilpatrick's troopers from the right wing to the left and had them demonstrate toward Augusta. Sherman had no intention of going to Wheeler's home town, but Kilpatrick's feint was highly effective. Leaving Iverson with the main body to dog the infantry's heels, Wheeler pursued the cavalry and overtook it short of its presumed objective. Attacking Kilpatrick's bivouacs just after midnight, November 27–28, Wheeler roused the slumbering enemy from their bedrolls and drove them from the Augusta road into nearby woods.

Once beyond pursuit, Kilpatrick's men turned south toward Waynesborough, where, as they boasted to the local people, they intended to burn the town, wreck the railroad, and burn the trestle that carried the tracks of the Augusta & Savannah over Brier Creek. In fact, the bridge was not burned; yet by the time Wheeler reached the town many of its buildings were afire and the Yankees were prying up rails and demolishing ties. Wheeler's men quickly set about extinguishing the flames and succeeded in saving all but one building. At the front of the rest of his command the War Child swept down upon the railroad vandals, forcing them to abandon their work and flee for their lives.[52]

Wheeler kept up his pursuit through the morning of the twenty-eighth. When his enemy paused to catch its breath, he launched what Kilpatrick himself called "one of the most desperate cavalry charges I have ever witnessed." Again his troopers took to their heels, racing Wheeler's men to Buckhead Creek, which they crossed before setting fire to the bridge. While some pursuers forded the stream to keep pressure on the enemy, Wheeler put the main body to work smothering the flames. Although apparently intact, the bridge, which had been weakened by the fire, proved too fragile to support the passage of men and mounts. Refusing to be stymied, Wheeler had his men strip the wood from the walls and pews of a nearby Baptist church. Under the supervision of his engineer officer, the materials were fashioned into replacement planks that eventually made the bridge usable. The troopers crossed it as soon as the last plank had been laid.[53]

After setting the bridge on fire, Kilpatrick had directed his two brigades to fall back within supporting range of their army's foot soldiers. But before they could enjoy the protective embrace of their less mobile comrades, Wheeler struck twice more before darkness closed the fighting of the twenty-eighth. Both attacks took a substantial toll, especially in prisoners. Enraged by the wanton destruction for which the bluecoats were clearly responsible, some of their captors threatened their prisoners with death, but Wheeler, sensing that unless checked his men might commit atrocities, restrained them from retaliating against the unarmed POWs.[54]

While unaware of—or unwilling to acknowledge—its magnitude, Wheeler already had a major disciplinary problem on his hands. Since the earliest hours of the pursuit, detachments had broken ranks—either against the orders of their officers or with their connivance—to loot some of the same homes and businesses that Sherman's foot soldiers and Kilpatrick's troopers had terrorized. Unaccompanied by supply wagons or pack-mules, Wheeler's corps had been living for many days on half-rations, quarter-rations, and, on more than a few occasions, no rations at all. Forced to live off the land, they realized that if they did not take what they and their mounts needed, they faced having to beg for their daily fare, something the majority swore they would never do.

The attitude of the citizenry was a factor in the growing willingness to loot and plunder. Unlike the civilians Wheeler's men had encountered in Tennessee and Alabama, many Georgians appeared not only inhospitable but openly hostile to the graycoats' presence. Thus it became ever easy for Wheeler's men to disregard tears, pleas, and protests as they vandalized chicken coops, smokehouses, and corn cribs. Others salved their consciences by reflecting on the orders issued at the outset of the campaign: to confiscate or destroy everything the enemy might appropriate for his own sustenance. Still other men considered it their duty to take what they required to keep in the fight, arguing that, as an officer in the 8th Confederate Cavalry put it, "it was depredation or desertion and in devotion to the cause for which they had fought and bled and suffered for three years, they scorned the latter and chose the former."[55]

The inevitable result was that Sherman's pursuers acquired a reputation for marauding on a par with—even above the level of—their hated opponents. For the duration of their service in Georgia, a loud and prolonged outcry assailed the ears of state officials, prompting Governor Brown to publicly condemn "Wheeler's robbers" and call for their removal from his state. By the end of 1864, General D. H. Hill, then commanding at Augusta, was declaring that "the whole of Georgia is full of bitter complaints of Wheeler's cavalry," while General Beauregard, who was personally responsible for Wheeler's presence in Georgia, was advising that unless a more stringent disciplinarian was placed over it, the cavalry should be dismounted: "Its conduct in front of the enemy, and its depredations on private property, renders it worse than useless." Another vocal critic, a noncommissioned officer from Georgia, offered a somewhat more balanced assessment: "Wheeler's cavalry . . . have done many villaneous [sic] things and some deserve to be shot, but [their crimes] were somewhat excusable as they were ordered to destroy everything in the route of the enemy."[56]

Not every outrage perpetrated on Georgians by Confederate soldierly was the work of Wheeler's much-maligned troopers. Many historians contend that the worst depredations were committed by deserters, guerrillas, and "Joe Brown's Pets"—members of those state militia units who, armed and often leaderless, roamed almost as freely over the countryside as the mounted regulars who derided them as summer soldiers. Still, Wheeler's troopers were among the most visible malefactors, and they made a convenient target for the complaints of Georgians outraged by the prospect of being assaulted and pillaged by friend and foe alike.[57]

— — — — —

By the onset of December, chill winds were buffeting the invaders of Georgia and their pursuers as Sherman's columns—Howard's two corps on the right, the two corps of Maj. Gen. Henry W. Slocum on the left, with Kilpatrick's horsemen guarding the flanks and rear of both—neared Savannah and the Atlantic coast. Frustrated by their inability to slow, let alone halt, their enemy, Wheeler's men had begun to lash out more frequently and indiscriminately, assailing infantry as well as mounted units. On the second, for example, they squared off at Rock Spring Church, near Louisville, against both Kilpatrick's troopers and elements of Brig. Gen. Absalom Baird's division of the XIV Corps (the latter had been ordered to shove Wheeler out of Slocum's way once and for all). Perhaps realizing that he was tempting fate by fighting dismounted against both cavalry and infantry, Wheeler withdrew from one position after another as far as Waynesborough. He sallied forth the next day, however, to halt temporarily a new round of railroad demolition, although on the fifth Baird and Kilpatrick advanced on him yet again, driving in his pickets near Thomas Station.

This time Wheeler battened down behind hastily built field works that proved formidable enough to stop a mounted attack. When his troops abandoned the position for another farther to the rear, Baird and Kilpatrick, believing their enemy in retreat, advanced in force. Again Wheeler's dismounted troopers stanched the blue tide, although by late in the day the growing presence of infantry on his flanks persuaded the Confederate leader to disengage and withdraw in good order.[58]

After this confrontation, the Union infantry, apparently believing that Wheeler had been sufficiently chastised, turned their backs and resumed their eastward journey. Over the next week Wheeler followed as closely as he thought prudent, cutting off slices of Slocum's rear guard and taking dozens of prisoners. On the evening of the eighth, he ran his horse artillery to the front and shelled a XIV Corps bivouac near Ebenezer Creek. A participant in the surprise attack called its effect "beautiful to behold. . . . As shot after shot plunged into them, our men would give a long yell. The cutthroats couldn't stand it; they fled in utter rout for the narrow bridge over the creek, leaving horses, arms and the entire camp equipage behind." Wheeler not only appropriated these spoils but prevented the escape of some 2,000 fugitive slaves who had attached themselves to Sherman's left wing in the hope of being led out of bondage. These unfortunates were herded together and sent under escort to the slave pens at Macon preparatory to being returned to their masters. Charges of committing atrocities were later directed at Wheeler's men, some of whom shot down helpless slaves in cold blood. Wheeler did not condone the killings, but he was unable to rein in his more obstreperous troopers.[59]

Earlier that same day, Wheeler's men nabbed a courier carrying a dispatch that confirmed Sherman's intent to attack or besiege Savannah. Wheeler promptly spurred around the flank of Slocum's column and got ahead of it on the main road to the city. In this advantageous position he resumed his harassment, which he kept up until within ten miles of the Savannah line. At that point, "finding it impossible to do any further harm to the enemy," he crossed the body of his command over the Savannah River in transports furnished by Flag Officer W. W. Hunter of the Confederate Navy. While the main body moved inland on the South Carolina shore, Iverson's small division remained on the Georgia side to watch Sherman in case he turned toward Augusta.[60]

Once over the river Wheeler established contact with General Hardee, who had moved his headquarters into Savannah, and was directed by him to supervise "the defense of New River and adjacent landings, and . . . the duty of holding the line of communication from Huger's Landing to Hardeeville. This we succeeded in doing, although the enemy held the South Carolina side of the river with a division of infantry."[61]

Wheeler could only guess as to what Hardee intended to accomplish in a city Sherman could invest and bottle up with relative ease. Whether he elected to hold the place or to evacuate it, Hardee would inflict little harm on his opponent. Wheeler must have realized that the same held true for his own command. It had become painfully clear that the enemy could not be halted by cavalry and militia alone. Such units were incapable of preventing the marauding leader from turning in any direction he chose—south toward Pensacola or north for a rampage through the Carolinas to Petersburg. If he chose the latter course, as Wheeler suspected he would, he would join Meade in making short work of the defense forces of Virginia. With the demise of Robert E. Lee's army, the war would effectively be at an end not only on the Virginia front but everywhere else.

With the onset of winter, the days were becoming noticeably shorter. So were those of the Confederate States of America.

12

ALL THAT HUMAN EXERTION COULD ACCOMPLISH

*I*f at year's end the future looked bleak for Wheeler, his army, and his nation, the first days of 1865 would do nothing to dispel the gloom. By now Wheeler's men had learned that Hood's much-heralded invasion of Kentucky had gotten no farther than Nashville before collapsing in ruins. Having been outmaneuvered and frustrated by elements of Thomas's army at Pulaski, Columbia, and Spring Hill (November 19–28) and violently repulsed at Franklin on the thirtieth, Hood had made the egregious mistake of besieging Nashville with an army weakened by battle losses, desertion, winter weather, and the ill-timed detaching of Forrest and most of his horsemen. On December 15 Thomas's 50,000-man army, which included several well-appointed divisions of cavalry, attacked out of its fortified stronghold and over the next two days smashed and thrashed its adversary, killing perhaps 2,000 Rebels, taking 4,500 prisoners, and propelling the rest across the Tennessee River. The disorganized, demoralized survivors were in no shape to withstand another campaign, although a few thousand die-hards would make their way to North Carolina in a desperate attempt to fight on.[1]

Five days after Hood's army stumbled away from Nashville dazed and bleeding, General Hardee determined to evacuate Savannah. Since reaching the city on December 9, Sherman had extended and strengthened his lines until he had the place and its 10,000-man garrison in a vice-like grip. His position was greatly strengthened on the thirteenth, when a division of the XV Corps assaulted and captured Fort McAllister on the Ogeechee River. By this point Sherman had made contact with a Union fleet that had been blockading the Georgia coast, from which he gained enough supplies to support an all-out attack or a debilitating siege. Believing he could withstand neither, on the twenty-first, only days after refusing to surrender the city, Hardee led his 10,000 across the river into South Carolina.

Even in its weakened state, Wheeler's cavalry did an effective job of covering the withdrawal. While some troopers engaged Union pickets from across the river, others helped to clear the streets of troops and civilians who wished to evacuate, while carrying off stores that would otherwise fall into enemy hands. Members of Crews's brigade were among the last to depart, only a few steps ahead of the invaders. Early on the twenty-second Sherman's legions marched in to the music of military bands and the cheers of Unionist citizens, military prisoners, and liberated slaves.[2]

Although hundreds crossed the river to South Carolina, most of Sherman's troops remained in Savannah for the next four weeks, resting and refitting. Wheeler's scouts kept an eye on them but could not discern their intentions. For a time, Sherman himself was unsure of his next move. From his headquarters in Virginia Grant had proposed shipping Sherman's 62,000 officers and men up the coast to join Meade, but the commanding general decided to give his subordinate his choice of routes north and mode of travel. Georgia's conqueror opted for an overland march through the Carolinas, a move that would sever the supply lines that connected Petersburg and Richmond to the Confederate interior. The overland route would also enable Sherman to make the first of the seceding states pay for her role in bringing on the war.[3]

Sherman did not depart Savannah in full force till the close of January. During the interim, Wheeler and Hardee not only skirmished with the occupiers but strove to overcome the deficiencies plaguing what was still considered the cavalry of the Army of Tennessee. In early January Hardee asserted in a letter to Jefferson Davis that "Wheeler's cavalry has been reorganized under my supervision. . . . It is a well-organized and efficient body. The reports of its disorganization and demoralization are without foundation and the depredations ascribed to this command can generally be ascribed to marauders, claiming to belong to it." As far as Hardee knew, all that remained to be done was to secure the promotion of those brigade and division commanders whose rank was not on a par with their positions.[4]

Hardee's claims appear to have been based on mistaken assumptions, for the problems Wheeler's command had faced since its fiasco of a raid through Tennessee had not been dealt with effectively. The reorganization Hardee spoke of had produced a single discernable effect: the addition to Wheeler's corps of a tenth brigade, even smaller and weaker than the other nine—two understrength regiments and two battalions under Colonel M. W. Hammond. But even a wholesale revamping of its table of organization would not have improved the physical condition of the command. Hundreds of its men remained lost to it through lack of a horse. Forced to serve as foot guards to their supply train, these unfortunates were known throughout the corps as Wheeler's "wagon dogs." Another 1,100 were unarmed, having lost their weapons in battle, to mechanical failure, or to a lack of ammunition specific to the carbines they had taken from dead or captured Federals. Despite Hardee's best efforts, many horsemen—in common with their comrades in the infantry, artillery, and support units of the army—continued to suffer from a lack of adequate clothing and regular rations, while their horses were breaking down from overwork and a lack of regular forage.[5]

Nor had the sunken morale and unraveling discipline of the command been addressed. In South Carolina Wheeler's troopers added new stains to the reputation they had tarnished all the way across Georgia. The complaints lodged against them by private citizens and politicos increased in frequency and stridency, and the corps's notoriety spread to every corner of the Confederacy. From Richmond a well-educated South Carolinian serving in Lee's army responded to the anguished pleas of his family, caught in the path of both armies: "The attention of our soldiers in the Army [of Northern Virginia] is now turned, not so much to the cruel treatment visited upon our people by Sherman's forces (this was expected) as to the strange and unanticipated conduct of 'Wheeler's cavalry,' which may . . . very properly be denominated 'the robber band.' We were not prepared for this promiscuous plundering of our houses at the hands of Confederate soldiers. We would not say a single word against their action if it was authorized by our government for its safety and protection. . . . but as there is every reason to believe that they are not earnestly and energetically engaged in the service of our common country, we most decidedly enter our protest against their unwarranted and barbarous operations. If I mistake not the character of our soldiers here, this 'Wheeler's Cavalry' will yet, if possible, meet with the punishment it so richly deserves." He closed by instructing his sister that if Wheeler's men "attempt to take our horses or something else without proper authority" she should "defend it to the last," presumably even to shooting down the pillagers.[6]

Precedent for the use of deadly force against Wheeler's men was set a few weeks after this man wrote when a provost detail from a North Carolina infantry regiment was called on to overawe a detachment of troopers who, as one foot soldier claimed, "*charged* [our] commissary . . . as we rushed up and ordered them to disperse, some few of them wheeled, drew their pistols and fired upon us, but without hurting anybody. We immediately returned the fire. . . . We killed two men and one horse and wounded one other man. Then they took flight, running off at the quickest possible speed in every direction."[7]

Belatedly—perhaps at Hardee's insistence—Wheeler had begun to confront the lawless ways of so many of his men. In the waning days of 1864 (two days before issuing a proclamation lauding his "brave men" for the fighting skills they had displayed over the past several months) he published a general order that addressed "the continued and grave complaints made by citizens against this command." The order called for "the most stringent efforts . . . by all officers, to prevent the slightest depredations of any character in [the] future."[8]

The prohibitions Wheeler laid down appeared properly strict. Henceforth, no officer or enlisted man would be allowed to enter a private dwelling "under any pretense whatever, unless invited by the occupants." Division, brigade,

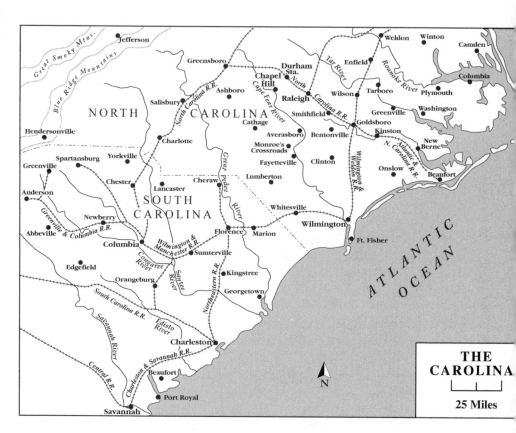

and regimental commanders would exercise the closest supervision over their troops, especially when their units were detached from the main body. Each division was to form a regiment-size unit of provost guards that, when on the march, would ride in advance of the main force and when in camp would post a guard at every house for miles around. These and other actions enumerated in the order had a dual purpose. Wheeler declared that "besides doing my duty to protect citizens and the families of your fellow soldiers, it is also my duty to protect your honor and your fair names, and I am determined at any cost to accomplish these objects."[9]

Wheeler's effort, however well intentioned, came too late to forestall official censure of the command's conduct and of his failure to rein it in. On January 2, 1865, Col. Alfred Roman of Beauregard's staff arrived at Wheeler's headquarters to inspect the corps and report on its strengths and weaknesses. Because Roman's superior had publicly condemned the command's lawlessness, Wheeler probably suspected the report would be critical of the corps's condition and perhaps also of his leadership.[10]

His concern undoubtedly increased when he learned that Roman's first stop was the Robertsville, South Carolina, camp of Ferguson's brigade. Wheeler and Ferguson had been on poor terms ever since the former criticized the latter's command for twice giving way before McPherson's army north of Atlanta. Not surprisingly, when he received the inspector, Ferguson "endeavor[ed] to point out some of the causes of the present demoralization in Wheelers Corps." On this subject the brigadier may be supposed to have waxed eloquent, for, as he admitted, he had "many grievances" against his corps commander. Some of these had only recently boiled over, causing Ferguson "to understand now, how it was that Wharton & Forrest & Armstrong & Martin could not serve under Wheeler." Ferguson was "desirous of getting out of the disorganized and undisciplined mass which is called his Corps, and which receives the curses of our people through the length and breadth of the land."[11]

Roman's inspection tour lasted almost two weeks. He departed Wheeler's command to return to departmental headquarters on January 16; six days later, he submitted his report to General Beauregard. It confirmed Wheeler's worst fears, critical as it was of almost every aspect of the command's condition. First of all, it was too small to support three divisions and ten brigades. Most of its regiments had shrunk to a quarter or less of their paper strength; some companies were composed of one, two, or three men, some regiments of as few as twenty-seven and thirty-two. Junior officers commanded at levels well above their effective rank while senior subordinates occupied lowly positions. Although he did not say so in plain words, Roman clearly believed that Wheeler rewarded favored subordinates such as Allen and Humes with high station while virtually demoting those officers, such as Ferguson, who were not his intimates.

Other criticisms had a less direct connection to Wheeler. The command's deficiency in weapons had grown to 1,447 shoulder arms and 3,747 pistols. There were no more than sixty sabers in the entire corps—not even the officers carried them. Shortages in accoutrements—waist belts, cartridge boxes, cap pouches, and the like—were widespread. Roman was charitable, however, in assessing the condition of the horses. He took no note of the many dismounted men, observing that with few exceptions the existing supply of horseflesh was in "very serviceable condition. The fact is the men seem to take better care of their horses than they do of themselves." Command hygiene was deemed to be satisfactory, although lice, cooties, and the "camp itch" were prevalent in every brigade. Clothing was "very deficient." The only thing in shorter supply was pay—the men had now gone without it for more than a year.[12]

Roman reserved his harshest commentary for the state of efficiency and discipline in the command. The appearance of both officers and men was exceedingly unmilitary, regulations were commonly neglected or ignored, and routine duties such as roll call were not attended to. In general, there was "an independent careless way about most of the officers and men which plainly indicates how little they value the details of army regulations and of tactics in general." Furthermore, training had lapsed to the degree that the majority of the men "are badly instructed, or not instructed at all."[13]

On the critical issue of discipline, Roman pulled his punches. When addressing the corps's "alleged depredations and straggling propensities, and their reported brutal interference with private property," he admitted that "much truth is hidden under some of the rumor" of bad conduct. Even so he believed, or professed to believe, that most of the complaints lodged against the command by the good citizens of Georgia were exaggerated, inaccurate, or misleading. A certain number of troopers, including some of the officers, had acted reprehensibly, besmirching the good name of the command. Still, these truants "form only a small proportion of the corps to which they belong."[14]

These conclusions notwithstanding, the inspector acknowledged the "undisciplined tone and relative inefficiency" of the corps and tried to determine its source. He considered a number of possibilities including the negligence and incompetence of "many" regimental and company commanders, the inefficiency of Wheeler's commissary, the absence of pay, and the government's policy of forcing troopers to procure their own mounts and remounts. To this list he added, quite pointedly, "the excessive leniency of the corps commander." While claiming that "no one admires General Wheeler more than I do," especially for his combativeness and courage, Roman found him "wanting in firmness. His mind and his will are not in proper relation to one another. He is too gentle, too lenient, and we know how easily leniency can degenerate into weakness. General Wheeler's men like him, but do not appear to be proud of him. They know he will always fight well, but seem to feel he cannot make them fight as well."[15]

Roman's concluding comment was no less harsh for being wrapped in faint praise: "Had I the power to act in the matter, I would relieve General Wheeler from his command, not as a rebuke, not as a punishment, for he surely deserves neither, but on higher grounds, that is, for the good of the cause, and for his own reputation." Had he thrust a bayonet into the general's chest, Roman could not have drawn more blood.[16]

———— ———— ———— ————

For reasons of his own—quite possibly because he lacked an acceptable replacement—Beauregard failed to follow his inspector's recommendations. He neither fired nor demoted Wheeler, although he did try to supersede him. Beginning the previous November, Maj. Gen. Wade Hampton had expressed a desire to relinquish command of the cavalry of Robert E. Lee's army to return to South Carolina and help defend his home state against Sherman's imminent invasion. Before the war Hampton had been regarded as one of the wealthiest men in the Deep South as well as one of its largest slaveholders. Though old for a cavalryman (forty-three at the war's start) and lacking military training, he had forged a reputation as one of the most talented and successful mounted leaders on either side. His stature and influence were such that both Lee—who in January became general-in-chief of the armies of the Confederacy—and South

Carolina Governor Andrew G. Magrath supported Hampton's desire to go home, and Jefferson Davis, with Beauregard's blessing, approved the transfer. On January 28, 1865, Hampton arrived at Charleston to assume an as-yet-undefined command in General Hardee's department.

At first the hulking, heavily bearded patrician exercised authority only over two of the units he had commanded in Virginia. One had preceded him south—Brig. Gen. Pierce M. B. Young's Georgia brigade—and the other—the South Carolina brigade of Brig. Gen. M. Calbraith Butler, Hampton's long-time subordinate and close friend—had accompanied him to Charleston. While the troop transfer was intended to strengthen the defense forces of the Carolinas, Hampton's coming was an indirect result of Richmond's growing dissatisfaction with Wheeler's leadership. Both Lee and Davis desired that the South Carolinian—whose character and demeanor demanded respect and obedience—take charge of all mounted forces in the path of Sherman's armies, including Wheeler's corps.[17]

The only sticking-point was that Wheeler was senior to Hampton as a major general. To circumvent this obstacle, on the eve of Hampton's departure Davis nominated him for higher rank. Responding to the president's sense of urgency, in less than a month the Confederate Congress confirmed Hampton's promotion to lieutenant general. The appointment enabled Hampton to head a command consisting of Wheeler's corps and a separate body comprising the cavalry that had come down from Virginia, commanded by Butler.[18]

Given Joe Wheeler's strong feelings about the privileges of rank, one might suppose the relationship thus imposed on him would create friction and perhaps bad blood between him and his new superior. But because Wheeler also prized decorum and restraint, this did not happen. Although rivalries consumed some of their subordinates and staff officers, from the start the two principals forged a cordial working arrangement, one sustained by mutual respect and trust as well as by a shared commitment to assist their beleaguered nation in its hour of crisis. In later years, however, Wheeler evidently felt embarrassed that he had been superseded by a volunteer officer who lacked prewar military experience and a West Point diploma. In order to enhance his own image, he would claim that in the final weeks of the war he too had been appointed a lieutenant general. The record fails to sustain his contention.

Whether either Hampton or Wheeler admitted it, the task ahead of them had an unmistakable air of futility. For one thing, demoralization was spreading like a flash-fire through the cavalry's ranks. Despite (or because of) Wheeler's recent efforts to tighten discipline and curtail unlawful behavior, by January 1865 his command was losing dozens of men daily to desertion. The microbe of disaffection was infecting entire regiments. In early February General Ferguson, who himself feared the end was near, was forced to use every argument he could conjure up to persuade two of his outfits to give up the idea of deserting en masse.[19]

Even those who nerved themselves to remain and fight found it increasingly difficult to ward off gloomy thoughts. "It looks like the yankes has got the upper hand of us," a 10th Confederate trooper wrote his wife. "I would like to here of some terms of pece before the[y] runn clear over us. . . . Our soldiers are very much dishartened and the most of them say we are whiped." A newly commissioned officer in the 1st Georgia was only slightly more optimistic, informing his father that "our present situation . . . appears gloomy enough, but I hope and think we will yet be independent. . . . [On the] patriotism of our Soldiers we must depend, and as we have few of them in comparison to the enemy we should foster and protect them as much as possible." The Georgian sounded a theme that was becoming popular among troops who yearned for a well-known and respected commander: "This is only to be done by putting men of heart and feeling in command like Johnston."[20]

In fact, a tremendous amount of pressure was being applied to President Davis to reinstate an officer he had relieved from command for not saluting him enough. His personal dislike of the man and distrust of his abilities caused Davis to persist in opposing the groundswell of support for Johnston. By early February, his resistance appeared to weaken, but even those who favored Johnston's return had to wonder what good it would achieve at this late date.

———————

The month-long lull in heavy fighting that had begun with Sherman's occupation of Savannah ended with his long-anticipated entrance into South Carolina. He expected the coming campaign to be "one of the most horrible things in the history of the world. . . . the Devil himself couldn't restrain my men." Joe Wheeler nevertheless attempted to do so. His men had been in near-constant contact with the Yankees ever since Savannah's fall, skirmishing with Kilpatrick's troopers and occasionally with their infantry friends at places including Hardeeville, Robertsville, Purysburg, Bowling Church, and various points on the Savannah River. Now he would challenge Kilpatrick in open combat and on a much grander scale. He would make his old classmate fight—and pay in blood—for every mile of Carolina countryside.[21]

Despite putting up all the opposition he could muster, Wheeler was unable to halt the Union juggernaut. By the end of January elements of Sherman's command had penetrated deeply enough into the Palmetto State to occupy strategic points including Lawtonville and Pocotaligo. On February 2, Humes's division made an all-out effort to prevent Sherman's crossing of the Big Salkehatchie River near the village of Buford. The spirited engagement gave evidence that the cavalry still had fight in it, but grit and determination failed to carry the day. Slocum's hardened veterans waded the stream under fire, straggled through a swamp, muscled Humes aside, and continued on toward an apparent junction with Howard's wing, which was then fifty miles to the northeast, moving inland from Beaufort. The general heading of Sherman's march appeared to be in the direction of the state capital at Columbia. Many local observers, however, feared that one or both of his columns would turn toward the coast to strike Charleston, where Hardee had gone with most of the troops who had fled Savannah.[22]

Suddenly and mysteriously, Kilpatrick, at the head of Slocum's wing, took off on a more westerly route. Followed by a substantial force of foot soldiers, he trotted along the railroad to Augusta, apparently intending to attack the logistical hub that Wheeler had prevented him from striking weeks ago. Having stretched his ranks across a wide area to oppose both of Sherman's wings, Wheeler could devote fewer than 2,000 of Humes's and Allen's troopers to the task of safeguarding the city of his birth. At the head of this compact force he hastened toward Kilpatrick's objective by a more direct route than available to his opponent. His opposition this day consisted of 5,068 troopers and six artillery pieces.

On the morning of February 11 Wheeler succeeded in getting across his enemy's path at Aiken, twelve miles northeast of Augusta. He positioned Humes's command, mounted, south of town and deployed Allen's men on foot to strike as the Yankees entered the city. His careful preparations paid dividends almost as soon as Kill-Cavalry arrived. Halfway through the city, he suddenly found every street and alley filled with shouting, shooting Rebels.

Unable to deploy effectively, Kilpatrick called a retreat after suffering two dozen casualties and fell back upon his infantry supports. There he rallied his units but turned about and resumed the northward march. Wheeler wished to pursue but, as he informed General Beauregard, "here our ammunition gave out and we had to halt and reload, having no sabers." Even so, he pronounced the fight a great success. News of Kilpatrick's ambush served to relieve the anxiety of Augusta's residents (including Wheeler's father and his maiden sister), raised the spirits of Confederate units elsewhere in the state, and won Wheeler and his men the thanks of Governor Magrath.[23]

After this miscue, Sherman permitted no deviation from the advance on South Carolina's capital. He was less restrictive when it came to governing his men's behavior on the march. As they penetrated the cradle of secession, his "bummers" (foragers) stepped up their depredations. Even more so than in Georgia, they were liberal and indiscriminate in their destruction of property, public and private. Whole villages including Erwinton, Treadaway, and Barnwell ("Burnwell," Kilpatrick's troopers dubbed it) had already gone up in flames. Barns, houses, stables, and outbuildings were razed at the whim of a bummer, but only after everything of value—animal, vegetable, perhaps even mineral— had been removed and carried off.

Here, as in Georgia, Sherman had no monopoly on looting and burning. Wheeler's men also descended upon helpless civilians, stealing their horses, appropriating their crops, and doing enough damage to make South Carolinians fear their coming almost as much as they did Sherman's approach. Both armies were guilty of atrocities, and some were perpetrated by Wheeler's outriders. A member of Shannon's Scouts, an elite reconnaissance unit that had gained a reputation for dealing harshly with enemy stragglers and foragers, confessed that "the smoke and flames of a dwelling [set afire by bummers] prevents the prayers of the Yankees for their lives, even when on their knees, being heard, and steadies my nerves to kill them all if possible."[24]

The wanton destruction inflicted on South Carolinians appeared to reach its height as Sherman closed in on Columbia. By the fourteenth, his main body was pushing northwestward from Orangeburg, dismantling railroad track as it went. That date marked the start of a several-day period of combat for Wheeler's cavalry, minus only a portion of Iverson's division that had been detached to support the transfer to the Carolinas of what remained of the Army of Tennessee, under A. P. Stewart. On the first day, Wheeler seized the opportunity to take in flank the advance echelon of the XIV Corps along the North Edisto River. The attack broke the Union battle line and gained Wheeler forty prisoners. The following day part of his command assaulted a Federal force approaching Bates's Ferry on the Congaree River, the last water barrier to Columbia. Later that same day other horsemen tangled with a Yankee column near Lexington, only twenty miles west of the capital.[25]

Slowly, grudgingly, but inexorably, Wheeler's troopers fell back to the outskirts of Columbia. Here for the first time they came under the authority of Wade Hampton, who had been placed in command of the city and its environs. Although Columbia had no natural defenses and was held only by the men of Wheeler and Butler plus a few thousand of Stewart's men, Hampton initially refused to surrender it to the enemy. He could not have said how he would hold the place; his only defensive effort was to pile in the streets thousands of bales of cotton removed from local storehouses. He would later regret this expedient, which would backfire—literally.[26]

Hampton directed Wheeler's and Butler's troopers to work in close cooperation to prevent Sherman's entrance into the capital. This was by any measure a Herculean task. Although some historians claim that Wheeler's recent aggressiveness had stalled the Union drive, by the morning of the sixteenth Sherman's wings had united on the left bank of the Congaree. Unwilling to attack across that deep and bridgeless stream, the Union leader ordered his XV Corps across the Saluda and Broad Rivers to take the city from the north.

Despite spirited resistance from the cavalry in their front, a formidable array of artillery on the south bank enabled the Federals to cross the Saluda without difficulty. When they pushed on to the bridge over the Broad River, however, they found that Wheeler had piled combustible materials on its pine-timbered floor and atop its shingled roof, while deploying dismounted skirmishers on a bluff in advance of the span. From behind hastily constructed works the troopers blasted the advancing enemy with their short Enfields.

Although initially stymied, the XV Corps rallied, re-formed, and came on in greater numbers than before. When they had gotten to within 100 yards of his position, Wheeler gave the word to retreat across the bridge. He had left orders that as soon the last man had crossed, the structure was to be burned. But through a miscommunication, the combustibles were touched off prematurely; within minutes, the wooden timbers were engulfed in flames.[27]

The skirmishers, whom Wheeler had accompanied, hastily remounted and made for the bridge at an extended gallop. As Wheeler crossed the bridge, his facial hair was singed, as was his horse's mane. Many of his troopers did not get off so easily; one recalled that "although bullets and splinters flew thick around, not a man was wounded, but all nearly suffocated and [were] scorched and ten or fifteen of the boys, who stumbled and fell, got hands and faces so badly burned that they had to go to the hospital."[28]

Once in the streets of Columbia, Wheeler's people joined Butler's in moving toward the northern suburbs through a demoralized mass of humanity and livestock. An officer in Butler's command found the citizenry "leaving in every direction. Such moving of cattle, hogs, sheep, etc. I never saw the like of, nor never want to see again." Hampton, finally convinced he could hold Columbia no longer, ordered every soldier to evacuate, but only after resistance became futile. Most of Butler's troopers appear to have complied, holding their ground to the last. In contrast, a majority of Wheeler's men retreated without a backward glance. Hampton would claim they did not fire a single shot on their way out of town.[29]

It would appear that the only troopers who delayed their departure did so in order to get a head start on their enemy in pillaging banks, shops, warehouses, and private homes. Happening upon one horde of plunderers, Hampton cursed them and drew his saber, only to have them level their pistols at him. Undoubtedly the men resented his intrusion in their affairs, but they may also have acted in response to a rumor that Hampton was responsible for the untimely burning of the Broad River Bridge. More embarrassed than fearful, the lieutenant general beat a quick retreat. He never forgot the incident, which forever colored his opinion of the material at Wheeler's disposal.[30]

Once the city's defense force had vacated, angry, hungry, thirsty Federals took possession of Columbia. Many promptly ran amuck, scouring streets and alleys for something to steal or break and someone to hurt. A two-day orgy of destruction ended with fully one-third of the city in ashes. The proximate cause of the conflagration was the indiscriminate torching of the cotton-bale barricades, which sent flames shooting in many directions. Inadvertently started by Confederate soldiers or local citizens, the blaze was joined by smaller, individual fires deliberately set by vengeful invaders.

The depredations of Sherman's men extended beyond the city to outlying regions, including the several plantations east of Columbia owned by Wade Hampton and his family. In an attempt to add insult to injury, Sherman later claimed that the fires had been the work of Hampton himself. Sherman knew the accusation to be false, but he would not admit it until years after the war.[31]

—— —— —— ——

Five days after Hampton and Wheeler evacuated Columbia, they came under the command of Joe Johnston, who had retaken the field despite Jefferson Davis's qualms. Johnston had been given command of everyone who had been opposing Sherman, including the remnants of his old army. To this force he would add Hardee's command, which had evacuated Charleston on the day Columbia fell, as well as a division of North Carolina troops under Maj. Gen. Robert F. Hoke, which Braxton Bragg had led down from Virginia. The latter, which would bring Johnston's effective force to about 25,000, had been sent to North Carolina to counter an army-navy expedition against Wilmington, the Confederacy's last operating seaport of any value. That effort had ended badly; the fate of the coastal city had been sealed on Christmas day with the capture of its most formidable work, Fort Fisher, by white and black troops under Maj. Gen. Alfred H. Terry.[32]

After capturing Columbia, Sherman made with all speed for the North Carolina border. He was now in position to advance on any of several potential objectives including Raleigh, Charlotte, and Goldsboro. Lacking the numbers to cover more than one target, Johnston moved ahead of his enemy, keeping his options open while trying to concentrate his far-flung troops. Even as they fell back, Wheeler and Butler lashed out at Sherman's wings—Slocum's XIV and XX corps on the west, Howard's XV and XVII to the east. They gained no lasting advantage, but by maintaining contact with the enemy they kept up the morale of their men, of the army as a whole, and, to a lesser extent, of the civilians in Sherman's path.

By the close of February it seemed apparent that the invaders were making for Fayetteville, North Carolina. Wheeler moved in that direction with Allen's and Humes's divisions (General Iverson, with the brigades of Ferguson, Lewis, Hannon, and Crews, remained detached in South Carolina even as Sherman's main body prepared to leave the state). With the 3,000 effectives left to him, Wheeler cut across the Yankees' path, drawing blood whenever possible although aware that any success he gained would be temporary. On March 4 he met Kilpatrick's cavalry at Phillips Cross Roads, South Carolina, and in a day-long slugging match took fifty prisoners. Still, he failed to prevent Sherman from evicting Hardee's command from nearby Cheraw and pursuing it northward with an energy and spirit suggestive of boundless confidence.[33]

On March 6—two days after Abraham Lincoln, during his second inaugural, asked the people of the North to "strive on to finish the work we are in"— Sherman crossed the Pee Dee River and entered the Tarheel State. Grudgingly, Hampton, Wheeler, and Butler withdrew toward Fayetteville. There Johnston planned to concentrate and make a stand in defiance of the odds against him.

Hampton, however, did not intend to wait that long. Noting that Kilpatrick's horsemen—who showed no inclination to curb their lust for terrorizing helpless citizens—were incautiously riding ahead of Sherman's infantry, the South Carolinian hoped for a chance to exact retribution. On the ninth, when his scouts reported that Kilpatrick had divided his command, placing half of it in camp near Monroe's Cross Roads, a few miles northwest of Fayetteville and an hour or more from Sherman's main force, Hampton vowed to act. He planned a multicolumn attack on Kilpatrick's swamp-bordered bivouac, intending not only to scatter Kilpatrick's men but to seize their leader and carry him off bodily.

After dark, acting on information personally gathered by Wheeler during a reconnaissance in company with Shannon's Scouts, the Confederates moved into positions from which to attack the Union camp. Three large detachments would strike from as many directions, converging toward the log farmhouse that Kill-Cavalry had appropriated for his headquarters. Just after sunrise on the cold, clear morning of March 10, Wheeler, at Hampton's request, put the plan into operation. At his signal, the northernmost detachment, under General Butler, galloped across Morganton Road and through the first lines of Yankee tents. Minutes later, Allen's division, accompanied by Wheeler himself, charged in from the northwest, and Humes's division, Harrison's brigade in the forefront, attacked from the west.[34]

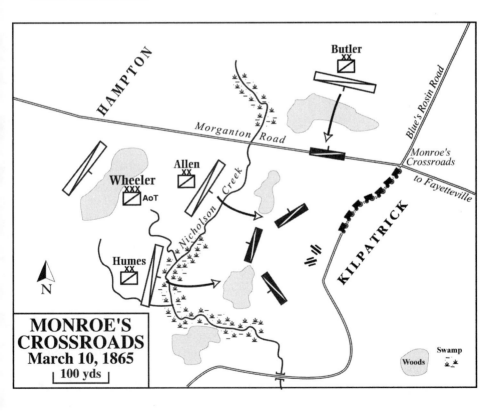

MONROE'S CROSSROADS
March 10, 1865
100 yds

As Hampton had hoped, the sleeping enemy was taken wholly by surprise. Half-dressed Yankees stumbled out of their bedrolls as hollering riders galloped through their midst, cutting them down with pistol fire before they could fight back. Feeble resistance quickly gave way to flight. Most of those who managed to mount galloped off in the only direction open to them: south. Within perhaps twenty minutes every unit encamped north and northwest of Kilpatrick's headquarters was in retreat, accompanied by their leader. Awakened either by the shooting or by a premonition of doom, Kill-Cavalry had bolted from his cabin clad in nightshirt, pants, and boots. He escaped only because the detachment charged with hunting him down mistook him for a private soldier not worth pursuing.[35]

By seven o'clock, the men of Butler's and Allen's divisions had secured the ground they had overrun. Some were pursuing the enemy; others were corralling prisoners; still others were helping themselves to the rations, equipment, arms, and ammunition their befuddled enemy had abandoned. This unauthorized halt combined with two other mistakes—both caused by untimely changes of position—to prevent Hampton and Wheeler from exploiting their initial success. Butler's second brigade, which for unknown reasons had been pulled out of line shortly before the attack began, failed to advance on the heels of the troops in front. And owing to a nigh-impenetrable swamp in its path, Humes's contingent failed to fight its way through to Kilpatrick's headquarters until the battle was almost over.[36]

The result of these miscues was that when a body of foot soldiers and artillerymen from the XIV Corps, awakened by the assault, reached the crossroads some time after 8 AM, the Confederates were thrust quickly backward and Hampton called retreat. By then, however, Kilpatrick's division had suffered nearly 200 losses, more than half of them in prisoners, while it had lost its hold on an even larger number of Confederate POWs. But the attackers' success had come at high cost, too, especially in high-ranking officers. General Humes and Colonels Hannon and Hagan had taken wounds, while General Allen and Colonel Ashby had been disabled when their horses were shot from under them. Allen remounted on a captured horse that had been Judson Kilpatrick's. Another mount belonging to the fugitive brigadier—a spotted stallion reported to be Kilpatrick's favorite steed—was presented to Wheeler by Shannon's Scouts, who had pooled their meager pay to purchase it from its captor.[37]

——— ——— ———

If the raid on Monroe's Cross Roads had been a victory, it was the last the army to which Wheeler belonged would ever claim. From the scene of "Kilpatrick's Shirttail Skedaddle," the Confederates moved to Fayetteville, from which Sherman's foot soldiers drove them the next day. Hampton would claim that Wheeler's troopers galloped through the streets without putting up a fight, just as they had at Columbia. As proof they had performed effectively their rear-guard duties Wheeler would cite the several casualties his command suffered on this occasion—including the severe wounding of General Anderson, his second while serving under Wheeler—and his men's demolition of the Cape Fear River bridge.[38]

On the fourteenth, Wheeler crossed Black River, fending off blows to the rear of Johnston's still-incomplete command along the roads to Raleigh. Two days later, Wheeler heard sounds of battle coming from the area south of Averasboro on the Cape Fear River. There Hardee's command, straining to join Johnston, had encountered the vanguard of Slocum's wing. Wheeler sought and gained Hampton's permission to take part in the fight. Galloping to the field of battle, he arrived to find a Union turning-movement in progress. "This I met," he reported matter-of-factly, "and held in check until night, when General Hardee withdrew his troops, leaving me to cover his retreat."[39]

The following evening, as Wheeler marched to rejoin Hampton, the latter conferred by courier with General Johnston, who was seeking suitable ground for his intended stand. Hampton suggested that the place where he had established his headquarters, about two miles south of Bentonville, met the relevant criteria; accordingly, Johnston ordered his divided command to concentrate there.[40]

Wheeler's corps, minus a large detachment assigned to escort Hardee from Averasboro, reached Hampton in time to fortify a position on the right of the Confederate battle line near Bentonville. The next day, March 19, Wheeler helped open the battle by resisting Slocum's advance on the road to Goldsboro. The fighting soon moved south, however, the warmest action taking place on the left, where Johnston attacked and tried mightily to overwhelm the XIV Corps. He had intended to hold the Yankees in check with a frontal assault, then crush their flank with Hardee's troops and the truncated Army of Tennessee, Wheeler's horsemen in support. But because Hardee was late getting into position the flank drive was critically delayed and fell short of success. Compounding Johnston's woes, Wheeler reported himself "prevented from engaging the enemy warmly the latter part of the day on account of meeting a stream over which it was impossible to cross." When Sherman rushed the XX Corps to the scene to reinforce his embattled flank, the fighting reached stalemate and Johnston withdrew to his original line. His men had made a worthy effort but had come up short.[41]

Throughout the twentieth both armies maneuvered but neither seized the initiative. Early in the day Hampton shifted Wheeler's main body to the left flank, where it skirmished briskly with blue infantry moving up the Goldsboro road. Wheeler was more heavily engaged on the twenty-first, when Sherman launched a major attack. At about 4 PM, a XVII Corps division under Bvt. Maj. Gen. Joseph A. Mower cut through a woods and plunged into a swamp that led to Johnston's left flank and rear. By this movement the aggressive Mower hoped to seize and hold the bridge over Mill Creek, his adversary's only route of retreat.

Hampton detected the movement but to counter it could call on only a skeletonized infantry brigade, some artillery, and Wheeler's troopers. While Wheeler attacked Mower's left flank with Hagan's brigade, under the command of Wirt Allen, General Hardee hurled at the enemy as a forlorn hope the 8th Texas Cavalry of Harrison's brigade, Humes's division. The result was a stunning reaffirmation of the effectiveness of a well-conducted mounted attack, even when launched against foot soldiers. As Wheeler reported proudly, "my gallant Texas Rangers . . . galloped across an open field and bore down most beautifully in an oblique direction upon their [the enemy's] left and front. . . . The rangers broke through the line of skirmishers without breaking their [own] impetus and pushed on, striking the main line almost the same moment with Allen's gallant Alabamians, which threw the entire force of the enemy in a most rapid and disorderly retreat, Gen. Mower . . . narrowly escaping capture." Wheeler may have exaggerated the role his command played in halting Mower's advance, but Humes and Allen did help check the turning movement and save the Mill Creek bridge, over which Johnston led his hard-pressed army near day's end. The relieved but exhausted Rebels then fell back through heavy woods in the direction of Smithfield.[42]

The timber through which they passed was so thick and constricting that by the morning of the twenty-second the rear of the army had not yet cleared Bentonville. To enable the rear guard to escape, Wheeler opposed Sherman's pursuit through the tried and true process of fighting as he retreated. The enemy pressed him so stoutly that by ten o'clock Wheeler had to halt and make a prolonged stand where the road to Smithville crossed Black Creek. After his carbineers fell back over the bridge, however, the Federals abruptly drew off "and made no further pursuit whatever." Thankful for this reprieve, Wheeler moved on to Smithfield, where he set about picketing the length of Johnston's shrunken, battered, and nearly exhausted army.[43]

———   ———   ———   ———

For more than a week, the War Child's warriors remained in the Smithfield area, where their contact with Sherman was limited to intermittent skirmishing with foraging and scouting parties. While Johnston's infantrymen and cannoneers caught their breath and treated their wounds, part of Sherman's massive army turned east and marched to the rail hub at Goldsboro. There his troops linked with forces under John M. Schofield, who had come all the way from Tennessee, as well as Terry's corps, fresh from its capture and occupation of Wilmington. The combined forces then turned northwestward and headed for Raleigh.[44]

By then Wheeler's troopers were already in the North Carolina capital, sent there by Hampton to guard the far rear. Almost immediately, however, the order was countermanded and they returned to Johnston's headquarters to resume the task of guarding the army's rear and flanks. On the way, they heard some troubling rumors out of Virginia: Grant and Meade were pressing Lee's attenuated lines at Petersburg, and Lee, either of his own volition or through compulsion, was evacuating the position he had occupied for the past ten months. Neither then nor later, however, did Johnston's army receive official word of Lee's abandonment of Petersburg or the April 3 evacuation and occupation of Richmond.

By the tenth Wheeler's horsemen were again moving north, this time in company with the rest of Johnston's forces. They managed to keep ahead of Sherman's infantry, now intent on taking Raleigh, but they skirmished briskly with Kilpatrick and temporarily stymied him by burning a bridge over Swift Creek. North of the stream, the retreat continued. Johnston had no intention of slugging it out with an enemy now almost 100,000 strong following its acquisition of Schofield's and Terry's troops.[45]

Presently Wheeler entered Raleigh for the second time in little over a week. He would remember the city as the place where he received the most disheartening news of his Confederate career. On the afternoon of the eleventh, army headquarters learned that Lee's army had surrendered to Grant at Appomattox Court House, Virginia, two days earlier. The next morning, Johnston broke the news to the rank and file. That same day, Judson Kilpatrick sent confirmation of the report through Wheeler's lines and requested that his West Point classmate suspend all aggressive acts toward the forces of the United States.

Wheeler was in no mood to cease hostilities, nor—for now, at least—was his commander. Refusing to stand down, Johnston led his soldiers out of Raleigh just before Sherman closed in. The Union infantry occupation of the capital began on the thirteenth; almost immediately, however, Kilpatrick resumed the pursuit, encountering Wheeler's rear guard on the road to Morrisville. Charges and countercharges in a driving rain produced casualties on both sides. Finally Kill-Cavalry broke contact and fell back upon Raleigh while his opponents headed toward Durham Station on the North Carolina Railroad.[46]

On the fourteenth Wheeler's command reached the college town of Chapel Hill, where Kilpatrick's men came up, apparently spoiling for a fight. Wheeler obliged, but after some light sparring, the Yankees retired. When they failed to reappear over the next several hours, a rumor began to spread through the ranks that Johnston and Sherman were communicating under a truce flag with a view to ending the fighting in North Carolina. The rumor appeared to be confirmed on the fifteenth, when army headquarters ordered Wheeler to refrain from engaging the enemy unless attacked. Two days later, the ranking antagonists met at a farmer's house near Durham Station to negotiate an armistice.

Fairly quickly the two men—who despite having warred against each other for many months were capable of mutual respect—agreed on terms under which Johnston's troops would disarm and disband. The conditions had been arrived at in an atmosphere made tense by a coded message that had just arrived from Washington that Sherman shared with his adversary: on the fourteenth

Abraham Lincoln had been assassinated by a Southern sympathizer while attending a play at a Washington theater.[47]

In an effort to end the fighting as quickly as possible, Sherman not only offered Johnston terms considered overly lenient by his political superiors but attempted to settle political questions concerning the postwar South. In so doing he exceeded the authority to negotiate given him by Grant. Within hours of the Durham Station conference, Lincoln's successor, Andrew Johnson, and Secretary of War Stanton would overturn the agreement Sherman and Johnston had hammered out. When word of this action reached North Carolina, the armistice that had taken effect came to an abrupt end.[48]

Although many on both sides were disappointed by this turn of events, most of Wheeler's men stood ready to carry on the fight from Chapel Hill, a prospect that pleased not only their commander but also his immediate superior. Having lost a brother and a son to Yankee bullets (a second son had been severely wounded), having seen his plantations razed and property seized, and having learned of his family's desperate flight from Columbia, Wade Hampton was determined to find a way to fight on. Wheeler, whose brother William had died in Confederate service and whose father and sister had been caught in the path of Sherman's invasion, likewise harbored too much bitterness and resentment to lay down his arms and go home. As he informed Johnston on the eighteenth, he would have preferred "ten thousand times to have been killed" in battle than be made a party to a surrender agreement.[49]

Hampton's and Wheeler's preferences notwithstanding, no sustained fighting occurred between the government's rejection of Sherman's initial terms and the convening of a second parlay at Durham Station on the twenty-sixth, which produced a surrender accord acceptable to Washington. Even so, during the interim both generals gained an opportunity to carry on the struggle. Shortly before Richmond was occupied, Jefferson Davis, members of his cabinet, and other civilian and military officials had fled the city by a special train that carried them first to Danville, Virginia, then to Greensboro, North Carolina, thirty-some miles west of Durham Station. Hampton, who hoped to join the fugitives in escaping to Mexico, another foreign country, or the Trans-Mississippi Department, wrote Davis of his desire to escort the president's party through enemy lines.[50]

Failing to meet Davis at Greensboro, Hampton left the army by train on the twenty-sixth—even as Sherman and Johnston were reaching an agreement on surrender terms—to confer with the president at his new location, Charlotte. Wheeler accompanied him on the trip, which ended with the president and his generals agreeing on a plan to flee to Texas, where Confederate forces under Kirby Smith continued to fight on. When the meeting broke up, Hampton and Wheeler returned to Durham to form an escort for Davis from the men of their commands.

The cavalry leaders got as far as Greensboro before learning that Johnston had accepted Sherman's terms. The news disrupted, at least briefly, Hampton's plan to accompany the presidential party to a safe haven. It had no discernable effect on Wheeler, who considered neither himself nor his command bound by the surrender agreement. Many of his men shared his view. Immediately after the first Sherman-Johnston parlay, Wheeler had found "that half my command had saddled up & left during the night in detached parties . . . to save themselves from surrender." At the time he had felt obligated to recall those still within his reach. Now he looked the other way when additional troopers rode off to evade surrender.[51]

To those who elected to remain, he issued an address, dated April 29, in which he praised the fortitude and fidelity they and their comrades had shown in camp, on the march, and in battle through three weary, bloody years of conflict. "You have fought your last fight," he told them, "your task is done. . . . You have done all that human exertion could accomplish. In bidding you adieu I desire to tender thanks for your gallantry in battle, your fortitude under suffering, and your devotion at all times to the holy cause you have done so much to maintain."[52]

Wheeler himself was not ready to relinquish the "holy cause." Having parted ways with Hampton, he had returned to the camp of his command at Company Shops, a railroad repair depot a few miles east of Greensboro. There he set about raising an escort for Davis and his party, at the head of which he expected to join the fugitives at Cokesboro, South Carolina. Wheeler would claim that everyone still a part of his command volunteered for the duty, of whom he selected 600 officers and men. This number seems too high—such a large force would attract unwanted attention from those troops already scouring the Carolinas, Georgia, and Florida for the fugitive president. Wheeler's aide, Maj. William E. Wales, suggests that the force was in fact much smaller, being limited to men who hailed from beyond the Mississippi.

On or before the day his farewell address was issued, Wheeler bade a poignant farewell to those who would not accompany him, and with the rest departed Company Shops. Apparently he started out in civilian attire—he had boxed up the major general's uniform he had worn for the past two years and had left directions that it be sent to his sister in Augusta. He also had a new destination. In response to a message from the president, he was now headed for Washington, a village in the midst of a sparsely settled section of Georgia. There, it was thought, the enemy's dragnet would be less active and extensive than the one in operation in South Carolina.[53]

Marching night and day, Wheeler covered the 250 miles to the rendezvous by the first days in May. It must have been a nerve-wracking trip as well as an arduous and debilitating one, for he and his men would have been careful to evade the squads of Union cavalry combing the Carolinas in hopes of claiming the reward Secretary Stanton had offered to anyone involved in Davis's apprehending.

Wheeler's uncertain journey reunited him with Wade Hampton, who had also departed the army in hopes of locating Davis but who had counseled his men to abide by the terms of the surrender pact. Accompanied by a small escort, Hampton had searched for Davis at Charlotte but failed to hook up with the president, who had decamped for points south. Despite failing health and the defection of all but one or two of his party, Hampton had trailed the presidential party as far as Yorkville, South Carolina, where his own family had fled after being driven from Columbia. Reaching Yorkville on May 1, Wheeler found his superior virtually incapacitated by physical and mental stress. Concerned for his health, Wheeler helped Mrs. Hampton persuade her husband to remain at home until he regained his strength.[54]

For Wheeler, the most frustrating part of his journey occurred at the finale. From Yorkville, he traveled south with only a handful of men. Fearing detection, he had split his escort into small parties, most of whose members, as soon as they left Wheeler's side, gave up the ghost and made their way home as best they could. Because his self-respect would not permit him to follow suit, a nearly exhausted Wheeler forged on to Washington only to discover that Davis, his family, a few other officials, and perhaps ten soldiers had left there the previous night for points unknown.[55]

This frustrating denouement should have ended his attempt to find and join the president, but Wheeler refused to concede defeat. He forged on, even though the area he now traversed, contrary to Davis's expectations, swarmed with cavalrymen seeking fugitive Confederates. It was not long before a force of about forty horsemen was tracking Wheeler's little band. Through hard riding and good luck they outdistanced their pursuers, but, as Wheeler feared, only temporarily. "I saw at once the danger that menaced us," he later recalled, "and, calling my men to the saddles, told them we could not remain a moment where we were."[56]

At his urging, they plunged into the Georgia countryside and rode through the night. But no matter how fast they traveled or how often they detoured or doubled back, they sensed the hounds closing in. The life span of the would-be escort had been reduced, it appeared, to a matter of days.

It proved to be a matter of hours. The next morning, believing the road behind him clear of Yankees, Wheeler and his companions sought essential rest in an open area that offered a panoramic view of approaching Yankees. A recently liberated slave who lived nearby was compelled to furnish them with a "steaming breakfast." The meal put the exhausted riders to sleep in violation of every survival instinct. After a brief slumber, they were awakened by a series of kicks from spurred boots and a chorus of shouts. As they regained their feet, they found themselves staring into the business end of pistols and carbines in the hands of Union cavalrymen.[57]

The War Child's war was over.

13

NEW FIELDS OF BATTLE

Wheeler's journey to imprisonment in the North was long and circuitous. From the place of his capture he and the three staff officers taken with him were escorted under guard to Conyers, Georgia, and from there to Athens, the seat of the local occupation district. At Athens the general was finally reunited with Jefferson Davis, whose party had been overtaken by Union cavalry near Irwinsville on May 10. Accompanying Davis were other distinguished prisoners, including Vice President Alexander H. Stephens, Postmaster General John H. Reagan, (Confederate) Senator Clement C. Clay, and Francis R. Lubbock, the former governor of Texas.

After a brief interrogation by the local commander, the fugitives were put aboard a train bound for Wheeler's native city. At Augusta, a large crowd turned out to view the political and military notables. Presumably Wheeler had a tearful reunion with his father and sister, but it must have been painfully brief. His request to be paroled having been denied, he and the other prisoners were ushered aboard a tug in the Savannah River, which was soon steaming downriver escorted by a warship "with guns primed and sailors standing by."[1]

Upon arriving at Savannah, the carefully guarded passengers were transferred to a more commodious steamer for the run to Hilton Head, headquarters of the Department of the South. Although still under guard, Wheeler was able to stroll the decks of the *William P. Clyde*. While so occupied he developed a plan to overawe the few sentries left above deck when the rest of the guards took dinner below. He communicated his scheme to some of the other prisoners, who thought it worth trying, but President Davis argued against it as too dangerous and the opportunity passed.[2]

On May 19 the *Clyde* docked at Fort Monroe, on the tip of the Virginia Peninsula. The following day some of the other prisoners were taken ashore, to be incarcerated locally or to be transported by other vessels to prisons in Boston and Washington, D.C. Davis and Clay would be locked up at Fort Monroe, the ex-president for the next two years. Never brought to trial, he would be released through the efforts of prominent Northerners who defied the wishes of government officials to let Davis rot in confinement.[3]

Wheeler and several other prisoners were kept aboard ship. Transported northward, they finally debarked—presumably in chains—on Pea Patch Island at the mouth of the Delaware River. The only structure of any substance on this desolate, marshy expanse was Fort Delaware, a foreboding citadel of masonry and iron in which Confederate POWs—including most of Lee's troops captured at Gettysburg—and political prisoners had been held since the war's early days. Conditions here rivaled those obtaining at the most notorious lockups in the South, including Andersonville. Rations were meager and often inedible, the clothing issued to the prisoners provided inadequate protection against the vicissitudes of the local weather, sanitary facilities were sadly lacking, and the inmates, many of whom were undernourished and ill, were put to hard labor on a daily basis.

Wheeler had to endure the rigors of solitary confinement in this forbidding place for less than a month. He was fortunate to have as his jailor a soldier who in prewar days had served under him in the 1st Dragoons. The man saw to it that his former superior received certain amenities including a regular issuance of newspapers. He even offered to help Wheeler escape from the island. The prisoner demurred for fear of the consequences should the effort fail—fear not for himself but for his benefactor.

On June 8, Wheeler was abruptly released from Fort Delaware upon "an arbitrary order from the Secretary of War" paroling him on the same terms as had been offered to Johnston's army. The action no doubt surprised him almost as much as it gratified him. Until then he must have wondered if—given the vengeful mood of Northern officials in the wake of Lincoln's murder—he would face a court-martial followed by a date with the gallows or the firing squad.[4]

Upon his release, Wheeler appears to have been in a quandary as to his next destination and how he should get there. His dilemma was solved, at least temporarily, by two ladies of Philadelphia, Southern sympathizers who were daily visitors to the prison population. At their insistence, he followed them to their home, "where they gave me the first good meal I had in many a day, and a comfortable bed to sleep in, and they saw me safely on my journey to New York the next morning." He forever remembered his hostesses as "noble women" and noted proudly that the South "had thousands like them."[5]

—————

Although details are lacking, Wheeler undoubtedly went north to visit his sister Lucy, in whose Brooklyn home he stayed until he had recovered the health that had been compromised by his stressful attempts to avoid capture, then by the rigors of his confinement. Wheeler's brother-in-law, whose business ventures continued to prosper, probably funded his trip home to Georgia. Upon his return to Augusta, he enjoyed a longer and more joyous reunion with his elderly father and maiden sister. Although happy to be back in the family fold, he must have been depressed by the debilitated condition of his native region. The war had decimated the local economy as it had the Wheeler family fortune, and he saw he had little chance of beginning his life anew—as he must in order to survive—in such surroundings.

By late August Wheeler had left home for Nashville, Tennessee, where he appeared as a witness before a military tribunal deliberating the fate of Champ Ferguson, a notorious guerrilla who on occasion had scouted for Wheeler's cavalry. Wheeler knew the accused only as a faithful soldier. No doubt he testified to this fact; but it did Ferguson no good. The unrepentant killer, who had dispatched dozens of soldiers and civilians in cold blood, was hanged in late October.[6]

If Ferguson's trial did not do so, a violent incident during Wheeler's stay in Nashville must have brought home to him how much bitterness the war had stirred up in states like Tennessee where loyalties were sharply divided. One night, two men in civilian clothes knocked on the door of Wheeler's hotel room. When let in, they identified themselves as officers recently discharged from the 4th Tennessee Mounted Infantry, a Unionist regiment that had frequently engaged in hand-to-hand combat with Wheeler's corps.

Wheeler's visitors—a Colonel Blackburn and a Captain Quinn—were carrying a year-old grudge against him. They accused Wheeler of issuing to his cavalry an order that every member of the 4th Tennessee captured in battle was to be hanged, ostensibly in retaliation for past atrocities. Now Wheeler was going to pay for this heinous act. Before their host could react, Quinn drew a pistol and Blackburn struck Wheeler in the face with a walking stick. The colonel continued to rain blows about the head and shoulders of his unarmed victim until Wheeler broke free and fled past Quinn through the hallway, shouting for help. Aroused guests and hotel employees intervened, and the assailants were taken into custody. They were released, however, when the local military commander, Sherman's old subordinate George H. Thomas, cited legal restrictions on his ability to hold discharged soldiers for trial. When the civil authorities failed to indict, Blackburn and Quinn went free, and a bruised and aching Wheeler returned to Georgia.[7]

Once again he rested and tried to regain his health. How long it took remains unknown, but when, late that summer or early in the fall, he left Georgia to visit a certain young woman in Courtland, Alabama, he probably carried the scars of his recent (and final) encounter with armed Yankees. Perhaps he hoped his wounds would arouse the sympathy of Daniella Jones Sherrod and assist him in his effort to win her hand in marriage. If so, he was mistaken, for he returned from the Jones estate without a commitment from his beloved. On the other hand, she had not rejected his proposal. They continued to correspond, and he continued to press his suit at long distance.

He was in a better position to take a bride than most unmarried ex-Confederates without employment experience in civilian life. The many commercial interests of his New York brother-in-law, Sterling Smith, included a hardware store and livery stable in New Orleans, which he had engaged Wheeler to manage for him. Despite his lack of a business background, in time Wheeler made the concern a profitable enterprise. Within three years he joined Smith and one of his New York associates as a partner in the business. One year later, along with a partner of his own, Wheeler bought out the original owners and took over the store and stable.[8]

His interest had been funded by an influx of capital in the form of a dowry. Not long after he had left Courtland an unmarried man, the widow Sherrod made up her mind and accepted his suit. On February 8, 1866, the couple was joined in wedlock in the parlor of Caledonia, the Jones's plantation house. Their union—a happy one, by all indications—would endure for thirty years. It would produce two sons, Joseph Jr. and Thomas Harrison Wheeler, and five daughters, Lucy Louise, Annie Early, Ella (who would die in early youth), Julia Knox Hull, and Carrie Payton Wheeler. The general, whom close friends described as "a fond and loving father and husband," took tremendous pride and comfort in his family and never felt himself complete when apart from home. Although required to leave it numerous times over the years in response to commercial, political, and military demands, he was never so happy as when he returned to his family, and he seized every opportunity to linger in its loving embrace.[9]

Almost as soon as Wheeler and his bride settled in New Orleans, his father-in-law began to agitate for Daniella's return to Alabama. Richard Jones appealed to his son-in-law's desire for financial stability by promising to set him up as a local planter: "I will furnish the farm outfit and give you half of the net proceeds." The colonel not only missed his only daughter, he feared that her health would suffer from the lowland ills common to the Crescent City and its environs. Conceivably, he was also disturbed by the social and political climate in the South. Military Reconstruction was well under way in Louisiana, as it was in Alabama and the rest of the occupied South, and ex-Confederate generals and their families had become targets of abuse from occupation troops, editors, and politicians, especially those Unionists who had seized control of the local government. Then, too, five months after the newlyweds settled in New Orleans, one of the most violent race riots in the nation's history broke out in the streets of the city. Before it ran its course, more than 150 African American and white residents had been killed or severely injured.[10]

Because his commercial ventures were so profitable, and because he doubted he could succeed at farming, for more than two years Wheeler resisted Richard Jones's attempts to regain the daughter he had given away. But, early in 1869, he finally succumbed to the desires of Daniella and her father. He sold his hardware and livery business and moved his growing family—which now included three-year-old Lucy, one-year-old Annie, and a couple of black servants—to Courtland.

They settled on Pond Spring, the 1,760-acre plantation Daniella had inherited from her late husband. The estate appears to have lacked a manor house—the original dwelling may have fallen victim to Yankee troops who overran that area late in the war—and Wheeler refused to board with his father-in-law any longer than he had to. As soon as possible, he began work on a modest farmhouse that went up a few miles east of Caledonia. Next to it he erected a building that housed a general store, a hedge against failure of his efforts at farming. The store proved to be a valuable investment, for Wheeler made a good living from it, especially—if his tax records are any indication—from liquor sales.[11]

From modest beginnings, the Wheeler family holdings grew to stately proportions. By 1870, Wheeler owned $2,000 worth of real estate in his own name; his wife's property—most of it in the form of land—was valued at nine times that amount. Soon he was using the profits he coaxed from the soil to expand his land holdings. The acquisition of new land—before the close of 1870 Pond Spring had grown to more than 7,000 acres—enabled him to lease parcels of it to sharecroppers both white and black, including former slaves of the Jones family. To help with the farming and to assist Daniella with household chores Wheeler hired additional servants. He added to the staff by persuading the probate court of Lawrence County to assign to his custody the underage children of indigent black families. The same tactic was adopted by Wheeler's father-in-law and Daniella's brother, Tom. The abolition of slavery had been written into the new constitution Alabama had adopted as a perquisite for its readmission to the Union in June 1868. Even so, a form of legalized slavery flourished in the state and elsewhere in the South under the so-called "black codes" enacted to control the legal, social, and economic status of freedmen.[12]

Although a novice at farming, Wheeler knew which crops would yield the highest return. In 1869 he began to plant cotton. Before the year's end he had picked enough to fill a storehouse that he built at the not inconsiderable cost of $900. In the early 1870s he began to invest surplus profits in bonds in the venerable but somewhat dilapidated Memphis & Charleston Railroad, which ran through Courtland. The value of these securities increased considerably after 1877, when the railroad was leased to a larger and more prosperous line. By late 1871 the road had erected a depot only a hundred yards from the front door of the manor house at Pond Spring. Built for the convenience of the general and his family, the depot was dubbed "Wheeler Station" in his honor. As people moved into the area and its infrastructure expanded, it became incorporated as the town of Wheeler, Alabama.[13]

As if farming and retail did not occupy enough of his time, by 1871 Wheeler was considering expanding into other commercial enterprises. Early

that year Jefferson Davis, who upon his release from prison had entered the
insurance business, offered to make Wheeler an agent for the firm he headed,
the Carolina Life Insurance Company. The general seriously considered the offer, initially believing "I could arrange to do justice to the business." That June,
however, he turned Davis down, pleading "family afflictions and a combination
of unforeseen accidents." One such accident was so severe that it threatened his
financial well-being, his reputation as a law-abiding citizen, and even his own
life. It also guided him into a new career—as a practicing attorney.[14]

———— ———— ———— ————

The incident revolved around a modest blacksmith shop in neighboring Decatur, which Wheeler owned in partnership with his brother-in-law, the
generally good-natured but occasionally hot-tempered Thomas Harrison Jones.
Their chief employee, blacksmith Dandrige T. Galey, had long been a hard worker
and faithful employee. By May 1871, however, the man had begun to act, as
Wheeler put it, in "a very insubordinate and threatening manner." Wheeler could
not pinpoint a cause, but Galey's confrontational behavior forced the partners to
fire him and then evict him, his wife, and their son from the house they had
occupied on the grounds of the shop.[15]

On the rainy morning of May 3, Galey and his son, John, who had yet
to evacuate the premises, returned to the shop to reclaim their tools, which
Wheeler and his brother-in-law had impounded. Both employers suddenly appeared, Jones with pistol in hand, and confronted the Galeys. What happened
next is a matter of dispute, but it is uncontestable that within minutes Galey lay
dead and his son, a bullet wound in his side, was fighting for his life.

Although Thomas Jones claimed self-defense, the circumstances of the
shooting were so unclear that state authorities arrested and arraigned Wheeler as
well as his brother-in-law. The following March, both were indicted for murder
in the circuit court of Lawrence County, then in session at Moulton. After pleading
not guilty to a charge that Jones declared "a ridiculous farce," the defendants
were released on $20,000 bond.[16]

Apparently local officials agreed—at least to a degree—with Jones's assessment of the case. While the court believed there was clear cause to prosecute
the man who fired the fatal shot (Galey's son would survive his wound), it did
not desire to try a celebrated soldier of the Confederacy. Over the next few
months, through legal maneuvering the details of which remain unclear, the
charge against Wheeler was dropped, leaving Jones as the sole defendant. In fact,
Wheeler managed to expunge from the record almost every reference to his involvement in the case. Furthermore, he succeeded in obtaining a change of venue
from the county seat, where the Galey family was well-known and Wheeler and
Jones were regarded as outsiders, to the court of law and equity in Courtland,
where both men—and many of their friends and business associates—resided.

Wheeler's success in these endeavors was attributable to the crash course he took in the law. For months he pored over legal texts, the contents of which he assimilated thanks to the coaching of practicing attorneys well known to him. He passed the rather perfunctory bar examination and in August 1872, just as his brother-in-law's trial began, he was admitted to the practice of law. Although never a brilliant legal mind, he would practice his new profession intermittently through the rest of his life. In time he would become a legal representative of railroads and other major commercial interests. He would even qualify to argue cases before the Supreme Court of the United States, although it does not appear that he availed himself of that opportunity.[17]

Despite his inexperience, Wheeler was permitted to represent Thomas Jones at his trial. Winning an acquittal for him turned out to be little more than a formality. A few witnesses gave testimony beneficial to the victim and his family and damaging to the accused. Yet the novice attorney managed to discredit at least one witness as "an excitable and vindictive woman, who was five months advanced in pregnancy, who was a friend to the Galeys, and who expressed animosity against Jones and his family."[18]

The defendant's cause received a major assist when the only eyewitness to the shooting, John Galey, who had implicated both Wheeler and Jones in his pretrial deposition, failed to appear in court. Later it was learned that shortly before the trial began Thomas Jones visited the young man and his mother and handed them a black satchel. What the bag contained never became public knowledge, but rumor had it that hours before, Jones had seen his banker in Huntsville. Mrs. Galey accepted the satchel, Jones departed, and a couple of days later mother and son caught a train at Wheeler Station bound for Texas. They never returned to Lawrence County.

Spared rebuttal testimony, Wheeler was able to portray his brother-in-law as a peaceable man compelled to shoot a former employee he believed to be armed and ready to draw his own weapon to back up repeated threats of violence. After a brief deliberation, the jury returned a verdict of not guilty, thus permitting Thomas Jones to return to the bosom of his greatly relieved family. There the episode ended, although accusations of conflict of interest and manipulation of the legal system would dog both the defendant and his unseasoned but clever and resourceful counsel.[19]

——— ——— ———

Wheeler's accelerated entrance into the legal profession opened doors to a political career. When downturns in the local economy brought him "only partial success" at farming, he devoted increasing attention to the law practice he had established in Courtland. His legal dealings created relationships with state and county officials, some of whom, impressed by his military and legal reputation, urged him to run for a seat in the Alabama legislature. Initially he was prevented from doing so by legislation enacted by the postwar Congress, which forbade former high Confederate officials from holding public office. In May 1872, however, an amnesty bill that removed this prohibition went into effect, and almost immediately, former Confederate military and civilian officials began to be elected not only to state offices but to the U.S. House and Senate. In the case of Alabama, "home rule" was reestablished during the elections of November 1874 when the victory of the entire Democratic state ticket swept out of office all "Radicals" (Republicans), former Unionists, carpetbaggers, and scalawags.[20]

These events, as well as the continued urging of power brokers, made Wheeler consider running for office. Yet he resisted the urge until he believed his family's finances were in a condition to support a hiatus from farming and his law practice. In 1880 he finally made himself available as a Democratic candidate for the U.S. House of Representatives from Alabama's Eighth Congressional District. On July 21 of that year he delivered his first political speech in a bid to win the Democratic Party's nomination and the right to oppose the current office-holder, William M. Lowe, the candidate of the state's Greenbacker-Laborite party, who was also supported by black and white Republicans. Although far from a polished orator, from the start Wheeler made a respectable showing on the speaker's platform. Two months later, won over by the image of honesty and candor he projected as well as by the magic in the Wheeler name, the "Bourbon" (old-line aristocratic) wing of his party made him its candidate.[21]

During the ensuing campaign Wheeler declared that a reelection of Lowe would be a return to Radicalism and carpetbagger rule. The power in this message carried the day, and in November the Democratic standard-bearer prevailed—barely. Out of almost 25,000 votes cast, Wheeler won by a margin of forty-three, but only, it would seem, because state canvassers disqualified more than 600 votes cast for his opponent.[22]

Lowe angrily contested the outcome, but in December Wheeler, accompanied by his family, left Courtland for Washington, D.C., where on the first Monday in December he answered the roll prior to the opening session of the Forty-seventh Congress. Almost immediately he plunged into efforts to promote an issue that would remain at the top of his legislative agenda throughout his long career in the House: the improvement of navigation on that stretch of the Tennessee River around Muscle, Colbert, and Bee Tree shoals, where the river dropped 140 feet in thirty miles, imperiling traffic. In time he would introduce legislation not only calling for the removal of rapids, reefs, and other obstructions but also promoting flood control, reforestation, and the agricultural and industrial development of his home region, which abounded in raw materials such as nitrate and phosphorus.

Wheeler viewed the promotion of river commerce as a means not only of improving the quality of life of his constituents, the great majority of whom were small farmers who transported their crops to market by water, but of enhancing the economic well-being of the nation as a whole. As he put it during a debate before the Committee on Rivers and Harbors, "every dollar spent in that character of improvement is a certain and good investment, giving a positive return, and the work will be permanent and for all time." His efforts would result in the completion of the Muscle Shoals Canal and the building of bridges and dams (one of the latter would be named for him), not only on the Tennessee but also along the Mississippi and other great highways of water commerce. At the end of his congressional career he would take tremendous pride in having secured more than three and a quarter million dollars in appropriations for Tennessee River improvements alone.[23]

He did not confine his river amelioration efforts to floor debates. As John Dyer notes, "almost any week day while Congress was in recess General Wheeler could be seen alone or in the company of an army engineer in a small boat on the river [Tennessee] taking measurements, making observations, planning locks." Wheeler could not foresee the establishment of the Tennessee Valley Authority or the Rural Electrification Program that seventy years hence would transform life in his district as well as in many other quarters of the American South. Yet, as Dyer observes, "he did envision a region in which the industry of the miner, the skill of the artisan, and the labor of the farmer would be correlated in such a manner that a well-balanced and sound economic system would be the result."[24]

For a time, it appeared that he would not retain his House seat long enough to make more than a dent in his ambitious agenda. By appealing to the U.S. district court in Huntsville and citing examples of voter fraud, William Lowe succeeded in obtaining a recount of the 1880 election, the results of which nevertheless failed to settle the question definitively. Still, in May 1882—by which time Wheeler had served in the Forty-seventh Congress for eleven of the twelve months it had been in session—the House Committee on Elections, in which Republicans predominated, declared Lowe entitled to Wheeler's seat. The general reacted angrily to the decision, which he assailed in a two-hour speech. The following month, however, the full chamber upheld the committee vote and Wheeler sullenly left Washington for his home district.[25]

Lowe's victory was short-lived—he died of tuberculosis four months after unseating Wheeler. Although still smarting over what he considered his unfair ouster, Wheeler agreed to enter the special election called to fill the unexpired portion of Lowe's term. Running unopposed, he returned to the capital in January 1883 at the outset of the short session of the Forty-seventh Congress. He immediately joined in a heated debate over providing pensions for Mexican War veterans who had later served in the Confederate army. He lost this battle, but he continued to fight for causes dear to his heart and of importance to his constituents. These included lowering tariff duties that Southern farmers considered excessive and even ruinous; promoting the circulation of a national monetary standard backed by silver, which would enable agrarians to pay their debts in depreciated currency; and opposing attempts by the federal government to intervene in state elections.[26]

Wheeler's popularity among the voters of his district had been highlighted by his easy victory in the special election. Even so, party leaders held him responsible for the lengthy legal battle that had distracted attention from the party's agenda. They punished him by refusing to support him for reelection in 1883. Wheeler was forced to mend fences, which he did by returning home, publicly admitting tactical errors in his fight to retain his seat, calling for "unanimity and harmony" within the Bourbon Democracy, and actively supporting his party's candidate for the Forty-eighth Congress. During the two years his successor served, Wheeler returned to practicing law, farming, and tending to his various commercial interests, which now included a directorship of the Southern Railroad.[27]

His *mea culpa* had the desired effect, and he regained his House seat in March 1885. He retained it through the succeeding seven Congresses, a period that ended with his resignation in April 1900. During that extended career—he would leave the House as the senior member of his party in Congress—he failed to win distinction as a solon of the highest order. Nevertheless, he established a solid record of achievement on behalf of his constituents, not only in the area of river and harbor improvement, but on many other issues of regional and national significance as well. He was appointed to several House panels, including one of the most powerful, the Ways and Means Committee, on which he sat from 1894 to 1897; and he rose to become chairman of the Committee on Expenditures in the Department of the Treasury. Among the noncongressional appointments he coveted most were those that made him a visitor to the U.S. Military Academy and a regent of the Smithsonian Institution.[28]

Of his many House assignments, the old soldier was most proud of his service on the Military Affairs Committee. On this panel he continued his advocacy of pensions for veterans of the U.S. Army and Navy who had fought for the Confederacy. He also strove to upgrade the nation's coastal and inland fortifications, to expand and improve the West Point curriculum, and to maintain adequate funding of the armed services regardless of the fluctuating economic condition of the nation.[29]

His advocacy of the interests of Civil War veterans was not limited to the needs of those who had worn the gray. He advanced the pension claims of Union veterans, including African Americans. He championed the cause of Maj. Gen. Fitz John Porter, who had been dismissed from the U.S. Army in 1863 on what many observers considered trumped-up charges heavy with political overtones. He also showed becoming respect to some of those who had directly opposed him on the battlefields of 1862 to 1865. He publicly conveyed his condolences to the family of Philip Sheridan upon his death in 1888 and of William T. Sherman upon his passing three years later. And in 1897 he formed a committee of House members to attend the dedication of the tomb of Ulysses S. Grant in New York City.[30]

When Congress was not in session, Wheeler attended Confederate veterans' reunions and appeared at the unveiling of war memorials in various Southern cities. As the years went by, such gatherings included increasing numbers of guests who had fought for the Union. In these and other ways, Wheeler's public behavior bespoke a spirit of conciliation and reunion. The gentleman from Alabama, once viewed by his Northern colleagues as an unreconstructed Rebel, acquired an image as a political moderate, a nationalist rather than a regionalist, one who could be counted on to help defuse those war-related tensions that continued to vex the country years after Appomattox and Durham Station.

Along with his sectional orientation, Wheeler's political interests changed during the course of his House career. At the outset, he championed those causes such as tariff reform and free silver that had the greatest impact on small farmers, a group he considered himself a member of. Over time—as befitted his intimate involvement in river and railroad commerce—he allied himself with the relatively small group of "Southern liberals" in Congress who were less concerned with agrarian issues than with promoting industrial, commercial, and educational progress. He championed the industrial potential of Alaska when most Americans considered the recently acquired territory productive of nothing except permafrost and pneumonia. He sought to fund a canal through Central America fifteen years before it became a reality under President Theodore Roosevelt. He favored legislation to establish weather signal stations across the country and especially in those locations vulnerable to hurricanes and tornadoes. He consistently promoted common schools as a means of fulfilling "the duty of ingrafting the human mind with knowledge," and he fought the hostility to public education that was an element of the political ideology of many of his Southern colleagues. During the second session of the Forty-ninth Congress he even advocated an appropriation "for the purpose of ascertaining the peculiarities of the formation and structure of the earth's crust."[31]

——— ——— ———

Wheeler's dogged pursuit of facts and statistics on subjects that might appear to be of narrow or theoretical interest did not always translate into an effective legislative agenda. As one historian has observed, the congressman "excelled in research and presentation of the evidence to the public, but was lacking in his ability to continually sway his peers' votes." Yet, because he was widely read and well informed on a host of subjects, was open to new ideas and approaches, and sought the advice of experts in many fields, Wheeler became adept at identifying political issues before they became popular causes.[32]

During his seventh term in Congress, he began to champion the efforts of Cubans to seek relief from the oppressive rule of their Spanish overlords. In a House speech delivered on April 4, 1896, not long after an armed rebellion broke out on the island, he declared that "a nation like Spain, which at one time controlled two-thirds of this continent, and has been driven step by step till now she has only that beautiful island upon which to wreak her oppression—I believe that the sooner such a nation is driven from that island, lying as it does within two hours' sail of the coast of the United States, the sooner Cuba becomes free and independent or a member of this great Commonwealth, [and] the sooner will the cause of civilization and of Christianity receive the vindication to which it is entitled."[33]

In delivering such a ringing indictment of Spanish misrule, Wheeler appeared to occupy solid ground. It was an incontrovertible fact that the mother country had treated her North American crown colony with extreme harshness. For years the Cuban people had been subjected to arbitrary arrests and imprisonments; rapes, murders, and other atrocities perpetrated by colonial forces; and a "reconcentration" program under which Spanish forces ravaged the countryside while forcing the inhabitants of rural villages into squalid camps on the edge of more populous areas where the government could better control their movements. Even as her 150,000 troops oppressed the island (another 30,000 occupied Puerto Rico and the Philippines), Spain regularly promised the Cuban people greater political freedom and, eventually, home rule. But as Wheeler would later argue in a book on which he collaborated with Gen. Fitzhugh Lee, a former Confederate cavalry colleague and a postwar governor of Virginia, all such pledges "down to the latest and present autonomy scheme, have been the merest subterfuges, [de]void of the true essence of local self-government."[34]

When Wheeler first called for Cuban autonomy, American public opinion had not yet coalesced around the issue. Over the next two years, however, the plight of the suffering people on America's doorstep received breathless and often lurid coverage in the press, which helped create a groundswell of popular support for the Cuban people. Although Wheeler's voice was silent for a time after Daniella's sudden death in the spring of 1896, he addressed the issue with increasing frequency as the decade progressed and atrocities attributed to Cuba's rulers increasingly provoked the American public. By mid-1897 the congressman was urging the House to adopt a resolution proclaiming that a state of war existed in Cuba. In later months he advocated making preparations for military intervention.[35]

Wheeler's confrontational style offended many members of both parties, especially in the early days of the debate. It greatly troubled the Democratic administration of Grover Cleveland, which was committed to keeping the lid on Cuba. When Cleveland's Republican successor, William McKinley, a Union army veteran, took office in March 1897, he too attempted to contain the tide of imperialism rising in the country and in his own party. But the tide became a flood after February 15, 1898, when the battleship *Maine*, sent to Havana harbor to monitor the volatile local situation, exploded and sank, with the loss of 266 American lives. The cause of the disaster was never determined to the satisfaction of all concerned, but most Americans suspected Spanish involvement.[36]

Public reaction was swift and decisive. On March 8 a bill was introduced in the House appropriating fifty million dollars to support national defense—the first official step in the march toward war. Party differences were forgotten as Democrats and Republicans vied with one another to put their support for the measure on record. Congressman Wheeler added materially to his jingoist image when, rising to speak on behalf of the bill, he declared that many thousands of "brave and true hearts" throughout the South "join me in most earnest support of this resolution. . . . For a century American mothers have taught their sons that an ounce of glory earned in battle was worth more than a million pounds of gold!" He punctuated his marks by suddenly letting loose with what reporters considered a worthy rendition of the Rebel Yell. When he retook his seat it was to the accompaniment of wild applause from the chamber floor as well as from the galleries crammed with visitors overcome by the drama and excitement of the hour. Three weeks later Wheeler followed up his raucous call to action by introducing a resolution providing for U.S. intervention in Cuba. As Dyer points out, the measure joined "twenty-nine similar ones then reposing in the rooms of the Committee on Foreign Affairs."[37]

His peacekeeping efforts having failed, on April 11 McKinley asked Congress to grant him the authority to do what Wheeler's resolution had proposed. Both houses responded enthusiastically, and on the twenty-fifth a war declaration was sent to the White House. Wheeler was plainly delighted. For the past three years, he had been applying and reapplying to the army for active duty in the event of war with Spain. Now he reaffirmed his intention to serve in whatever capacity the commander in chief considered him capable of filling.[38]

In fact, the president was amenable to tendering Wheeler a major command. Viewing a war against a foreign power as an effective way to promote national reunion and sectional harmony, the McKinley administration had decided to offer commissions to prominent veterans of the blue and the gray considered spry enough to shoulder the burden of field service. Ex-Confederate officers given this opportunity included several cavalry veterans: Fitz Lee, most recently the U.S. consul-general in Havana; Thomas Rosser of Virginia, one of J. E. B. Stuart's most talented subordinates; and M. C. Butler of South Carolina, a colleague of Wheeler's during the Carolinas Campaign of 1865.

The same invitation was extended to the senior U.S. representative from Alabama, who on the evening of April 26 was called to the White House, where he met with McKinley, Secretary of War Russell A. Alger, Attorney General John W. Griggs, and officials of both major political parties. After some small talk, the president announced that he had been empowered to appoint fifteen major generals in the volunteer army for service in Cuba: "I have sent for you to ask if you want to go, and if you feel able to go." He had already broached the matter to Secretary Alger and other administration officials, "and it would have given you great pleasure to have heard the pleasant things said about you while we were discussing the matter yesterday."[39]

One account of this meeting has Wheeler initially declining the honor on grounds of age, whereupon McKinley explains that he has to appoint some ex-Confederates: "There must be a symbol that the old days are gone. You are needed." By his own account, Wheeler hesitated not at all, telling the president that "while I was sixty-one years old, I felt as strong and capable as when I was forty, or even much younger, and that I desired very much to have another opportunity to serve my country."[40]

As soon as the bargain was sealed, Wheeler left Washington for Alabama to await orders and plan his departure for the seat of war. Reports of his return to military service, this time in a United States army uniform, stirred public interest not only in the South but around the country. A *New York Times* headline proclaimed, "Blue and Gray United—Grizzled Joe Wheeler Draws His Sword Again." His constituents' reaction to the news was overwhelmingly positive, for by this time, thirty-three years after the most divisive war in American history, most ex-Confederates appeared just as eager as their former enemies to reunite in a common cause, proclaim their love of country, and heal old wounds.[41]

Wheeler's pledge of military service met less resistance from the Southern public as a whole than it did from his own family. Upon his return to Pond Spring he found he had to fend off the gentle but insistent objections of his children to the course to which he had committed himself. Thirty-year-old Annie—who had already made up her mind to go to Cuba as a volunteer nurse—repeatedly asked her father if he had not "had fighting enough to do from sixty-one to sixty-five."

For a time the old veteran avoided answering. When the inquiries kept coming, he finally took Annie aside and in a quiet voice and with a sly smile, told her, "Daughter, if a fish had been out of water for thirty-three years, and suddenly came in sight of a great pond, he'd wriggle a little, at any rate."[42]

14

A SOLDIER TO THE LAST

On May 2, 1898, while at home at Pond Spring, Wheeler was notified that his appointment to two-star command had been forwarded to the Senate. Two days later the nomination was confirmed, and five days after that he was ordered to report for duty at the training rendezvous that had been established on the old Chickamauga battlefield in Georgia. Tickled by the thought that his return to duty should begin on a field on which he had fought thirty-five years ago, he packed his trunk and, accompanied by members of his hastily assembled staff, including 2nd Lt. Joseph Wheeler Jr. of the 4th United States Artillery (USMA Class of 1895), entrained for Camp George H. Thomas.[1]

He arrived on the eleventh, and left at 2:07 the following afternoon. During that brief interval an order reached him to report at once to the commanding general of the army, Nelson A. Miles, at Tampa, Florida, the point of embarkation for Cuba. The same order informed Wheeler that he had been assigned "to command the cavalry in the expedition now leaving." For an old trooper, it was the most desirable posting imaginable.[2]

When Wheeler reached Tampa on the thirteenth, the sense of urgency inherent in his orders seemed to evaporate. Details of his assignment had not reached Florida, his interview with Miles was both belated and brief, and it was some days before Wheeler met with the expeditionary commander, William R. Shafter, a Civil War Medal of Honor winner and veteran of thirty-one years in the Regular Army. Their pairing must have turned heads, for no two major generals could have been more dissimilar in mien or stature—the wispy old volunteer and the gargantuan regular, his uniform coat straining to hold back some of his 300 pounds of flesh.[3]

While waiting for more information about his role in the campaigning that lay ahead, Wheeler and his son took rooms in the Tampa Bay Hotel. There they mingled with scores of gilt-encrusted officers of the regular and volunteer services, government officials in ice-cream suits, and rumpled-looking reporters seeking war stories. At first the newcomers moved inconspicuously through this crowd of the important and the self-important. As a junior officer young Joseph attracted little attention, and his father had left Alabama so hastily that his uniform was still at the tailor's, being altered to fit his compact physique, which continued to rise no more than two inches above five feet in height and encompass little more than 100 pounds. In fact, the only visible changes in Wheeler's physiognomy since the Civil War were his nearly bald head and the whiteness of his spade-shaped beard.

Until the woolen tunic with the twin stars on the shoulders arrived, Wheeler clothed himself in what war correspondent Stephen Bonsal described as "a linen duster of undoubted antiquity." So attired, "no one knew him, and no one paid any attention to him. He was given a small room on the sunny side of the hotel, where the thermometer was 110 degrees, and when with some embarrassment he slipped into the dining-room for luncheon, he was placed at the last table, the rendezvous of transients of little consequence and of short purse. . . . He went to bed at an early hour in a ramshackle cot that any lieutenant of volunteers would have disdained. . . . We thought the little old man was a devoted father, who had come perhaps to say 'good-by' to his son who was going to the war."[4]

Everything changed on the day his uniform arrived and for the first time in thirty-seven years he donned the blue of the United States Army. Suddenly everyone at the Tampa Bay Hotel wanted to meet and converse with the distinguished old warrior. Waiters and desk clerks fell over themselves to serve him and find more luxurious accommodations for him. Lesser-ranking officers saluted him profusely. Politicians pumped his hand, forced cigars on him, and sought favors for constituents recently gone into the ranks. Journalists pestered him for interviews and had him pose for their box cameras.

Any man rescued from deepest obscurity might have reveled in this sudden taste of celebrity, but Wheeler remained true to his nature. The famous war correspondent Richard Harding Davis described him as a man "on whom politics had left no mark, who was courteous because he could not help being so, who stood up when a second lieutenant was introduced to him, and who ran as lightly as a boy to help a woman move a chair, or to assist her to step from a carriage."[5]

One of the most memorable and evocative days in Wheeler's life began on the humid May morning when, with orders finally in hand, he reported at the rendezvous of his command. Stephen Bonsal observed him as stood at attention before a flagpole from which flew the Stars and Stripes "like the most formal subaltern of them all. His bare head was bowed more reverently forward, and a mist of tears veiled his eyes as he gazed steadfastly at the flag under which our army was to fight." A cavalry troop, trotting past, brought him out of his reverie and drew from him a cry of recognition: the horsemen belonged to the regiment he had joined immediately after leaving West Point. Memories of his service in the pre–Civil War army flooded over him, and when he spoke of them he did so in what Bonsal called "a voice quivering with emotion." As he told his son, "I feel as though I had been away on three weeks' furlough, and had but just come back to my own colors."[6]

Wheeler had been assigned command of the Cavalry Division of the 5th Army Corps. Its six regiments had been grouped into brigades commanded by seasoned veterans of the horse cavalry: Brig. Gens. Samuel S. Sumner and Samuel B. M. Young. The composition of the division may have given an old Confederate like Wheeler pause, at least initially. Two of its regular outfits—the 9th Cavalry of Sumner's brigade and the 10th Cavalry of Young's—were composed of African-American enlisted men and white officers. By far the most striking component of the command was its single volunteer regiment, a motley collection of cowboys, Ivy League athletes, and polo-playing socialites officially styled the 1st United States Volunteer Cavalry but already known to the newspaper-reading public by a name as colorful as the recruits themselves—the Rough Riders.

This aggregation of adventurous youth and grim-eyed frontiersmen was commanded by Col. Leonard Wood, a former contract surgeon and White House physician who twelve years hence would become chief of staff of the United States Army. Wood's executive officer was Lt. Col. Theodore Roosevelt, who in less than three years would make his home in the White House. An unlikely warrior in his walrus mustache and thick spectacles, Roosevelt lacked a military background but, as Richard Harding Davis observed, exuded "energy and brains and enthusiasm enough to inspire a whole regiment."[7]

From the first, Wheeler found his subordinates to be officers of ability and good sense, and their soldiers—the black troops included—worthy specimens of American manhood. The elderly ex-Confederate made differing impressions on the Northerners and Westerners he was to lead into battle. One noncommissioned officer was struck by Wheeler's "remarkably shaped head, and wonderfully expressive eyes . . . eyes that seemed to be looking a thousand years into the future." Some of the officers, especially those in the Rough Riders, were less impressed with his physiognomy or sagacity than with his obvious age and apparent frailty. Colonel Wood found him charming and courageous but too old for field service. His second-in-command agreed, calling Wheeler "an old dear, but he is very little more fit than Shafter to command."[8]

Roosevelt's opinion may have been ungenerous, but he was entitled to it. The well-heeled New Yorker had already made a substantial contribution to America's role in this war as assistant secretary of the navy, a post he had held for almost a year before his recent resignation. Largely through his efforts the nation had acquired the ships, the armament, and the seamen that had made her a first-class naval power. That power had been dramatically demonstrated on May 1 by Adm. George Dewey's Asiatic Squadron, which in less than four hours of fighting sank and crippled a Spanish fleet on the waters of Manila Bay. A second flotilla of fast, heavily armed warships under Adm. William T. Sampson would soon duplicate Dewey's feat thousands of miles from the Philippines.[9]

It was Sampson's North Atlantic Squadron that was responsible for the War Department's decision to send Wheeler's division off to war. The Spanish fleet ensconced in the harbor of Santiago, Cuba, held no terrors for Sampson, but the land batteries that commanded the entrance to the anchorage prevented him from engaging the enemy ships. When Sampson called on the army for assistance, Washington responded by ordering the 5th Corps to sail at once for Cuba.[10]

Wheeler received embarkation orders on the evening of June 7. Just before midnight he packed his regulars and Rough Riders aboard a train that shuttled them down to the wharves of Port Tampa. The next morning officers and men crowded aboard four transports and prepared to cast off. For a week, however, they went nowhere. Unfounded reports of Spanish cruisers lying in ambush kept Shafter's corps in port until the fourteenth. The delay was vexing enough, but Wheeler was more distressed to learn that a shortage of transportation meant that when the 5th Corps did sail it would be at less than full strength. A total of 2,822 members of the Cavalry Division would make the trip, less than half the paper strength of the command. A crowning indignity—a blow to the pride of any self-respecting trooper—was the necessity of taking only enough horses to mount some of the officers. When the division entered the fight in Cuba it would be in the role of dismounted cavalry.[11]

When finally under way, Shafter's fifty-ship flotilla churned south in three columns. Wheeler's transport, the *Allegheny*, led the column sailing nearest to Cuba. From the foredeck the general marveled at the night sky, which he described as "beautiful, the stars very bright, and . . . much more numerous than in more northern latitudes. At dusk we see Tortugas Light, and pass, leaving it to our right."[12]

By the seventeenth the transports were moving parallel to the Cuban coast. On shore they could discern Spanish fortifications and some of the troops that occupied them. The passengers expected to debark soon, but the voyage continued for nearly a week. Delays caused by the slowness of some vessels and the need to coordinate landing operations with Sampson's fleet, as well as with officers of Cuba's revolutionary army, prevented the expedition from making land until the twenty-third.

The troops came ashore at Daiquiri, a ramshackle hamlet at the southern tip of the island. What Wheeler called "serious difficulties," including a high surf that capsized landing craft and drowned some horses, plagued the disembarkation. The infantry brigade of Brig. Gen. Henry W. Lawton was first to land, Wheeler's men straggling ashore in its rear. When he reached dry ground, Wheeler found that the local defenders, infantry units under Lt. Gen. Arsenio Linares, had evacuated the area. At once he had a Rough Rider raise the American flag over an abandoned Spanish blockhouse just off the beach. The gesture, Wheeler wrote, "was responded to by shrill whistles from the entire fleet."[13]

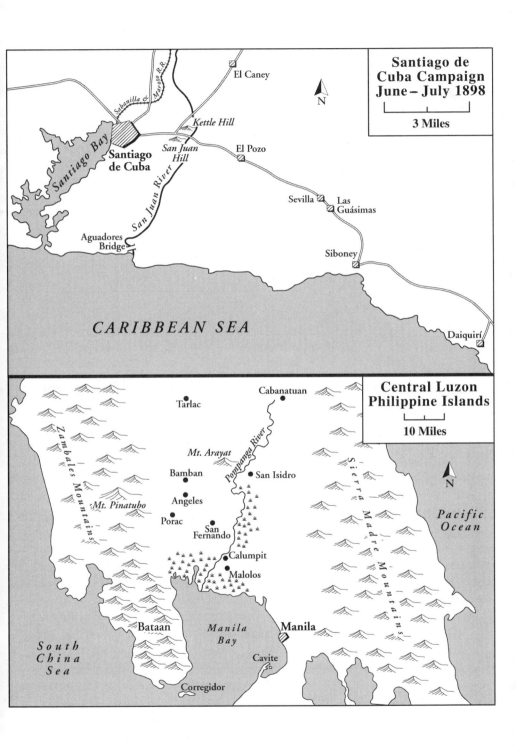

Santiago de
Cuba Campaign
June – July 1898

3 Miles

El Caney

N

Kettle Hill

San Juan
Hill

El Pozo

Santiago Bay

Santiago
de Cuba

San Juan River

Sabanilla & Maroto R.R.

Sevilla

Las
Guásimas

Aguadores
Bridge

Siboney

Daiquirí

CARIBBEAN SEA

Central Luzon
Philippine Islands

10 Miles

Cabanatuan

Tarlac

Mt. Arayat

Pompanga River

Bamban

San Isidro

Zambales Mountains

Angeles

Mt. Pinatubo

Porac

San
Fernando

Sierra Madre Mountains

Pacific
Ocean

N

Calumpit

Malolos

Bataan

Manila
Bay

Manila

South
China
Sea

Cavite

Corregidor

Acting on both impulse and instinct, Shafter rode several miles into the Cuban interior, to and beyond the point secured by Lawton's troops. By the time he returned from his spur-of-the-moment reconnaissance, it was after dark. It had been a risky undertaking, for Linares's men had not retreated far from shore; but it helped orient him to this sector of the island, especially in the direction of his next destination. That would be the port village of Siboney, about eleven miles up the coast. As expected, Shafter ordered the cavalry to march there the next morning to secure another point of disembarkation. With much of his command still aboard ship, Wheeler rode on ahead to Siboney accompanied by eight companies of Rough Riders and four companies each of the 1st and 3rd Cavalry—fewer than 1,000 officers and men—as well as three lightweight, rapid-fire Hotchkiss guns.[14]

When the contingent reached Siboney some time after 8 AM, it found Lawton's men already there. Shafter had determined to move against the main Spanish position outside Santiago rather than oppose the harbor forts, as the navy had desired. He had given Lawton the advance—the post of honor—and the brigadier expected the next morning to make contact with an enemy force that Cuban scouts estimated at 2,000 officers and men. Supported by a pair of German-made field guns, these troops had taken up a fortified position four miles from Siboney. When Lawton encountered them, Wheeler, as befitted his status as the least experienced (but highest ranking) of Shafter's three division commanders, was to remain in a reserve position well to the rear. Only if called upon was he to move up, and only if Lawton acquiesced would he see action. It seemed clear that this war was intended to be fought and won by the stalwarts of the regular service.

But Wheeler had other ideas. Shafter having decided to supervise the landing from aboard ship (his constitution might not survive hours of exposure to the tropical sun ashore), Wheeler was the ranking general on the scene. Over the course of a long—if long-ago—military career, the erstwhile War Child had never been one to hang in the rear when combat and glory lay just ahead, as they appeared to do. Nor had he come hundreds of miles from home to salute an officer of lesser rank and meekly do his bidding.

Therefore, at 5 AM on the twenty-fourth, before Lawton put his men on the road, Wheeler had his buglers blow reveille. Assembling everyone who had made the trek from Daiquiri, he and General Young led their foot cavalry up the road to Santiago. When he learned of Wheeler's end-run around him, Lawton was suitably furious but could do nothing except fume inwardly.[15]

By two routes—the main road and a more westerly coastal trail—Wheeler marched to Sevilla (which the Americans chose to call Las Guasimas), approaching the village at about seven-thirty. Approximately 460 members of the 1st and 10th Cavalry occupied the road, while some 500 of Wood's Rough Riders had taken the coastal trail. When Young's scouts reported sighting stone breastworks on a lofty eminence just up ahead, Wheeler had his artillerymen lob a few shells in that direction. The Spaniards returned the fire, and both of Wheeler's columns buried themselves in the jungle-like undergrowth that lined their roads. Having staked out a perimeter as near the enemy position as possible, for the next several hours the widely separated columns held up their end of the first sustained clash between the principal antagonists on Cuba.

The firefight took a heavy toll on the Americans, the inevitable result of the enemy's advantages in strength, armament, and position. Gen. Antero Rubin's garrison outnumbered Wheeler's combined force and was ensconced behind fixed works that could not easily be taken in flank or rear. Moreover, the Spaniards were wielding state-of-the-art weaponry—not only those Krupp-made cannons, but also Mauser repeating rifles fed by ammo clips and firing smokeless powder. Both of Wheeler's columns were also armed with foreign-made shoulder arms—Krag-Jorgensen carbines—but their effective range was shorter and they fired fewer rounds per minute. Wheeler was mightily impressed by the enemy's firepower, remarking that in his long experience he had never witnessed such sustained musketry.[16]

For most of the fight his men were very much on the defensive and so hard-pressed that before the day was over their leader was forced to swallow his pride and petition Lawton for help. It proved to be unneeded, however, for just as the reinforcements arrived, Wheeler's regulars advanced slowly but implacably toward the top of the hill. Their intimidating climb appeared to drive the Spaniards away. In actuality, Rubin, fearing he would soon be surrounded by American reinforcements, had begun to fall back before the cavalry neared his works. From his imperfect vantage point, Wheeler only saw that the summit was suddenly clear of the enemy. As he rode forward in pursuit, he forgot himself. For an exhilarating moment, he was back on the battlefields of Tennessee or Georgia, leading his Rebels in a wildly successful attack. Regulars and Rough Riders observed him as he stood up in the stirrups and shouted at the top of his voice, "We've got the damned Yankees on the run!" One of his staff officers called it "an embarrassing moment for the General," but added that everyone around him laughed, "and he joined [in] and the incident was closed."[17]

Many of those who read news accounts of the battle considered the utterance the fruit of a reporter's imagination. But when asked to verify the incident Wheeler would admit to having used the term "Yankee." Devout Christian that he was, however, he would make a point of denying he had preceded it with a profanity.[18]

——— ——— ———

When word of Wheeler's success flashed to the rear, it was quickly relayed to Washington and the American public. This, the first triumph of American arms on foreign soil since the Mexican War, not only added to the Wheeler legend but had a profound effect on the morale of his command and, in fact, of the entire expeditionary force. By their courage and determination Wheeler's regulars and volunteers had captured a strategic position that appeared to afford access to the main enemy force east of Santiago. The seizure of Las Guasimas also cleared the interior, thus safeguarding the continuing debarkation of Shafter's corps.[19]

These achievements notwithstanding, Wheeler's willingness to rush to the front without explicit instructions and his calculated effort to outmaneuver a fellow division commander brought him a certain amount of censure, most of it emanating from General Lawton's staff and from newspapermen sympathetic to the regular army. Stephen Bonsal, for one, would claim in dispatches from the field and, later, in a book-length study of the Santiago Campaign that Wheeler had blundered with near-disastrous results: his "direct disobedience to orders" had permitted his command to be ambushed and suffer needlessly. With better planning, the army could have advanced toward Santiago without being drawn into a defensive struggle. Wheeler would feel compelled to defend his actions through newspaper interviews as well as in a book of his own, *The Santiago Campaign, 1898*, which he knocked out during a two-week stretch that summer with the assistance of his military secretary, Leonard Wilson, and which was published before year's end.[20]

After Las Guasimas, General Shafter, who had finally come ashore to exercise command from a carriage, forbade Wheeler from launching any more offensives unless specifically ordered to do so. But there was no friction between him and his elderly subordinate. In fact, they immediately collaborated on a strategy for operating against Santiago. Eventually it was decided that Lawton's men would attack the 1,200 Spaniards holed up in the fortified village of El Caney, northeast of the city—an effort expected to take no more than a couple of hours—after which the division of Brig. Gen. J. Ford Kent, supported by the now-intact Cavalry Division, would assault San Juan Heights, the key to the entire enemy position. This latter operation would involve driving General Linares's troops from blockhouses and rifle pits at the summit of what became known as Kettle Hill, on the north side of the road to Santiago, and San Juan Hill, across the road to the south and west.[21]

Through scouting missions Wheeler conducted in company with his own troops and Cuban guides, he gained a great deal of intelligence about enemy positions and numbers, which was factored into the battle plan. But when Shafter put that plan into execution on the morning of July 1, Wheeler was not on the field. His health undermined by the unremitting heat, mosquitoes and other tropical vermin, poor quality rations, and overexertion, he fell victim to a form of malaria that left him so groggy and debilitated that General Sumner had to lead the Cavalry Division into action against Kettle Hill. (General Young having also been felled by illness, Colonel Wood commanded his brigade this day, Lieutenant Colonel Roosevelt moving up to lead the Rough Riders.)[22]

Late on the morning of the first, with the fighting at Kettle Hill at full fury, Wheeler responded to the beckoning call of the guns. Thanks to the ministrations of his private nurse—his daughter Annie—the general made enough of a recovery to buckle on his saber and mount his war horse. Galloping to the front, he not only reassumed command of his division but, at Shafter's order, he directed the operations of Kent's division on the cavalry's left flank.

By the time Wheeler arrived, the battle had turned in the Americans' favor. As at Las Guasimas, they had overcome early setbacks—including Lawton's unexpectedly extended (eleven-hours-long) reduction of El Caney—through a triumphant late-afternoon attack up Kettle and San Juan Hills. Many participants had distinguished themselves, most particularly the black troopers of the 9th and 10th Cavalry, Roosevelt's Rough Riders, and the foot soldiers under Kent who went up the heights alongside the volunteers. A young lieutenant in the 10th Cavalry named Pershing, who during a later war would command an American army in France, recalled that "white regiments, black regiments, Regulars and Rough Riders, representing the young manhood of the North and South, fought shoulder to shoulder, unmindful of race or color, unmindful of whether commanded by ex-Confederates or not, and mindful only of their common duty as Americans."[23]

Although once again they took a grievous toll of the attackers—upwards of 1,400 American and Cuban casualties—the Spaniards were finally dislodged from San Juan Heights. They did not consider themselves vanquished; when forced from the crest, they simply redeployed closer to Santiago, where they dug in and resumed firing. The fighting extended well into July 2, following a night-long rain that made the tired soldiers utterly miserable and churned into soup the roads by which reinforcements and supplies would have to reach the front.

By noon on the second Lawton and his division had finally joined Shafter, Wheeler, and Kent on San Juan Heights, taking position on the cavalry's right flank. But although the 5th Corps was now intact, Shafter made no effort to advance, aware that the troops were still recovering from their labors of the previous twenty-four hours. For their part, the Spaniards—now under General Jose Toral—made no attempt to retake the ground they had lost.

Discouraged by his recent losses, Shafter began to fear that his command had been fought out. At 6 PM on the second, after day-long fighting intense enough to inflict another 150 American casualties, he conferred with Wheeler and his other senior subordinates. To them he expressed the conviction that reports of an imminent influx of Spanish reinforcements were accurate. He also confided that, despite repeated entreaties, Admiral Sampson had refused to attack the forts at the mouth of the harbor, a move that might relieve the army of some pressure. In this crisis atmosphere, Shafter appeared to favor abandoning the captured heights and falling back. Although his own officers had urged him to withdraw, Wheeler joined Lawton and Kent in advising their superior to hold on. Shafter agreed to do so but reserved the right to decide otherwise if twenty-four hours passed without any improvement in their situation. The following day, assailed by illness, he again gave way to pessimism, cabling the War Department that, given the enemy's unexpectedly stout opposition, Santiago might be unassailable with his force on hand (even so, he went through the motions of demanding Toral's surrender). He even suggested that he might have to withdraw five miles, a move that would enable his corps to be more regularly supplied by rail.[24]

Shafter's dark assessment of his plight—especially his reference to a possible retreat—left official Washington in a state of uncertainty and depression. But the crisis proved to be short-lived. Concerned that his generals were contemplating a surrender, the island's governor general ordered the Spanish fleet to break out of Santiago Harbor and make a run for open water. The attempt, made late on the third, was a disastrous mistake; Sampson's heavier and more seaworthy ships, this day commanded by Adm. Winfield Scott Schley, made quick work of the enemy, most of whose vessels they sent to the bottom of the harbor or forced to run aground.[25]

The navy's victory stiffened the army's spine, as did a message from General Toral suggesting a willingness to discuss surrender terms. Shafter informed a relieved War Department and White House that he had changed his mind and would hold his position on Santiago's doorstep. His mental condition restored and his physical condition improving, he began to envision a quick capitulation by Toral. In the interim, he issued a general order commending his officers and men for their gallant conduct in the recent operations. Although Wheeler—now fully recovered from his bout with malaria—had been absent during the critical phase of the fighting on San Juan Heights, he was cited for having ably performed "the most difficult task" assigned to any division commander on July 1.[26]

Shafter's convictions notwithstanding, surrender negotiations dragged on for two weeks. They were not expedited until after General Miles reached the island on July 13 and entered into the discussions alongside Shafter, Wheeler, and other senior officers. When Toral agreed to lay down his arms if acceptable terms could be worked out, Wheeler was appointed to head a three-man commission that would draft a surrender agreement. Assisted by his secretary, Wilson, he prepared the papers, presented them to Toral, then haggled with the general and his staff over nomenclature and protocol.

Early on the sixteenth Toral announced his acceptance of the terms. The following morning at nine o'clock a surrender ceremony, attended by nearly 200 members of both armies, was held in a grove of trees between the lines. After Toral signed the document Wheeler had prepared, the opponents shook hands and exchanged pleasantries and cigars, an incongruous demonstration of goodwill that a reporter likened to "a meeting of old friends and not the acknowledgment of defeat." Then followed a military procession through the streets of Santiago—Shafter and Wheeler at the head of the column—as the Americans took formal possession of the city. At high noon the Stars and Stripes was run up the flagpole in the plaza in front of the governor's palace.[27]

The war to liberate Cuba was at an end, but the expansion of America's overseas empire had just begun. Under the terms of the surrender pact, Cuba would be granted her independence from Spain, which would also cede to the United States Puerto Rico (another battleground between American and Spanish forces) and the island of Guam, important to the U.S. Navy as a coaling and repair station. The fate of the Philippines, yet another arena of the war, was to be determined at a peace conference to be held two and a half months hence in Paris. Many political and diplomatic hurdles had to be cleared before the United States could fully embrace the results of its success in overseas combat. These difficulties, however, did not trouble the great majority of the blue-clad soldiers on Cuba. To them what counted was that the fighting was at an end and they would soon be on their way home.[28]

——— ——— ———

Wheeler was content to leave the Caribbean behind, but only if the job was over. For nearly a month after Cuba's surrender, fighting continued on Puerto Rico until the Spanish forces there were persuaded to cease firing. In common with subordinates including Wood and Roosevelt, Wheeler petitioned the War Department to transfer him to that theater. Instead he was sent, along with the greater part of the army but in advance of most of it, to Montauk Point on the tip of Long Island, some 120 miles northeast of New York City.[29]

At Montauk a rendezvous for returning troops, Camp Wikoff, had been established; it included a hastily constructed, inadequately supplied, and woefully understaffed hospital. The hospital would be the focal point of attention at the camp over the next several months, because almost as soon as the first transport docked off Montauk Point a veritable army of the sick, the invalid, and the dying came ashore—the fruit of summer campaigning in a tropical theater alive with rank vegetation, devoid of potable water, and infested with insects carrying diseases the medical science of the day was virtually powerless to combat.

The baleful effects of the recent campaigning had not been manifest to Shafter until the shooting stopped, by which time he had a major health crisis on its hands. He failed to notify the War Department of the gravity of the situation until early August, at which time his reports were so alarming that Washington ordered almost every soldier eligible for discharge to be returned to the States at once. The hurried embarkation allowed no time for setting up medical facilities capable of handling the seemingly endless wave of soldiers who arrived on crutches and stretchers.[30]

General Wheeler, accompanied by 700 of his officers and men—many of them ill or soon to become ill—left Santiago harbor aboard the transport

Miami on August 6 and reached Montauk Point eight days later. On the morning of the fifteenth, Wheeler bounded down the gangplank into the arms of his waiting family. Immediately after, he was mobbed by reporters and news photographers. Within hours, banner headlines in both northern and southern newspapers were announcing his triumphal return and recounting in glowing terms his Cuban adventures. Not even disease had stilled his fighting spirit and his determined courage. Even his slip-of-the-tongue reference to skedaddling Yankees was fashioned into a reminder of his faithful service in two wars more than thirty years apart.[31]

His celebrity status quickly gave way to unwanted notoriety. Two days after reaching Long Island he was called to Washington for conferences at the White House and War Department. The president and his secretary of war praised Wheeler's contributions to victory and thanked him for his services, military and political. McKinley did Wheeler no favor, however, when he returned him to Montauk Point in the role of commander of Camp Wikoff until the demobilization of the 5th Corps was complete, at which time General Shafter would supersede him.

The assignment placed Wheeler in a position he was not qualified to fill by training, experience, or mindset. Military administration had never been his forte, and he knew next to nothing about running a hospital, especially one so lacking in infrastructure. The inevitable result was that over the next six weeks he was widely criticized by editors, politicians, and the families of patients, who blamed him for the inadequate medical care available at Wikoff—much of which was neither his fault nor within his power to remedy.

His reputation could have been irredeemably damaged by the misery that overflowed Wikoff in common with the leaky latrines and the summer downpours that turned the camp into a world of mud (and provided its only safe supply of drinking water). In the end, several events intervened to save his good name. He received vocal and unqualified support from Alger and McKinley, especially during their much-publicized visits to Wikoff on August 27 and September 3, respectively. Interviews Wheeler gave to the press publicized his well-meaning and increasingly effective efforts to ameliorate the suffering of the sick and disabled ("everything was done," he insisted, "which hand could do and brain devise for the well-being of the soldiers"). All told, 257 of Wikoff's patients would succumb to tropical diseases or other maladies, but the mortality rate never rose above 2 percent during Wheeler's tenure, an extremely low figure given the variety of diseases from which the veterans suffered and the inadequacies of current medical knowledge.[32]

Other events worked in his favor as well. A blue-ribbon panel formed by a reluctant McKinley to investigate charges of mismanagement and corruption cleared the general of the most serious charges that had been lodged against him. He benefited from the camp-wide admiration accorded his daughter, Annie, whose unstinting efforts to nurse the sick and provide for their every comfort gained her the nickname "Army Angel." And he received the sympathy of thousands upon the death of his youngest son, Thomas, a Naval Academy cadet just returned from the war, who on September 7 drowned while bathing in the surf off Montauk. Consumed by grief, Thomas's father shipped his body to Wheeler Station for burial next to his mother in the family cemetery.[33]

Wheeler's service at Camp Wikoff ended on September 23, when he was relieved by General Shafter, recently recovered from a virulent illness. Wheeler's next assignment was a happy contrast to the one he had just completed: command of the 4th Army Corps, headquartered at Huntsville, Alabama. The prestigious sinecure, whose location close to his home would enable him to attend to both professional and personal interests, was clearly a reward for his contributions to the nation, and a token of McKinley's gratitude for the unflagging support Wheeler had given his administration.[34]

McKinley also ensured that the general realized how much his services were appreciated by the general public. Beginning in late October, he spent an increasing amount of time away from Huntsville, being ordered to attend a series of "peace jubilees" held in cities north and south. During the first of these, at Philadelphia, he joined McKinley and General Miles at a review of hundreds of returned veterans. Watching him ride at the head of the procession, acknowledging the cheers of spectators who knew him not as the villain of the Camp Wikoff fiasco but as a hero of the Santiago Campaign, a reporter described him as "the picture of wiry activity and cool courage."[35]

In later weeks the general appeared at similar celebrations in Atlanta, Nashville, and elsewhere in the South. During this same period he became the recipient of awards and honors granted by various organizations and institutions. The Tennessee chapter of the Daughters of the American Revolution presented him with a gift sword. Georgetown College in Washington, D.C., conferred on him the degree of doctor of laws. He was a featured speaker before civic, fraternal, and professional organizations in Richmond, Chattanooga, Birmingham, Mobile, and elsewhere. And he continued to be a much sought-after guest at veterans' reunions, especially the gatherings of the United Confederate Veterans and the Society of the Army of Tennessee.[36]

In many of his public addresses, Wheeler trumpeted his views on international affairs including his fervent belief that America should acquire not just Puerto Rico, Guam, and the Philippines but every available overseas territory that would contribute to her security and prosperity. Annexation, he told a Nashville audience in early December 1898, was an issue "that has passed beyond the point of discussion. The logic of events has visited upon us these colonies, and it is our duty now to legislate and to do the most possible for the benefit of the inhabitants of these islands and the United States."[37]

Over time, utterances of this sort made him a *persona non grata* in the ranks of the political party of which he had been a lifelong adherent. He was more popular than ever with his constituents—in the summer of '98 he easily won renomination for an eighth term in the House, and he cruised to victory that November. Democratic leaders, however, reacted sharply to his ardent support of a war that had been run by a Republican administration. When charged with mismanagement and neglect of patients at Camp Wikoff, Wheeler had defended not only himself but also, by extension, McKinley, Alger, and other G.O.P. officials. And his advocacy of an overseas empire ran counter to the growing antiexpansionist orientation of the national Democratic party.

Soon after Wheeler—who remained a major general of volunteers—reclaimed his House seat during the opening session of the Fifty-fifth Congress, party leaders took their revenge. Citing a constitutional provision that forbade any member of Congress from holding another public office including a military command, leading Democrats called for a vote to expel him. Wheeler survived the vote, thanks largely to the support of the House's Republican majority. Party leaders, however, continued to oppose and thwart him in any way possible. They helped defeat an amendment that would have enlarged the Regular Army to include a fourth major generalship, a position McKinley intended to fill with Wheeler. He suffered a particularly embarrassing defeat when House leaders rebuked him for inviting his former commander, Shafter, to address the chamber, an invitation they promptly revoked. Stung by these petty acts of retaliation, and finding his influence in Democratic circles increasingly circumscribed, Wheeler would resign his seat before his term was out.[38]

Not wishing to see one of his most popular and effective supporters forced to leave the army, whose volunteer force was undergoing a sharp reduction, McKinley in April 1899 outflanked the House leadership by appointing him a brigadier general in the Regular Army. Wheeler, who was willing to accept a demotion from two-star rank, wished to take on one more combat assignment. He sought a command in the Philippines, which the United States had annexed under terms of the peace treaty with Spain, signed in Paris on December 10, 1898. Two months later fighting had broken out between occupation forces and Filipino rebels determined to win independence for their archipelago.[39]

By mid-1899 the Philippine Insurrection was raging at white heat, pitting 4,000 poorly armed and equipped but fanatically inspired followers of Emilio Aguinaldo against the 8th Army Corps of Maj. Gen. Elwell S. Otis. At first the fighting more or less followed the pattern of conventional warfare, but before the year was out Aguinaldo would disband his "Army of Liberation" and commence guerrilla operations. For America, the result would be a war of conquest ten times as long and far more costly than the "splendid little war" on Cuba and Puerto Rico.

On June 20, 1899, Wheeler's repeated applications for service paid off with his assignment to command the 1st Brigade, 2nd Division of Otis's corps. In mid-August he relinquished his post at Huntsville and, accompanied by Joe Jr. and Annie (who had become his constant companion), traveled to San Francisco, where he took ship for central Luzon. He arrived in Manila on August 21 and immediately joined his command, which consisted principally of the 9th and 12th United States Infantry.[40]

Wheeler's service in the Philippines would prove to be less satisfying and successful than his campaigning in Cuba. From the first, he clashed not only with Otis but with the latter's ranking subordinate and future successor, Maj. Gen. Arthur McArthur. Late in October, barely two months after reaching Luzon, Wheeler was complaining to President McKinley that Otis was unaccountably delaying a decisive confrontation with Aguinaldo. When Otis finally launched his offensive the following month and Wheeler got his first taste of combat, he angered his immediate superior, McArthur, during the 2nd Division's crossing of the Paruao River near the village of Bamban. Wheeler had been ordered to make a diversion to distract the principal enemy force while McArthur's main body maneuvered around its flank. Instead, Wheeler—with the same streak of impetuosity that had won him praise and condemnation at Las Guasimas— attacked the Filipinos head-on. Ignoring McArthur's order to halt, he fought his way across the river, but once on the other side lost control of his brigade. Having outrun their support, the badly scattered Regulars might have been surrounded and crushed. As it was, the day ended in success for their division, an outcome that spared Wheeler the consequences of his impulsiveness.[41]

Despite the fortunate outcome, McArthur thereafter confined his independent-minded subordinate to a rear sector. In later weeks, Wheeler performed capably in a support role. His most notable accomplishment was a bamboo bridge his troops built across a half-mile washout near Tarlac over which arms, ammunition, and thousands of rations reached the troops at the front. The supply flow enabled Otis's offensive to continue. Eventually it drove the enemy across the Luzon plains and into the island's northern mountains. It was at this point that Aguinaldo, convinced he could not prevail in conventional campaigning, initiated guerilla operations. By this stratagem he would prolong the war for another year and a half. It would not wind down until early 1900, when his capture, combined with a series of rebel defeats at the hands of the resourceful, determined McArthur, brought on the collapse of the insurgent cause.[42]

———————

Joe Wheeler was not on hand to witness the successful conclusion of the U.S. war effort. When he saw that he would not be permitted to resume front-line duty, he requested to be relieved of his command. On January 15, 1900, he and Annie left Luzon for the States. Joe Jr. stayed behind to win distinction in command of both conventional forces and scouting detachments composed of pro-American Filipinos.[43]

Wheeler still held his congressional seat, which he intended to reclaim, albeit unenthusiastically, until McKinley offered him one last military assignment, command of the Department of the Lakes. Realizing he could complete his army career in that position, Wheeler accepted the appointment and moved with Annie to departmental headquarters in Chicago. The assignment, which lasted less than three months, was not taxing to the general's health, which had begun to wane under the burdens imposed by his overseas campaigning and his political difficulties. On September 10, 1900, his sixty-fourth birthday, he retired from active military service and returned with his daughter to Pond Spring, to live out the remaining six years of his life.[44]

When at home, Wheeler received visitors and well-wishers on a weekly—sometimes a daily—basis. He reentered business life as the agent of a firearms manufacturer. In his free time, he worked on literary projects. A few years earlier he had assembled his military memoirs, which, with the assistance of former staff officers with whom he kept in close touch and under the editorship of one of his old soldiers, had been published in 1899 under the title *Campaigns of Wheeler and His Cavalry, 1862–1865*. At about this same time, his history of Cuba and the war there, written in collaboration with Fitzhugh Lee, appeared in print. Earlier literary works included his memoir of Shiloh, published in the *Southern Historical Society Papers* for 1896; an article titled "An Effort to Rescue Jefferson Davis," which ran in *Century Illustrated Magazine* two years later; and a lengthy study of the Perryville Campaign, the lead article in volume three of the well-known anthology *Battles and Leaders of the Civil War*. He and his wife also produced a pamphlet of Wheeler and Jones genealogy, published shortly before Daniella's death.[45]

Although he cherished his home life, Wheeler spent many of his final years traveling in the States and abroad. He spoke before numerous groups throughout the East. He visited his sister Lucy and her family in New York, was feted at a banquet by his old prep school in Connecticut, and summered in Rhode Island, where he became known as the "Social Lion" of Newport. In 1901 he traveled to Europe. In London he was guest of honor at a gala reception; in Paris he observed the maneuvers of the French army and toured Napoleon's battlefields. He returned to England in 1902, but his sightseeing was cut short by a bout with rheumatism. In 1904–5 he spent several months in Mexico, where "every honor was shown him" and he forged a friendship with President Porforio Diaz.[46]

In January 1906, while at his sister's home in Brooklyn, the old general fell ill with pleurisy. At first his condition was not considered serious, but within three days he was battling pneumonia, which rapidly drained his strength. He had not been well for some months, and in his weakened condition he was no match for the virulent disease. Nevertheless, he fought his unseen enemy—against which he and medical science had few weapons—with the same courage and resolve he had displayed on countless fields of combat, in the uniforms of two armies. At first a faint hope was entertained for his recovery but by Thursday, the twenty-fifth, his breathing became shallow and he began to drift into delirium. By early evening the struggle had neared its inevitable conclusion.

Family members would later recall that up to this time his mind had been clear. Suddenly, however, "it wandered back and he heard the bugle call and the battle cry." Like the good soldier he had always been, he answered both, and reported to his Superior.[47]

NOTES

ABBREVIATIONS USED IN NOTES

ADA&H   Alabama Department of Archives and History
B&L   Battles and Leaders of the Civil War
C-, F-   container, folder
CAH   Center for American History, University of Texas Library
CR   Congressional Record
CV   Confederate Veteran
CWH   Civil War History
CWTI   Civil War Times Illustrated
DU   William R. Perkins Library, Duke University
EU   Robert W. Woodruff Library, Emory University
GHQ   Georgia Historical Quarterly
GLC   Gilder Lehrman Collection
GSA   Georgia State Archives
HU   Dearborn Collection, Houghton Library, Harvard University
JW   Joseph Wheeler
MC   Eleanor S. Brockenbrough Library, Museum of the Confederacy
MDA&H   Mississippi Department of Archives and History
MSS   correspondence, papers
NA   National Archives
N-YHS   New-York Historical Society
OR   War of the Rebellion: A Compilation of the Official Records of the Union and
         Confederate Armies
RG-, E- record group, entry
SB   Southern Bivouac
SHC   Southern Historical Collection, Wilson Library, University of North Carolina
SHSP   Southern Historical Society Papers
THQ   Tennessee Historical Quarterly
TSL&A   Tennessee State Library and Archives
USAMHI   U.S. Army Military History Institute
USMAA   U.S. Military Academy Archives
WRHS   Western Reserve Historical Society

1. Not Length or Breadth or Thickness

1. William C. Harris, *Leroy Pope Walker, Confederate Secretary of War* (Tuscaloosa, Ala.: Confederate Publishing Co., Inc., 1962), 7–18.
2. Harris, *Leroy Pope Walker*, 104–20; *OR*, ser. 1, vol. 4: 416, 440, 445; vol. 6: 793; vol. 52, pt. 2: 152, 192.
3. *OR*, ser. 1, vol. 4: 416; John Witherspoon Du Bose, *General Joseph Wheeler and the Army of Tennessee* (New York: Neale Publishing Co., 1912), 54–55.
4. Wheeler Family History, JW MSS, C-1, F-1, ADA&H; *OR*, ser. 1, vol. 52, pt. 2: 149, 152, 169; Harris, *Leroy Pope Walker*, 99–100.
5. George Washington Cullum, comp., *Biographical Register of the Officers and Graduates of the United States Military Academy at West Point, New York . . .* (Boston: Houghton Mifflin Co., 1891), 2: 730.
6. Charles Rice, *Hard Times: The Civil War in Huntsville and Northern Alabama, 1861–1865* (Huntsville, Ala.: Old Huntsville Magazine, 1994), 13–14.
7. Rice, *Hard Times*, 13–14.
8. Du Bose, *Wheeler and the Army of Tennessee*, 55–56.
9. *OR*, ser. 1, vol. 4:416–17, 440; vol. 6:761.
10. Du Bose, *Wheeler and the Army of Tennessee*, 53–54; John P. Dyer, *"Fightin' Joe" Wheeler* (Baton Rouge: Louisiana State University Press, 1941), 23–24.
11. *OR*, ser. 1, vol. 6:744.
12. *OR*, ser. 1, vol. 52, pt. 2:169.
13. *OR*, ser. 1, vol. 6:758–60.
14. *OR*, ser. 1, vol. 6:761, 764, 772, 793, 810, 815–16, 820; vol. 52, pt. 2: 202, 265; Du Bose, *Wheeler and the Army of Tennessee*, 54.
15. Wheeler Family History, JW MSS, C-1, F-1, 2, ADA&H; Dyer, *"Fightin' Joe" Wheeler*, 8–9; John P. Dyer, "The Civil War Career of General Joseph Wheeler," *GHQ* 19 (1935): 17; Du Bose, *Wheeler and the Army of Tennessee*, 49–50; "Sketch of Lieutenant-General [sic] Joseph Wheeler," *SB* 2 (1884): 241–42.
16. Wheeler Family History, JW MSS, C-1, F-1, ADA& H; Dyer, *"Fightin' Joe" Wheeler*, 8–9.
17. Dyer, *"Fightin' Joe" Wheeler*, 10.
18. Dyer, *"Fightin' Joe" Wheeler*, 11; Thomas C. DeLeon, *Joseph Wheeler, the Man, the Statesman, the Soldier* (Atlanta: Byrd Printing Co., 1899), 52.
19. Dyer, *"Fightin' Joe" Wheeler*, 11–12; Du Bose, *Wheeler and the Army of Tennessee*, 50; Wheeler Family History, JW MSS, C-1, F-1, ADA& H.
20. Dyer, *"Fightin' Joe" Wheeler*, 12; Jefferson Davis to JW, June 15, 1854 (with endorsement by Mrs. Augusta Hull Platt), Cadet Application MSS, USMAA.
21. Du Bose, *Wheeler and the Army of Tennessee*, 49–51; Francis B. Heitman, comp., *Historical Register and Dictionary of the United States Army, from Its Organization, September 29, 1789, to March 2, 1903* (Washington, D.C.: Government Printing Office, 1903), 1: 553.
22. JW to Joseph G. Totten, Apr. 28, May 16, 1853; John Wheeler to Jefferson Davis, June 6, 1854 (with endorsement by Davis, June 8, 1854); Rev. Francis Vinton to Joseph G. Totten, Nov. 8, 1853; all, Cadet Application MSS, USMAA.
23. Jefferson Davis to JW, June 15, 1854 (with endorsement by Mrs. Augusta Hull Platt); JW to Joseph G. Totten, June 15, 1864; both, Cadet Application MSS, USMAA.
24. Academic Record of Joseph Wheeler Jr. USMA Class of 1859, USMAA; JW's USMA Records, JW MSS, C-127, F-1, ADA&H. A record of JW's grades may also be found in the *Official Register of the Officers and Cadets of the U.S. Military Academy,*

West Point, New York (West Point, New York), 1855–59.

25. Dyer, *"Fightin" Joe" Wheeler*, 6; Cadet Delinquency Log, USMAA; Deborah McKeon-Pogue, Special Collections and Archives, U.S. Military Academy, to the author, Feb. 27, 2004.

26. Du Bose, *Wheeler and the Army of Tennessee*, 51.

27. DeLeon, *Wheeler, the Man, the Statesman, the Soldier*, 26.

28. Academic Record of Joseph Wheeler Jr., USMA Class of 1859, USMAA; *Official Register of Officers and Cadets of U.S. Military Academy*, 1859, 7; Dyer, *"Fightin' Joe" Wheeler*, 13–14.

29. Academic Record of Joseph Wheeler Jr., USMA Class of 1859, USMAA; Cullum, *Biographical Register of United States Military Academy*, 2: 730.

30. Theophilus F. Rodenbough and William L. Haskin, eds., *The Army of the United States: Historical Sketches of Staff and Line* . . . (New York: Merrill & Co., 1896), 153–58; K. Jack Bauer, *The Mexican War, 1846–1848* (New York: Macmillan Publishing Co., Inc., 1974), 212, 215.

31. Rodenbough and Haskin, *Army of the United States*, 174, 193, 221; James R. Arnold, *Jeff Davis's Own: Cavalry, Comanches, and the Battle for the Texas Frontier* (New York: John Wiley & Sons, Inc., 2000), 13–19.

32. Wheeler Family History, JW MSS, C-1, F-1, 2, ADA&H; Cullum, *Biographical Register of United States Military Academy*, 2: 730; William W. Averell, *Ten Years in the Saddle: The Memoir of William Woods Averell, 1851–1862*, ed. Edward K. Eckert and Nicholas J. Amato (San Rafael, Calif.: Presidio Press, 1978), 57–58.

33. Averell, *Ten Years in the Saddle*, 59.

34. Cullum, *Biographical Register of United States Military Academy*, 2: 730; DeLeon, *Wheeler, the Man, the Statesman, the Soldier*, 24.

35. Robert W. Frazer, *Forts of the West: Military Forts* . . . *West of the Mississippi River to 1898* (Norman: University of Oklahoma Press, 1965), 98–99, 105–06.

36. Dyer, *"Fightin' Joe" Wheeler*, 16–17.

37. Dyer, *"Fightin' Joe" Wheeler*, 17–18; *Synopsis of the Military Career of Gen. Joseph Wheeler, Commander of the Cavalry Corps, Army of the West* (New York: privately issued, 1865), 5–6.

38. Heitman, *Historical Register and Dictionary*, 2: 405.

39. Dyer, *"Fightin' Joe"" Wheeler*, 18–19.

40. James M. McPherson, *Ordeal by Fire: The Civil War and Reconstruction* (New York: Alfred A. Knopf, 1982), 121–29; William Carey Dodson, ed., *Campaigns of Wheeler and His Cavalry, 1862–1865* (Atlanta: Hudgins Publishing Co., 1899), 2.

41. Dyer, *"Fightin' Joe" Wheeler*, 19–20.

42. Wheeler Family History, JW MSS, C-1, F-1, ADA&H.

2. AN EXAMPLE OF COOL, HEROIC COURAGE

1. Wheeler Family History, JW MSS, C-1, F-1, ADA&H; Patricia L. Faust, ed., *Historical Times Illustrated Encyclopedia of the Civil War* (New York: Harper & Row, 1986), 604, 621–22. For additional details on Confederate Regulars, see Richard P. Weinert Jr., *The Confederate Regular Army* (Shippensburg, Pa.: White Mane Publishing Co., Inc., 1991).

2. Dyer, *"Fightin' Joe" Wheeler*, 22–23; Du Bose, *Wheeler and the Army of Tennessee*, 53; J. H. Gilman, "With Slemmer in Pensacola Harbor," *B&L* 1:26–32.

3. Dyer, *"Fightin' Joe" Wheeler*, 26–27; Du Bose, *Wheeler and the Army of Tennessee*, 53–54; J. R. Soley, "Early Operations in the Gulf," *B&L* 2:13.

4. Du Bose, *Wheeler and the Army of Tennessee*, 55; *OR*, ser. I, vol. 6:793.
5. Dodson, *Campaigns of Wheeler*, 373.
6. Grady McWhiney and Perry D. Jamieson, *Attack and Die: Civil War Military Tactics and the Southern Heritage* (University: University of Alabama Press, 1982), 49–54.
7. McWhiney and Jamieson, *Attack and Die*, 55–58.
8. McPherson, *Ordeal by Fire*, 154–61, 177–78, 206–15.
9. Gilman, "With Slemmer in Pensacola Harbor," 32n.
10. McPherson, *Ordeal by Fire*, 161–62, 222–25.
11. Wiley Sword, *Shiloh: Bloody April* (New York: William Morrow & Co., Inc., 1974), 58–72, 84–98.
12. *OR*, ser. 1, vol. 6:826–27.
13. *OR*, ser. 1, vol. 6:828.
14. *OR*, ser. 1, vol. 6:772, 815–16; Ezra J. Warner, *Generals in Gray: Lives of the Confederate Commanders* (Baton Rouge: Louisiana State University Press, 1959), 107, 321.
15. Du Bose, *Wheeler and the Army of Tennessee*, 56; *OR*, ser. 1, vol. 10, pt. 2:307; JW, "The Battle of Shiloh: A Graphic Description of That Sanguinary Engagement," *SHSP* 24 (1896): 120.
16. JW, "Battle of Shiloh," 120.
17. *OR*, ser. 1, vol. 10, pt. 2:375–76; Du Bose, *Wheeler and the Army of Tennessee*, 63–64; Sword, *Shiloh*, 82–86; Warner, *Generals in Gray*, 31, 124, 242–43.
18. Warner, *Generals in Gray*, 150; *OR*, ser. 1, vol. 10, pt. 1:383.
19. *OR*, ser. 1, vol. 10, pt. 2:389.
20. Du Bose, *Wheeler and the Army of Tennessee*, 64–65.
21. Du Bose, *Wheeler and the Army of Tennessee*, 65; Sword, *Shiloh*, 99–106; Larry J. Daniel, *Shiloh: The Battle That Changed the Civil War* (New York: Simon & Schuster, 1997), 121–27.
22. Daniel, *Shiloh*, 128–30.
23. Du Bose, *Wheeler and the Army of Tennessee*, 65.
24. Daniel, *Shiloh*, 118–20, 143–201; Sword, *Shiloh*, 141–233.
25. Daniel, *Shiloh*, 202–14; Sword, *Shiloh*, 234–56.
26. Du Bose, *Wheeler and the Army of Tennessee*, 68.
27. JW, "Battle of Shiloh," 121; Daniel, *Shiloh*, 269.
28. *OR*, ser. 1, vol. 10, pt. 1:558; Daniel, *Shiloh*, 235.
29. *OR*, ser. 1, vol. 10, pt. 1:558.
30. *OR*, ser. 1, vol. 10, pt. 1:558.
31. *OR*, ser. 1, vol. 10, pt. 1: 551–52, 558.
32. *OR*, ser. 1, vol. 10, pt. 1: 558; Sword, *Shiloh*, 269–73.
33. *OR*, ser. 1, vol. 10, pt. 1:558; Sword, *Shiloh*, 285–86.
34. *OR*, ser. 1, vol. 10, pt. 1:558.
35. JW, "Battle of Shiloh," 131.
36. JW, "Battle of Shiloh," 124; *OR*, ser. 1, vol. 10. pt. 1:559.
37. JW, "Battle of Shiloh," 124; *OR*, ser. 1, vol. 10, pt. 1:551–52, 555, 559.
38. Sword, *Shiloh*, 364–66.
39. Ulysses S. Grant, *Personal Memoirs*, ed. E. B. Long (New York: Da Capo Press, 2001), 178–81.
40. Sword, *Shiloh*, 380–88; Daniel, *Shiloh*, 276–72; JW, "Battle of Shiloh," 124–25.
41. *OR*, ser. 1, vol. 10, pt. 1:552, 559; JW, "Battle of Shiloh," 125–26.
42. JW, "Battle of Shiloh," 125–26; *OR*, ser. 1, vol. 10, pt. 1:559.
43. *OR*, ser. 1, vol. 10, pt. 1:468, 535, 552, 559; Dyer, *"Fightin' Joe" Wheeler*, 38; Daniel, *Shiloh*, 269.

3. BLUEGRASS BOUND

1. *OR*, ser. 1, vol. 10, pt. 2:398.
2. *OR*, ser. 1, vol. 10, pt. 2:, 400, 403.
3. *OR*, ser. 1, vol. 10, pt. 2:, 399.
4. *OR*, ser. 1, vol. 10, pt. 2:, 400, 403.
5. *OR*, ser. 1, vol. 10, pt. 1:109, 253–54; pt. 2: 97, 414.
6. *OR*, ser. 1, vol. 10, pt. 2:414; Dyer, *"Fightin" Joe" Wheeler*, 39.
7. Barnes F. Lathrop, "A Confederate Artilleryman at Shiloh," *CWH* 8 (1962): 385.
8. Alfred Roman, *The Military Operations of General Beauregard in the War Between the States* (New York: Harper & Brothers, 1884), 1:380–84; Stanley F. Horn, *The Army of Tennessee* (Norman: University of Oklahoma Press, 1953), 149–51.
9. *OR*, ser. 1, vol. 10, pt. 1:839; Warner, *Generals in Gray*, 260–61.
10. *OR*, ser. 1, vol. 10, pt. 1:852–54; Du Bose, *Wheeler and the Army of Tennessee*, 76–77.
11. *OR*, ser. 1, vol. 10, pt. 1:854–55; Dodson, *Campaigns of Wheeler*, 6–8; JW, typescript memoir of war service, JW MSS, C-156, F-2, ADA&H, 11–12.
12. *OR*, ser. 1, vol. 10, pt. 1:853.
13. Dyer, *"Fightin" Joe" Wheeler*, 44; Thomas L. Connelly, *Army of the Heartland: The Army of Tennessee, 1861–1862* (Baton Rouge: Louisiana State University Press, 1967), 177; George K. Miller memoirs, 7-8, MDA&H.
14. Dyer, *"Fightin' Joe" Wheeler*, 45; Roman, *Military Operations of Beauregard*, 1:400–08; Connelly, *Army of the Heartland*, 178–83.
15. Grady McWhiney, *Braxton Bragg and Confederate Defeat*, vol. 1, *Field Command* (New York: Columbia University Press, 1969), 264–65.
16. Connelly, *Army of the Heartland*, 196–97.
17. Dyer, *"Fightin' Joe" Wheeler*, 45; JW, "Bragg's Invasion of Kentucky," *B&L* 3:1–2.
18. Warner, *Generals in Gray*, 279–80; Connelly, *Army of the Heartland*, 187–93.
19. Connelly, *Army of the Heartland*, 181-94.
20. Don Carlos Buell, "East Tennessee and the Campaign of Perryville," *B&L* 3:31–38.
21. Buell, "East Tennessee and the Campaign of Perryville," 38; Basil W. Duke, *History of Morgan's Cavalry* (Cincinnati: Miami Printing & Publishing Co., 1867), 182–204; Cecil F. Holland, *Morgan and His Raiders* (New York: Macmillan Co., 1943), 116–26; William R. Brooksher and David K. Snider, "Stampede in Kentucky: John Hunt Morgan's Summer Raid," *CWTI* 17 (June 1978): 4–10, 43–46; Kenneth A. Hafendorfer, *They Died by Twos and Tens: The Confederate Cavalry in the Kentucky Campaign* (Louisville: KH Press, 1995), 122–31, 137–48; John Allan Wyeth, *Life of General Nathan Bedford Forrest* (New York: Harper & Brothers, 1899), 83–103; Charles F. Bryan Jr., "'I Mean to Have Them All': Forrest's Murfreesboro Raid," *CWTI* 12 (Jan. 1974): 27–34.
22. JW, "Bragg's Invasion of Kentucky," 3; Connelly, *Army of the Heartland*, 196–97; McWhiney, *Braxton Bragg*, 267–68; *OR*, ser. 1, vol. 17, pt. 2:656–57.
23. *OR*, ser. 1, vol. 17, pt. 1:22.
24. *OR*, ser. 1, vol. 17, pt. 1:22; Dyer, *"Fightin' Joe" Wheeler*, 46–47.
25. *OR*, ser. 1, vol. 17, pt. 1:23; Dyer, *"Fightin' Joe" Wheeler*, 48n.; Du Bose, *Wheeler and the Army of Tennessee*, 79–80.
26. George K. Miller memoirs, 12, MDA&H.
27. *OR*, ser. 1, vol. 17, pt. 1:23; pt. 2:667.
28. *OR*, ser. 1, vol. 17, pt. 1:23–24.

29. *OR,* ser. 1, vol. 17, pt. 1:24; JW, "Bragg's Invasion of Kentucky," 3–4.

30. Dyer, *"Fightin' Joe" Wheeler,* 47.

31. *OR,* ser. 1, vol. 17, pt. 1:24.

32. *OR,* ser. 1, vol. 17, pt. 2:124–26, 128–31, 133–39; Richard L. Kiper, *Major General John Alexander McClernand, Politician in Uniform* (Kent, Ohio: Kent State University Press, 1999), 126–28.

33. *OR,* ser. 1, vol. 17, pt. 1: 24–25; Dyer, *"Fightin' Joe" Wheeler,* 48; Dodson, *Campaigns of Wheeler,* 9; George K. Miller memoirs, 12, MDA&H.

34. Connelly, *Army of the Heartland,* 205–06; McWhiney, *Braxton Bragg,* 272–73.

35. Connelly, *Army of the Heartland,* 207–10.

36. Connelly, *Army of the Heartland,* 208, 221–23; McWhiney, *Braxton Bragg,* 274.

37. Connelly, *Army of the Heartland,* 211; Dyer, *"Fightin' Joe" Wheeler,* 48–49; Thomas Jordan and J. P. Pryor, *The Campaigns of Lieut.-Gen. N. B. Forrest and of Forrest's Cavalry* (New Orleans: Blelock & Co., 1868), 174–81; Brian Steel Wills, *A Battle From the Start: The Life of Nathan Bedford Forrest* (New York: HarperCollins, 1992), 79–82; Jack Hurst, *Nathan Bedford Forrest: A Biography* (New York: Alfred A. Knopf, 1993), 104–05.

38. *OR,* ser. 1, vol. 16, pt. 1:893; pt. 2:781–82.

39. *OR,* ser. 1, vol. 16, pt. 1:887–91, 893; pt. 2:781, 785; Hafendorfer, *They Died by Twos and Tens,* 245.

40. *OR,* ser. 1, vol. 16, pt. 1:893; JW, "Bragg's Invasion of Kentucky," 7–8; Hafendorfer, *They Died by Twos and Tens,* 245–54; Earl J. Hess, *Banners in the Breeze: The Kentucky Campaign, Corinth, and Stones River* (Lincoln: University of Nebraska Press, 2000), 60.

41. *OR,* ser. 1, vol. 16, pt. 1:893; pt. 2:801; JW, "Bragg's Invasion of Kentucky," 8.

42. Baxter Smith memoirs, 2, USAMHI.

43. *OR,* ser. 1, vol. 16, pt. 1:893–94; Hafendorfer, *They Died by Twos and Tens,* 368–73.

44. Jordan and Pryor, *Campaigns of Forrest,* 182–84; Hafendorfer, *They Died by Twos and Tens,* 378; *OR,* ser. 1, vol. 16, pt. 1:894.

45. Steven E. Woodworth, *No Band of Brothers: Problems in the Rebel High Command* (Columbia: University of Missouri Press, 1999), 152–55; *OR,* ser. 1, vol. 16, pt. 2:824.

46. Jordan and Pryor, *Campaigns of Forrest,* 184–86; Wills, *Battle From the Start,* 83–84.

47. *OR,* ser. 1, vol. 16, pt. 2:876–77. For a discussion of Bragg's reasoning in detaching Forrest, see Hafendorfer, *They Died by Twos and Tens,* 508–11.

4. Praise and Promotion

1. *OR,* ser. 1, vol. 16, pt. 1:894.

2. Connelly, *Army of the Heartland,* 215–17, 230–31.

3. Connelly, *Army of the Heartland,* 228–30; Hess, *Banners in the Breeze,* 63–88; Horn, *Army of Tennessee,* 168–69.

4. *OR,* ser. 1, vol. 16, pt. 1:894.

5. *OR,* ser. 1, vol. 16, pt. 1:894; Connelly, *Army of the Heartland,* 231–32.

6. JW, "Bragg's Invasion of Kentucky," 10; Basil W. Duke, "Bragg's Campaign in Kentucky," *SB* 4 (1885): 167.

7. Connelly, *Army of the Heartland,* 232; JW, "Bragg's Invasion of Kentucky," 10.

8. *OR,* ser. 1, vol. 16, pt. 1:894; pt. 2:878–79.

9. *OR,* ser. 1, vol. 16, pt. 1:895; JW, "Bragg's Invasion of Kentucky," 10–11.

10. *OR*, ser. 1, vol. 16, pt. 1:895–96.
11. *OR*, ser. 1, vol. 16, pt. 1:896, 1016–18.
12. Connelly, *Army of the Heartland*, 234–42.
13. Horn, *Army of Tennessee*, 167–68; McWhiney, *Braxton Bragg*, 297–99; Buell, "East Tennessee and Perryville," 46–47; JW, "Bragg's Invasion of Kentucky," 11.
14. *OR*, ser. 1, vol. 16, pt. 1:896; pt. 2:884; JW, "Bragg's Invasion of Kentucky," 14; Connelly, *Army of the Heartland*, 247–56.
15. *OR*, ser. 1, vol. 16, pt. 1:896; pt. 2:900–06.
16. *OR*, ser. 1, vol. 16, pt. 1:896; JW, "Bragg's Invasion of Kentucky," 14–15; Hafendorfer, *They Died by Twos and Tens*, 682–85; John R. Poole, *Cracker Cavaliers: The 2nd Georgia Cavalry Under Wheeler and Forrest* (Macon, Ga.: Mercer University Press, 2000), 40–41.
17. *OR*, ser. 1, vol. 16, pt. 1:896–97; JW, "Bragg's Invasion of Kentucky," 15; Hafendorfer, *They Died by Twos and Tens*, 680–85.
18. St. John Richardson Liddell, *Liddell's Record . . .*, ed. Nathaniel Cheairs Hughes Jr. (Baton Rouge: Louisiana State University Press, 1985), 87–88; *OR*, ser. 1, vol. 16, pt. 1:897; Hafendorfer, *They Died by Twos and Tens*, 694–702.
19. Hafendorfer, *They Died by Twos and Tens*, 695, 736–38; JW to Thomas B. Roy, Oct. 7, 1862, Braxton Bragg MSS, WRHS.
20. Connelly, *Army of the Heartland*, 257–58; Horn, *Army of Tennessee*, 179–80.
21. Connelly, *Army of the Heartland*, 259–63; McWhiney, *Braxton Bragg*, 309–12; *OR*, ser. 1, vol. 16, pt. 2:925.
22. JW, "Bragg's Invasion of Kentucky," 16; Dyer, *"Fightin' Joe" Wheeler*, 63; James Hagan, History of the 3rd Alabama Cavalry, 6, ADA&H, *Synopsis of Career of Wheeler*, 7; Kenneth W. Noe, *Perryville: This Grand Havoc of Battle* (Lexington: University Press of Kentucky, 2001), 236.
23. Hafendorfer, *They Died by Twos and Tens*, 714–16; Dodson, *Campaigns of Wheeler*, 23–24; *OR*, ser. 1, vol. 16, pt. 1:897.
24. *OR*, ser. 1, vol. 16, pt. 1:898.
25. Noe, *Perryville*, 236.
26. Noe, *Perryville*, 236.
27. Noe, *Perryville*, 237.
28. Connelly, *Army of the Heartland*, 266–68; Horn, *Army of Tennessee*, 186–87; McWhiney, *Braxton Bragg*, 319; JW, "Bragg's Invasion of Kentucky," 17–18.
29. *OR*, ser. 1, vol. 16, pt. 1:898, 1136–44; pt. 2:930–31.
30. *OR*, ser. 1, vol. 16, pt. 2:940; Dyer, *"Fightin' Joe" Wheeler*, 64–65; Hafendorfer, *They Died by Twos and Tens*, 689.
31. *OR*, ser. 1, vol. 20, pt. 2:388; Warner, *Generals in Gray*, 332–33.
32. *OR*, ser. 1, vol. 16, pt. 2:930.
33. JW, "Bragg's Invasion of Kentucky," 18; McWhiney, *Braxton Bragg*, 320–21; Connelly, *Army of the Heartland*, 267–72.
34. Connelly, *Army of the Heartland*, 267; Horn, *Army of Tennessee*, 186–87; Buell, "East Tennessee and Perryville," 49.
35. *OR*, ser. 1, vol. 16, pt. 1:898; pt. 2:935, 939, 941–52; JW, "Bragg's Invasion of Kentucky," 18–19.
36. Dyer, *"Fightin' Joe" Wheeler*, 66; *OR*, ser. 1, vol. 16, pt. 1:11, 199, 1028–29.
37. Baxter Smith memoirs, 6, USAMHI.
38. JW, "Bragg's Invasion of Kentucky," 19; Du Bose, *Wheeler and the Army of Tennessee*, 104.
39. *OR*, ser. 1, vol. 16, pt. 2:965.

5. Defending in Front, Attacking in Rear

1. Thomas L. Connelly, *Autumn of Glory: The Army of Tennessee, 1862–1865* (Baton Rouge: Louisiana State University Press, 1971), 16.
2. *OR*, ser. 1, vol. 16, pt. 2:976–77.
3. Connelly, *Autumn of Glory*, 13–15; McWhiney, *Braxton Bragg*, 337.
4. McWhiney, *Braxton Bragg*, 325–29; Horn, *Army of Tennessee*, 190–92; Connelly, *Autumn of Glory*, 14–16, 31–32.
5. Connelly, *Autumn of Glory*, 33–37; Joseph E. Johnston, *Narrative of Military Operations During the Civil War* (New York: D. Appleton & Co., 1874), 149–50; Warner, *Generals in Gray*, 162.
6. *OR*, ser. 1, vol. 20, pt. 2:411–12.
7. *OR*, ser. 1, vol. 20, pt. 2:420, 422.
8. Jordan and Pryor, *Campaigns of Forrest*, 193–222; James R. Chalmers, "Forrest and His Campaigns," *SHSP* 7 (1879): 460; Dale S. Snair, ed., "This Looked But Little Like Trying to Catch the Enemy," *CWTI* 23 (Sept. 1984): 21–24, 28–33.
9. John G. Deupree, "The Capture of Holly Springs, Mississippi, Dec. 20, 1862," *Publications of the Mississippi Historical Society* 4 (1901): 49–61; A. F. Brown, "Van Dorn's Operations in Northern Mississippi—Recollections of a Cavalryman," *SHSP* 6 (1878): 151–61; Edward G. Longacre, *Mounted Raids of the Civil War* (South Brunswick, N.J.: A. S. Barnes & Co., Inc., 1975), 46–65; William R. Brooksher and David K. Snider, "A Visit to Holly Springs," *CWTI* 14 (June 1975): 4–9, 40–44.
10. *OR*, ser. 1, vol. 16, pt. 2:654–55; John Allan Wyeth, "Morgan's Christmas Raid, 1862–63," in *The Photographic History of the Civil War* (New York: Review of Reviews Co., 1911), 4: 144–56; Howard Swiggett, *The Rebel Raider: A Life of John Hunt Morgan* (Indianapolis: Bobbs-Merrill Co., 1934), 92–100; Holland, *Morgan and His Raiders*, 179–87; D. Alexander Brown, *The Bold Cavaliers: Morgan's Kentucky Cavalry Raiders* (Philadelphia: J. B. Lippincott Co., 1959), 142–61; James A. Ramage, *Rebel Raider: The Life of General John Hunt Morgan* (Lexington: University Press of Kentucky, 1986), 134–48.
11. Hafendorfer, *They Died by Twos and Tens*, 863; Warner, *Generals in Gray*, 39, 232; Connelly, *Autumn of Glory*, 27, 57.
12. *OR*, ser. 1, vol. 20, pt. 2:402, 404, 414, 416; Dyer, *"Fightin' Joe" Wheeler*, 71n.
13. Poole, *Cracker Cavaliers*, 55; Connelly, *Autumn of Glory*, 25–26.
14. *OR*, ser. 1, vol. 20, pt. 2: 422.
15. *OR*, ser. 1, vol. 20, pt. 2: 404.
16. *OR*, ser. 1, vol. 20, pt. 2: 427.
17. *OR*, ser. 1, vol. 20, pt. 1:15–19; *Synopsis of Career of Wheeler*, 8; *Gen. Joseph Wheeler: Proceedings in Statuary Hall of the United States Capitol Upon the Unveiling and Presentation of the Statue of Gen. Joseph Wheeler by the State of Alabama* (Washington, D.C.: Government Printing Office, 1926), 6.
18. Nimrod W. E. Long to his wife, Dec. 7, 1862, Long MSS, EU; Dodson, *Campaigns of Wheeler*, 46–47; George K. Miller memoirs, 16, MDA&H.
19. Benjamin F. Batchelor and George Q. Turner, *Batchelor-Turner Letters, 1861–1864, Written by Two of Terry's Texas Rangers*, ed. Helen J. H. Rugeley (Austin, Tex.: Steck Co., 1961), 37; George K. Miller memoirs, 15–16, MDA&H.
20. *OR*, ser. 1, vol. 20, pt. 1:77–78; pt. 2:457; John H. Fisher, *They Rode With Forrest and Wheeler: A Chronicle of Five Tennessee Brothers' Service in the Confederate Western Cavalry* (Jefferson, N.C.: McFarland & Co., Inc., 1995), 27.
21. *OR*, ser. 1, vol. 20, pt. 1:163–65, 958.

22. Edwin C. Bearss, "Cavalry Operations in the Battle of Stone's River," *THQ* 19 (1960): 25–26.

23. Bearss, "Cavalry Operations in the Battle of Stone's River," 27–33; *OR*, ser. 1, vol. 20, pt. 1:958. For criticism of Wheeler's intelligence-gathering activities on Dec. 26, see Peter Cozzens, *No Better Place to Die: The Battle of Stones River* (Urbana: University of Illinois Press, 1990), 55.

24. Du Bose, *Wheeler and the Army of Tennessee*, 120; Dodson, *Campaigns of Wheeler*, 50.

25. *OR*, ser. 1, vol. 20, pt. 1:958.

26. Robert F. Bunting to "Editor Telegraph," Jan. 6, 1863, Bunting MSS, CAH.

27. *OR*, ser. 1, vol. 20, pt. 1:958; pt. 2:467; Bearss, "Cavalry in Battle of Stone's River," 43–48; Du Bose, *Wheeler and the Army of Tennessee*, 140–41; George K. Miller memoirs, 18, MDA&H; Batchelor and Turner, *Letters*, 41.

28. Du Bose, *Wheeler and the Army of Tennessee*, 123–24; Dodson, *Campaigns of Wheeler*, 50.

29. Bearss, "Cavalry in Battle of Stone's River," 52–53.

30. Bearss, "Cavalry in Battle of Stone's River," 110; *OR*, ser. 1, vol. 20, pt. 1:664, 958, 960; Dyer, *"Fightin' Joe" Wheeler*, 81; Du Bose, *Wheeler and the Army of Tennessee*, 126–27; George K. Miller memoirs, 18, MDA&H; William R. Brooksher and David K. Snider, "The 'War Child' Rides: Joe Wheeler at Stones River," *CWTI* 14 (Jan. 1976): 8.

31. *OR*, ser. 1, vol. 20, pt. 1:958, 960; Bearss, "Cavalry in Battle of Stone's River," 110; Dyer, *"Fightin' Joe" Wheeler*, 81; Du Bose, *Wheeler and the Army of Tennessee*, 141–42; Dodson, *Campaigns of Wheeler*, 51; Poole, *Cracker Cavaliers*, 59; Isaac B. Ulmer, Memoir of 3rd Alabama Cavalry, 2–3, SHC.

32. *OR*, ser. 1, vol. 20, pt. 1:958, 960; Bearss, "Cavalry in Battle of Stone's River," 111–12; Brooksher and Snider, "'War Child' Rides," 8–9.

33. Bearss, "Cavalry in Battle of Stone's River," 112–14; George K. Miller memoirs, MDA&H, 18.

34. George K. Miller memoirs, 18, MDA&H; *OR*, ser. 1, vol. 20, pt. 1:959–60; Bearss, "Cavalry in Battle of Stone's River," 114–15; Du Bose, *Wheeler and the Army of Tennessee*, 142.

35. *OR*, ser. 1, vol. 20, pt. 1:959–60; Bearss, "Cavalry in Battle of Stone's River," 115; Dyer, *"Fightin' Joe" Wheeler*, 82–83; George K. Miller memoirs, 18, MDA&H; Du Bose, *Wheeler and the Army of Tennessee*, 142–43; Brooksher and Snider, "'War Child' Rides," 10, 44.

36. G. C. Kniffin, "The Battle of Stone's River," *B&L* 3: 618–28; Connelly, *Autumn of Glory*, 54–58; Horn, *Army of Tennessee*, 199–201; McWhiney, *Braxton Bragg*, 352–61; Bearss, "Cavalry in Battle of Stone's River," 118–24; *OR*, ser. 1, vol. 20, pt. 1:664–67, 966; Dyer, *"Fightin' Joe" Wheeler*, 84; Du Bose, *Wheeler and the Army of Tennessee*, 129–31; Batchelor and Turner, *Letters*, 41; Cozzens, *No Better Place to Die*, 104–07; Gustave Cook to his wife, Jan. 13, 1863, Cook MSS, GLC; W. B. Corbit diary Dec. 30–31, 1862, EU.

37. *OR*, ser. 1, vol. 20, pt. 1:959–60, 970; Bearss, "Cavalry in Battle of Stone's River," 125–27; Dodson, *Campaigns of Wheeler*, 52–53; George K. Miller memoirs, 19, MDA&H; *Synopsis of Career of Wheeler*, 9.

38. *OR*, ser. 1, vol. 20, pt. 1:959-60; Bearss, "Cavalry in Battle of Stone's River," 127-28.

39. David Urquhart, "Bragg's Advance and Retreat," *B&L* 3: 607; Horn, *Army of Tennessee*, 201–06; Connelly, *Autumn of Glory*, 58–62; McWhiney, *Braxton Bragg*, 361–66; Dyer, *"Fightin' Joe" Wheeler*, 84–85.

40. *OR*, ser. 1, vol. 20, pt. 1:959–60, 968–69; vol. 52, pt. 2:402; Bearss, "Cavalry in

Battle of Stone's River," 131–32; Dyer, *"Fightin' Joe" Wheeler*, 85; Du Bose, *Wheeler and the Army of Tennessee*, 143; Dodson, *Campaigns of Wheeler*, 54; George K. Miller memoirs, 19, MDA&H; Batchelor and Turner, *Letters*, 42; Brooksher and Snider, "'War Child' Rides," 44–45; Gustave Cook to his wife, Jan. 13, 1863, Cooke MSS, GLC.

41. *OR*, ser. 1, vol. 20, pt. 1:959; Bearss, "Cavalry in Battle of Stone's River," 132–34; Du Bose, *Wheeler and the Army of Tennessee*, 143.

42. *OR*, ser. 1, vol. 20, pt. 1:959–60, 969; Bearss, "Cavalry in Battle of Stone's River," 134–36.

43. *OR*, ser. 1, vol. 20, pt. 1:667-68; Kniffin, "Battle of Stone's River," 630-32; Horn, *Army of Tennessee*, 206-08; Connelly, *Autumn of Glory*, 62-65; McWhiney, *Braxton Bragg*, 366-70.

6. TARGETING SHIPS, FORTS, AND TRAINS

1. Connelly, *Autumn of Glory*, 66–68.
2. McWhiney, *Braxton Bragg*, 371 and n.; Liddell, *Liddell's Record*, 114–15.
3. *OR*, ser. 1, vol. 20, pt. 1:957, 959–61, 970; Bearss, "Cavalry in Battle of Stone's River," 137–40.
4. *OR*, ser. 1, vol. 20, pt. 1:957–61; Bearss, "Cavalry in Battle of Stone's River," 140–42.
5. *OR*, ser. 1, vol. 20, pt. 1:674, 958.
6. Bearss, "Cavalry in Battle of Stone's River," 142–43.
7. Bearss, "Cavalry in Battle of Stone's River," 143.
8. Bearss, "Cavalry in Battle of Stone's River," 143; James Lee McDonough, *Stones River—Bloody Winter in Tennessee* (Knoxville: University of Tennessee Press, 1980), 136–40; H. B. Clay, "On the Right at Murfreesboro," *CV* 21 (1913): 588–89.
9. *OR*, ser. 1, vol. 20, pt. 1:670.
10. Batchelor and Turner, *Letters*, 42; Robert W. Williams Jr. and Ralph A. Wooster, eds., "With Terry's Texas Rangers: The Letters of Isaac Dunbar Affleck," *CWH* 9 (1963): 313.
11. *OR*, ser. 1, vol. 20, pt. 2:488; Du Bose, *Wheeler and the Army of Tennessee*, 151.
12. Dodson, *Campaigns of Wheeler*, 61.
13. Dodson, *Campaigns of Wheeler*, 61; *OR*, ser. 1, vol. 20, pt. 1:961, 983.
14. Du Bose, *Wheeler and the Army of Tennessee*, 151; Dyer, *"Fightin' Joe" Wheeler*, 87–88; George K. Miller memoirs, 20, MDA&H.
15. Dyer, *"Fightin' Joe" Wheeler*, 88; Du Bose, *Wheeler and the Army of Tennessee*, 151–52; F. W. Flood, "Captures by Eighth Confederate Cavalry," *CV* 13 (1905): 458; George K. Miller memoirs, 20–21, MDA&H; Dodson, *Campaigns of Wheeler*, 62.
16. Dyer, *"Fightin' Joe" Wheeler*, 89–90; Du Bose, *Wheeler and the Army of Tennessee*, 152–53; Flood, "Captures by Eighth Confederate," 458–59; George K. Miller memoirs, 21, MDA&H; Dodson, *Campaigns of Wheeler*, 62.
17. Du Bose, *Wheeler and the Army of Tennessee*, 153–54; George K. Miller memoirs, 21–22, MDA&H; Dodson, *Campaigns of Wheeler*, 62–63.
18. *OR*, ser. 1, vol. 20, pt. 1:961, 983–84; Dodson, *Campaigns of Wheeler*, 64–67; *Synopsis of Career of Wheeler*, 10–11.
19. George K. Miller memoirs, 22, MDA&H.
20. *OR*, ser. 1, vol. 20, pt. 1:961, 983; pt. 2:504; George K. Miller memoirs, 22, MDA&H; Dyer, *"Fightin' Joe" Wheeler*, 90n. In later years, Wheeler recalled the date of his promotion as Jan. 19, 1863: JW to Charles C. Jones, July 6, 1871, Charles C. Jones MSS, DU.

21. Jordan and Pryor, *Campaigns of Forrest*, 223–24; Dyer, *"Fightin' Joe" Wheeler*, 91. The most detailed modern account of the operation is Benjamin F. Cooling, *Fort Donelson's Legacy: War and Society in Kentucky and Tennessee, 1852–1863* (Knoxville: University of Tennessee Press, 1997), 192–206.
22. *OR*, ser. 1, vol. 23, pt. 1:40.
23. Dyer, *"Fightin' Joe" Wheeler*, 92; Benjamin F. Cooling, "The Attack on Dover, Tenn.," *CWTI* 2 (Aug. 1963): 11; Wills, *Battle From the Start*, 98; Wyeth, *Life of Forrest*, 146–47; Michael Cotton, *The Williamson County Cavalry: A History of Company F, Fourth Tennessee Cavalry Regiment, C.S.A.* (n.p.: privately issued, 1994), 85.
24. *OR*, ser. 1, vol. 23, pt. 1:40; Dodson, *Campaigns of Wheeler*, 69–70.
25. *OR*, ser. 1, vol. 23, pt. 1:35–38, 40–41; Dodson, *Campaigns of Wheeler*, 70; Jordan and Pryor, *Campaigns of Forrest*, 227–28; Wills, *Battle From the Start*, 98–100; Cooling, "Attack on Dover, Tenn.," 12; Poole, *Cracker Cavaliers*, 76; Batchelor and Turner, *Letters*, 46.
26. *OR*, ser. 1, vol. 23, pt. 1:41.
27. *OR*, ser. 1, vol. 23, pt. 1:33, 38, 41; Jordan and Pryor, *Campaigns of Forrest*, 229–30.
28. Dyer, *"Fightin' Joe" Wheeler*, 94–96; Wills, *Battle From the Start*, 102; Wyeth, *Life of Forrest*, 151.
29. Dyer, *"Fightin' Joe" Wheeler*, 96–97.
30. Cooling, *Fort Donelson's Legacy*, 247; Du Bose, *Wheeler and the Army of Tennessee*, 160; Fisher, *They Rode With Forrest and Wheeler*, 32; Robert G. Hartje, *Van Dorn: The Life and Times of a Confederate General* (Nashville, Tenn.: Vanderbilt University Press, 1967), 275–78; Warner, *Generals in Gray*, 314–15.
31. *OR*, ser. 1, vol. 20, pt. 2:326; vol. 23, pt. 2:14, 22–23, 31, 34, 59, 81, 154–55.
32. JW, *A Revised System of Cavalry Tactics, for the Use of the Cavalry and Mounted Infantry, C.S.A.* (Mobile, Ala.: S. H. Goetzel & Co., 1863).
33. McWhiney and Jamieson, *Attack and Die*, 66; Dyer, *"Fightin' Joe" Wheeler*, 101–02; Dodson, *Campaigns of Wheeler*, 81.
34. *OR*, ser. 1, vol. 23, pt. 2:684, 695, 701, 711; Dodson, *Campaigns of Wheeler*, 76; Du Bose, *Wheeler and the Army of Tennessee*, 160; Warner, *Generals in Gray*, 214–15.
35. Poole, *Cracker Cavaliers*, 77.
36. *OR*, ser. 1, vol. 23, pt. 2:668–69, 684.
37. *OR*, ser. 1, vol. 23, pt. 1:116–22; Jordan and Pryor, *Campaigns of Forrest*, 232–38; Wills, *Battle From the Start*, 104–05; Hartje, *Van Dorn*, 279–90.
38. *OR*, ser. 1, vol. 23, pt. 1:218–19; Robert L. Willett, "We Rushed With a Yell," *CWTI* 8 (Feb. 1970): 17–18.
39. *OR*, ser. 1, vol. 23, pt. 1:219.
40. *OR*, ser. 1, vol. 23, pt. 1:219–20.
41. *OR*, ser. 1, vol. 23, pt. 1:219; Batchelor and Turner, *Letters*, 48.
42. *OR*, ser. 1, vol. 23, pt. 1:219; Willett, "We Rushed With a Yell," 18–19.
43. *OR*, ser. 1, vol. 23, pt. 1:219–20; Willett, "We Rushed With a Yell," 20; Batchelor and Turner, *Letters*, 48–49.
44. *OR*, ser. 1, vol. 23, pt. 1:219, 221; Willett, "We Rushed With a Yell," 21.

7. At Long Last, Victory

1. Longacre, *Mounted Raids*, 66–90. The most comprehensive account of this expedition is Robert L. Willett, *The Lightning Mule Brigade: Abel Streight's 1863 Raid Into Alabama* (Carmel, Ind.: Guild Press, 1999).
2. Longacre, *Mounted Raids*, 91–122. The definitive source on this operation is D.

Alexander Brown, *Grierson's Raid: A Cavalry Adventure of the Civil War* (Urbana: University of Illinois Press, 1954).

3. L. Virginia French diary, Mar. 1, May 3, 1863, TSL&A.
4. *OR*, ser. 1, vol. 23, pt. 1:151; Sydney K. Smith, *Life, Army Record, and Public Services of D. Howard Smith* (Louisville: Bradley & Gilbert Co., 1890), 43–47; John B. Castleman, *Active Service* (Louisville: Courier-Journal Printing Co., 1917), 106–08; Ramage, *Rebel Raider*, 152–54.
5. Ramage, *Rebel Raider*, 154–56; Cooling, *Fort Donelson's Legacy*, 248.
6. Ramage, *Rebel Raider*, 156–57.
7. Cooling, *Fort Donelson's Legacy*, 248; *OR*, ser. 1, vol. 23, pt. 1:817-18; pt. 2:844; Lester V. Horowitz, *The Longest Raid of the Civil War: Little-Known and Untold Stories of Morgan's Raid Into Kentucky, Indiana and Ohio* (Cincinnati: Farmcourt Publications, 1999), 4, 14; Edison H. Thomas, *John Hunt Morgan and His Raiders* (Lexington: University Press of Kentucky, 1985), 75–76; Dyer, *"Fightin' Joe" Wheeler*, 102–03.
8. Longacre, *Mounted Raids*, 175–201. Horowitz, *The Longest Raid of the Civil War*, is the most thorough study of this expedition; see also Allan Keller, *Morgan's Raid* (Indianapolis: Bobbs-Merrill Co., Inc., 1961).
9. *OR*, ser. 1, vol. 23, pt. 1:585-86; vol. 24, pt. 1:242-44; vol. 52, pt. 2:472; Dyer, *"Fightin' Joe" Wheeler*, 103; Connelly, *Autumn of Glory*, 125.
10. Bachelor and Turner, *Letters*, 50; Williams and Wooster, "With Terry's Texas Rangers," 318.
11. *OR*, ser. 1, vol. 23, pt. 1:403–05; Horn, *Army of Tennessee*, 235–36; Dyer, *"Fightin' Joe" Wheeler*, 104; Steven E. Woodworth, *Six Armies in Tennessee: The Chickamauga and Chattanooga Campaigns* (Lincoln: University of Nebraska Press, 1998), 26.
12. Connelly, *Autumn of Glory*, 116–22; *OR*, ser. 1, vol. 23, pt. 2:883; Woodworth, *Six Armies in Tennessee*, 28–29; Dodson, *Campaigns of Wheeler*, 83; George K. Miller memoirs, MDA&H, 25.
13. *OR*, ser. 1, vol. 23, pt. 1:405–06, 457–59, 611–12; Connelly, *Autumn of Glory*, 123–27.
14. Connelly, *Army of the Heartland*, 127–28; Dodson, *Campaigns of Wheeler*, 86; *OR*, ser. 1, vol. 23, pt. 2:891–92.
15. Connelly, *Autumn of Glory*, 128–29; Horn, *Army of Tennessee*, 235.
16. Dodson, *Campaigns of Wheeler*, 86–87; Jordan and Pryor, *Campaigns of Forrest*, 291.
17. Dodson, *Campaigns of Wheeler*, 87–88; Dyer, *"Fightin' Joe" Wheeler*, 105; Julius L. Dowda memoirs, 4, GSA.
18. Dodson, *Campaigns of Wheeler*, 88.
19. Dodson, *Campaigns of Wheeler*, 88–90; Jordan and Pryor, *Campaigns of Forrest*, 291; Thomas J. Gray to his wife, July 16, 1863, Gray MSS, TSL&A; W. R. Dyer diary, June 28, 1863, TSL&A; Robert Selph Henry, *"First With the Most" Forrest* (Indianapolis: Bobbs-Merrill Co., 1944), 165–66; Du Bose, *Wheeler and the Army of Tennessee*, 176–77.
20. Dodson, *Campaigns of Wheeler*, 90–91; Dyer, *"Fightin' Joe" Wheeler*, 106–07; Du Bose, *Wheeler and the Army of Tennessee*, 177.
21. Connelly, *Autumn of Glory*, 129–31.
22. Connelly, *Autumn of Glory*, 132–33.
23. Connelly, *Autumn of Glory*, 131–33; *OR*, ser. 1, vol. 23, pt. 1:615–17.
24. Batchelor and Turner, *Letters*, 61; Thomas J. Gray to his wife, July 16, 1863, Gray MSS, TSL&A.
25. Batchelor and Turner, *Letters*, 58; Nimrod W. E. Long to his wife, July 17, 1863, Long MSS, EU.

26. *OR*, ser. 1, vol. 23, pt. 2:902, 916, 925–26; vol. 30, pt. 2:519–20; Dodson, *Campaigns of Wheeler*, 99; Dyer, *"Fightin' Joe" Wheeler*, 110–11; George K. Miller memoirs, 27, MDA&H; Poole, *Cracker Cavaliers*, 85.

27. *OR*, ser. 1, vol. 23, pt. 2:944, 954, 961; vol. 30, pt. 2:20.

28. *OR*, ser. 1, vol. 23, pt. 2:938; Judith Lee Hallock, *Braxton Bragg and Confederate Defeat: Volume II* (Tuscaloosa: University of Alabama Press, 1991), 34–35.

29. Hallock, *Braxton Bragg*, 44–45; Connelly, *Autumn of Glory*, 163–65.

30. Hallock, *Braxton Bragg*, 35, 45.

31. Hallock, *Braxton Bragg*, 46; Connelly, *Autumn of Glory*, 146–49, 171–73; Horn, *Army of Tennessee*, 239–44; William T. Martin to "Dear Jess," Aug. 28, 1863, CAH; Poole, *Cracker Cavaliers*, 86; *OR*, ser. 1, vol. 30, pt. 2:27; pt. 4:627.

32. *OR*, ser. 1, vol. 30, pt. 2:27–31; Connelly, *Autumn of Glory*, 150–62, 174–200; Horn, *Army of Tennessee*, 245–59.

33. *OR*, ser. 1, vol. 30, pt. 2:520; pt. 4:602, 614–15; Dyer, *"Fightin' Joe" Wheeler*, 114–15.

34. *OR*, ser. 1, vol. 30, pt. 2:520, 524; Connelly, *Autumn of Glory*, 197–99; Horn, *Army of Tennessee*, 256–57.

35. *OR*, ser. 1, vol. 30, pt. 2:32–33, 520; pt. 4:666; Horn, *Army of Tennessee*, 257–58.

36. Daniel H. Hill, "Chickamauga—The Great Battle of the West," *B&L* 3:649–51.

37. *OR*, ser. 1, vol. 30, pt. 2:520; John Allan Wyeth, *With Sabre and Scalpel: The Autobiography of a Soldier and Surgeon* (New York: Harper & Brothers, 1914), 244; Robert F. Bunting to "Ed[itor] Telegraph," Sept. 29, 1863, Bunting MSS, CAH.

38. Hill, "Chickamauga," 651–61; Connelly, *Autumn of Glory*, 221–26; Horn, *Army of Tennessee*, 260–70; *OR*, ser. 1, vol. 30, pt. 2:33-34.

39. *OR*, ser. 1, vol. 30, pt. 2:520; Wyeth, *With Sabre and Scalpel*, 247.

40. *OR*, ser. 1, vol. 30, pt. 2:34, 520; Dyer, *"Fightin' Joe" Wheeler*, 120–21; Dodson, *Campaigns of Wheeler*, 107; Peter Cozzens, *This Terrible Sound: The Battle of Chickamauga* (Urbana: University of Illinois Press, 1992), 464–65; Poole, *Cracker Cavaliers*, 87.

41. *OR*, ser. 1, vol. 30, pt. 2:521.

42. *OR*, ser. 1, vol. 30, pt. 2:521; Wyeth, *With Sabre and Scalpel*, 248.

8. WAR CHILD

1. Horn, *Army of Tennessee*, 272–79.

2. Connelly, *Autumn of Glory*, 227–31; Woodworth, *Six Armies in Tennessee*, 132–33.

3. *OR*, ser. 1, vol. 30, pt. 4:681; Jordan and Pryor, *Campaigns of Forrest*, 350–52.

4. Connelly, *Autumn of Glory*, 235–37.

5. Horn, *Army of Tennessee*, 285–90.

6. *OR*, ser. 1, vol. 30, pt. 2:521; pt. 4:679, 682.

7. *OR*, ser. 1, vol. 30, pt. 2: 521–22; pt. 4: 694–95.

8. *OR*, ser. 1, vol. 30, pt. 2:522; pt. 4:698–99, 711; Jordan and Pryor, *Campaigns of Forrest*, 354–56; Dodson, *Campaigns of Wheeler*, 109–10; Robert F. Bunting to "Ed[itor] Telegraph," Sept. 29, 1863, Bunting MSS, CAH.

9. *OR*, ser. 1, vol. 30, pt. 4:695.

10. Horn, *Army of Tennessee*, 242–43, 296–97.

11. *OR*, ser. 1, vol. 30, pt. 4:710; Henry, *"First with the Most" Forrest*, 198–99; Wyeth, *Life of Forrest*, 205–06.

12. Steven E. Woodworth, *Jefferson Davis and His Generals: The Failure of Confederate Command in the West* (Lawrence: University Press of Kansas, 1990), 243–44.

13. *OR*, ser. 1, vol. 30, pt. 2:722-23; pt. 4:711; Calvin L. Collier, *The War Child's Children:*

The Story of the Third Regiment, Arkansas Cavalry, Confederate States Army (Little Rock: Pioneer Press, 1965), 71.

14. *OR*, ser. 1, vol. 30, pt. 2:669, 684–85, 723; Dyer, *"Fightin' Joe" Wheeler*, 127–28; Dodson, *Campaigns of Wheeler*, 117–21; William R. Brooksher and David K Snider, "A Ride Down the Sequatchie Valley," *CWTI* 22 (Mar. 1983): 33–34.

15. *OR*, ser. 1, vol. 30, pt. 2:723; Du Bose, *Wheeler and the Army of Tennessee*, 208.

16. Du Bose, *Wheeler and the Army of Tennessee*, 208.

17. George B. Guild, *A Brief Narrative of the Fourth Tennessee Cavalry Regiment, Wheeler's Corps, Army of Tennessee* (Nashville, Tenn.: privately issued, 1913), 37–38; *Synopsis of Career of Wheeler*, 14–15.

18. *OR*, ser. 1, vol. 30, pt. 2:723; John Allan Wyeth, "The Destruction of Rosecrans' Great Wagon Train," in *The Photographic History of the Civil War*, 4:160, 162; Wilbur F. Mims, *War History of the Prattville Dragoons . . . 1861–1865* (Thurber, Tex.: Journal Printery, n.d.), 11.

19. *OR*, ser. 1, vol. 30, pt. 2:723; Wyeth, "Destruction of Rosecrans' Train," 162; *Synopsis of Career of Wheeler*, 15; John W. Du Bose, "Wheeler's Raid into Tennessee," *CV* 24 (1916): 12.

20. *OR*, ser. 1, vol. 30, pt. 2:723–24, 726–27; Dyer, *"Fightin' Joe" Wheeler*, 131; Batchelor and Turner, *Letters*, 71; Julius L. Dowda memoirs, 8, GSA; L. Virginia French diary, Nov. 12, 1863, TSL&A.

21. *OR*, ser. 1, vol. 30, pt. 2:724.

22. *OR*, ser. 1, vol. 30, pt. 2:666, 685–87, 724; JW to Braxton Bragg, Oct. 12, 1863, Wheeler MSS, RG-109, E-136, NA; Dodson, *Campaigns of Wheeler*, 125–26; Guild, *Fourth Tennessee Cavalry*, 43–44; Batchelor and Turner, *Letters*, 71; Julius L. Dowda memoirs, GSA, 8.

23. *OR*, ser. 1, vol. 30, pt. 2:666, 724, 727; Collier, *War Child's Children*, 77–78.

24. *OR*, ser. 1, vol. 30, pt. 2:666, 687–88, 724–25; Collier, *War Child's Children*, 78–79.

25. Grant, *Personal Memoirs*, 310–16.

26. Grant, *Personal Memoirs*, 317–19; Longacre, *Mounted Raids*, 224; Cooling, *Fort Donelson's Legacy*, 310–11.

27. DeLeon, *Wheeler, the Man, the Statesman, the Soldier*, 56–57; Dyer, *"Fightin' Joe" Wheeler*, 135–37.

28. Batchelor and Turner, *Letters*, 71.

29. JW to Braxton Bragg, Oct. 12, 1863, Wheeler MSS, RG-109, E-136, NA; *OR*, ser. 1, vol. 30, pt. 2:664–66, 725.

30. Cooling, *Fort Donelson's Legacy*, 310–11; Hallock, *Braxton Bragg*, 111–12.

31. *OR*, ser. 1, vol. 30, pt. 4:746–47.

32. Elisha S. Burford to "Dear Atkison," Oct. 10, 1863, Burford MSS, RG-109, E-136, NA.

33. Elisha S. Burford to "Dear Atkison," Oct. 10, 1863, Burford MSS, RG-109, E-136, NA.

34. *OR*, ser. 1, vol. 31, pt. 2:662–64.

35. *OR*, ser. 1, vol. 31, pt. 2: 666; Batchelor and Turner, *Letters*, 71; Robert F. Bunting to "Editor Telegraph," Oct. 29, 1863, Bunting MSS, CAH; JW to Braxton Bragg, Dec. 20, 1863, Bragg MSS, DU.

36. JW to Braxton Bragg, Dec. 20, 1863, Bragg MSS, DU.

37. Elisha S. Burford to his wife, Oct. 12, 1863, Burford MSS, RG-109, E-136, NA; *OR*, ser. 1, vol. 30, pt. 4:743, 763; Ellen Virginia Saunders, "War-Time Journal of a 'Little Rebel'," *CV* 28 (1920): 11.

38. Connelly, *Autumn of Glory*, 262–64; Horn, *Army of Tennessee*, 294–95.

39. Connelly, *Autumn of Glory*, 264–65; *OR*, ser. 1, vol. 31, pt. 1:453–56; pt. 3:634–35; Jeffry D. Wert, *General James Longstreet, the Confederacy's Most Controversial Soldier: A Biography* (New York, 1993), 338–39; Cooling, *Fort Donelson's Legacy*, 320–21.
40. *OR*, ser. 1, vol. 31, pt. 1:456, 540–41; pt. 3:679, 686–88, 696; James Longstreet to JW, Nov. 12, 14, 1863, Longstreet MSS, GLC; Dodson, *Campaigns of Wheeler*, 145–46; Julius L. Dowda memoirs, 10, GSA; Collier, *War Child's Children*, 82–83; J. W. Minnich, "The Cavalry at Knoxville," *CV* 32 (1924): 11.
41. *OR*, ser. 1, vol. 31, pt. 1:541; *Synopsis of Career of Wheeler*, 17.
42. *OR*, ser. 1, vol. 31, pt. 1:541.
43. *OR*, ser. 1, vol. 31, pt. 1: 457–58.
44. *OR*, ser. 1, vol. 31, pt. 1: 459, 542; pt. 3:696, 704, 708, 719–20, 732–33; James Longstreet to JW, Dec. 20, 1863, Longstreet MSS, GLC.
45. *OR*, ser. 1, vol. 31, pt. 1:543–44; pt. 3:733–34, 737; Du Bose, *Wheeler and the Army of Tennessee*, 217–18; Hagan, History of 3rd Alabama Cavalry, 8.
46. *OR*, ser. 1, vol. 31, pt. 1:460–61, 544, 546.
47. *OR*, ser. 1, vol. 31, pt. 1: 460, 544–45; pt. 3: 740–41.

9. ESSENTIAL TO THE EFFICIENCY OF THE CAVALRY

1. *OR*, ser. 1, vol. 31, pt. 2:680–81; pt. 3: 760.
2. *OR*, ser. 1, vol. 31, pt. 2: 664–67; Grant, *Personal Memoirs*, 331–42.
3. *OR*, ser. 1, vol. 31, pt. 3:755, 760–62, 771, 780–81.
4. Horn, *Army of Tennessee*, 311; Du Bose, *Wheeler and the Army of Tennessee*, 266; Grant, *Personal Memoirs*, 357–59.
5. Connelly, *Autumn of Glory*, 277–78; Horn, *Army of Tennessee*, 303–06; *OR*, ser. 1, vol. 31, pt. 3:771.
6. Andrew Haughton, *Training, Tactics and Leadership in the Confederate Army of Tennessee: Seeds of Failure* (Portland, Ore.: Frank Cass, 2000), 137; Guild, *Fourth Tennessee Cavalry*, 57.
7. *OR*, ser. 1, vol. 32, pt. 2:799; Connelly, *Autumn of Glory*, 278; Horn, *Army of Tennessee*, 306.
8. George K. Miller memoirs, 28, MDA&H; John W. Rowell, "The Battle of Mossy Creek," *CWTI* 8 (July 1969): 11–16.
9. Dodson, *Campaigns of Wheeler*, 156; *Synopsis of Career of Wheeler*, 17–18.
10. *OR*, ser. 1, vol. 31, pt. 1:641–44; Dodson, *Campaigns of Wheeler*, 157–59; George K. Miller memoirs, 29, MDA&H; John W. Cotton, *"Yours Till Death": Civil War Letters of John W. Cotton*, ed. Lucille Griffith (University: University of Alabama Press, 1951), 99.
11. George K. Miller memoirs, 29, MDA&H.
12. *OR*, ser. 1, vol. 31, pt. 3:842–43; Connelly, *Autumn of Glory*, 281–83; Horn, *Army of Tennessee*, 308–09; Richard M. McMurry, *Two Great Rebel Armies: An Essay in Confederate Military History* (Chapel Hill: University of North Carolina Press, 1989), 127–30.
13. Connelly, *Autumn of Glory*, 283–89.
14. Dyer, *"Fightin' Joe" Wheeler*, 153–54; *OR*, ser. 1, vol. 32, pt. 3:683; Recruiting broadside, headquarters, Cavalry District, North Alabama, Mar. 31, 1864, GLC; Nathaniel Cheairs Hughes Jr. and Roy P. Stonesifer Jr., *The Life and Wars of Gideon J. Pillow* (Chapel Hill: University of North Carolina Press, 1993), 152–54, 260–76.
15. George K. Miller memoirs, 27, MDA&H; Poole, *Cracker Cavaliers*, 118; Richard M. McMurry, *Atlanta, 1864: Last Chance for the Confederacy* (Lincoln: University of

Nebraska Press, 2000), 132.

16. Dyer, *"Fightin' Joe" Wheeler*, 155–56; Du Bose, *Wheeler and the Army of Tennessee*, 274–75; Horn, *Army of Tennessee*, 314–15; Haughton, *Training in Army of Tennessee*, 147–48; Philip L. Secrist, "The Role of Cavalry in the Atlanta Campaign, 1864," *GHQ* 56 (1972): 510; *OR*, ser. 1, vol. 32, pt. 2:759.

17. Dodson, *Campaigns of Wheeler*, 407.

18. Alexander P. Stewart, "The Army of Tennessee: A Sketch," in John Berrien Lindsley, ed., *The Military Annals of Tennessee, Confederate*... (Nashville, Tenn.: J. M. Lindsley & Co., 1886), 85; Howell Carter, *A Cavalryman's Reminiscences of the Civil War* (New Orleans: American Printing Co., 1900), 102–03; J.P. Austin, *The Blue and the Gray: Sketches of a Portion of the Unwritten History of the Great American Civil War*... (Atlanta: Franklin Printing & Publishing Co., 1899), 119; George K. Miller memoirs, 30, MDA&H.

19. *OR*, ser. 1, vol. 32, pt. 2:510; Mims, *Prattville Dragoons*, 13.

20. Fisher, *They Rode With Forrest and Wheeler*, 73; Collier, *War Child's Children*, 90–91; McMurry, *Atlanta, 1864*, 59; *OR*, ser. 1, vol. 32, pt. 3:795.

21. *OR*, ser. 1, vol. 32, pt. 2:699; vol. 38, pt. 3:642; James Lee McDonough and James Pickett Jones, *War So Terrible: Sherman and Atlanta* (New York: W. W. Norton & Co., 1987), 65–67; Woodworth, *Davis and His Generals*, 266.

22. Warner, *Generals in Gray*, 332.

23. *OR*, ser. 1, vol. 32, pt. 3:866; John P. Dyer, "Some Aspects of Cavalry Operations in the Army of Tennessee," *Journal of Southern History* 8 (1942): 212. In *Autumn of Glory* (384–86), Connelly attempts to explain the inconsistencies in Wheeler's reporting of cavalry strength throughout the Atlanta Campaign.

24. *OR*, ser. 1, vol. 38, pt. 1:115.

25. *OR*, ser. 1, vol. 52, pt. 2:606–07.

26. *OR*, ser. 1, vol. 32, pt. 1:173–94; Dyer, *"Fightin' Joe" Wheeler*, 157–58; Du Bose, *Wheeler and the Army of Tennessee*, 266–68.

27. *OR*, ser. 1, vol. 52, pt. 1:611–14; Connelly, *Autumn of Glory*, 316.

28. *OR*, ser. 1, vol. 52, pt. 1:606.

29. Connelly, *Autumn of Glory*, 289–92.

30. Connelly, *Autumn of Glory*, 292–312.

31. Connelly, *Autumn of Glory*, 307–08.

32. Connelly, *Autumn of Glory*, 317, 410.

33. Connelly, *Autumn of Glory*, 322–24.

34. Connelly, *Autumn of Glory*, 318–21; Horn, *Army of Tennessee*, 313–14.

35. Connelly, *Autumn of Glory*, 319–20; *OR*, ser. 1, vol. 51, pt. 1:606–07; JW to Braxton Bragg, Feb. 14, 1864, JW MSS, HU.

36. Horn, *Army of Tennessee*, 314; Connelly, *Autumn of Glory*, 320–21.

37. Batchelor and Turner, *Letters*, 75; Du Bose, *Wheeler and the Army of Tennessee*, 268–69.

38. Johnston, *Narrative of Military Operations*, 282–85; Dodson, *Campaigns of Wheeler*, 162–68; Austin, *Blue and Gray*, 121–22; *OR*, ser. 1, vol. 32, pt. 1:10, 484; pt. 2:798.

39. Connelly, *Autumn of Glory*, 326–30; McMurry, *Atlanta, 1864*, 58–59; Craig L. Symonds, *Joseph E. Johnston: A Civil War Biography* (New York: W. W. Norton & Co., 1992), 273–74.

40. Dodson, *Campaigns of Wheeler*, 169.

41. Dodson, *Campaigns of Wheeler*, 169–71; Poole, *Cracker Cavaliers*, 119.

42. Grant, *Personal Memoirs*, 374–77; Secrist, "Cavalry in Atlanta Campaign," 510–11; Connelly, *Autumn of Glory*, 331–34; Dyer, *"Fightin' Joe" Wheeler*, 159–62; *OR*, ser. 1, vol. 38, pt. 3:943–44; pt. 4:656–57, 660–64, 672–73.

43. Connelly, *Autumn of Glory*, 335; Secrist, "Cavalry in Atlanta Campaign," 511; McMurry, *Atlanta, 1864*, 62–63.
44. McDonough and Jones, *War So Terrible*, 96.
45. *OR*, ser. 1, vol. 38, pt. 3:944; pt. 4:672–73; Connelly, *Autumn of Glory*, 335–38; Secrist, "Cavalry in Atlanta Campaign," 512; Gustave Cook to his wife, May 9, 1864, Cook MSS, GLC.
46. *OR*, ser. 1, vol. 38, pt. 3:944; Dodson, *Campaigns of Wheeler*, 176–77.
47. Connelly, *Autumn of Glory*, 338–39; *OR*, ser. 1, vol. 38, pt. 3:944; pt. 4:681–82.
48. *OR*, ser. 1, vol. 38, pt. 3:944; pt. 4:710; Secrist, "Cavalry in Atlanta Campaign," 512.
49. *OR*, ser. 1, vol. 38, pt. 3:944–45.

10. COUNTERMARCHING THROUGH GEORGIA

1. Dyer, *"Fightin' Joe" Wheeler*, 166–67; Dodson, *Campaigns of Wheeler*, 178; William S. Ward to "My Dear Cousin," May 28, 1864, Ward MSS, USAMHI.
2. *OR*, ser. 1, vol. 38, pt. 3:945; pt. 4:707.
3. *OR*, ser. 1, vol. 38, pt. 3: 945; Johnston, *Narrative of Military Operations*, 310–11; Dyer, *"Fightin' Joe" Wheeler*, 166–67.
4. Albert Castel, *Decision in the West: The Atlanta Campaign of 1864* (Lawrence: University Press of Kansas, 1992), 172, 175–81; McDonough and Jones, *War So Terrible*, 284; *OR*, ser. 1, vol. 38, pt. 3:945; pt. 4:713; Secrist, "Cavalry in Atlanta Campaign," 513.
5. Dodson, *Campaigns of Wheeler*, 179–80; George K. Miller memoirs, 36–37, MDA&H.
6. *OR*, ser. 1, vol. 38, pt. 3:945–46; James Cooper Nisbet, *Four Years on the Firing Line* (Jackson, Tenn.: McCowat-Mercer Press, 1963), 187–91.
7. Castel, *Decision in the West*, 193–95; Connelly, *Autumn of Glory*, 332, 334, 341, 344–45; *OR*, ser. 1, vol. 38, pt. 3:946.
8. *OR*, ser. 1 vol. 38, pt. 3:646, 650; Warner, *Generals in Gray*, 9–10, 338–39; John T. Morgan to Isaac W. Avery, June 7, 8, July 20, 1864, and Avery's answers to John T. Morgan's "Interrogatories," July 28, 1864, Avery MSS, USAMHI.
9. *OR*, ser. 1, vol. 38, pt. 3:946; pt. 4:728; Dodson, *Campaigns of Wheeler*, 183, 200–06.
10. *OR*, ser. 1, vol. 38, pt. 3:946; pt. 4:729; 222 185; Johnston, *Narrative of Military Operations*, 325.
11. Dodson, *Campaigns of Wheeler*, 186; Austin, *Blue and Gray*, 125.
12. *OR*, ser. 1, vol. 38, pt. 3:947; George K. Miller memoirs, 38, MDA&H; Collier, *War Child's Children*, 98–99.
13. Cotton, *"Yours Till Death,"* 108–09; Du Bose, *Wheeler and the Army of Tennessee*, 304–05; Adam Henry Whetstone, *History of the Fifty-third Alabama Volunteer Infantry (Mounted)*, ed. William Stanley Hoole (University, Ala.: Confederate Publishing Co., 1985), 53.
14. Connelly, *Autumn of Glory*, 353–55; Horn, *Army of Tennessee*, 329–30; Castel, *Decision in the West*, 221–26.
15. *OR*, ser. 1, vol. 38, pt. 3:948; Dyer, *"Fightin' Joe" Wheeler*, 171–72; Castel, *Decision in the West*, 233–41.
16. Gustave Cook to his wife, July 7, 1864, Cook MSS, GLC; Secrist, "Cavalry in Atlanta Campaign," 516–17.
17. *OR*, ser. 1, vol. 38, pt. 3:949. In *Autumn of Glory* (389) Connelly, incorrectly suggests that Wheeler's May 1864 losses (548, including men captured or missing) were relatively few.

18. *OR*, ser. 1, vol. 38, pt. 4:681–82; Connelly, *Autumn of Glory*, 338.

19. Connelly, *Autumn of Glory*, 372–90; McMurry, *Atlanta, 1864*, 97–99, 111, 131–36, 198–202; McDonough and Jones, *War So Terrible*, 124–26; Johnston, *Narrative of Military Operations*, 359–62; Dyer, *"Fightin' Joe" Wheeler*, 172–73; *OR*, ser. 1, vol. 52, pt. 2:704–07.

20. Jordan and Pryor, *Campaigns of Forrest*, 457–553; Wills, *Battle From the Start*, 200–46; Hurst, *Nathan Bedford Forrest*, 182–215.

21. JW to Braxton Bragg, July [?], 1864, Bragg MSS, DU.

22. Dodson, *Campaigns of Wheeler*, 380–86; *OR*, ser. 1, vol. 38, pt. 4:751; vol. 52, pt. 2:676.

23. *OR*, ser. 1, vol. 38, pt. 3:948–49; Secrist, "Cavalry in Atlanta Campaign," 517; Sidney S. Champion to his wife, May 31, 1864, Champion MSS, EU.

24. Connelly, *Autumn of Glory*, 355–56; Castel, *Decision in the West*, 242–77.

25. Poole, *Cracker Cavaliers*, 122–23; Dodson, *Campaigns of Wheeler*, 190; Secrist, "Cavalry in Atlanta Campaign," 518–19.

26. Sidney S. Champion to anon., June 9, 1864, Champion MSS, EU; *Synopsis of Career of Wheeler*, 23; Castel, *Decision in the West*, 285–86.

27. *OR*, ser. 1, vol. 38, pt. 4:783; Poole, *Cracker Cavaliers*, 124–25; William A. Fleming memoirs, 29, USAMHI; Glenn W. Sunderland, *Lightning at Hoover's Gap: The Story of Wilder's Brigade* (New York: Thomas Yoseloff, 1969), 155–58; Richard A. Baumgartner and Larry M. Strayer, *Kennesaw Mountain, June 1864* (Huntington, W.Va.: Blue Acorn Press, 1998), 55. Although details remain in dispute, at Noonday Creek Wheeler narrowly avoided being killed or badly wounded when a captured member of Wilder's brigade, en route to the rear, attempted to shoot him at point-blank range with a concealed pistol whose percussion cap proved defective; see David Evans, *Sherman's Horsemen: Union Cavalry Operations in the Atlanta Campaign* (Bloomington: Indiana University Press, 1996), 242–43, 536n; and O. P. Hargis, "We Came Very Near Capturing General Wilder," *CWTI* 7 (Nov. 1968): 40.

28. Castel, *Decision in the West*, 303–24; Connelly, *Autumn of Glory*, 359–60; Sidney S. Champion to his wife, June 27, 1864, Champion MSS; Samuel H. Brodnax memoirs, 5–6, Filson Historical Society, Louisville, Ky.; Janet Hewett, et al., eds., *Supplement to the Official Records of the Union and Confederate Armies* (Wilmington, N.C.: Broadfoot Publishing Co., 1994–2001), 7:147–50.

29. Sidney S. Champion to his wife, July 11, 1864, Champion MSS, EU; Connelly, *Autumn of Glory*, 361–71.

30. Connelly, *Autumn of Glory*, 393–99; *OR*, ser. 1, vol. 38, pt. 5:861–63, 872; Dodson, *Campaigns of Wheeler*, 195–97; Secrist, "Cavalry in Atlanta Campaign," 519–21; Poole, *Cracker Cavaliers*, 127–28; Timothy Daiss, *In the Saddle: Exploits of the 5th Georgia Cavalry During the Civil War* (Atglen, Pa.: Schiffer Publishing, Ltd., 1999), 104–07; George K. Miller memoirs, 40–41, MDA&H; John H. Ash diary, July 5–8, 1864, EU.

31. *OR*, ser. 1, vol. 38, pt. 5:885, 887–89; Johnston, *Narrative of Military Operations*, 348–49; Connelly, *Autumn of Glory*, 399–422.

32. Guild, *Fourth Tennessee Cavalry*, 66; John G. Deupree, "The Noxubee Squadron of the First Mississippi Cavalry, C.S.A., 1861–1865," *Publications of the Mississippi Historical Society, Centenary Series* 2 (1918): 101; William T. Sherman, "The Grand Strategy of the Last Year of the War," *B&L* 4: 253.

33. Evans, *Sherman's Horsemen*, 77–84, 87–88; Secrist, "Cavalry in Atlanta Campaign," 521; Dyer, *"Fightin' Joe" Wheeler*, 176–77; Dodson, *Campaigns of Wheeler*, 199, 205–06.

34. *OR*, ser. 1, vol. 38, pt. 3:951–52; pt. 5:894–95; Castel, *Decision in the West*, 369–71; Connelly, *Autumn of Glory*, 439–40.

35. *OR*, ser. 1, vol. 38, pt. 3:952; Castel, *Decision in the West*, 372–83; Connelly, *Autumn of Glory*, 440–44; Dyer, *"Fightin' Joe" Wheeler*, 177–78; Dodson, *Campaigns of Wheeler*, 209; Poole, *Cracker Cavaliers*, 129–30.

36. *OR*, ser. 1, vol. 38, pt. 3:952; Castel, *Decision in the West*, 383–88; Connelly, *Autumn of Glory*, 444; Dyer, *"Fightin' Joe" Wheeler*, 178; Dodson, *Campaigns of Wheeler*, 209–10; Poole, *Cracker Cavaliers*, 131–32.

37. Castel, *Decision in the West*, 389–413; Connelly, *Autumn of Glory*, 445–49.

38. *OR*, ser. 1, vol. 38, pt. 3:952; Dyer, *"Fightin' Joe" Wheeler*, 179; Poole, *Cracker Cavaliers*, 132–32; John H. Ash diary, July 22, 1864, EU; William L. Nugent, *My Dear Nellie: The Civil War Letters of William L. Nugent to Eleanor Smith Nugent*, ed. William M. Cash and Lucy Somerville Howorth (Jackson: University Press of Mississippi, 1977), 189–90; Du Bose, *Wheeler and the Army of Tennessee*, 373–74.

39. *OR*, ser. 1, vol. 38, pt. 3:952–53; pt. 5:901; Dyer, *"Fightin' Joe" Wheeler*, 179–80; Dodson, *Campaigns of Wheeler*, 211–12.

40. *OR*, ser. 1, vol. 38, pt. 3:953; pt. 5:905, 910–11, 913–15, 921; Evans, *Sherman's Horsemen*, 209–11; Dodson, *Campaigns of Wheeler*, 217–19; John H. Ash diary, July 23–27, 1864, EU; Nugent, *My Dear Nellie*, 190.

41. Evans, *Sherman's Horsemen*, 212–16; Secrist, "Cavalry in Atlanta Campaign," 522; Dodson, *Campaigns of Wheeler*, 220–22.

42. *OR*, ser. 1, vol. 38, pt. 3:953; Dyer, *"Fightin' Joe" Wheeler*, 182.

43. *OR*, ser. 1, vol. 38, pt. 3:953; Dodson, *Campaigns of Wheeler*, 223.

11. THE PURSUER AND THE PURSUED

1. *OR*, ser. 1, vol. 38, pt. 3:953–54; pt. 5:922; Secrist, "Cavalry in Atlanta Campaign," 522–23.

2. *OR*, ser. 1, vol. 38, pt. 3:954; pt. 5:927-28; Mims, *Prattville Dragoons*, 14; Lee Kennett, *Marching through Georgia: The Story of Soldiers and Civilians during Sherman's Campaign* (New York: HarperCollins, 1995), 134; Evans, *Sherman's Horsemen*, 217–37, 243–44; John W. Rowell, "McCook's Raid," *CWTI* 13 (July 1974): 8–9, 42–43; John H. Ash diary, July 29, 1864, EU.

3. *OR*, ser. 1, vol. 38, pt. 3:954; 5:927–29; Dyer, *"Fightin' Joe" Wheeler*, 183; Evans, *Sherman's Horsemen*, 244–49; Du Bose, *Wheeler and the Army of Tennessee*, 377–78.

4. *OR*, ser. 1, vol. 38, pt. 3:954; Dodson, *Campaigns of Wheeler*, 225; Evans, *Sherman's Horsemen*, 249–51; George K. Miller memoirs, 43–44, MDA&H; John H. Ash diary, July 30, 1864, EU.

5. *OR*, ser. 1, vol. 38, pt. 3:955, 964; Dodson, *Campaigns of Wheeler*, 226–27; Dyer, *"Fightin' Joe" Wheeler*, 183–84; Evans, *Sherman's Horsemen*, 252–61.

6. *OR*, ser. 1, vol. 38, pt. 3:955, 964; Evans, *Sherman's Horsemen*, 262–64; Rowell, "McCook's Raid," 44–45; Du Bose, *Wheeler and the Army of Tennessee*, 378–79; George L. Griscom, *Fighting With Ross' Texas Cavalry Brigade, C.S.A.: The Diary of George L. Griscom, Adjutant, 9th Texas Cavalry Regiment*, ed. Homer L. Kerr (Hillsboro, Tex.: Hill Junior College Press, 1976), 161–62; Martha L. Crabb, *All Afire to Fight: The Untold Tale of the Civil War's Ninth Texas Cavalry* (New York: Post Road Publishing, 2000), 236–37.

7. *OR*, ser. 1, vol. 38, pt. 3:955–56; Evans, *Sherman's Horsemen*, 265–71; Guild, *Fourth Tennessee Cavalry*, 70–71.

8. *OR*, ser. 1, vol. 38, pt. 3:956; Dodson, *Campaigns of Wheeler*, 228–29; Evans, *Sherman's Horsemen*, 271–77; Rowell, "McCook's Raid," 46–48; Du Bose, *Wheeler and the Army of Tennessee*, 379.

9. Evans, *Sherman's Horsemen*, 291–319; George K. Miller memoirs, 44, MDA&H.

10. *OR*, ser. 1, vol. 38, pt. 3:936, 938–39; Secrist, "Cavalry in Atlanta Campaign," 523–24; Evans, *Sherman's Horsemen*, 320–76; Hargis, "We Came Very Near Capturing General Wilder," 41; Poole, *Cracker Cavaliers*, 133–35, 141–44; Gilbert C. Kniffin, *General Capron's Narrative of Stoneman's Raid South of Atlanta* (Washington, D.C.: Military Order of the Loyal Legion, Commandery of the District of Columbia, 1899), 11–20.

11. *OR*, ser. 1, vol. 38, pt. 3:957.

12. Dyer, *"Fightin' Joe" Wheeler*, 187; Castel, *Decision in the West*, 425–36; Connelly, *Autumn of Glory*, 453–55.

13. Dodson, *Campaigns of Wheeler*, 234; Connelly, *Autumn of Glory*, 455–57.

14. *OR*, ser. 1, vol. 38, pt. 3:957; Dyer, *"Fightin' Joe" Wheeler*, 187–88; Dodson, *Campaigns of Wheeler*, 249; Cotton, *"Yours Till Death,"* 117.

15. *OR*, ser. 1, vol. 38, pt. 3:957; Connelly, *Autumn of Glory*, 434, 457–58.

16. *OR*, ser. 1, vol. 38, pt. 3:957; Dodson, *Campaigns of Wheeler*, 249; Connelly, *Autumn of Glory*, 436–37; Du Bose, *Wheeler and the Army of Tennessee*, 383.

17. *OR*, ser. 1, vol. 38, pt. 3:957; Dyer, *"Fightin' Joe" Wheeler*, 190; Whetstone, *Fifty-third Alabama*, 56.

18. *OR*, ser. 1, vol. 38, pt. 3:958; Dodson, *Campaigns of Wheeler*, 250.

19. *OR*, ser. 1, vol. 38, pt. 3:958; Warner, *Generals in Gray*, 214–15.

20. *OR*, ser. 1, vol. 38, pt. 3:958; Dodson, *Campaigns of Wheeler*, 250–51; Dyer, *"Fightin' Joe" Wheeler*, 190–91.

21. *OR*, ser. 1, vol. 38, pt. 3:958; J. C. Williamson, ed., "Diary of John Coffee Williamson," *THQ* 15 (1956): 66.

22. *OR*, ser. 1, vol. 38, pt. 3:958–59; Dyer, *"Fightin' Joe" Wheeler*, 191–92; Connelly, *Autumn of Glory*, 435; George K. Miller memoirs, 46, MDA&H.

23. *OR*, ser. 1, vol. 38, pt. 3:959; Dyer, *"Fightin' Joe" Wheeler*, 192–93; Dodson, *Campaigns of Wheeler*, 252, 254; Du Bose, *Wheeler and the Army of Tennessee*, 385; Whetstone, *Fifty-third Alabama*, 60.

24. Du Bose, *Wheeler and the Army of Tennessee*, 387–89; George K. Miller memoirs, 46–50, MDA&H; Whetstone, *Fifty-third Alabama*, 60–73; Felix H. Robertson, "On Wheeler's Last Raid in Middle Tennessee," *CV* 30 (1922): 334–35; *OR*, ser. 1, vol. 39, pt. 3:801; vol. 45, pt. 1:240; pt. 2:775–77.

25. *OR*, ser. 1, vol. 38, pt. 3:959–60; Dodson, *Campaigns of Wheeler*, 252–53; Collier, *War Child's Children*, 113–14; Williamson, "Diary of John Coffee Williamson," 66.

26. *OR*, ser. 1, vol. 38, pt. 3:960; Fisher, *They Rode with Forrest and Wheeler*, 99–100; Guild, *Fourth Tennessee Cavalry*, 97–98; Daiss, *In the Saddle*, 60, 63.

27. Dyer, *"Fightin' Joe" Wheeler*, 193–94; DeLeon, *Wheeler, the Man, the Statesman, the Soldier*, 32–34.

28. *OR*, ser. 1, vol. 38, pt. 3:961; Dyer, *"Fightin' Joe" Wheeler*, 194–95; Dodson, *Campaigns of Wheeler*, 253; Du Bose, *Wheeler and the Army of Tennessee*, 386; J. C. Witherspoon, "Confederate Cavalry Leaders," *CV* 27 (1919): 416–17.

29. *OR*, ser. 1, vol. 38, pt. 3:960.

30. *OR*, ser. 1, vol. 38, pt. 3:960–61; Connelly, *Autumn of Glory*, 435, 458; McDonough and Jones, *War So Terrible*, 288.

31. *OR*, ser. 1, vol. 38, pt. 3:960–61; Evans, *Sherman's Horsemen*, 404–37; Connelly, *Autumn of Glory*, 435–36; William A. Fletcher, *Rebel Private, Front and Rear: Mem-*

oirs of a Confederate Soldier (New York: E. P. Dutton, 1995), 128; Armin E. Mruck, "The Role of Railroads in the Atlanta Campaign," *CWH* 7 (1961): 269.

32. Dyer, *"Fightin' Joe" Wheeler*, 197–98; Connelly, *Autumn of Glory*, 458–69; Castel, *Decision in the West*, 501–24.
33. McPherson, *Ordeal by Fire*, 412–13.
34. McPherson, *Ordeal by Fire*, 414–28.
35. McPherson, *Ordeal by Fire*, 437–42.
36. McPherson, *Ordeal by Fire*, 442–46; Connelly, *Autumn of Glory*, 469.
37. Cotton, *"Yours Till Death"*, 118; McDonough and Jones, *War So Terrible*, 287.
38. *OR*, ser. 1, vol. 38, pt. 3:960; vol. 39, pt. 2:859; Dyer, *"Fightin' Joe" Wheeler*, 195–96; Hurst, *Nathan Bedford Forrest*, 216.
39. *OR*, ser. 1, vol. 36, pt. 5:1,010, 1,029; vol. 39, pt. 2:834, 849; Dyer, *"Fightin' Joe" Wheeler*, 196; Dodson, *Campaigns of Wheeler*, 257.
40. Williamson, "Diary of John Coffee Williamson," 69.
41. Williamson, "Diary of John Coffee Williamson," 71; *OR*, ser. 1, vol. 38, pt. 3:960; vol. 39, pt. 2:861; Dyer, *"Fightin' Joe" Wheeler*, 200–01; Dodson, *Campaigns of Wheeler*, 258; *Synopsis of Career of Wheeler*, 29; Fisher, *They Rode with Forrest and Wheeler*, 119.
42. John Bell Hood, *Advance and Retreat: Personal Experiences in the United States and Confederate States Armies* (New Orleans: Hood Orphan Memorial Fund, 1880), 243–48; John P. Dyer, *The Gallant Hood* (Indianapolis: Bobbs-Merrill Co., 1950), 279–80; Connelly, *Autumn of Glory*, 470–72, 477–79.
43. Connelly, *Autumn of Glory*, 479–85; Hood, *Advance and Retreat*, 252; Anne J. Bailey, *The Chessboard of War: Sherman and Hood in the Autumn Campaigns of 1864* (Lincoln: University of Nebraska Press, 2000), 41; *OR*, ser. 1, vol. 39, pt. 3:843, 891; vol. 44: 931–33; vol. 52, pt. 2:768.
44. *OR*, ser. 1, vol. 39, pt. 3:842, 859, 882–83, 892. In a postwar biography of his former commander, one of Wheeler's staff officers asserts that Wheeler, a native Georgian, foresaw Sherman's march to Savannah and lobbied for authority to oppose it: "With great difficulty [he] gained permission to take a portion of his command to Georgia, to assist in its defence" (*Synopsis of Career of Wheeler*, 29).
45. *OR*, 39, pt. 1: 580–86.
46. Poole, *Cracker Cavaliers*, 160–61.
47. Du Bose, *Wheeler and the Army of Tennessee*, 407–08; William C. Davis, *The Orphan Brigade: The Kentucky Confederates Who Couldn't Go Home* (Garden City, N.Y.: Doubleday & Co., Inc., 1980), 237–39.
48. *OR*, ser. 1, vol. 44:7–8, 406; Dyer, *"Fightin' Joe" Wheeler*, 207; Dodson, *Campaigns of Wheeler*, 284–87; Edward G. Longacre, "Judson Kilpatrick," *CWTI* 10 (Apr. 1971): 25–33.
49. *OR*, ser. 1, vol. 44:362–63, 406.
50. *OR*, ser. 1, vol. 44: 363, 406–07; Poole, *Cracker Cavaliers*, 164–65; Guild, *Fourth Tennessee Cavalry*, 106–07; Samuel J. Martin, *"Kill-Cavalry," Sherman's Merchant of Terror: The Life of Union General Hugh Judson Kilpatrick* (Madison, N.J.: Fairleigh Dickinson University Press, 1996), 196; William A. Fleming memoirs, 30, USAMHI.
51. *OR*, ser. 1, vol. 44:363, 407, 898; Dodson, *Campaigns of Wheeler*, 288–89; Poole, *Cracker Cavaliers*, 165; Burke Davis, *Sherman's March* (New York: Random House, 1980), 57–68.
52. *OR*, ser. 1, vol. 44:363, 408, 900–01, 903; Dodson, *Campaigns of Wheeler*, 289–90; Dyer, *"Fightin' Joe" Wheeler*, 208; Guild, *Fourth Tennessee Cavalry*, 107–08; William A. Fleming memoirs, 30, USAMHI; Davis, *Sherman's March*, 82–83.

53. *OR*, ser. 1, vol. 44:363–64, 408–09, 910; Dodson, *Campaigns of Wheeler*, 290–93; Fisher, *They Rode with Forrest and Wheeler*, 123; Guild, *Fourth Tennessee Cavalry*, 108–09; Martin, *"Kill-Cavalry,"* 198–99; Joseph T. Glatthaar, *The March to the Sea and Beyond: Sherman's Troops in the Savannah and Carolinas Campaigns* (New York: New York University Press, 1985), 160.

54. *OR*, ser. 1, vol. 44:364, 409; Nugent, *My Dear Nellie*, 224; Guild, *Fourth Tennessee Cavalry*, 107.

55. *Charleston Mercury*, Jan. 14, 1865; Dyer, *"Fightin' Joe" Wheeler*, 210–11; Poole, *Cracker Cavaliers*, 172; Kennett, *Marching Through Georgia*, 278; Bailey, *Chessboard of War*, 59; Glatthaar, *March to the Sea and Beyond*, 120, 152; John G. Barrett, *Sherman's March through the Carolinas* (Chapel Hill: University of North Carolina Press, 1956), 58; George K. Miller memoirs, 51, MDA&H.

56. *OR*, ser. 1, vol. 44:979, 998; vol. 47, pt. 2:1,047; ser. 4, pt. 3:967–68; Lavender R. Ray to his father, Dec. 5, 1864, Ray MSS, EU.

57. *OR*, ser. 1, vol. 44:998–99; Dyer, *"Fightin' Joe" Wheeler*, 212; Kennett, *Marching Through Georgia*, 312. Du Bose, in *Wheeler and the Army of Tennessee* (421) asserts that when looting and burning their way through Georgia, Union cavalrymen (presumably clothed in nondescript attire) often represented themselves as members of Wheeler's corps.

58. *OR*, ser. 1, vol. 44: 364–65, 409–10; Dodson, *Campaigns of Wheeler*, 297–301; Du Bose, *Wheeler and the Army of Tennessee*, 414–15; Paul R. Scott, "On the Road to the Sea: Shannon's Scouts," *CWTI* 21 (Jan. 1983): 29; Fisher, *They Rode With Forrest and Wheeler*, 123–24; Martin, *"Kill-Cavalry,"* 199–200; Bailey, *Chessboard of War*, 113.

59. *OR*, ser. 1, vol. 44:365, 410; Fisher, *They Rode With Forrest and Wheeler*, 124; Du Bose, *Wheeler and the Army of Tennessee*, 416–17.

60. *OR*, ser. 1, vol. 44:410–11, 941, 955; Dodson, *Campaigns of Wheeler*, 307–08.

61. *OR*, ser. 1, vol. 44:411.

12. All That Human Exertion Could Accomplish

1. Connelly, *Autumn of Glory*, 485–514; Horn, *Army of Tennessee*, 381–424.

2. *OR*, ser. 1, vol. 44:9–12, 411, 967; Charles C. Jones Jr., "The Siege and Evacuation of Savannah, Georgia, in December, 1864," *SHSP* 17 (1889): 80–84; Davis, *Sherman's March*, 102–19.

3. *OR*, ser. 1, vol. 44:12–13; vol. 47, pt. 1:17–19; Davis, *Sherman's March*, 120–40.

4. *OR*, ser. 1, vol. 47, pt. 2:1,000.

5. *OR*, ser. 1, vol. 47, pt. 2:980; Poole, *Cracker Cavaliers*, 172; Donald A. Hopkins, *The Little Jeff: The Jeff Davis Legion, Cavalry, Army of Northern Virginia* (Shippensburg, Pa.: White Mane Books, 1999), 251; Nugent, *My Dear Nellie*, 231.

6. James Spratt White to "My Dear Sister," Mar. 8, 1865, White Family MSS, Archives and Special Collections, Winthrop College, Rock Hill, S. C.

7. Joseph Mullen Jr. diary, Apr. 15, 1865, MC.

8. JW to "My Brave Soldiers," Dec. 31, 1864, Civil War Collection, TSL&A (a copy is in Wheeler MSS, RG-109, E-136, NA); *OR*, ser. 1, vol. 44:1,002.

9. *OR*, ser. 1, vol. 44:1,002–03.

10. Special order, number unknown, Headquarters Military Division of the West, Nov. 26, 1864, GLC; *OR*, ser. 1, vol. 44:898; Dyer, *"Fightin' Joe" Wheeler*, 213.

11. Samuel W. Ferguson diary, Jan. 3, 5–7, 1865; Samuel W. Ferguson to H. C. Chambers, Jan. 12, 1865; both, Ferguson MSS, MDA&H; *OR*, ser. 1, vol. 47, pt. 2:1,004.

12. Alfred Roman, "Inspection Report of Wheeler's Cavalry Corps in Obedience to Instructions from Headquarters Military Division of the West, Dated December 28, 1864," Jan. 22, 1865, Roman MSS, Library of Congress, Washington, D.C.
13. Roman, "Inspection Report."
14. Roman, "Inspection Report."
15. Roman, "Inspection Report."
16. Roman, "Inspection Report."
17. Edward G. Longacre, *Gentleman and Soldier: A Biography of Wade Hampton III* (Nashville, Tenn.: Rutledge Hill Press, 2003), 220–23; *OR*, ser. 1, vol. 47, pt. 2:1,054.
18. Longacre, *Gentleman and Soldier*, 223–24.
19. Du Bose, *Wheeler and the Army of Tennessee*, 430; JW to Charles C. Jones, July 6, 1871, Charles C. Jones MSS, DU; Samuel W. Ferguson diary, Jan. 5, 7, Feb. 12, 1865, Ferguson MSS, MDA&H.
20. Cotton, *"Yours Till Death"*, 125; Lavender R. Ray to "Dear Brother," Jan. 20, 1865, Ray MSS, EU.
21. Davis, *Sherman's March*, 141; *OR*, ser. 1, vol. 47, pt. 1:1,115–21.
22. JW to William J. Hardee, Feb. 1, 1865, Hardee MSS, DU; Davis, *Sherman's March*, 146–47; *OR*, ser. 1, vol. 47, pt. 1:1,121; pt. 2:1,079; Dodson, *Campaigns of Wheeler*, 318–19; Collier, *War Child's Children*, 127.
23. *OR*, ser. 1, vol. 47, pt. 1:858; pt. 2:1,163–64, 1,170, 1,295; JW to Braxton Bragg, Feb. 9, 1865, and JW to P. G. T. Beauregard, Feb. 10, 1865, JW MSS, HU; JW to P. G. T. Beauregard, Feb. 11, 1865, MC; George K. Miller memoirs, 53, MDA&H; Dodson, *Campaigns of Wheeler*, 321–24; D. B. Morgan, "Incidents of the Fighting at Aiken, S. C.," *CV* 32 (1924): 300–01; Barrett, *Sherman's March Through the Carolinas*, 56–57; Collier, *War Child's Children*, 128.
24. Scott, "On the Road to the Sea," 29.
25. Dodson, *Campaigns of Wheeler*, 326–27; W. C. Dodson, "Burning of Broad River Bridge . . .," *CV* 17 (1909): 463; George K. Miller memoirs, 55, MDA&H; Henry L. Stone diary, Feb. 15, 1865, MC; John W. Dyer, *Reminiscences; or, Four Years in the Confederate Army . . .* (Evansville, Ind.: Keller Printing & Publishing Co., 1898), 280–81; Barrett, *Sherman's March Through the Carolinas*, 59–60.
26. *OR*, ser. 1, vol. 47, pt. 2:1,186; Longacre, *Gentleman and Soldier*, 225–26.
27. *OR*, ser. 1, vol. 47, pt. 2:1,207; Dodson, *Campaigns of Wheeler*, 327–28; Dodson, "Burning of Broad River Bridge," 464–65; Clement Saussy, "Two Bridges Burned Near Columbia," *CV* 17 (1909): 553; G. W. F. Harper, "Sherman at Columbia," *CV* 18 (1910): 32.
28. Dyer, *"Fightin' Joe" Wheeler*, 220; Dodson, "Burning of Broad River Bridge," 465; Fletcher, *Rebel Private, Front and Rear*, 189; Zachariah T. DeLoach memoirs, 5, GSA; John H. Ash diary, Feb. 16, 1865, EU; Henry L. Stone diary, Feb. 16, 1865, MC; Dyer, *Reminiscences*, 282–83.
29. JW to Albert Ferry, Feb. 17, 1865, JW MSS, HU; William Stokes, *Saddle Soldiers: The Civil War Correspondence of General William Stokes of the 4th South Carolina Cavalry*, ed. Lloyd Halliburton (Orangeburg, S.C.: Sandlapper Publishing Co., Inc., 1993), 193; Wade Hampton to Edward L. Wells, Mar. 25, 1900, Wells MSS, Charleston Library Society, Charleston, S.C. William Carey Dodson, in "More About the Defense of Columbia" (*CV* 18 [1910]: 75–78), attempts to refute the charge that Wheeler's men did no fighting, and suffered no casualties, during the evacuation of the city.
30. Barrett, *Sherman's March Through the Carolinas*, 68; Longacre, *Gentleman and Soldier*, 227.

31. Barrett, *Sherman's March Through the Carolinas*, 71–92; Longacre, *Gentleman and Soldier*, 227–29; William T. Sherman, *Memoirs of General William T. Sherman, Written by Himself* (New York: D. Appleton & Co., 1875), 2:287.

32. *OR*, ser. 1, vol. 47, pt. 2:1,247–48, 1,256–57, 1,261–62, 1,270; Connelly, *Autumn of Glory*, 517–20.

33. *OR*, ser. 1, vol. 47, pt. 1:122–24; pt. 2:1,281; pt. 3:704; Dyer, *"Fightin' Joe" Wheeler*, 221, 223; Dodson, *Campaigns of Wheeler*, 342–43; Barrett, *Sherman's March Through the Carolinas*, 107–08, 113.

34. *OR*, ser. 1, vol. 47, pt. 1:1,124–25, 1,130; Dodson, *Campaigns of Wheeler*, 343–45; Du Bose, *Wheeler and the Army of Tennessee*, 443–45; Davis, *Sherman's March*, 206–07; Barrett, *Sherman's March Through the Carolinas*, 114, 126–27.

35. *OR*, ser. 1, vol. 47, pt. 1:861, 1,130; Dyer, *"Fightin' Joe" Wheeler*, 223–24; Edward L. Wells, *Hampton and His Cavalry in '64* (Richmond, Va.: B. F. Johnson Publishing Co., 1899), 406–07; Longacre, *Gentleman and Soldier*, 233–34; Sharyn Kane and Richard Keeton, *Fiery Dawn: The Civil War Battle at Monroe's Crossroads, North Carolina* (Tallahassee, Fla.: Southeast Archeological Center, National Park Service, 1999), 64, 66; Barrett, *Sherman's March Through the Carolinas*, 127–30.

36. Wells, *Hampton and His Cavalry*, 412–13; Kane and Keeton, *Fiery Dawn*, 59, 67–68, 71–72, 75; J. C. Witcher, "Shannon's Scouts—Kilpatrick," *CV* 14 (1906): 511–12; George K. Miller memoirs, 57, MDA&H.

37. *OR*, ser. 1, vol. 47, pt. 1:861–62, 1,130; Dodson, *Campaigns of Wheeler*, 345; Du Bose, *Wheeler and the Army of Tennessee*, 448; Kane and Keeton, *Fiery Dawn*, 75, 79; Witcher, "Shannon's Scouts," 512; A. E. Jenkins, "Kilpatrick's Spotted Horse," *CV* 13 (1905): 315; W. G. Caruthers, "More About Kilpatrick's Horses," *CV* 13 (1905): 456; W. H. Davis, "Kilpatrick's Spotted Horse," *CV* 14 (1906): 62; "The Kilpatrick Spotted Horse Affair," *CV* 14 (1906): 309.

38. *OR*, ser. 1, vol. 47, pt. 1:1,130; pt. 2:1,361, 1,375; E. L. Wells, "Hampton at Fayetteville," *SHSP* 13 (1885): 144–48.

39. *OR*, ser. 1, vol. 47, pt. 1:1,130; pt. 2:1,409, 1,415; Dodson, *Campaigns of Wheeler*, 347; Barrett, *Sherman's March Through the Carolinas*, 149–58; Guild, *Fourth Tennessee Cavalry*, 127–28; Nathaniel Cheairs Hughes Jr., *Bentonville: The Final Battle of Sherman and Johnston* (Chapel Hill: University of North Carolina Press, 1996), 33–34.

40. Wade Hampton, "The Battle of Bentonville," *B&L* 4: 701–02; Longacre, *Gentleman and Soldier*, 236.

41. *OR*, ser. 1, vol. 47, pt. 1:1,130–31; pt. 2:1,428–33, 1,438–39; Dodson, *Campaigns of Wheeler*, 350; Hampton, "Battle of Bentonville," 702–04; Jay Luvaas, "Bentonville—Last Chance to Stop Sherman," *CWTI* 2 (Oct. 1963): 8–9, 38–39.

42. *OR*, ser. 1, vol. 47, pt. 1:1,131; pt. 2:1,443, 1,447; Dodson, *Campaigns of Wheeler*, 351–52; Du Bose, *Wheeler and the Army of Tennessee*, 452; Fletcher, *Rebel Private, Front and Rear*, 192–93; Hampton, "Battle of Bentonville," 704–05; Luvaas, "Bentonville," 39–40; George K. Miller memoirs, 58, MDA&H.

43. *OR*, ser. 1, vol. 47, pt. 1:1,131–32; pt. 2:1,451–52; Dodson, *Campaigns of Wheeler*, 352–53; Du Bose, *Wheeler and the Army of Tennessee*, 452–53; Hampton, "Battle of Bentonville," 705; Luvaas, "Bentonville," 40; Hughes, *Bentonville*, 189–210, 225; George K. Miller memoirs, 58–59, MDA&H; Hagan, History of 3rd Alabama Cavalry, 13; Guild, *Fourth Tennessee Cavalry*, 130–33; Mark L. Bradley, *Last Stand in the Carolinas: The Battle of Bentonville* (Mason City, Ia.: Savas Publishing Co., 1996), 374–92.

44. *OR*, ser. 1, vol. 47, pt. 1:27, 862.

45. *OR*, ser. 1, vol. 47, pt. 1:1,132; pt. 3:771–73, 783–84; Dodson, *Campaigns of Wheeler*, 355–56.
46. Dodson, *Campaigns of Wheeler*, 357; Mims, *Prattville Dragoons*, 15; George K. Miller memoirs, 60, MDA&H.
47. *OR*, ser. 1, vol. 47, pt. 1:1,132; pt. 3:798–99, 802–03, 805, 808; Barrett, *Sherman's March Through the Carolinas*, 256–57; Guild, *Fourth Tennessee Cavalry*, 145.
48. Davis, *Sherman's March*, 259–65, 269–72.
49. Longacre, *Gentleman and Soldier*, 238–43; JW to Joseph E. Johnston, Apr. 18, 1865, JW MSS, GLC.
50. *OR*, ser. 1, vol. 47, pt. 3:813–14; Dyer, *"Fightin' Joe" Wheeler*, 227–28.
51. JW, "An Effort to Rescue Jefferson Davis," *Century Illustrated Magazine* 56 (1898): 85–86; Longacre, *Gentleman and Soldier*, 243–44; JW to Joseph E. Johnston, Apr. 18, 1865, JW MSS, GLC; *OR*, ser. 1, vol. 47, pt. 3:851.
52. JW, Address of Apr. 25, 1865, Pope-Carter MSS, DU; Dodson, *Campaigns of Wheeler*, 359–60.
53. Dyer, *"Fightin' Joe" Wheeler*, 229–30; Dodson, *Campaigns of Wheeler*, 360–61; Du Bose, *Wheeler and the Army of Tennessee*, 470.
54. JW, "Effort to Rescue Jefferson Davis," 86–87; Dyer, *"Fightin' Joe" Wheeler*, 230–31; Dodson, *Campaigns of Wheeler*, 361; Wade Hampton, "An Effort to Rescue Jefferson Davis," *SHSP* 37 (1899): 135–36; *OR*, ser. 1, vol. 47, pt. 3:841; Longacre, *Gentleman and Soldier*, 245–46.
55. Dyer, *"Fightin' Joe" Wheeler*, 231–32; JW, "Effort to Rescue Jefferson Davis," 87.
56. JW, "Effort to Rescue Jefferson Davis," 87–88.
57. JW, "Effort to Rescue Jefferson Davis," 88.

13. New Fields of Battle

1. JW, "Effort to Rescue Jefferson Davis," 88; "Alexander H. Stephens' Prison Life," *CV* 1 (1893): 169; Dyer, *"Fightin' Joe" Wheeler*, 234–35.
2. JW, "Effort to Rescue Jefferson Davis," 88–89.
3. JW, "Effort to Rescue Jefferson Davis," 89–90; "Alexander H. Stephens' Prison Life," 170; Charles M. Blackford, "The Trials and Trial of Jefferson Davis," *SHSP* 29 (1901): 49; McPherson, *Ordeal by Fire*, 486.
4. JW, "Effort to Rescue Jefferson Davis," 90–91; "Alexander H. Stephens' Prison Life," 171; Dyer, *"Fightin' Joe" Wheeler*, 239–41; Wheeler Family History, JW MSS, C-1, F-1, ADA&H.
5. Dyer, *"Fightin' Joe" Wheeler*, 242.
6. Dyer, *"Fightin' Joe" Wheeler*, 242; Fisher, *They Rode With Forrest and Wheeler*, 115–18.
7. *OR*, ser. 1, vol. 8:726–29; *Nashville Dispatch*, Aug. 22, 1865; Du Bose, *Wheeler and the Army of Tennessee*, 470; Dyer, *"Fightin' Joe" Wheeler*, 242–44; "The General Takes a Beating," *Decatur* [Ala.] *Daily*, Dec. 9, 2003.
8. Dyer, *"Fightin' Joe" Wheeler*, 244; John Witherspoon Du Bose, *Alabama's Tragic Decade: The Years of Alabama, 1865–1874*, ed. James K. Greer (Birmingham, Ala.: Webb Book Co., 1940), 14.
9. Dyer, *"Fightin' Joe" Wheeler*, 244; Dodson, *Campaigns of Wheeler*, 75–76; DeLeon, *Wheeler, the Man, the Statesman, the Soldier*, 57; *Gen. Joseph Wheeler: Proceedings in Statuary Hall*, 6–7; Wheeler Family History, JW MSS, C-1, F-1, ADA&H; "The Wheeler Legacy," *Decatur Daily*, Dec. 7, 2003.
10. Richard Jones to JW, Sept. 30, 1866, JW MSS, C-5, F-6, ADA&H; James G.

Hollandsworth Jr., *An Absolute Massacre: The New Orleans Race Riot of July 30, 1866* (Baton Rouge: Louisiana State University Press, 2001), 140–45.

11. Dyer, *"Fightin' Joe" Wheeler*, 245–46; "Wheeler Legacy," *Decatur Daily*, Dec. 7, 2003; "Pond Spring's Potential," *Decatur Daily*, Dec. 13, 2003; Legal MSS, 1866–69, JW MSS, C-31, F-7, ADA&H. Wheeler later claimed that he left New Orleans "as the climate did not agree with me." (JW to Joseph E. Johnston, June 18, 1874, Johnston MSS, Earl Gregg Swem Library, College of William and Mary, Williamsburg, Va.)

12. "Wheeler Legacy," *Decatur Daily*, Dec. 7, 2003.

13. Dyer, *"Fightin' Joe" Wheeler*, 246; JW to Charles C. Jones, July 6, 1871, Jones MSS, DU; Wheeler Family History, C-1, F-1, C-31, F-7, JW MSS, ADA&H; JW to Jefferson Davis, Nov. 23, 1871, Davis MSS, MC.

14. JW to Jefferson Davis, June 8, 1871, Davis MSS, MC.

15. "On Trial for Killing," *Decatur Daily*, Dec. 10, 2003.

16. Dyer, *"Fightin' Joe" Wheeler*, 246–47; Peter Branum, "General Joe Wheeler and the Dandrige Galey Murder Trial, 1871–1873," *Alabama Review* 50 (July 1997): 163–66.

17. Branum, "Wheeler and Galey Murder Trial," 166–67.

18. Branum, "Wheeler and Galey Murder Trial," 167–71.

19. Branum, "Wheeler and Galey Murder Trial," 169–73.

20. McPherson, *Ordeal by Fire*, 568–71; John B. Clark, *Populism in Alabama* (Auburn, Ala.: Auburn Printing Co., 1927), 12; Du Bose, *Alabama's Tragic Decade*, 426.

21. Dyer, *"Fightin' Joe" Wheeler*, 249–52; "Wheeler the Politician," *Decatur Daily*, Dec. 11, 2003.

22. Clark, *Populism in Alabama*, 25–26; Dyer, *"Fightin' Joe" Wheeler*, 253–59.

23. *CR*, 48th Cong., 1st Sess., 1,213; 49th Cong., 1st Sess., 151; 49th Cong., 2nd Sess., 1,453, 2,456–57; 50th Cong., 1st Sess., 8; 51st Cong., 1st Sess., 5,154; appendix, 667–72; 51st Cong., 2nd Sess., 195, 1,114, 3,028; 52nd Cong., 1st Sess., 4,018–19; 55th Cong., 1st Sess., 91–93; Dyer, *"Fightin' Joe" Wheeler*, 259–61, 301–02.

24. Dyer, *"Fightin' Joe" Wheeler*, 302.

25. Dyer, *"Fightin' Joe" Wheeler*, 260–65; *CR*, 47th Cong., 1st Sess., 13, 222, 238, 417, 724, 2,160, 2,296, 4,058, 4,445–48, 4,487–90, 4,501–05.

26. Dyer, *"Fightin' Joe" Wheeler*, 266–70, 275–78, 290–96, 308–12, 320–22. For some of JW's more important remarks and floor speeches on the tariff issue, see the following *CR* references: 48th Cong., 1st Sess., 2,462, 2,521; 50th Cong., 1st Sess., 9,306–11, 9,595–99; appendix, 120–50, 620; 51st Cong., 1st Sess., appendix, 703–06; 54th Cong., 1st Sess., 312–14; 55th Cong., 1st Sess., 128–30, 343–45, 414, 447, 471, 481, 502–03, 503–06, 522, 569, 971–78, 2,655–60; appendix, 394–415. For his views on silver coinage, see the following: 51st Cong., 2nd Sess., 12; 52nd Cong., 1st Sess., appendix, 215–16, 532–35; 54th Cong., 1st Sess., 360–62, 365–67, 3,367–68; appendix, 204–16. On limiting federal election laws, see 51st Cong., 1st Sess., appendix, 681–700.

27. Dyer, *"Fightin' Joe" Wheeler*, 246, 278–81.

28. Dyer, *"Fightin' Joe" Wheeler*, 281, 325–26; *CR*, 53rd Cong., 3rd Sess., 84, 2,564; 54th Cong., 1st Sess., 271, 284; 55th Cong., 1st Sess., 20, 2,974.

29. *CR*, 48th Cong., 1st Sess., 1,758; 49th Cong., 1st Sess., 366, 538; 49th Cong., 2nd Sess., 379; 50th Cong., 2nd Sess., 2,493; 51st Cong., 2nd Sess., 1,259, 1,928–29, 1,940–41.

30. *CR*, 47th Cong., 2nd Sess., appendix, 251–78; 49th Cong., 1st Sess., 367; 50th Cong., 1st Sess., 7,273; 51st Cong., 2nd Sess., 2,767; 55th Cong., 1st Sess., 678; Dyer, *"Fightin' Joe" Wheeler*, 272–74, 283–84.

31. *CR*, 47th Cong., 2nd Sess., appendix, 281–90; 49th Cong., 1st Sess., 366; 49th Cong., 2nd Sess., 494; 50th Cong., 2nd Sess., 92, 1,573; 53rd Cong., 3rd Sess., 888, 1,051; Dyer, *"Fightin' Joe" Wheeler*, 285.

32. Anders Michael Kinney, *Joseph Wheeler: Uniting the Blue and Gray* (Lincoln, Neb.: Writers Club Press, 2002), 32.

33. *CR*, 54th Cong., 1st Sess., appendix, 453.

34. Fitzhugh Lee and Joseph Wheeler, *Cuba's Struggle Against Spain, With the Causes for American Intervention . . .* (New York: American Historical Press, 1899), 78–79.

35. Dyer, *"Fightin' Joe" Wheeler*, 327–31; *Gen. Joseph Wheeler: Proceedings in Statuary Hall*, 6; Wheeler Family History, JW MSS, C-1, F-1, ADA&H; "Gen. Joseph Wheeler and Family," *CV* 6 (1898): 404; *CR*, 55th Cong., 1st Sess., 1,196–98; "Wheeler the Politician," *Decatur Daily*, Dec. 11, 2003.

36. Dyer, *"Fightin' Joe" Wheeler*, 332; David F. Trask, *The War With Spain in 1898* (New York: Macmillan Publishing Co., Inc., 1981), 24–25; Michael Blow, *A Ship to Remember: The Maine and the Spanish-American War* (New York: William Morrow & Co., Inc., 1992), 187–88.

37. Margaret Leech, *In the Days of McKinley* (New York: Harper & Brothers, 1959), 169; Blow, *Ship to Remember*, 279; Dyer, *"Fightin' Joe" Wheeler*, 333.

38. Dyer, *"Fightin' Joe" Wheeler*, 333.

39. Dyer, *"Fightin' Joe" Wheeler*, 334–35; JW, *The Santiago Campaign, 1898* (Boston: Lamson, Wolffe & Co., 1898), 3–4.

40. Charles Johnson Post, *The Little War of Private Post: The Spanish-American War Up Close* (Boston: Little, Brown Co., 1960), 214–15; JW, *Santiago Campaign*, 4.

41. Dyer, *"Fightin' Joe" Wheeler*, 333–34; *New York Times*, Apr. 30, 1898.

42. Dyer, *"Fightin' Joe" Wheeler*, 334.

14. A Soldier to the Last

1. JW, *Santiago Campaign*, 4–5; Heitman, *Historical Register and Dictionary*, 1:1,024.

2. JW, *Santiago Campaign*, 5.

3. JW, *Santiago Campaign*, 6.

4. Stephen Bonsal, *The Fight for Santiago: The Story of the Soldier in the Cuban Campaign From Tampa to the Surrender* (New York: Doubleday & McClure Co., 1899), 54–55; Virgil Carrington Jones, *Roosevelt's Rough Riders* (Garden City, N.Y.: Doubleday & Co., Inc. 1971), 52–53.

5. Richard Harding Davis, *The Cuban and Porto Rican Campaigns* (New York: Charles Scribner's Sons, 1898), 55–56.

6. Bonsal, *Fight for Santiago*, 56–57.

7. Davis, *Cuban and Porto Rican Campaigns*, 56.

8. Charles Herner, *The Arizona Rough Riders* (Tucson: University of Arizona Press, 1970), 78; Trask, *War With Spain*, 315; Jones, *Roosevelt's Rough Riders*, 224.

9. Allan R. Millett and Peter Maslowski, *For the Common Defense: A Military History of the United States of America* (New York: Free Press, 1984), 288, 292.

10. Millet and Maslowski, *For the Common Defense*, 293–94.

11. JW, *Santiago Campaign*, 6–8, 15; J. T. Dickman, ed., *The Santiago Campaign: Reminiscences of the Operations for the Capture of Santiago de Cuba in the Spanish-American War, June and July, 1898* (Richmond, Va.: Williams Printing Co., 1927), 4–5.

12. JW, *Santiago Campaign*, 8.

13. JW, *Santiago Campaign*, 10–11, 13–14, 240–41; JW to "Captain V. Nickerson," June 22, 23, 1898, Leonard Wilson MSS, WRHS; Theodore Roosevelt, *The Rough*

Riders (New York: Charles Scribner's Sons, 1899), 70; G. J. A. O'Toole, *The Spanish War: An American Epic—1898* (New York: W. W. Norton & Co., 1984), 265–68; Tom Hall, *The Fun and Fighting of the Rough Riders* (New York: Frederick A. Stokes Co., 1899), 108–11; Jones, *Roosevelt's Rough Riders*, 103.

14. JW, *Santiago Campaign*, 16, 18; Dickman, *Santiago Campaign*, 407; G. Creighton Webb to William McKittrick, Mar. 25, 1899, Webb MSS, N-YHS.

15. JW, *Santiago Campaign*, 16–17, 242–44; G. Creighton Webb to William McKittrick, Mar. 25, 1899, JW to Webb, May 18, 1899, and Webb to Phillip Reade, July 19, 1901; all, Webb MSS, N-YHS; Roosevelt, *Rough Riders*, 76; Hall, *Fun and Fighting of Rough Riders*, 132–34; Jones, *Roosevelt's Rough Riders*, 115–16; Jack Cameron Dierks, *A Leap to Arms: The Cuban Campaign of 1898* (Philadelphia: J. B. Lippincott Co., 1970), 88–89.

16. JW, *Santiago Campaign*, 17–31, 134; JW to William Shafter, June 24, 1898, and draft of JW's report of battle of Las Guasimas, June 26, 1898, Leonard Wilson MSS, WRHS; G. Creighton Webb to William McKittrick, Mar. 25, 1899, Webb MSS, N-YHS; Dyer, *"Fightin' Joe" Wheeler*, 350–53; Trask, *War With Spain*, 220–22; Dierks, *Leap to Arms*, 89–92; Walter Millis, *The Martial Spirit: A Study of Our War With Spain* (Boston: Houghton Mifflin Co., 1931), 272–75; Jones, *Roosevelt's Rough Riders*, 122–39.

17. Dyer, *"Fightin' Joe" Wheeler*, 352, 353n; Dickman, *Santiago Campaign*, 411.

18. Nisbet, *Four Years on the Firing Line*, 191–92; "Additional Tributes to General Wheeler," *CV* 14 (1906): 300.

19. Dierks, *Leap to Arms*, 93; Trask, *War With Spain*, 222–23; Herner, *Arizona Rough Riders*, 121; Russell A. Alger, *The Spanish-American War* (New York: Harper & Brothers, 1901), 112–17.

20. Bonsal, *Fight for Santiago*, 88–90, 103–04; *New York Sun*, Mar. 21, 1899; G. Creighton Webb to William McKittrick, Mar. 25, 1899; Webb to Phillip Reade, July 19, 1901; Webb, "Critique of JW's Operations During the Santiago Campaign," n.d.; JW to Webb, May 18, 1899, all, Webb MSS, N-YHS.

21. JW, *Santiago Campaign*, 40–42, 243; O'Toole, *Spanish War*, 294–95; Jones, *Roosevelt's Rough Riders*, 160–61.

22. Dyer, *"Fightin' Joe" Wheeler*, 354–55; Davis, *Cuban and Porto Rican Campaigns*, 188; G. Creighton Webb to JW, Apr. 25, 1899, Webb MSS, N-YHS.

23. William R. Shafter to JW, July 1, 1898, JW to Samuel S. Sumner, July 1, 1898, and JW to "Lt. [Col.] Miley," July 1, 1898; all, Leonard Wilson MSS, WRHS; G. Creighton Webb to JW, May 1, 1899, Webb MSS, N-YHS; JW, *Santiago Campaign*, 43–52, 271–79; Roosevelt, *Rough Riders*, 126–48; Dyer, *"Fightin' Joe" Wheeler*, 355–59; Alger, *Spanish-American War*, 151–67; James R. Young and J. Hampton Moore, eds., *Reminiscences and Thrilling Stories of the* [Spanish-American] *War by Returned Heroes . . .* (Chicago: Wabash Publishing House, 1898), 166–73; Jones, *Roosevelt's Rough Riders*, 182.

24. JW, *Santiago Campaign*, 49–54, 118, 280–89; Dyer, *"Fightin' Joe" Wheeler*, 359–61; G. Creighton Webb to JW, May 1, 1899, Webb MSS, N-YHS; Bonsal, *Fight for Santiago*, 256n–57n; Dickman, *Santiago Campaign*, 36–37; Trask, *War With Spain*, 248–52; Young and Moore, *Reminiscences and Thrilling Stories*, 177.

25. JW, *Santiago Campaign*, 87–90; Millett and Maslowski, *For the Common Defense*, 297–98.

26. Millett and Maslowski, *For the Common Defense*, 298; Dyer, *"Fightin' Joe" Wheeler*, 361–62.

27. JW, *Santiago Campaign*, 122–82; JW to William R. Shafter, July 9 and 15, 1898;

William R. Shafter to JW and J. Ford Kent, July 14, 1898; "Preliminary Agreement for the Capitulation of the Spanish Forces," n.d.; "Terms of the Military Convention for the Capitulation of the Spanish Forces," n.d.; and Nelson A. Miles to Russell A. Alger, July 14, 1898; all, Leonard Wilson MSS, WRHS; Dyer, *"Fightin' Joe" Wheeler*, 362–66; O'Toole, *Spanish War*, 348–51; Herbert H. Sargent, *The Campaign of Santiago de Cuba*, (Chicago: A. C. McClurg & Co., 1907), 3:36–48.

28. Millett and Maslowski, *For the Common Defense*, 300–301.
29. JW, *Santiago Campaign*, 205; Theodore Roosevelt to JW, July 31, 1898, and JW to Col. Commanding 2nd Brigade, Cavalry Division, Aug. 1, 1898, Webb MSS, N-YHS; Jones, *Roosevelt's Rough Riders*, 241, 253–54.
30. Millett and Maslowski, *For the Common Defense*, 301–02; O'Toole, *Spanish War*, 362.
31. JW, *Santiago Campaign*, 205–206; Dyer, *"Fightin' Joe" Wheeler*, 367–68; Jones, *Roosevelt's Rough Riders*, 265–66; Herner, *Arizona Rough Riders*, 197–98.
32. JW, *Santiago Campaign*, 207–22; Spanish-American War—Reports (covering JW's service at Camp Wikoff), JW MSS, C-134, F-4, 5, 6, ADA&H; Dyer, *"Fightin' Joe" Wheeler*, 369–75; JW to G. Creighton Webb, May 18, 1899, Webb MSS, N-YHS; Post, *Little War*, 305–35; O'Toole, *Spanish War*, 374–76; Trask, *War With Spain*, 334.
33. Dyer, *"Fightin' Joe" Wheeler*, 375–80; O'Toole, *Spanish War*, 376; Leech, *In the Days of McKinley*, 308–09; Post, *Little War*, 282; Dodson, *Campaigns of Wheeler*, 61–67, 76–77; Jones, *Roosevelt's Rough Riders*, 275–76; "Gen. Joseph Wheeler and Family," 404.
34. Dyer, *"Fightin' Joe" Wheeler*, 385; Kinney, *Joseph Wheeler: Uniting Blue and Gray*, 158–59.
35. Dyer, *"Fightin' Joe" Wheeler*, 380–81; JW to Mrs. J. M. Dickinson, Nov. 2, 1898, Jacob McGavock Dickinson MSS, TSL&A.
36. Dyer, *"Fightin' Joe" Wheeler*, 381; Leech, *In the Days of McKinley*, 348; "Gen. Joseph Wheeler," *CV* 14 (1906): 248; "General Joseph Wheeler: The Visit of the Hero to Richmond, Va. . . .," *SHSP* 26 (1899): 291–92; George Washington Cullum, comp., *Biographical Register of the Officers and Graduates of the U. S. Military Academy at West Point, New York: Supplement, Volume IV, 1890–1900*, ed. Edward S. Holden (Cambridge, Mass.: Riverside Press, 1901), 115.
37. Dyer, *"Fightin' Joe" Wheeler*, 381–82.
38. Dyer, *"Fightin' Joe" Wheeler*, 382–85; JW to William McKinley, Mar. 4, 1899, Leonard Wilson MSS, WRHS.
39. Heitman, *Historical Register and Dictionary*, 1:1,024; Millett and Maslowski, *For the Common Defense*, 306; John Morgan Gates, *Schoolbooks and Krags: The United States Army in the Philippines, 1898–1902* (Westport, Conn.: Greenwood Press, 1973), 76–77.
40. Brian McAllister Linn, *The Philippine War, 1899–1902* (Lawrence: University Press of Kansas, 2000), 136–37, 152; Dyer, *"Fightin' Joe" Wheeler*, 386; Wheeler Family History and "Philippine Islands—Special Orders," JW MSS, C-1, F-1 and C-138, F-1, 2, 3, ADA&H.
41. Dyer, *"Fightin' Joe" Wheeler*, 386–88; Gates, *Schoolbooks and Krags*, 108; Linn, *Philippine War*, 152–53.
42. Linn, *Philippine War*, 153; Millett and Maslowski, *For the Common Defense*, 307–13.
43. Dyer, *"Fightin' Joe" Wheeler*, 389; Philippine Islands—Special Orders, JW MSS, C-138, F-1, 2, ADA&H; Frederick Funston, *Memories of Two Wars: Cuban and Philippine Experiences* (New York: Charles Scribner's Sons, 1911), 323–24, 338, 371–72; *Gen. Joseph Wheeler: Proceedings in Statuary Hall*, 6–7.

44. Heitman, *Historical Register and Dictionary*, 1:1,024; Dyer, *"Fightin' Joe" Wheeler*, 389; Wheeler Family History, JW MSS, C-1, F-1, ADA&H. In 1994 the Alabama Historical Commission acquired from Wheeler's descendants fifty acres of the Pond Spring plantation including the general's home, a log cabin that served as slave quarters when the Sherrod family owned the land, a log barn, a nineteenth-century icehouse, and the Wheeler family cemetery. Immediately after the transaction, state officials made plans to restore the plantation as a tourist attraction. The ongoing project, estimated to cost as much as ten million dollars, has been called "the most challenging restoration" the state has ever undertaken. Wheeler's contributions to his adopted region of northwestern Alabama are commemorated not only in Pond Spring and the Wheeler Dam but also in Wheeler State Park and the Wheeler Wildlife Refuge.

45. Dyer, *"Fightin' Joe" Wheeler*, 389. The bibliography to the present volume includes a complete listing of Wheeler's books and articles.

46. Dyer, *"Fightin' Joe" Wheeler*, 389; *Washington Times*, Aug. 31, 1901; JW to Charles Edgeworth Jones, Apr. 6, 1902, and June 24, 1903, Charles C. Jones MSS, DU; JW to Mrs. W. R. Smith, June 12, 1902, and July 13, 1903, William Russell Smith MSS, SHC; "Additional Tributes to General Wheeler," *CV* 14 (1906): 300; "Fifteenth Annual Reunion [of United Confederate Veterans]," *CV* 18 (1910): 157; *Reception and Dinner Rendered to Major-General Joseph Wheeler, U.S.A., by the Alumni of the Episcopal Academy of Connecticut: Monday Evening, April Fifteenth* (Cheshire, Conn.: Episcopal Academy of Connecticut, 1901); *Joe Wheeler, C.S.A., Songster: April Fifteenth, 1901* (Cheshire, Conn.: Episcopal Academy of Connecticut, 1901); *Gen. Joseph Wheeler: Proceedings in Statuary Hall*, 10.

47. Dyer, *"Fightin' Joe" Wheeler*, 390; "Action of Sons [of Confederate Veterans] on the Death of Gen. Wheeler," *CV* 14 (1906): 103; "Gen. Joseph Wheeler," *CV* 14 (1906): 154; "Tributes to Gen. Wheeler and Mrs. Davis," *CV* 15 (1907): 32; *Gen. Joseph Wheeler: Proceedings in Statuary Hall*, 10–11. In recognition of his military services to the United States during the Spanish-American War and the Philippine Insurrection, Wheeler was laid to rest in Arlington National Cemetery, in Arlington, Va. In March 1925 a life-size likeness, the work of Swiss sculptor Berthold Nebel, was placed in National Statuary Hall in the U.S. Capitol Building. The statue was unveiled by the general's granddaughter, Julia Wheeler Harris, daughter of the former Julia Knox Wheeler and her husband, Senator William J. Harris of Georgia.

BIBLIOGRAPHY

UNPUBLISHED MATERIALS

Allen, William Gibbs. Memoirs. Tennessee State Library and Archives, Nashville.
Allen, William Wirt. Correspondence. Dearborn Collection, Houghton Library, Harvard University, Cambridge, Mass.
Ash, John H. Correspondence and Diaries, 1861–65. Robert W. Woodruff Library, Emory University, Atlanta, Ga.
Avery, Isaac W. Papers. U.S. Army Military History Institute, Carlisle Barracks, Pa.
Bragg, Braxton. Papers. Southern Historical Collection, Wilson Library, University of North Carolina, Chapel Hill.
———. Papers. William R. Perkins Library, Duke University, Durham, N.C.
———. Papers. Western Reserve Historical Society, Cleveland, Ohio.
Brodnax, Samuel H. Memoirs. Filson Historical Society, Louisville, Ky.
Bunting, Robert F. Correspondence. Center for American History, University of Texas, Austin.
Burford, Elisha S. Correspondence. National Archives, Washington, D.C.
Cartmell, Robert H. Diaries. Tennessee State Library and Archives.
Champion, Sidney S. Correspondence. Robert W. Woodruff Library, Emory University.
Corbit, W. B. Diaries, 1862–63, and Memoirs. Robert W. Woodruff Library, Emory University.
DeLoach, Zachariah T. Memoirs. Georgia State Archives, Atlanta.
Dowda, Julius L. Memoirs. Georgia State Archives.
Dyer, W. R. Diaries, 1863–64. Tennessee State Library and Archives.
Ferguson, Samuel W. Correspondence and Diary, 1865. Mississippi Department of Archives and History, Jackson.
Fleming, William A. Memoirs. U.S. Army Military History Institute.
Forrest, Nathan Bedford. Papers. Louisiana State Museum, New Orleans.
———. Papers. Tennessee State Library and Archives.
———. Papers. William R. Perkins Library, Duke University.
French, L. Virginia. Diaries and Memoirs. Tennessee State Library and Archives.
Fussell, Joseph H. Papers. Tennessee State Library and Archives.
Gray, Thomas J. Letter of July 16, 1863. Tennessee State Library and Archives.
Hagan, James. History of the 3rd Alabama Cavalry. Alabama Department of Archives and History, Montgomery.

Hampton, Wade. Correspondence. Edward L. Wells Papers, Charleston Library Society, Charleston, S.C.

———. Correspondence. Gilder Lehrman Collection, New York, N.Y.

———. Correspondence. South Caroliniana Library, University of South Carolina, Columbia.

Hardee, William J. Papers. William R. Perkins Library, Duke University.

Harder, William H. Memoirs. Tennessee State Library and Archives.

Jackson, William H. Papers. Tennessee State Library and Archives.

Johnston, Joseph E. Papers. Earl Gregg Swem Library, College of William and Mary, Williamsburg, Va.

Jordan, John L. "Triune [Tennessee] in the Civil War." Tennessee State Library and Archives.

Long, Nimrod W. E. Correspondence. Robert W. Woodruff Library, Emory University.

Longstreet, James. Correspondence. Gilder Lehrman Collection.

Martin, William T. Correspondence. Dearborn Collection, Houghton Library, Harvard University.

———. Letter of August 28, 1863. Center for American History, University of Texas.

Miller, George K. Memoirs. Mississippi Department of Archives and History.

Mullen, Joseph Jr. Diary, 1865. Eleanor S. Brockenbrough Library, Museum of the Confederacy, Richmond, Va.

Roman, Alfred. Papers. Library of Congress, Washington. D.C.

Simpson, Samuel R. Papers. Tennessee State Library and Archives.

Sloan, William E. Diaries. Tennessee State Library and Archives.

Smith, Baxter. Memoirs. U.S. Army Military History Institute.

Special Order, number unknown, Headquarters Military Division of the West, Nov. 26, 1864, Gilder Lehrman Collection.

Stone, Henry L. Diary, 1865. Eleanor S. Brockenbrough Library, Museum of the Confederacy.

Ward, William S. Correspondence. U.S. Army Military History Institute.

Webb, G. Creighton. Papers. New-York Historical Society, New York, N.Y.

Wharton, John A. Letter of December 12, 1862. Dearborn Collection, Houghton Library, Harvard University.

Wheeler, Joseph. Academic Record of Joseph Wheeler Jr., USMA Class of 1859. U.S. Military Academy Archives, West Point, N.Y.

———. Address of April 25, 1865. Pope-Carter Papers, William R. Perkins Library, Duke University.

———. Cadet Application Papers. U. S. Military Academy Archives.

———. Cadet Delinquency Log. U. S. Military Academy Archives.

———. Correspondence. Bradley T. Johnson Papers, William R. Perkins Library, Duke University.

———. Correspondence. Braxton Bragg Papers, William R. Perkins Library, Duke University.

———. Correspondence. Charles C. Jones Papers, William R. Perkins Library, Duke University.

———. Correspondence. Confederate Officers' Papers, William R. Perkins Library, Duke University.

———. Correspondence. Dearborn Collection, Houghton Library, Harvard University.

———. Correspondence. George St. Leger Grenfell Papers, National Archives.

———. Correspondence. Jefferson Davis Papers, Eleanor S. Brockenbrough Library, Museum of the Confederacy.

———. Correspondence. Joseph E. Johnston Papers, Earl Gregg Swem Library, College of William and Mary.

———. Correspondence. Leonard Wilson Papers, Western Reserve Historical Society.

———. Correspondence. Mrs. J. L. Brent Papers, Richard Taylor Collection, Louisiana State Museum.

———. Correspondence. National Archives.

———. Correspondence. Papers of the Cuban Educational Association of the United States of America, Library of Congress.

———. Correspondence. William Russell Smith Papers, Southern Historical Collection, Wilson Library, University of North Carolina.

———. Correspondence. William R. Shafter Papers, C. H. Green Library, Stanford University, Stanford, Calif.

———. Letter of April 17, 1898. George Houston Papers, William R. Perkins Library, Duke University.

———. Letter of April 30, 1867. Itzer Collection, New-York Historical Society.

———. Letter of December 31, 1864. Civil War Collection, Tennessee State Library and Archives.

———. Letter of December 4, 1905. Chattanooga-Hamilton County Bicentennial Library, Chattanooga, Tenn.

———. Letter of February 1, 1865. William J. Hardee Papers, William R. Perkins Library, Duke University.

———. Letter of February 11, 1865. Eleanor S. Brockenbrough Library, Museum of the Confederacy.

———. Letter of July 28, 1885. Elizabeth Comstock Papers, Murphy Library, University of Wisconsin, La Crosse, Wis.

———. Letter of June 16, 1886. W. S. Hoole Library, University of Alabama, Tuscaloosa.

———. Letter of March 15, 1898. Thomas Nelson Page Papers, William R. Perkins Library, Duke University.

———. Letter of May 7, 1887. Boteler Papers, William R. Perkins Library, Duke University.

———. Letter of May 18, 1899. G. Creighton Webb Papers, New-York Historical Society.

———. Letter of November 2, 1898. Jacob McGavock Dickinson Papers, Tennessee State Library and Archives.

———. Letter of November 29, 1882. Ruth Jackson Bland Papers, Tennessee State Library and Archives.

———. Papers. Alabama Department of Archives and History.

———. Papers. Gilder Lehrman Collection.

———. Papers. William R. Perkins Library, Duke University.

———. Telegrams. P. G. T. Beauregard Papers, William R. Perkins Library, Duke University.

White, James Spratt. Letter of March 8, 1865. White Family Papers, Archives and Special Collections, Winthrop University, Rock Hill, S.C.

Wilson, Leonard. Papers. Western Reserve Historical Society.

NEWSPAPERS

Charleston Mercury
Decatur [Ala.] *Daily*
Nashville Daily Press and Times
Nashville Dispatch
New York Sun
New York Times
Washington Times

ARTICLES AND ESSAYS

"Action of Sons [of Confederate Veterans] on the Death of Gen. Wheeler." *Confederate Veteran* 14 (1906): 103.

"Additional Tributes to General Wheeler." *Confederate Veteran* 14 (1906): 300.

"Alexander H. Stephens' Prison Life." *Confederate Veteran* 1 (1893): 169–71.

Barron, S. B. "Wheeler's Cavalry in the Georgia Campaign." *Confederate Veteran* 14 (1906): 70.

Bearss, Edwin C. "Cavalry Operations in the Battle of Stone's River." *Tennessee Historical Quarterly* 19 (1960): 23–53, 110–44.

Blackford, Charles M. "The Trials and Trial of Jefferson Davis." *Southern Historical Society Papers* 29 (1901): 45–81.

Branum, Peter. "General Joe Wheeler and the Dandrige Galey Murder Trial, 1871– 1873." *Alabama Review* 50 (July 1997): 163–73.

Brooksher, William R., and David K. Snider. "Bold Cavalry Raid: Ride Down the Sequatchie Valley." *Civil War Times Illustrated* 22 (March 1983): 32–39.

———. "Stampede in Kentucky: John Hunt Morgan's Summer Raid." *Civil War Times Illustrated* 17 (June 1978): 4–10, 43–46.

———. "A Visit to Holly Springs." *Civil War Times Illustrated* 14 (June 1975): 4–9, 40–44.

———. "The 'War Child' Rides: Joe Wheeler at Stones River." *Civil War Times Illustrated* 14 (January 1976): 5–10, 44–46.

Brown, A. F. "Van Dorn's Operations in Northern Mississippi—Recollections of a Cavalryman." *Southern Historical Society Papers* 6 (1878): 151–61

Bryan, Charles F., Jr. "'I Mean to Have Them All': Forrest's Murfreesboro Raid." *Civil War Times Illustrated* 12 (January 1974): 27–34.

Buell, Don Carlos. "East Tennessee and the Campaign of Perryville." In *Battles and Leaders of the Civil War* (New York: Century Co., 1887–88), 3:31–51.

Calhoun, C. M. "Credit to Wheeler Claimed for Others." *Confederate Veteran* 20 (1912): 82–83.

Caruthers, W. G. "More About Kilpatrick's Horses." *Confederate Veteran* 13 (1905): 456.

Chalmers, James R. "Forrest and His Campaigns." *Southern Historical Society Papers* 7 (1879): 451–86.

Clay, H. B. "On the Right at Murfreesboro." *Confederate Veteran* 21 (1913): 588–89.

Cooling, Benjamin F. "The Attack on Dover, Tenn." *Civil War Times Illustrated* 2 (August 1963): 11–13.

Curry, William L. "Raid of the Confederate Cavalry Through Central Tennessee." *Journal of the U. S. Cavalry Association* 19 (1908–09): 815–35.

Davis, George B. "The Cavalry Operations in Middle Tennessee in October, 1863." *Journal of the U. S. Cavalry Association* 24 (1913–14): 879–91.

Davis, W. H. "Kilpatrick's Spotted Horses." *Confederate Veteran* 14 (1906): 62.

Deupree, John G. "The Capture of Holly Springs, Mississippi, Dec. 20, 1862." *Publications of the Mississippi Historical Society* 4 (1901): 49–61.

———. "The Noxubee Squadron of the First Mississippi Cavalry, C.S.A., 1861–1865." *Publications of the Mississippi Historical Society, Centenary Series* 2 (1918): 12–143.

Dodson, W. C. "Burning of Broad River Bridge . . ." *Confederate Veteran* 17 (1909): 462- 65.

———. "More About the Defense of Columbia." *Confederate Veteran* 18 (1910): 75–78.

Du Bose, John W. "Wheeler's Raid Into Tennessee." *Confederate Veteran* 24 (1916): 10–12.

Dyer, John P. "The Civil War Career of General Joseph Wheeler." *Georgia Historical Quarterly* 19 (1935): 17–46.

———. "Some Aspects of Cavalry Operations in the Army of Tennessee." *Journal of Southern History* 8 (1942): 210–25.

"Fifteenth Annual Reunion [of United Confederate Veterans]." *Confederate Veteran* 18 (1910): 157.

"Fighting at Columbia, S.C." *Confederate Veteran* 18 (1910): 420–21.

"Fighting Joe Wheeler Traded His Confederate Gray for Army Blue in the Spanish- American War." *America's Civil War* 8 (May 1995): 6.

Flood, F. W. "Captures by Eighth Confederate Cavalry." *Confederate Veteran* 13 (1905): 458–59.

"General Joseph Wheeler: The Visit of the Hero to Richmond, Va., . . ." *Southern Historical Society Papers* 26 (1899): 291–305.

"Gen. Joseph Wheeler." *Confederate Veteran* 14 (1906): 248–49.

"Gen. Joseph Wheeler and Army of Tennessee." *Confederate Veteran* 20 (1912): 540–41.

"Gen. Joseph Wheeler and Family." *Confederate Veteran* 6 (1898): 404.

Gilman, J. H. "With Slemmer in Pensacola Harbor." In *Battles and Leaders of the Civil War* (New York: Century Co., 1887–88), 1:26–32.

Hampton, Wade. "The Battle of Bentonville." In *Battles and Leaders of the Civil War* (New York: Century Co., 1887–88), 4:700–705.

———. "An Effort to Rescue Jefferson Davis." *Southern Historical Society Papers* 37 (1899): 132–36.

Hargis, O. P. "We Came Very Near Capturing General Wilder." *Civil War Times Illustrated* 7 (November 1968): 36–41.

———. "We Kept Fighting and Falling Back." *Civil War Times Illustrated* 7 (December 1968): 37–42.

Harper, G. W. F. "Sherman at Columbia." *Confederate Veteran* 18 (1910): 32–33.

Hartje, Robert. "Van Dorn Conducts a Raid on Holly Springs and Enters Tennessee." *Tennessee Historical Quarterly* 18 (1959): 120–33.

Hill, Daniel H. "Chickamauga—The Great Battle of the West." In *Battles and Leaders of the Civil War* (New York: Century Co., 1887–88), 3:638–62.

Jenkins, A. E. "Kilpatrick's Spotted Horse." *Confederate Veteran* 13 (1905): 315.

Johnston, Joseph E. "Opposing Sherman's Advance to Atlanta." In *Battles and Leaders of the Civil War* (New York: Century Co., 1887–88), 4:260–77.

Johnston, William Preston. "Albert Sidney Johnston at Shiloh." In *Battles and Leaders of the Civil War* (New York: Century Co., 1887–88), 1:540–68.

Jones, Charles C. Jr. "The Siege and Evacuation of Savannah, Georgia, in December, 1864." *Southern Historical Society Papers* 17 (1889): 60–85.

Keenan, Jerry. "Final Cavalry Operations [of the Atlanta Campaign]." *Civil War Times Illustrated* 3 (July 1964): 50.

Kennedy, Edward. "Last Work of Wheeler's Special Confederate Scouts." *Confederate Veteran* 32 (1924): 60–61.

"The Kilpatrick Spotted Horse Affair." *Confederate Veteran* 14 (1906): 309.

Kniffin, Gilbert C. "The Battle of Stone's River." In *Battles and Leaders of the Civil War* (New York: Century Co., 1887–88), 3:613–32.

Lathrop, Barnes F. "A Confederate Artilleryman at Shiloh." *Civil War History* 8 (1962): 373–85.

Longacre, Edward G. "Judson Kilpatrick." *Civil War Times Illustrated* 10 (April 1971): 25–33.

Luvaas, Jay. "Bentonville—Last Chance to Stop Sherman." *Civil War Times Illustrated* 2 (October 1963): 7–9, 38–42.

"Major Gen. Joseph Wheeler, Jr." *Southern Literary Messenger* 38 (1864): 222–32.

McDonald, William N. "Sketch of Lieutenant-General [sic] Joseph Wheeler." *Southern Bivouac* 2 (1884): 241–46.

McMahon, Mrs. C. W. "General Joseph Wheeler." *Confederate Veteran* 33 (1925): 454– 56.

McWhiney, Grady C. "Controversy in Kentucky: Braxton Bragg's Campaign of 1862." *Civil War History* 6 (1960): 5–42.

Minnich, J. W. "The Cavalry at Knoxville." *Confederate Veteran* 32 (1924): 10–13.

Morgan. D. B. "Incidents of the Fighting at Aiken, S. C." *Confederate Veteran* 32 (1924): 300–301.

Mruck, Armin E. "The Role of Railroads in the Atlanta Campaign." *Civil War History* 7 (1961): 264–71.

"Notes from Headquarters U.C.V." *Confederate Veteran* 14 (1906): 154–55.

Nye, Wilbur S. "Cavalry Operations Around Atlanta." *Civil War Times Illustrated* 3 (July 1964): 46–50.

Powles, James M. "Civil War Veterans of Both Sides Fought in the Spanish-American War . . ." *Military History* 21 (April 2004): 70, 72.

"Prison Life of Vice President Stephens." *Confederate Veteran* 14 (1906): 169–73.

Robertson, Felix H. "On Wheeler's Last Raid in Middle Tennessee." *Confederate Veteran* 30 (1922): 334–35.

Rowell, John W. "The Battle of Mossy Creek." *Civil War Times Illustrated* 8 (July 1969): 11–16.

———. "McCook's Raid." *Civil War Times Illustrated* 13 (July 1974): 5–9, 42–48.

Saunders, Ellen Virginia. "War-Time Journal of a 'Little Rebel'." *Confederate Veteran* 28 (1920): 11–12.

Saussy, Clement. "Two Bridges Burned Near Columbia." *Confederate Veteran* 17 (1909): 553–54.

Scott, Paul R. "On the Road to the Sea: Shannon's Scouts." *Civil War Times Illustrated* 21 (January 1983): 26–29.

Secrist, Philip L. "The Role of Cavalry in the Atlanta Campaign, 1864." *Georgia Historical Quarterly* 56 (1972): 510–28.

Sherman, William T. "The Grand Strategy of the Last Year of the War." In *Battles and Leaders of the Civil War* (New York: Century Co., 1887–88), 4:247–59.

Snair, Dale S., ed. "This Looked But Little Like Trying to Catch the Enemy." *Civil War Times Illustrated* 23 (September 1984): 21–24, 28–33.

Soley, J. R. "Early Operations in the Gulf." In *Battles and Leaders of the Civil War* (New York: Century Co., 1887–88), 2:13.

Speed, Thomas. "Cavalry Operations in the West Under Rosecrans and Sherman." In *Battles and Leaders of the Civil War* (New York: Century Co., 1887–88), 4:413–16.

Stewart, Alexander P. "The Army of Tennessee: A Sketch." In John Berrien Lindsley, ed., *The Military Annals of Tennessee, Confederate* . . . (Nashville: J. M. Lindsley & Co., 1886), 55–111.

Thomas, Edward J. "A Raid With Joe Wheeler." *Confederate Veteran* 30 (1932): 169–70.

"Tributes to Gen. Wheeler and Mrs. Davis." *Confederate Veteran* 15 (1907): 32.

Urquhart, David. "Bragg's Advance and Retreat." In *Battles and Leaders of the Civil War* (New York: Century Co., 1887–88), 3:600–609.

Wells, E. L. "Hampton at Fayetteville." *Southern Historical Society Papers* 13 (1885): 144–48.

Wheeler, Joseph. "The Battle of Shiloh: A Graphic Description of That Sanguinary Engagement." *Southern Historical Society Papers* 24 (1896): 119–31.

———. "Bragg's Invasion of Kentucky." In *Battles and Leaders of the Civil War* (New York: Century Co., 1887–88), 3:1–25.

———. "An Effort to Rescue Jefferson Davis." *Century Illustrated Magazine* 56 (1898): 85–91.

Willett, Robert L. "We Rushed With a Yell." *Civil War Times Illustrated* 8 (February 1970): 17–21.

Williams, Robert W. Jr., and Ralph A. Wooster, eds. "With Terry's Texas Rangers: The Letters of Isaac Dunbar Affleck." *Civil War History* 9 (1963): 299–319.

Williamson, J. C., ed. "The Civil War Diary of John Coffee Williamson." *Tennessee Historical Quarterly* 15 (1956): 61–74.

Witcher, J. C. "Shannon's Scouts—Kilpatrick." *Confederate Veteran* 14 (1906): 511–12.

Witherspoon, J. C. "Confederate Cavalry Leaders." *Confederate Veteran* 27 (1919): 414–17.

Womack, J. K. "Gen. Wheeler in the Sixties." *Confederate Veteran* 7 (1899): 72.

Wyeth, John Allan. "The Destruction of Rosecrans' Great Wagon Train." In *The Photographic History of the Civil War* (New York: Review of Reviews Co., 1911), 4:158–64.

———. "Morgan's Christmas Raid, 1862–63." In *The Photographic History of the Civil War* (New York: Review of Reviews Co., 1911), 4:144–56.

BOOKS

Alger, Russell A. *The Spanish-American War.* New York: Harper & Brothers, 1901.

Arnold, James R. *Jeff Davis's Own: Cavalry, Comanches, and the Battle for the Texas Frontier.* New York: John Wiley & Sons, Inc., 2000.

Austin, J. P. *The Blue and the Gray: Sketches of a Portion of the Unwritten History of the Great American Civil War . . .* Atlanta: Franklin Printing and Publishing Co., 1899.

Averell, William W. *Ten Years in the Saddle: The Memoir of William Woods Averell, 1851–1862.* Edited by Edward K. Eckert and Nicholas J. Amato. San Rafael, Calif.: Presidio Press, 1978.

Bailey, Anne J. *The Chessboard of War: Sherman and Hood in the Autumn Campaigns of 1864.* Lincoln: University of Nebraska Press, 2000.

Barrett, John G. *Sherman's March Through the Carolinas.* Chapel Hill: University of North Carolina Press, 1956.

Batchelor, Benjamin F., and George Q. Turner. *Batchelor-Turner Letters, 1861–1864, Written by Two of Terry's Texas Rangers.* Edited by Helen J. H. Rugeley. Austin: Steck Co., 1961.

Bauer, K. Jack. *The Mexican War, 1846–1848.* New York: Macmillan Publishing Co., Inc., 1974.

Baumgartner, Richard A., and Larry M. Strayer. *Kennesaw Mountain, June 1864.* Huntington, W.Va.: Blue Acorn Press, 1998.

Benner, Judith Ann. *Sul Ross, Soldier, Statesman, Educator.* College Station: Texas A&M University Press, 1983.

Blow, Michael. *A Ship to Remember: The* Maine *and the Spanish-American War.* New York: William Morrow & Co., Inc., 1992.

Bonsal, Stephen. *The Fight for Santiago: The Story of the Soldier in the Cuban Campaign From Tampa to the Surrender.* New York: Doubleday & McClure Co., 1899.

Brackett, Albert G. *History of the United States Cavalry, From the Formation of the Federal Government to the 1st of June, 1863.* New York: Harper & Brothers, 1865.

Bradley, Mark L. *Last Stand in the Carolinas: The Battle of Bentonville.* Mason City, Ia.: Savas Publishing Co., 1996.

———. *This Astounding Close: The Road to Bennett Place.* Chapel Hill: University of North Carolina Press, 2000.

Bradley, Michael R. *Tullahoma: The 1863 Campaign for the Control of Middle Tennessee.* Shippensburg, Pa.: White Mane Publishing Co., Inc., 2000.

Brooks, U. R. *Butler and His Cavalry in the War of Secession, 1861–1865.* Columbia, S.C.: State Co., 1909.

Brown, D. Alexander. *The Bold Cavaliers: Morgan's Kentucky Cavalry Raiders*. Philadelphia: J. B. Lippincott Co., 1959.

Carter, Howell. *A Cavalryman's Reminiscences of the Civil War*. New Orleans: American Printing Co., 1900.

Carter, Samuel. *The Last Cavaliers: Confederate and Union Cavalry in the Civil War*. New York: St. Martin's Press, 1979.

Castel, Albert. *Decision in the West: The Atlanta Campaign of 1864*. Lawrence: University Press of Kansas, 1996.

Castleman, John B. *Active Service*. Louisville: Courier-Journal Printing Co., 1917.

Clark, John B. *Populism in Alabama*. Auburn, Ala.: Auburn Printing Co., 1927.

Collier, Calvin L. *The War Child's Children: The Story of the Third Regiment, Arkansas Cavalry, Confederate States Army*. Little Rock: Pioneer Press, 1965.

Congressional Record. Washington, D.C.: Government Printing Office, 1880–98.

Connelly, Thomas L. *Army of the Heartland: The Army of Tennessee, 1861–1862*. Baton Rouge: Louisiana State University Press, 1967.

———. *Autumn of Glory: The Army of Tennessee, 1862–1865*. Baton Rouge: Louisiana State University Press, 1971.

Cooling, Benjamin F. *Fort Donelson's Legacy: War and Society in Kentucky and Tennessee, 1852–1863*. Knoxville: University of Tennessee Press, 1997.

Cotton, John W. *"Yours Till Death": Civil War Letters of John W. Cotton*. Edited by Lucille Griffith. University: University of Alabama Press, 1951.

Cotton, Michael. *The Williamson County Cavalry: A History of Company F, Fourth Tennessee Cavalry Regiment, C. S. A.* Privately issued, 1994.

Cozzens, Peter. *No Better Place to Die: The Battle of Stones River*. Urbana: University of Illinois Press, 1990.

———. *The Shipwreck of Their Hopes: The Battles for Chattanooga*. Urbana: University of Illinois Press, 1994.

———. *This Terrible Sound: The Battle of Chickamauga*. Urbana: University of Illinois Press, 1992.

Crabb, Martha L. *All Afire to Fight: The Untold Tale of the Civil War's Ninth Texas Cavalry*. New York: Post Road Publishing, 2000.

Cullum, George Washington comp., *Biographical Register of the Officers and Graduates of the United States Military Academy at West Point, New York . . .* 2 vols. Boston: Houghton Mifflin Co., 1891.

———. *Biographical Register of the Officers and Graduates of the U. S. Military Academy at West Point, New York: Supplement, Volume IV, 1890–1900*. Edited by Edward S. Holden. Cambridge, Mass.: Riverside Press, 1901.

Daiss, Timothy. *In the Saddle: Exploits of the 5th Georgia Cavalry During the Civil War*. Atglen, Pa.: Schiffer Publishing, Ltd., 1999.

Daniel, Larry J. *Shiloh: The Battle That Changed the Civil War*. New York: Simon & Schuster, 1997.

———. *Soldiering in the Army of Tennessee: A Portrait of Life in a Confederate Army*. Chapel Hill: University of North Carolina Press, 1991.

Davis, Burke. *Sherman's March*. New York: Random House, 1980.

Davis, Richard Harding. *The Cuban and Porto Rican Campaigns*. New York: Charles Scribner's Sons, 1898.

Davis, William C. *The Orphan Brigade: The Kentucky Confederates Who Couldn't Go Home*. Garden City, N.Y.: Doubleday & Co., Inc., 1980.

DeLeon, Thomas C. *Joseph Wheeler, the Man, the Statesman, the Soldier.* Atlanta: Byrd Printing Co., 1899.

Dickman, J. T., ed. *The Santiago Campaign: Reminiscences of the Operations for the Capture of Santiago de Cuba in the Spanish-American War, June and July, 1898.* Richmond, Va.: Williams Printing Co., 1927.

Dierks, Jack Cameron. *A Leap to Arms: The Cuban Campaign of 1898.* Philadelphia: J. B. Lippincott Co., 1970.

Dodson, William Carey, ed. *Campaigns of Wheeler and His Cavalry, 1862–1865.* Atlanta: Hudgins Publishing Co., 1899.

Du Bose, John Witherspoon. *Alabama's Tragic Decade: The Years of Alabama, 1865–1874.* Edited by James K. Greer. Birmingham, Ala.: Webb Book Co., 1940.

———. *General Joseph Wheeler and the Army of Tennessee.* New York: Neale Publishing Co., 1912.

Duke, Basil W. *History of Morgan's Cavalry.* Cincinnati: Miami Printing & Publishing Co., 1867.

Dyer, John P. *"Fightin' Joe" Wheeler.* Baton Rouge: Louisiana State University Press, 1941.

———. *The Gallant Hood.* Indianapolis: Bobbs-Merrill Co., 1950.

Dyer, John W. *Reminiscences; or, Four Years in the Confederate Army . . .* Evansville, Ind.: Keller Printing & Publishing Co.,1898.

Evans, Clement A., ed. *Confederate Military History: A Library of Confederate States History . . .* 12 vols. Atlanta: Confederate Publishing Co., 1899.

Faust, Patricia L., ed. *Historical Times Illustrated Encyclopedia of the Civil War.* New York: Harper & Row, 1986.

Fisher, John H. *They Rode With Forrest and Wheeler: A Chronicle of Five Tennessee Brothers' Service in the Confederate Western Cavalry.* Jefferson, N.C.: McFarland & Co., Inc., 1995.

Fleming, Walter L. *Civil War and Reconstruction in Alabama.* New York: Columbia University Press, 1905.

Fletcher, William A. *Rebel Private, Front and Rear: Memoirs of a Confederate Soldier.* New York: E. P. Dutton, 1995.

Frazer, Robert W. *Forts of the West: Military Forts . . . West of the Mississippi River to 1898.* Norman: University of Oklahoma Press, 1965.

Funston, Frederick. *Memories of Two Wars: Cuban and Philippine Experiences.* New York: Charles Scribner's Sons, 1911.

Gates, John Morgan. *Schoolbooks and Krags: The United States Army in the Philippines, 1898–1902.* Westport, Conn.: Greenwood Press, 1973.

General Orders, Confederate States of America: Army of Tennessee, Wheeler's Cavalry Corps. n.p., 1863.

Gen. Joseph Wheeler: Proceedings in Statuary Hall of the United States Capitol Upon the Unveiling and Presentation of the Statue of Gen. Joseph Wheeler by the State of Alabama. Washington, D.C.: Government Printing Office, 1926.

Glatthaar, Joseph T. *The March to the Sea and Beyond: Sherman's Troops in the Savannah and Carolinas Campaigns.* New York: New York University Press, 1985.

Govan, Gilbert E., and James W. Livingood. *A Different Valor: The Story of General Joseph E. Johnston, C. S. A.* Indianapolis: Bobbs-Merrill Co., 1956.

Grant, Ulysses S. *Personal Memoirs.* Edited by E. B. Long. New York: Da Capo Press, 2001.

Griscom, George L. *Fighting With Ross' Texas Cavalry Brigade, C. S. A.: The Diary of George L. Griscom, Adjutant, 9th Texas Cavalry Regiment.* Edited by Homer L. Kerr. Hillsboro, Tex.: Hill Junior College Press, 1976.

Guild, George B. *A Brief Narrative of the Fourth Tennessee Cavalry Regiment, Wheeler's Corps,*

Army of Tennessee. Nashville, Tenn.: privately issued, 1913.

Hafendorfer, Kenneth A. *They Died by Twos and Tens: The Confederate Cavalry in the Kentucky Campaign.* Louisville: KH Press, 1995.

Hall, Tom. *The Fun and Fighting of the Rough Riders.* New York: Frederick A. Stokes Co., 1899.

Hallock, Judith Lee. *Braxton Bragg and Confederate Defeat: Volume II.* Tuscaloosa: University of Alabama Press, 1991.

Harris, William C. *Leroy Pope Walker, Confederate Secretary of War.* Tuscaloosa, Ala.: Confederate Publishing Co., Inc., 1962.

Hartje, Robert G. *Van Dorn: The Life and Times of a Confederate General.* Nashville, Tenn.: Vanderbilt University Press, 1967.

Haughton, Andrew. *Training, Tactics and Leadership in the Confederate Army of Tennessee: Seeds of Failure.* Portland, Ore.: Frank Cass, 2000.

Heitman, Francis B., comp. *Historical Register and Dictionary of the United States Army, From Its Organization, September 29, 1789, to March 2, 1903.* 2 vols. Washington, D.C.: Government Printing Office, 1903.

Henry, Robert Selph. *"First With the Most" Forrest.* Indianapolis: Bobbs-Merrill Co., 1944.

Herner, Charles. *The Arizona Rough Riders.* Tucson: University of Arizona Press, 1970.

Hess, Earl J. *Banners in the Breeze: The Kentucky Campaign, Corinth, and Stones River.* Lincoln: University of Nebraska Press, 2000.

Hewett, Janet, et al., eds. *Supplement to the Official Records of the Union and Confederate Armies.* 3 pts., 99 vols. Wilmington, N.C.: Broadfoot Publishing Co., 1994–2001.

Holland, Cecil F. *Morgan and His Raiders.* New York: Macmillan Co., 1943.

Hollandsworth, James G., Jr. *An Absolute Massacre: The New Orleans Race Riot of July 30, 1866.* Baton Rouge: Louisiana State University Press, 2001.

Hood, John Bell. *Advance and Retreat: Personal Experiences in the United States and Confederate States Armies.* New Orleans: Hood Orphan Memorial Fund, 1880.

Hopkins, Donald A. *The Little Jeff: The Jeff Davis Legion, Cavalry, Army of Northern Virginia.* Shippensburg, Pa.: White Mane Books, 1999.

Horn, Stanley F. *The Army of Tennessee.* Norman: University of Oklahoma Press, 1953.

Horwitz, Lester V. *The Longest Raid of the Civil War: Little-Known & Untold Stories of Morgan's Raid Into Kentucky, Indiana and Ohio.* Cincinnati: Farmcourt Publications, 1999.

Hughes, Nathaniel Cheairs Jr. *Bentonville: The Final Battle of Sherman and Johnston.* Chapel Hill: University of North Carolina Press, 1996.

Hughes, Nathaniel Cheairs, Jr., and Roy P. Stonesifer Jr. *The Life and Wars of Gideon J. Pillow.* Chapel Hill: University of North Carolina Press, 1993.

Hurst, Jack. *Nathan Bedford Forrest: A Biography.* New York: Alfred A. Knopf, 1993.

Joe Wheeler, C.S.A., Songster: April Fifteenth, 1901. Cheshire, Conn.: Episcopal Academy of Connecticut, 1901.

Johnston, Joseph E. *Narrative of Military Operations During the Civil War.* New York: D. Appleton & Co., 1874.

Johnston, William Preston. *The Life of Gen. Albert Sidney Johnston . . .* New York: D. Appleton & Co., 1878.

Jones, Virgil Carrington. *Roosevelt's Rough Riders.* Garden City, N.Y.: Doubleday & Co., Inc., 1971.

Jordan, Thomas, and J. P. Pryor. *The Campaigns of Lieut.-Gen. N. B. Forrest and of Forrest's Cavalry.* New Orleans: Blelock & Co., 1868.

Kane, Sharyn, and Richard Keeton. *Fiery Dawn: The Civil War Battle at Monroe's Crossroads, North Carolina.* Tallahassee, Fla.: Southeast Archeological Center, National Park Service, 1999.

Kennett, Lee. *Marching Through Georgia: The Story of Soldiers and Civilians During Sherman's Campaign.* New York: HarperCollins, 1995.

Kinney, Anders Michael. *Joseph Wheeler: Uniting the Blue and Gray.* Lincoln, Neb.: Writers Club Press, 2002.

Kiper, Richard L. *Major General John Alexander McClernand, Politician in Uniform.* Kent, Ohio: Kent State University Press, 1999.

Kniffin, Gilbert C. *General Capron's Narrative of Stoneman's Raid South of Atlanta.* Washington, D.C.: Military Order of the Loyal Legion, Commandery of the District of Columbia, 1899.

Lawson, Lewis A. *Wheeler's Last Raid.* Greenwood, Fla.: Penkevill Publishing Co., 1986.

Lee, Fitzhugh, and Joseph Wheeler. *Cuba's Struggle Against Spain, With the Causes for American Intervention* . . . New York: American Historical Press, 1899.

Leech, Margaret. *In the Days of McKinley.* New York: Harper & Brothers, 1959.

Liddell, St. John Richardson. *Liddell's Record.* . . . Edited by Nathaniel Cheairs Hughes Jr. Baton Rouge: Louisiana State University Press, 1985.

Linn, Brian McAllister. *The Philippine War, 1899–1902.* Lawrence: University Press of Kansas, 2000.

Longacre, Edward G. *Gentleman and Soldier: A Biography of Wade Hampton III.* Nashville, Tenn.: Rutledge Hill Press, 2003.

———. *Mounted Raids of the Civil War.* South Brunswick, N.J.: A. S. Barnes & Co., Inc., 1975.

Martin, Samuel J. *"Kill-Cavalry," Sherman's Merchant of Terror: The Life of Union General Hugh Judson Kilpatrick.* Madison, N.J.: Fairleigh Dickinson University Press, 1996.

McDonough, James Lee. *Stones River—Bloody Winter in Tennessee.* Knoxville: University of Tennessee Press, 1980.

McDonough, James Lee, and James Pickett Jones. *War So Terrible: Sherman and Atlanta.* New York: W. W. Norton & Co., 1987.

McMurry, Richard M. *Atlanta, 1864: Last Chance for the Confederacy.* Lincoln: University of Nebraska Press, 2000.

———. *Two Great Rebel Armies: An Essay in Confederate Military History.* Chapel Hill: University of North Carolina Press, 1989.

McPherson, James M. *Ordeal by Fire: The Civil War and Reconstruction.* New York: Alfred A. Knopf, 1982.

McWhiney, Grady. *Braxton Bragg and Confederate Defeat—Volume I: Field Command.* New York: Columbia University Press, 1969.

McWhiney, Grady, and Perry D. Jamieson. *Attack and Die: Civil War Military Tactics and the Southern Heritage.* University: University of Alabama Press, 1982.

Miller, Rex. *Wheeler's Favorites: A Regimental History of the 51s Alabama Cavalry Regiment.* Depew, N.Y.: privately issued, 1991.

Millett, Allan R., and Peter Maslowski. *For the Common Defense: A Military History of the United States of America.* New York: Free Press, 1984.

Millis, Walter. *The Martial Spirit: A Study of Our War With Spain.* Boston: Houghton Mifflin Co., 1931.

Mims, Wilbur F. *War History of the Prattville Dragoons . . . 1861–1865.* Thurber, Tex.: Journal Printery, n.d.

Nisbet, James Cooper. *Four Years on the Firing Line.* Jackson, Tenn.: McCowat-Mercer Press, Inc., 1963.

Noe, Kenneth W. *Perryville: This Grand Havoc of Battle.* Lexington: University Press of Kentucky, 2001.

Nugent, William L. *My Dear Nellie: The Civil War Letters of William L. Nugent to Eleanor Smith Nugent.* Edited by William M. Cash and Lucy Somerville Howorth. Jackson: University Press of Mississippi, 1977.

Official Register of the Officers and Cadets of the U. S. Military Academy, West Point, New York. West Point, N. Y.: privately issued, 1855–59.

O'Toole, G. J. A. *The Spanish War: An American Epic—1898.* New York: W. W. Norton & Co., 1984.

Poole, John R. *Cracker Cavaliers: The 2nd Georgia Cavalry Under Wheeler and Forrest.* Macon, Ga.: Mercer University Press, 2000.

Post, Charles Johnson. *The Little War of Private Post: The Spanish-American War Up Close.* Boston: Little, Brown Co., 1960.

Ramage, James A. *Rebel Raider: The Life of General John Hunt Morgan.* Lexington: University Press of Kentucky, 1986.

Reception and Dinner Rendered to Major-General Joseph Wheeler, U. S. A., by the Alumni of the Episcopal Academy of Connecticut: Monday Evening, April Fifteenth. Cheshire, Conn.: Episcopal Academy of Connecticut, 1901.

Rice, Charles. *Hard Times: The Civil War in Huntsville and Northern Alabama, 1861– 1865.* Huntsville, Ala.: Old Huntsville Magazine, 1994.

Rodenbough, Theophilus F., and William L. Haskin, eds. *The Army of the United States: Historical Sketches of Staff and Line . . .* New York: Merrill & Co., 1896.

Roman, Alfred. *The Military Operations of General Beauregard in the War Between the States.* 2 vols. New York: Harper & Brothers, 1884.

Roosevelt, Theodore. *The Rough Riders.* New York: Charles Scribner's Sons, 1899.

Sargent, Herbert H. *The Campaign of Santiago de Cuba.* 3 vols. Chicago: A. C. McClurg & Co., 1907.

Sherman, William T. *Memoirs of General William T. Sherman.* 2 vols. New York: D. Appleton & Co., 1875.

Smith, Sydney K. *Life, Army Record, and Public Services of D. Howard Smith.* Louisville, Ky.: Bradley & Gilbert Co., 1890.

Stokes, William. *Saddle Soldiers: The Civil War Correspondence of General William Stokes of the 4th South Carolina Cavalry.* Edited by Lloyd Halliburton. Orangeburg, S.C.: Sandlapper Publishing Co., Inc., 1993.

Sunderland, Glenn W. *Lightning at Hoover's Gap: The Story of Wilder's Brigade.* New York: Thomas Yoseloff, 1969.

Swiggett, Howard. *The Rebel Raider: A Life of John Hunt Morgan.* Indianapolis: Bobbs-Merrill Co., 1934.

Sword, Wiley. *Shiloh: Bloody April.* New York: William Morrow & Co., Inc., 1974.

Symonds, Craig L. *Joseph E. Johnston: A Civil War Biography.* New York: W. W. Norton & Co., 1992.

Synopsis of the Military Career of Gen. Joseph Wheeler, Commander of the Cavalry Corps, Army of the West. New York: privately issued, 1865.

Thomas, Edison H. *John Hunt Morgan and His Raiders.* Lexington: University Press of Kentucky, 1985.

Trask, David F. *The War With Spain in 1898.* New York: Macmillan Publishing Co., Inc., 1981.

Warner, Ezra J. *Generals in Gray: Lives of the Confederate Commanders.* Baton Rouge: Louisiana State University Press, 1959.

The War of the Rebellion: A Compilation of the Official Records of the Union and Confederate

Armies. 4 series, 70 vols. in 128. Washington, D.C.: Government Printing Office, 1880–1901.

Weinert, Richard P., Jr. *The Confederate Regular Army.* Shippensburg, Pa.: White Mane Publishing Co., Inc., 1991.

Wells, Edward L. *Hampton and His Cavalry in '64.* Richmond, Va.: B. F. Johnson Publishing Co., 1899.

Wert, Jeffry D. *General James Longstreet, the Confederacy's Most Controversial Soldier: A Biography.* New York: Simon & Schuster, 1993.

Wheeler, Joseph. *A Revised System of Cavalry Tactics, for the Use of the Cavalry and Mounted Infantry, C.S.A.* Mobile, Ala.: S. H. Goetzel & Co., 1863.

———. *The Santiago Campaign, 1898.* Boston: Lamson, Wolffe & Co., 1898.

Wheeler, Joseph, and Daniella Jones Wheeler, comps. *American Ancestors of the Children of Joseph and Daniella Wheeler of Whom We Have Records . . .* Wheeler, Ala.: privately issued, ca. 1896.

Whetstone, Adam Henry. *History of the Fifty-third Alabama Volunteer Infantry (Mounted).* Edited by William Stanley Hoole. University, Ala.: Confederate Publishing Co., 1985.

Wills, Brian Steel. *A Battle From the Start: The Life of Nathan Bedford Forrest.* New York: HarperCollins, 1992.

Woodworth, Steven E. *Jefferson Davis and His Generals: The Failure of Confederate Command in the West.* Lawrence: University Press of Kansas, 1990.

———. *No Band of Brothers: Problems in the Rebel High Command.* Columbia: University of Missouri Press, 1999.

———. *Six Armies in Tennessee: The Chickamauga and Chattanooga Campaigns.* Lincoln: University of Nebraska Press, 1998.

Wyeth, John Allan. *Life of General Nathan Bedford Forrest.* New York: Harper & Brothers, 1899.

———. *With Sabre and Scalpel: The Autobiography of a Soldier and Surgeon.* New York: Harper & Brothers, 1914.

Young, James R., and J. Hampton Moore, eds. *Reminiscences and Thrilling Stories of the* [Spanish-American] *War by Returned Heroes . . .* Chicago: Wabash Publishing House, 1898.

INDEX

Adairsville, Ga., 150–52
Aguinaldo, Emilio, 232–33
Alger, Russell A., 217–18, 232
Allatoona Pass, 152–53
Allen, William Wirt, 46–47, 52–53, 57, 59, 61, 73, 140, 147, 150–51, 161, 163, 165, 179, 189, 193, 196–98, 200
Anderson, Robert Houston, 128, 152, 158, 165–67, 172, 179, 199
Andersonville Prison, 164, 168, 206
Antietam, Battle of, 52
Appomattox Court House, Va., 201, 215
Armstrong, Frank C., 42, 96, 101, 109, 129–31, 165–66, 189
Army of Kentucky, 67, 69
Army of Middle Tennessee, 69
Army of Mississippi, 110, 151
Army of Northern Virginia, 39, 67, 102, 135, 176, 184, 187
Army of Tennessee, 67, 69, 74, 86, 93, 102, 107–108, 110, 114, 117, 119, 127, 129, 132–34, 140, 142–44, 148–49, 153, 163, 169, 171, 174–75, 178–79, 186, 194, 199
Army of the Cumberland, 68, 75, 80, 90, 96, 102, 125, 136, 144, 147, 157, 175
Army of the Mississippi, 22–23, 31, 33, 37–38, 40, 42, 45, 49, 51, 55, 62, 65–66
Army of the Ohio, 44, 47, 54, 60, 68, 125, 146–47, 159
Army of the Potomac, 39, 71, 109, 125, 133–34, 146, 154, 175
Army of the Tennessee, 125, 146–48, 161, 180
Ashby, George H., 140, 165–67, 179, 198
Asiatic Squadron, U.S., 221
Athens, Ga., 205
Athens, Tenn., 118, 172
Atlanta, Battle of, 162
Atlanta, Ga., 43, 115, 146, 153–55, 159–62, 164–66, 168–69, 171, 173, 175–76, 178–80, 231

Atlanta & West Point Railroad, 163–66, 175
Atlanta Campaign, 146–75
Augusta, Ga., 7, 16–17, 23, 178, 181–82, 184, 193, 205, 207
Averasboro, Battle of, 199
Averell, William Woods, 13

Baird, Absalom, 183
Ball's Bluff, Battle of, 20
Bate, William B., 104
Beauregard, Pierre G. T., 22–24, 27, 30–31, 33–38, 41, 142, 176, 178, 182, 188–91, 183
Beckham, Robert F., 11
Belmont, Battle of, 20
Benjamin, Judah P., 6, 21–22
Bentonville, Battle of, 199–200
blockhouses, 108, 173
Blue Springs, Ala., 4
Bonsal, Stephen, 220–21, 226
Bragg, Braxton, 38, 135, 137; in Chattanooga Campaign, 115–16, 119–20, 125, 129, 132–35; at Chickamauga, 111–12, 114–15, 117; as Davis's military advisor, 135, 138, 142–43, 156; forms cavalry corps, 95; in Murfreesboro Campaign, 72–75, 79–80, 82–83, 86–87, 89–90; opposes Union raids, 99; at Pensacola, 2, 5–6, 17; in Perryville Campaign, 44–45, 47, 49–54–55, 58–63; reinforces A. S. Johnston, 21–22; reinforces J. E. Johnston, 196; relations with Forrest, 49–50, 62, 68–69, 93, 119; relations with Morgan, 68–69, 100–102; relieved of command, 134–35; sends Wheeler against Knoxville, 129; after Shiloh, 33, 38–42, 44; at Shiloh, 23–26, 29–31; in Tullahoma Campaign, 102–107; visits J. E. Johnston's headquarters, 159–60
Breckinridge, John C., 1, 23–26, 33–34, 54, 69, 74, 82, 86–87, 101
brevet rank, 12
Brice's Cross Roads, Battle of, 156
Brooklyn, N.Y., 8–9, 12, 206, 234

Brown, Joseph E., 3, 16, 155, 168, 182–83
Brown, T. B., 53
Brown's Ferry, 125
Buckner, Simon Bolivar, 53, 109–10
Buell, Don Carlos, 21, 30, 38–40, 42, 44–47, 51–60, 62–64, 68
Buena Vista, Battle of, 12
Buford, Abraham, 69, 79–81, 84, 86, 95
Bull Run, First Battle of. *See* Manassas, First Battle of
Bullock, Edward C., 2
"bummers," 193
Bunting, Robert F., 112
Burford, Elisha S., 85, 127
Burnside, Ambrose, 71, 109, 118–19, 129–30, 135, 146
Butler, Benjamin F., 175
Butler, M. Calbraith, 191, 194–98, 217

"Caledonia," 125–26, 208–209
Campaigns of Wheeler and His Cavalry, 73, 103–104, 234
camps: Bradford, 4, 6; Dick Robinson, 61; Jones, 4–5; Wikoff, 229–32
Canada de los Penavetitos, Battle of, 15
Cantey, James, 147–48
Carnifix Ferry, Battle of, 20
Carter, James E., 75
Cass Station, Skirmish at, 152–53
Cassville, Ga., 151–53, 160, 170
Cavalry School of Practice, 3, 12–14
Chalmers, James R., 25, 27–31, 41–42
Chancellorsville, Battle of, 102
Charleston, S.C., 1, 3, 16, 179, 191, 193, 196
Chattanooga, Tenn., 37–40, 42–46, 54, 61, 66–67, 69, 94, 99, 103–104, 107–11, 113–19, 121–22, 125, 127, 129, 132–34, 136–37, 144, 169, 173, 177, 179, 231
Chattanooga Campaign, 125–29, 133–34
Cheat Mountain, Battle of, 20
Cheatham, Frank, 161–62
Chickamauga, Battle of, 111–14, 125, 128–29, 219
Clanton, James H., 36
Clay, Clement C., 205–206
Cleburne, Patrick, 134, 143–44, 147, 154, 161
Clements, Jeremiah, 4
Cleveland, Grover, 216
Cold Harbor, Battle of, 175–76
Collins, Charles R., 11
Columbia, S.C., 192, 194–96, 199, 202, 204
Company Shops, 203
Confederate Congress, 90, 141
Cooke, Philip St. George, 95
Cooper, Samuel, 61, 135, 173
Corinth, Battle of, 34, 62, 68
Corinth, Miss., 21–24, 29, 31, 33–37, 41–42, 44, 54
Courtland, Ala., 125–26, 128–29, 177, 207–12
"Cracker Line," 125
Crawford, Martin J., 46, 54
Crews, Charles C., 127–28, 161, 165, 168, 179–80, 186, 196
Crittenden, George B., 15, 20
Crittenden, Thomas L., 47, 49, 58–59, 73–74, 82, 104,

112
Crook, George, 120, 123–24, 126
Cumberland Gap, 39, 44–45, 54, 62, 65
Cumberland Plateau, 46, 65, 95, 172
Cumberland River, 21, 70, 88–91, 97, 101, 109–10

Daiquiri, Cuba, 224
Dalton, Ga., 133–34, 136–37, 139–40, 142, 144–46, 148–49, 171, 177–78
Davidson, Henry B., 119, 121, 124, 126–27, 134
Davis, J. Lucius, 94
Davis, Jefferson, 1–2, 22, 39, 70; approves Hampton's transfer to South Carolina, 191; capture and imprisonment of, 205–206; flees Richmond, 202–204; and Knoxville Campaign, 129; and Perryville Campaign, 44; postwar occupation of, 210; praises Wheeler, 127; relations with Bragg, 38, 66, 110, 116–17, 135; relations with Forrest, 110; relations with J. E. Johnston, 137, 142–43, 146; relations with Joseph E. Brown, 155; relieves Johnston, 159; reinstates Johnston, 192, 196; as secretary of war, 19; supports Wheeler's confirmation, 141; visits Hood, 178
Davis, Richard Harding, 220–21
departments, military: Alabama and West Florida, 2; Alabama, Mississippi, and East Louisiana, 177; East Tennessee, 38–39, 95, 109, 129, 140; The Lakes, 233; Mississippi, Alabama, West Tennessee, and East Louisiana, 127; Mississippi and East Louisiana, 67, 141; The South, 205; South Carolina, Georgia, and Florida, 179
Derby, Conn., 8
Dewey, George, 221–22
Dibrell, George, 140, 147, 151, 158, 165, 173–74, 179
districts, military: The Gulf, 67; The Mississippi, 38; The Tennessee, 38, 42
Doctor's Fork, 55
Dodson, William Carey, 73, 87
Douglas, Stephen A., 1
Dover, Tenn., 90–93, 95
Du Bose, John Witherspoon, 4, 10, 18, 22, 25–26, 73, 179
Duke, Basil W., 53, 97–98, 100–101
Durham Station, 201–202, 215
Dyer, John P., 7, 13, 15, 43, 58, 63–64, 111, 140, 213, 217

El Caney, Battle of, 226–27
Elk River, 103, 106–107
Elliott, Washington L., 146–48
Enfield rifles, 43, 138, 194
Episcopal Academy of Connecticut, 8–9, 234
Ezra Church, Battle of, 168

Ferguson, Champ, 207
Ferguson, Samuel W., 161, 179, 188–89, 191, 196
Ferrill, Steven C., 97–98
Forrest, Nathan Bedford: assesses Wheeler and his men, 177; at Brice's Cross Roads, 156; at Chickamauga, 112, 115–17; as disciplinarian, 131; on Dover Expedition,

90–92; early service of, 21, 39–40; forms new brigade, 68– 70; feuds with Bragg, 119; gains Jackson's division, 101; leaves Army of Tennessee, 93; in Nashville Campaign, 178, 185; opposes Meridian Expedition, 141; in Perryville Campaign, 45, 47, 49, 53; pursues Streight, 99; raids Grant's lines, 68; raids Sherman's lines, 155–56; at Thompson's Station, 96; in Tullahoma Campaign, 103, 105–108

forts: Barrancas, 5, 17–18, 20; Craig, 14–15; Delaware, 206; Donelson, 21, 90, 100; Fillmore, 14; Fisher, 196; Gaines, 22; Henry, 21, 92; McAllister, 185; McRae, 17, 20; Monroe, 206; Morgan, 22; Pickens, 5, 18, 20; Sanders, 131–32; Sumter, 16, 22, 35; Union, 14

Frankfort, Ky., 45, 54–55, 58

Franklin, Battle of, 185

Fredericksburg, Battle of, 71, 109

French, Lucy, 100

Galey, Dandrige T., 210–11

Galey, John, 210–11

Galveston, Tex., 18

Garrard, Kenner, 157–58, 160, 162–65

Gay, Ebenezer, 56

Gettysburg, Battle of, 108, 206

Gilbert, Charles C., 55–56, 59

Girardey, I. P., 23, 27

Gladden, Adley H., 22, 25

Granger, Gordon, 104–105

Grant, Ulysses S.: besieges Petersburg, 176; calls Sherman to Virginia, 186; in Chattanooga Campaign, 125, 129, 131, 133–35; early service of, 20–21; forces Lee's surrender, 201; in Overland Campaign, 175–76; plans 1864 campaign, 146, 175; and Sherman-Johnston negotiations, 202; after Shiloh, 34–35, 38, 54; at Shiloh, 23–26, 29–31; tomb of, 215; transferred to Virginia, 134, 142; in Vicksburg Campaign, 68, 99, 101–102, 116, 155

Grierson, Benjamin H., 99, 101

Grigsby, J. Warren, 46, 128, 140, 147–48, 152

Hagan, James, 42, 46. 52, 57, 59, 95, 179, 198, 200

Halleck, Henry Wager, 34–35, 38–39, 94, 125

Hampton, Wade, 190–91, 194–200, 202–204

Hannon, Moses W., 140, 151, 170, 179, 196, 198

Hardee, William J.: at Averasboro, 199; at Battle of Atlanta, 162; befriends Morgan, 100; at Bentonville, 199–200; at Cassville, 152; commands at Savannah, 179–80, 184; evacuates Charleston, 196; evacuates Savannah, 185; gains corps under J. E. Johnston, 139; joined by Hampton, 191; in Murfreesboro Campaign, 73, 75, 78, 83–84, 86; at Peachtree Creek, 161; in Perryville Campaign, 45–47, 55, 57–58, 62, 66; relations with Hood, 160; reorganizes Wheeler's cavalry, 186–87; at Resaca, 150; sends Wheeler on raid, 135; at Shiloh, 23–26, 38; supports Cleburne's plan to recruit blacks, 144; temporarily succeeds Bragg, 135, 142; as theoretician, 19–20; transfers to Army of Mississippi, 110; in Tullahoma Campaign, 104–105, 107

Hardin, Martin D., 11

Harding, Abner C., 91–92

Harris, Julia W. (granddaughter of Joseph Wheeler), 266 n. 47

Harris, William J., 266 n. 47

Harrison, Thomas, 127, 120, 140, 149, 166, 179, 197, 200

Hawes, Richard C., 45, 54–55

Hazen, William B., 61

"Hell Hole," the, 153

Hill, Daniel Harvey, 110, 112, 116, 182

Hill, W. E., 4

Hilton Head, S. C., 205

Hindman, Thomas C., 116, 144

Hodge, George B., 124

Holly Springs, Miss., 40–44, 68, 93, 155

Holston River, 109, 130–31, 172

Hood, John Bell, 160; in Battle of Atlanta, 162; at Cassville, 152; at Chickamauga, 110, 112, 129; evacuates Atlanta, 175; at Ezra Church, 168; fails to attack Sherman, 157, 160; gains corps under J. E. Johnston, 139; intrigues against Johnston, 143; in Nashville Campaign, 185; at New Hope Church, 153; in opening of Atlanta Campaign, 148; at Peachtree Creek, 160–61; plans third sortie, 163; refuses to oppose March to the Sea, 178–79; replaces Johnston, 160; at Resaca, 149–50; sends Wheeler against Sherman's communications, 169, 174–75; sends Wheeler after Stoneman-McCook raiders, 163, 165, 168

Hooker, Joseph, 102, 125, 133, 146–47

Hoover's Gap, Battle of, 104

Horn, Stanley F., 115

"Hornet's Nest," 26–27

House Foreign Affairs Committee, 217

House Military Affairs Committee, 214

House Ways and Means Committee, 214

Howard, Oliver Otis, 146, 154, 180, 183, 192, 196

Hull, Abraham Fuller, 9

Hull, Richard, 7

Hull, William, 7, 9

Humes, William Y. C., 127–28, 139, 146, 150–53, 161, 163, 165, 169, 171, 179, 189, 192–93, 196–97, 200

Huntsville, Ala., 2–4, 6, 18, 213, 231–32

Infantry Tactics, 19

Iuka, Battle of, 54

Iverson, Alfred, 140, 151, 161, 165, 168, 171, 179–81, 184, 194, 196

Jackson, Andrew, 97

Jackson, John King, 23, 25–26, 29–31

Jackson, Miss., 42–44

Jackson, "Stonewall," 102

Jackson, William H. ("Red"), 42, 96, 101, 151, 157, 159–61, 163–67, 178

Johnson, Andrew, 122, 202

Johnston, Albert Sidney, 21–27, 30, 34

Johnston, Joseph Eggleston, 137–38; abandons Chattahoochee River, 159; at Adairsville, 151; at Bentonville, 199–200; at Cassville, 152; at Kennesaw

Mountain, 158–59; learns of Lee's surrender, 201; loses confidence of army, 157, 159; named theater commander, 67; at New Hope Church, 153–54; in opening of Atlanta Campaign, 145–48; plans for 1864 Campaign, 142–43; relieved of command, 159–60; refuses to raid Sherman's communications, 155; regains Army of Tennessee, 192, 196; reinforces Vicksburg, 101–102; reorganizes Van Dorn's cavalry, 93; at Resaca, 149–50; succeeds Bragg, 137–38; supports Wheeler's conformation, 141; surrenders to Sherman, 201–203, 206; upgrades Wheeler's cavalry, 138–39

Jones, Egbert J., 4

Jones, Richard (father-in-law of Joseph Wheeler), 125, 129, 208–209

Jones, Thomas (brother-in-law of Joseph Wheeler), 209–11

Jonesboro, Battle of, 175

Jonesboro, Ga., 165, 175, 180

Kelly, John H., 127–28, 134–36, 139–40, 144, 146–47, 149, 151–53, 161, 165, 169, 171, 174

Kennesaw Mountain, Battle of, 158–59

Kent, J. Ford, 226–27

Kettle Hill, 226–27

Kilpatrick, H. Judson, 175, 179–81, 183, 192–93, 196–98, 201

"Kilpatrick's Shirttail Skedaddle," 198

Knoxville, Tenn., 44, 54, 109–10, 119, 129–32, 134–36, 142–43, 146, 172

Knoxville Campaign, 129–32

Krag-Jorgensen firearms, 225

La Grange, Oscar H., 147–48

La Vergne, Tenn., 71, 73, 77, 80–82

Las Guasimas, Battle of, 224, 226–27, 233

Lawton, Henry W., 222, 224, 226–27

Lee, Fitzhugh, 234

Lee, Robert E., 20, 39, 52, 67, 71, 102, 108, 110, 116, 132, 134–35, 142, 146, 175–76, 184, 187, 190–91, 201, 206

Lee, Stephen Dill, 127, 141, 168

Lewis, Joseph H., 179–80, 196

Lexington, Ky., 45, 51–52, 54–55

Lexington, Siege of, 20

Liddell, St. John, 57

"Lightning Brigade," 104, 123, 158

Linaries, Arsenio, 222, 224, 226

Lincoln, Abraham, 1, 15, 53, 68, 94, 108, 176, 196, 202

Longstreet, James, 110, 112–13, 115–16, 129–35, 172

Lookout Mountain, 109, 111, 117–18, 129, 133, 135, 139–40, 142

Lookout Valley, 116, 125

Loring, William Wing, 15, 158

Louisville, Ky., 45, 49, 51–52, 54–55, 88–89, 96, 100–102

Louisville & Nashville Railroad, 47, 51, 68, 70, 96–97, 101

Lovejoy's Station, 165–66

Lowe, William M., 212–13

Lubbock, Francis R., 205

Lundy's Lane, Battle of, 9

Luzon, Philippine Islands, 232–33

Mackall, W. W., 104

Magrath, Andrew G., 191, 193

Mahan, Dennis Hart, 35

Maine (battleship), 217

Manassas, First Battle of, 20, 22, 35, 67

Maney, George, 72–73

Manila Bay, Battle of, 221

March to the Sea, 179–84, 257 n. 44

Martin, William Thompson, 95, 97, 103, 105, 108–109, 113, 121, 124, 126–27, 129–32, 139, 141, 145, 147, 150–51, 157–58, 161, 169, 171, 173, 189

Maryville, Tenn., 130

Mauser rifles, 225

McArthur, Arthur, 233

McClellan, George B., 20, 39

McCook, Alexander M., 46–47, 73–75, 77–78, 104

McCook, Edward M., 60, 113, 147, 155, 164–67, 169, 173

McKinley, William, 216–18, 230–33

McLaws, Lafayette, 110, 129

McPherson, James B., 146–49, 152, 158, 160–63, 189

Meade, George Gordon, 125, 142, 146, 175, 184, 186, 201

Memphis & Charleston Railroad, 209

Meridian Expedition, 141, 144

Mexican War, 12, 22, 152, 213, 225

Miles, Nelson A., 219, 228, 231

Military Academy, U.S., 3, 5, 9–12, 15, 19, 23, 35, 41, 49–50, 61, 175, 191, 201, 214, 221

Military Division of the Mississippi, 125, 134, 140

Mill Creek, 88, 199–200

Mill Creek Gap, 145, 147

Mill Springs, Battle of, 20–21

Milledgeville, Ga., 16, 168, 180–81

Minty, Robert H. G., 79, 158

Missionary Ridge, 118, 129, 133, 135

Mississippi River, 38, 67, 102, 108, 213

Mitchell, Robert B., 57, 120, 124

Mobile, Ala., 5, 18, 20–22, 43, 94, 231

Mobile Bay, 18, 22

Monroe's Cross Roads, 197–98

Montauk Point, N.Y., 229–31

Monterey, Skirmish at, 35–36

Montgomery, Ala., 1–2, 17

Moore, John C., 23, 32

Morgan, George W., 39, 54

Morgan, J. Pierpont, 8

Morgan, John Hunt, 39, 45, 53, 68, 87, 95, 100–101

Morgan, John Tyler, 70, 122, 127–28, 140, 151

Morgan, Mattie Ready, 68, 100

Mossy Creek, Battle of, 135–36

Mower, Joseph A., 199–200

"Mule Brigade," 99

Munfordville, Ky., 49, 51–54, 67

Murfreesboro, Battle of, 78–80, 83

Murfreesboro, Tenn., 39–40, 46, 66, 68–70, 73–75, 77,

79, 84–88, 96, 99, 102, 104–5, 123, 173
Murfreesboro Campaign, 69–87
Muscle Shoals, 124, 212
Muscle Shoals Canal, 213

Nashville, Battle of, 185
Nashville, Tenn., 40, 45, 50, 66, 69–72, 75, 77, 79–81,
    83–84, 86–88, 95–100, 142, 169, 173–74, 178–79,
    185, 207, 231
Nashville & Chattanooga Railroad, 88, 96–97, 123
Nebel, Berthold, 266 n. 47
Negley, James S., 111–13
Nelson, William, 30–31
New Hope Church, 153–54, 157, 160
New Hope Church, Battle of, 153–54
New Market, Battle of, 175
New Orleans, La., 21–22, 208
Newport, R.I., 234
Nisbet, James Cooper, 150–51
Noonday Creek, Skirmish at, 158, 254 n. 27
North Atlantic Blockading Squadron, 222

Otis, Elwell S., 232–33

Palmer, John M., 73, 146
Panic of 1837, 8
Patterson, Michael L., 122–23
Pea Patch Island, 206
Peachtree Creek, Battle of, 160–61
Pegram, John, 67, 69, 72–74, 84–86, 95, 109
Pemberton, John C., 67–68, 99, 108
Peninsula Campaign, 39
Pensacola, Fla., 2–3, 5, 17–18, 20–22, 62, 179, 184
Perryville, Battle of, 58–60, 82, 171
Perryville Campaign, 40, 45–47, 49–64, 70, 73, 118, 234
Pershing, John J., 227
Petersburg, Siege of, 176
Petersburg, Va., 175–76, 184, 186, 201
Philadelphia, Pa., 206, 231
Philippine Insurrection, 232–33
Pickett's Charge, 108
Pickett's Mill, Battle of, 154, 156
Pinson, R. A., 42–43
Platt, Augusta Hull (aunt of Joseph Wheeler), 8
Polk, Leonidas, 23; at Adairsville, 151; criticizes Bragg,
    116; at Cassville, 152; at Chickamauga, 111–12, 116;
    death of, 157; in Meridian Campaign, 141, 144; in
    Murfreesboro Campaign, 73–75, 83–84; in Perryville
    Campaign, 45–46, 49, 55, 58–59, 62; recommends J.
    E. Johnston succeed Bragg, 137; after Shiloh, 38; at
    Shiloh, 24–26; transfers to Army of Mississippi, 116,
    142; in Tullahoma Campaign, 104–105, 107
"Pond Spring," 125, 209, 219, 234, 266 n. 44
Port Hudson, La., 102, 108
Porter, Fitz John, 214
Potomac River, 20, 102
Powhatan (warship), 18
Prentiss, Benjamin F., 25–26, 28
Price, Sterling, 35, 38, 42, 46, 54, 62

"Quaker guns," 37

Raleigh, N.C., 196, 199–201
Red River Campaign, 146, 175
Resaca, Battle of, 149–50
Resaca, Ga., 134, 145, 147–50
Revised System of Cavalry Tactics, 94
Richmond, Va., 1–3, 37, 39, 64, 66, 102, 110, 128, 134–
    35, 138–39, 141–44, 146, 155–56, 159, 175, 178,
    186–87, 201–202, 231
Rifle and Light Infantry Tactics, 19
"Rock of Chickamauga," 125
Rocky Face Ridge, 134, 145–48
Roddey, Philip D., 108, 166–67
Roman, Alfred, 188–90
Rome, Ga., 99, 108, 139, 145, 147
Roosevelt, Theodore, 215, 221, 226–27, 229
Rosecrans, William S.: advances into Georgia, 108–11;
    besieged at Chattanooga, 115–16, 118, 120–22, 124–
    27; at Chickamauga, 113; commands Army of the
    Cumberland, 68; in Murfreesboro Campaign, 69–75,
    77–78, 80, 82–84, 86–87; raids Bragg's communica-
    tions, 99; relieved of command, 125; in Tullahoma
    Campaign, 102–104, 106–107; as victim of Wheeler's
    attacks, 88–89, 91, 94–95, 98
Ross, Lawrence S., 166–67
Rosser, Thomas, 217
Rough Riders. *See* units, cavalry, 1st U.S. Volunteers
Rousseau, Lovell, 164, 173
Rubin, Antero, 225

Sampson, William T., 222, 227–28
San Juan Heights, 226–28
San Juan Hill, Battle of, 226–27
Santiago, Cuba, 222, 224, 226–29, 231
Savannah, Ga., 179, 183–85, 192–93
Savannah River, 7, 184, 192, 205
Schofield, John M., 125, 146–47, 152, 159, 200–201
Scott, John, 45, 67
Scott, Winfield, 19
Seddon, James, 116, 137, 142, 144
Selfridge, Robert O., 40–41
Sequatchie Valley, 46–47, 118, 121, 125
Sequatchie Valley Raid, 119–26, 128, 135, 153, 166, 173
Seven Pines, Battle of, 67
Sewanee Mountain, 107
Shafter, William R., 219, 222, 224, 226–32
Shannon's Scouts, 194, 197–98
Shelbyville, Tenn., 83–84, 87, 94, 98, 102–106
Sheridan, Philip H., 40–41, 58, 78, 136, 154, 176, 215
Sherman, William T.: at Battle of Atlanta, 162; at
    Bentonville, 199–200; besieges Savannah, 184–86; burns
    Columbia, S.C., 194–96; in Carolinas Campaign, 187,
    190–201; at Cassville, 152; crosses Chattahoochee River,
    159; death of, 215; early service of, 23; fears cavalry
    raids, 155–56; fears cavalry weakness, 154; forces
    Johnston's surrender, 201–203; at Kennesaw Mountain,
    158–59; learns of Johnston's relief, 160; on March to
    the Sea, 179; in Meridian Expedition, 141; at New Hope

Church, 153; occupies Atlanta, 175; in opening of Atlanta Campaign, 144–48; at Peachtree Creek, 161; at Pickett's Mill, 154; plans Atlanta Campaign, 140; pursues Hood, 178–79; reinforces Chattanooga, 125; relieves Knoxville, 131–32; at Resaca, 149; shells Atlanta, 169; after Shiloh, 34; at Shiloh, 25; succeeds Grant, 134

Sherrod, Benjamin, 125

Shiloh, Battle of, 25–32, 119, 234

Shorter, Eli S., 23, 29

Shoup, Francis A., 163–64, 177

Slemmer, Adam J., 17–18, 20

Slemons, W. F., 42–43

Slocum, Henry W., 183, 192–93, 196, 199

Smith, Baxter, 63

Smith, Edmund Kirby, 38–40, 44–45, 54–55, 58, 60, 62–67, 69, 202

Smith, Lucy Wheeler (sister of Joseph Wheeler), 8, 234

Smith, Sterling S., 208

Southern Historical Society Papers, 26, 31, 234

Southern Railroad, 214

Spotsylvania, Battle of, 175

Stanley, David S., 72–73, 79, 81, 84–85, 99–100, 104–106

Stanton, Edwin M., 202–203, 206

Starkweather, John C., 76–77

Steedman, James B., 56, 171

Steen, Enoch, 12

Stewart, Alexander P., 112, 160–62, 194

Stoneman, George, 146, 148, 150, 153, 164–65, 167–68

Stoneman-McCook Raid, 163–68

Stones River, 72–74, 76, 78, 82, 84, 86, 97, 123

Stones River, Battle of. *See* Murfreesboro, Battle of

Stoughton, Edwin H., 11

Streight, Abel D., 99, 108

Stuart, David, 25–27

Stuart, J. E. B., 94–95

Sumner, Samuel S., 221, 226

Sunshine Church, Skirmish at, 168

Tampa Bay Hotel, 219–20

Taylor, Richard, 177–78

Tennessee River, 21, 24–26, 29–30, 40, 46, 66, 110, 115, 117–20, 125, 127–30, 142, 169, 172, 174, 178, 185, 212–13

Terry, Alfred H., 196, 200–201

Terry's Texas Rangers. *See* units, cavalry, 8th Texas

Thomas, George H., 20–21, 58–60, 74, 76–77, 79, 103–4, 110–13, 125–26, 133–34, 144–47, 152, 158, 167, 179, 185, 207

Thompson's Station, Skirmish at, 96

Tishomic Creek, Skirmish at, 36–37

Toral, Jose, 227–28

Tracy, E. D., 40–41

Trans-Mississippi Department, 20, 128, 140, 202

Treatise on Advanced-Guard, 35

Trooper's Manual, 94

Tullahoma Campaign, 102–107

Tunnel Hill, 134, 145–47, 171

Tupelo, Miss., 35–38, 40–41, 155

units, artillery: 1st U.S., 17; 4th U.S., 219; Girardey's Battery, 23, 26–27; Hanley's Battery, 2, 56–57; Pice's Battery, 97; Robertson's Battery, 35–37; White's Battery, 120, 124; Wiggins's Battery, 74, 77, 85, 120, 124

units, cavalry: 1st Alabama, 46–47, 52–53, 57, 59, 61, 95; 1st Confederate, 81, 95; 1st Georgia, 67, 192; 1st Kentucky, 46, 53, 57, 61, 103; 1st Kentucky (Union), 59, 61; 1st Louisiana, 67; 1st Mississippi, 42–43; 1st Tennessee, 75; 1st U.S., 224; 1st U.S. Volunteers, 221–22, 224, 226–27; 2nd Arkansas, 42–43; 2nd Georgia, 61, 95; 2nd Kentucky, 68; 2nd Michigan, 40; 2nd U.S., 84; 3rd Alabama, 42–43, 46, 52, 57, 59, 61, 95; 3rd Confederate, 95; 3rd Georgia, 46–47, 53–54, 61, 95; 3rd Kentucky, 69, 95; 3rd U.S., 224; 4th Alabama, 68, 95; 4th Georgia, 95; 4th Kentucky, 61; 4th Tennessee, 68, 81, 95; 4th U.S., 84; 5th Georgia, 152, 161; 5th Kentucky, 69; 5th Tennessee, 173; 6th Confederate, 52, 61; 6th Kentucky, 69; 7th Alabama, 95; 7th Kentucky, 68; 7th Pennsylvania, 59; 8th Confederate, 42, 46, 61, 75, 88–90, 95, 136, 139, 150, 182; 8th Kentucky, 68; 8th Tennessee, 68; 8th Texas, 49–50, 61, 71, 74, 95, 97, 107, 112, 147, 154, 180; 9th Kentucky, 88, 165; 9th Kentucky (Union), 56; 9th Tennessee, 47, 68; 9th U.S., 221, 227; 10th Confederate, 169, 192; 10th U.S., 221, 224, 227; 10th Virginia, 94; 11th Kentucky, 68; 11th Texas, 95; 14th Alabama (battalion), 81

units, dragoons: 1st U.S., 12, 206

units, infantry: 1st Alabama (battalion), 22; 2nd Texas, 23, 26, 32; 7th Alabama, 6; 9th U.S., 233; 12th U.S., 233; 14th Alabama, 2; 17th Alabama, 2, 23; 18th Alabama, 2, 22–23, 29; 19th Alabama, 2–6, 18–19, 22, 26–31, 35, 40–41; 21st Wisconsin, 77; 23rd Alabama, 22; 25th Alabama, 22, 35; 26th Alabama, 35; 55th Illinois, 26–27; 66th Georgia, 150; 79th Pennsylvania, 77

units, mounted infantry: 4th Tennessee (Union), 207; 51st Alabama, 70–71, 95, 108, 113

units, mounted rifles, U.S., 13–15

University of the South, 107

Van Dorn, Earl, 35, 38, 42, 46, 54, 62, 68, 93, 95–96, 101, 155

Vicksburg, Miss., 38, 67–68, 99, 101–102, 108, 116, 133, 141

Villepigue, John B., 42–43

Vinton, Francis, 9

Wade, W. B., 42–43, 46, 61, 88–89, 128, 136

Walden's Ridge, 46, 118, 121, 125

Wales, William E., 85, 203

Walker, Leroy P., 1–6, 18, 22

Walker, William H. T., 110, 144

Washington, D.C., 14, 20, 102, 125, 201–204, 206, 212–13, 218, 222, 228–31

Washington, Ga., 203

West Point. *See* Military Academy, U.S.

Western & Atlantic Railroad, 66, 99, 108, 133–34, 147, 157, 170–71, 178–79

Wharton, John Austin, 50, 53; at Chickamauga, 113; commands division, 95; on Dover Expedition, 90–93; intrigues against Wheeler, 128, 141; in Murfreesboro Campaign, 72–75, 78–82, 84, 86; replaces Morgan, 100; after Perryville, 66–67, 69; in Perryville Campaign, 53–54, 58, 61, 63; on railroads raid, 97–98; on Sequatchie Valley Raid, 121–22, 124, 126–27; in Tullahoma Campaign, 103, 105; wangles transfer to Louisiana, 140

Wheeler, Ala., 209

Wheeler, Annie Early (daughter of Joseph Wheeler), 208–209, 218, 227, 230, 232–34

Wheeler, Carrie Payton (daughter of Joseph Wheeler), 208

Wheeler, Daniella J. S. (wife of Joseph Wheeler), 125–26, 129, 177, 207–209, 216, 234

Wheeler, Ella (daughter of Joseph Wheeler), 208

Wheeler, John, 9

Wheeler, Joseph (father of Joseph Wheeler), 7–9, 193, 202, 205, 207

Wheeler, Joseph: accepts Confederate commission, 17; in advance to Shiloh, 24; assaulted in Nashville, 207; attacks Cass Station, Ga., 152–53; attacks Charleston, Tenn., 135–36; attacks Decatur, Ga., 162; attacks Kingston, Tenn., 131; at Bald Hill, 161; at Bentonville, 199–200; bids farewell to troops, 203; on Bolivar Expedition, 41–44; calls for war with Spain, 217; capture and imprisonment of, 204–206; at Cavalry School, 12–14; champions Cuban independence, 216–17; character and personality of, 7–9, 11, 32, 44, 61, 63, 71, 100, 126, 128, 131, 138, 140, 144, 150–51, 155–56, 160, 169, 173, 190–91, 215–16; at Chickamauga, 111–14; claims promotion to lieutenant general, 191; commands Bragg's cavalry, 61; commands Camp Wikoff, 230–31; commands cavalry in Cuba, 220–22, 224; commands infantry in Philippines, 232–33; compiles tactics manual, 94–95, 138; concludes military career, 233–34; condemns slave recruiting, 143–44; covers evacuation of Columbia, S. C., 194–96; covers evacuation of Chattanooga, 110–11; covers evacuation of Savannah, 186; covers retreat to Dalton, 134; covers retreat to Etowah River, 152; covers retreat to Raleigh and Chapel Hill, 201; covers retreat to Shelbyville, 83–85; criticized by military inspectors, 109, 188–90; criticized by politicians, 141; on Dover Expedition, 90–94; at Ebenezer Creek, 183–84; escapes trap at Shelbyville, 105–106; fails to discipline command, 131, 156, 182–84, 187–88, 258 n. 57; family of, 7–9; faults plans for 1864 campaign, 143; final years and death of, 234–35, 266 n. 47; forms escort for Jefferson Davis, 203; involved in murder case, 210–11; at Kennesaw Mountain, 158; at Kettle Hill, 227; on Knoxville Expedition, 129; at Las Guasimas, 224–25; lax bookkeeping of, 140; manages store in New Orleans, 208; marries and raises family, 208; meets future wife, 125–26; at Monroe's Cross Roads, 197–98; in Mounted Rifles, 14–16; at moves to Alabama, 209, 266 n. 44; Murfreesboro, 78–80; in Murfreesboro Campaign, 69–87; nicknames of, 15,

127; occupies Santiago, Cuba, 228–29; in opening of Atlanta Campaign, 144–49; opposes March to the Sea, 178–84, 257 n. 44; opposes Rosecrans's advance, 72–75; at Peachtree Creek, 161; at Perryville, 58–60; in Perryville Campaign, 46–47, 49–58; physical appearance of, 2, 7, 100; at Pickett's Mill, 154; political career of, 211–15; promotes Tennessee River improvements, 212–13; pursues McCook-Stoneman raiders, 163–68; raids Rosecrans's supply trains, 76–78, 80–82, 96–98; raids Sherman's communications, 169–78; raids Union shipping, 87–90; receives flag-of-truce party, 40–41; reconnoiters toward Chattanooga, 117–18; reconnoiters toward Nashville, 70–72; refits and enlarges command, 138–39; refutes criticism of "Wheeler's robbers," 182–83; relations with Bragg, 2–3, 5–6, 49–50, 62, 87, 109, 117, 138; relations with Forrest, 49, 91–94, 189; relations with Hampton, 191; relations with Hood, 160; relations with J. E. Johnston, 137–38, 142; relations with J. H. Morgan, 100; relations with Wharton, 53, 61, 121, 128, 189; at Resaca, 149–50; resigns from U.S. Army, 16–17; on retreat from Perryville, 60–64; on retreat to Chattanooga, 106–107; returns to U.S. Army (1898), 217–20; seeks new subordinates, 128; on Sequatchie Valley Raid, 119–27; service at Huntsville, Ala., 1–2, 231; service at Mobile, 18–19; service at Pensacola, 5–6; at Shiloh, 26–32; in skirmish at Aiken, Ga., 193; in skirmish at Noonday Creek, 158, 254 n. 27; in skirmishes at Monterey and Tishomic Creek, 23, 35–36; speeches and public appearances of, 231; in Tullahoma Campaign, 103–107; West Point career of, 9–11

Wheeler, Joseph, Jr. (son of Joseph Wheeler), 208, 219–20, 232–33

Wheeler, Julia Knox Hull (daughter of Joseph Wheeler), 208, 266 n. 47

Wheeler, Julia Knox Hull (mother of Joseph Wheeler), 7–8

Wheeler, Lucy Louise (daughter of Joseph Wheeler), 208–209

Wheeler, Sara Bradford, 7

Wheeler, Thomas Harrison (son of Joseph Wheeler), 208, 231

Wheeler, William (brother of Joseph Wheeler), 12, 16, 202

Wheeler Station, 211, 231

"Wheeler's Polka," 129

Wilder, John T., 103–104, 106–107, 123, 158

Wilderness, Battle of the, 175

Williams, John Stuart, 129, 158, 165, 172–74

Wilson, Leonard, 226, 228

Wilson's Creek, Battle of, 20

Withers, Jones M., 25–26, 29–31, 35

Wood, Leonard, 221, 224, 226, 229

Wood, Sterling, 72, 74

Wyeth, John Allan, 113–14, 122–23

Yorkville, S.C., 204

Young, Samuel M. B., 221, 224

Zahm, Louis, 81–82, 84

ABOUT THE AUTHOR

EDWARD G. LONGACRE is an historian for the U.S. Air Force, stationed at Headquarters Air Combat Command, Langley Air Force Base, Virginia. He has published twenty books and more than 100 journal and magazine articles on the American Civil War. His books have won the Fletcher Pratt Award and the Douglas Southall Freeman History Award. In 1993 he was historical advisor to Sam Elliott, who portrayed Union general John Buford in the Hollywood film *Gettysburg*. Since 2001 he has been an honorary director of the U.S. Cavalry Association. He and his wife, Ann, reside in Newport News, Virginia.